Programming Flex™ 2

Programming Flex™ 2

Chafic Kazoun and Joey Lott

O'REILLY®

Beijing · Cambridge · Farnham · Köln · Paris · Sebastopol · Taipei · Tokyo

Programming Flex 2™
by Chafic Kazoun and Joey Lott

Copyright © 2007 O'Reilly Media, Inc. All rights reserved.
Printed in the United States of America.

Published by O'Reilly Media, Inc., 1005 Gravenstein Highway North, Sebastopol, CA 95472.

O'Reilly books may be purchased for educational, business, or sales promotional use. Online editions are also available for most titles (*safari.oreilly.com*). For more information, contact our corporate/institutional sales department: (800) 998-9938 or *corporate@oreilly.com*.

Editor: Steve Weiss
Developmental Editor: Audrey Doyle
Production Editor: Philip Dangler
Indexer: Reg Aubry

Cover Designer: Karen Montgomery
Interior Designer: David Futato
Illustrators: Robert Romano and Jessamyn Read

Printing History:

April 2007:   First Edition.

Nutshell Handbook, the Nutshell Handbook logo, and the O'Reilly logo are registered trademarks of O'Reilly Media, Inc. *Programming Flex 2*, the image of a Krait Snake, and related trade dress are trademarks of O'Reilly Media, Inc.

Many of the designations used by manufacturers and sellers to distinguish their products are claimed as trademarks. Where those designations appear in this book, and O'Reilly Media, Inc. was aware of a trademark claim, the designations have been printed in caps or initial caps.

While every precaution has been taken in the preparation of this book, the publisher and authors assume no responsibility for errors or omissions, or for damages resulting from the use of the information contained herein.

RepKover™ This book uses RepKover™, a durable and flexible lay-flat binding.

ISBN-10: 0-596-52689-X
ISBN-13: 978-0-596-52689-4
[M]   [11/07]

Table of Contents

Foreword

Whenever I talk to people about Flex 2, the most common questions they ask are the basic ones: what is it, who is it for, and why did we build it? It turns out that although these questions are basic, they really get to the heart of what Flex 2 is all about.

Flex 2 is a new technology for building rich web applications and experiences that run on Flash Player, so they look great, are responsive, and are highly interactive. It was designed specifically to be comfortable and productive for those coming from a web or application development background, though it is suitable for anyone.

Why did we build it? Well that's a longer story.

This Shouldn't Be Too Hard

The genesis of my involvement with Flex 2 really started with a seed of inspiration. Like everyone who surfs the Web, I would occasionally come across an application that just blew me away. It would be responsive, look incredible, and have an almost cinematic quality to it. Being curious, I would poke around to figure out how it was built.

What I discovered was that it was almost always built with Flash. Because my background is in software development and I like to build things, this made me want to try Flash, so I did. The result was shocking and humbling. I failed miserably, and I came away unable to fathom how anybody built anything with Flash, never mind how they built the amazing creations that had inspired me.

Part of my problem was with the Flash authoring tool. Not only didn't it feel like the developer tools I'd used before, but also it didn't really seem to have been designed for what I was trying to do. For example, the Timeline is one of the most notable features of Flash. I could not, for the life of me, figure out how I would use it to build an application. Although developer tools often provide a toolbox of components, such as buttons and lists that you can drag onto the design surface, the Flash toolbox was different. Here the components were things such as a line, rectangle, pen, pencil, ink bottle, and paint bucket. How do I build an application with a pencil?

The other problem I had was with the terminology used to describe the concepts presented by Flash Player. In Flash, small reusable UI elements are called Movie Clips. The main display area is called the Stage. The output of compiling the project is a Movie. I can't tell you how weird it was to try to track down a problem by running the Debug Movie command.

Maybe We Need a Different Approach

From my experiment, I concluded that Flash simply was not designed for building applications, or for developers like me. However, rather than see this as a problem, I saw it as an opportunity. How many more great Flash applications would there be if it was easier for developers to build them?

I focused on this question, instead of just trying harder to use Flash, because my main interest in software is not so much in writing applications, but in improving the process of doing so. That is, I've been most concerned with what the code actually looks like. As a result, I've spent most of my career working on application frameworks and tools that simplify development.

My first framework was called zApp, and I began writing it in 1989. I had been developing for Windows for three years, starting with version 1.03, and had grown frustrated by how difficult it was. zApp not only made Windows development much easier, but also solved another key problem for developers. It allowed you to move your application to other platforms, such as OS/2 or Unix, simply by recompiling. zApp was released in 1991 and it became a popular cross-platform application framework.

During the mid-'90s, while working at Microsoft, I became more involved with web applications and was amazed at how hard it was to write them. So, in 1997, a colleague and I developed a prototype web development framework that we called XSP. Based on the prototype's success, I led a team to build a production version that we shipped in 2002 as ASP.NET.

So, as I thought about Flash, I felt the same level of excitement that I had in those previous projects, and I wanted to do something about it. Doing so would enable me to simultaneously explore two areas that I loved: web application development and rich, cross-platform UIs. Therefore, in mid-2004, I joined Macromedia to help make Flash a great platform for developers.

My First Meeting with Flex

At Macromedia, my first task was to learn about all of the projects underway that were related to Flash, and it was then that I first heard about Flex. Version 1.0 had been released a few months earlier, and it was described to me as a presentation server for experienced Java developers building enterprise applications. When I heard this and learned the price, which was very high, I realized why I had not previously noticed it. A high-priced enterprise server did not jump out at me as an easier way to build Flash applications.

However, as I learned the details of how Flex actually worked, I began to become more interested in it. The key thing Flex provided was a powerful, easy-to-use, developer-friendly framework for developing Flash applications. It also had a nice XML-based language for defining the UI structure that ironically felt very similar to programming in ASP.NET.

The server component of Flex provided two things. The first was the compiler that translated all of the code into a SWF file for the Flash Player to run. The compile-on-demand model was also very similar to how one built applications in ASP.NET. However, unlike ASP.NET, the code you wrote ran on the client, not on the server.

So, the main question I had at this point was why is Flex a server? You don't need a server to compile, and it seemed to me that that would be much more easily done on a developer's machine.

There was one other server component of Flex, which was a gateway that enabled Flash to talk to the server using an optimized binary protocol and integrated with backend Java code. This was the one component of Flex that really needed to be a server. However, it was used for only certain scenarios, and it really was optional. It also was not addressing the fundamental problem I was looking to solve: namely, making it easier and more intuitive for developers to build Flash applications.

Flex, Take 2

So, the biggest problem that I saw with Flex 1.0 was not with the technology per se, but with the packaging and positioning. Selling Flex as an expensive enterprise server made it irrelevant to developers who just wanted to build cool stuff in Flash. I just could not imagine anyone who went through what I did with Flash saying, "Hmmm, this isn't really for me, maybe I'll check out that multithousand-dollar enterprise presentation server." As a result, an opportunity was missed, because I had become convinced that if developers tried Flex, they would love it.

After I finished looking around, I made some recommendations as to what I thought should be done. The first was that the part of Flex used to build Flash applications (i. e., the Flex framework and compiler) should be offered separate from the server. I had no problem with the server, as it had a lot of value, but it should not be required.

I also recommended that we build a real developer-style tool for Flex that enabled a more traditional client development model. Flex 1.0 did have a development tool, called Flex Builder, but it was built as an extension to Dreamweaver and it lacked many features one expected in a real developer IDE. What I wanted was something that felt more like a tool such as Visual Studio or Eclipse.

The Flex 2 Framework

Fortunately, there was broad agreement, and my recommendations were reflected in what we actually did to create Flex 2. So, what is it?

The core of Flex 2 is the Flex framework, a library of ActionScript objects that provide a great foundation for building rich Internet applications that run on Flash. It is a developer-centric framework that provides a strong architecture and uses design patterns that will be familiar to developers coming from a .NET, Java, or web development background.

Flex 2 has a rich component model, similar to the ones found in Visual Basic, .NET, and Java. Components expose properties to enable configuration, provide methods to enable invoking their functionality, and fire events when their state changes. Flex 2 provides standard mechanisms for providing data to components, for customizing their look and feel, and for managing their layout.

But Flex doesn't just provide architecture. It also provides a wealth of useful components so that developers don't have to build everything from scratch. These include buttons, lists, menus, sliders, tabs, accordions, data grids, and more. Of course, it is easy to build your own components from scratch or customize the ones provided.

The primary way one programs with Flex is via a mix of ActionScript and an XML-based language called MXML. Each tag in MXML maps to a component, so unlike HTML, you don't have a fixed set of tags. If you write new components, you have new tags to use. Properties on a component become the tag's attributes. MXML also supports script blocks where you can put ActionScript event-handling code and utility functions.

One exciting decision we made was to provide the Flex Framework SDK, which includes the Flex framework with complete source, compilers, and other utilities, for free. We did this to encourage adoption and enable it to be freely used with non-Adobe tools. You can download it by going to the official Flex web site, *http://www. flex.org*.

Flex Builder 2

Flex Builder 2 is an IDE that makes using the Flex framework more productive. It provides a great code-editing environment for both ActionScript and MXML, a

WYSIWYG design view to allow you to build your UI visually, a powerful debugger, and a project system that automates compiling your application.

The source editors are especially valuable because they help you to write correct code more easily and they streamline learning the framework object model. We put a lot of work into code completion to make it always up-to-date, whether it's providing suggestions for built-in classes or for ones that you create.

One of the challenges in doing this was that because MXML and ActionScript are essentially two languages defining and using the same objects, what you do in one affects the other. For example, you can define a class in ActionScript and use it from MXML, and as you make changes to the class definition, they will be reflected in the hints you are offered when editing MXML code.

Because we wanted to make Flex Builder a tool that developers would really like, we built it on the Eclipse framework as a set of plug-ins. Eclipse is a widely adopted, open source tools framework originally developed by IBM. It has a huge extension-building community, and many of its extensions are free and open source and can easily be integrated into Flex Builder 2. You can install Flex Builder as a standalone tool, or as a set of plug-ins to an existing installation of Eclipse.

ActionScript 3

One of the most important aspects of Flex 2 is that it is written entirely in Action-Script 3, which was introduced as part of Flash Player 9. Both products shipped simultaneously. ActionScript 3 is an incredibly important new language for a number of reasons.

First, ActionScript has always been based on EcmaScript, which is the standard that JavaScript is based on, but in the past was not implemented 100% to specification. To better support the standard and help it move forward, Macromedia played an active role on the EcmaScript planning committee and made ActionScript 100% compatible with the next major revision of the standard.

One thing you'll find is that this is not the JavaScript you have in today's browsers, but rather is a much more modern and robust language. In fact, I find it to be much more like C# or Java and think it will really appeal to developers coming from either of those languages. A key feature that I really like is the option of strong typing. This results in much more useful error messages and enables you to produce much more correct and reliable code.

To provide a more robust execution environment for ActionScript 3, the Flash Player team developed a new virtual machine (VM), called ActionScript Virtual Machine 2, or AVM2 for short. It was created from the ground up to be fast and scalable, and it features a just-in-time (JIT) compiler that turns the ActionScript 3 bytecode into native code. In that respect, it is much more like a Java VM or the .NET CLR than the script engines in today's browsers. The result is that it is 10 times faster than the previous VM and it uses much less memory. Note that the previous version of the VM, now called AVM1, continues to be included within Flash Player to ensure backward compatibility.

We recently made AVM2 open source by donating it to the Mozilla Foundation for incorporation into Firefox. We believe this will speed adoption of the new standard, and help ensure compatibility with future implementations of JavaScript.

Flex Data Services

The final component of Flex 2 is Flex Data Services (FDS), which represents the evolution of the original Flex server. FDS has added an incredible array of features to enable richer, more responsive applications, including client server messaging, JMS integration, a rich data model and data synchronization framework, data paging, and proxy services.

One of the most intriguing features is that FDS supports bidirectional messaging between the client and the server. This allows the server to actually push data to the client without the client having to poll for updates. This solves one of the key problems in building rich web applications for real-time data display, such as for financial services.

Although FDS is not always required when building a Flex application, it is extremely valuable when it is required. To encourage easy adoption of FDS, we created a free Express edition that allows free, nonexpiring commercial use. The only limitation is that the applications can't be clustered or run across multiple CPUs.

Taking Another Look at Flash

After joining Macromedia, I was able to take another look at Flash and spend more time programming with it. This was important so that I could get a better understanding of how Flash developers work today. Over time, I was able to break through some of the barriers I had initially encountered and began to understand how Flash abstractions relate to those I was used to. As such, I gradually got the hang of the fact that a Movie Clip is just another type of component.

I also had the opportunity to meet a number of the world's top Flash developers, which was really great, because they were the ones who inspired me to learn about Flash in the first place. This was when I first met Chafic Kazoun and Joey Lott, the authors of the book you hold in your hands.

One of the things that I found interesting is that today's Flash developers are somewhat different from those in other communities. Some came to Flash from a creative background, without prior software experience, and got into programming Flash in order to enhance their work. Others came to Flash from a programming background, but were also interested in the aesthetic aspects of software. Whichever way they got there, however, they all had a mix of the creative and technical skills that is not typical.

I do believe that Flex will change this somewhat, because you no longer have to have great design skills to create something in Flash that looks fantastic. Flex applications look great out of the box.

One of the things I have been delighted with is that Flex has been enthusiastically received by Flash developers. One might have thought that they wouldn't care because they had already mastered the skills needed to use Flash, but they do care and they like it. In fact, I recently spoke at some conferences, and the other Flex presenters were almost all Flash developers who had gotten hooked on Flex.

In talking to them, I learned that they like that they can be more productive when they're building something that fits within the Flex paradigm. They find that the architecture is well done and solves comprehensively what they used to address in an ad hoc way. They love the fact that Flex Builder has a great coding environment. And of course, they love that Flex and Flash can work together, so they can use each where appropriate. Flex is not the right solution for everything they might want to build, but when it is the right solution, they love it as much as anyone.

Programming Flex 2

One of the things that makes frameworks such as Flex so great is that they provide a rich architecture and lots of prebuilt software components that enable you to build software much more quickly than if you had to write it yourself. And the best frameworks, of which Flex is one, allow you to deeply customize and extend the provided functionality so that you are not limited in your creations.

With all of this, however, comes a degree of complexity. We put a ton of effort into making sure that things are as consistent as possible, that the right design patterns are used, and that there is the right balance of ease of use and flexibility, all in an effort to make things as simple to learn and use as possible. With that said, there's nothing like a good book to take you through the concepts so that you can really understand what's going on.

What I really like about *Programming Flex 2* is that not only does it take you through the breadth of what Flex provides, but it also takes you deep into how it works. It explains the high-level concepts as well as points out the finer details of what's really happening.

I also like that *Programming Flex 2* takes a practical approach, explaining common techniques of how ActionScript programs typically work in ways that go beyond simply explaining the classes that Flex provides.

Both Chafic Kazoun and Joey Lott are ideal people to present this information. Both are long-time Flash developers, are well known in the Flash community, and are among the elite of the Flash development world. Each of them has been using Flex for a long time.

I think that the depth of their Flash experience is part of what makes *Programming Flex 2* so special. Their mastery of the Flash Player API combined with their extensive knowledge of Flex enable them to not just tell you how to leverage the features Flex provides, but to do so with a thorough understanding of the entire system.

Looking Ahead

When we shipped Flex 2 June 27, 2006, it was just a few days shy of 18 months since we had started developing it. It was a great accomplishment, because we built a new tool from scratch, rewrote the framework in ActionScript 3, which was still being developed, and shipped on schedule.

It was an amazing time, and a lot of fun. Of course, for us, probably the biggest thing that happened was that Macromedia was acquired by Adobe Systems. Although some Macromedia fans expressed concern that Adobe might not really support Flex, they couldn't have been more wrong. It was amazing to experience how excited Adobe employees were about Flex and all of the technology being created by the former Macromedia teams. And over the past year since the acquisition, this has been confirmed by what we've been able to accomplish.

January 4, 2007, just six months after shipping Flex 2, we released Flex 2.0.1. Although it sounds like a tiny update, it actually has a number of new features and improvements. One of the key things that we were able to deliver was Flex Builder 2 for the Mac, running on both PowerPC and Intel.

We followed this up January 16 with Flash Player 9 for Linux. What makes this so important is that it means you can now run Flex 2 applications that behave identically across Windows, the Mac, and Linux.

One of the most important extensions of what Flex can do is a project that was begun immediately after Adobe and Macromedia combined. Apollo is a technology that will allow developers to build desktop applications that run outside of the browser using the web technologies they use today, including Flex/Flash, HTML/AJAX, and PDF.

This means you can develop a Flex application and install it on either Windows or the Mac (Linux will come a little later) and it will behave like any other application on your system. On Windows, it can appear in the Start menu and in the taskbar, and on the Mac, it will appear in the Dock. Apollo will have additional APIs that enable you to interact with the system in ways you can't from within the browser. For example, you can open multiple windows, support drag and drop, and more directly access the filesystem.

What's more, you will be able to integrate full HTML into a Flex application. That is, you'll essentially be able to have the full HTML engine that powers the Mac Safari browser embedded within your Flex app.

So, I think we are doing a number of exciting things to move Flex forward. However, I'm most looking forward to being inspired by the incredible apps that you create with Flex 2. Good luck and happy coding!

—Mark Anders

Senior Principal Scientist,
Adobe Systems Incorporated

Preface

This book is a long time in the making. We first started talking about this book several years ago, when Flex 1.0 first hit the market. We recognized that Flex was something important, yet we knew the product hadn't matured enough at that point. However, we shortly thereafter heard the whispers of Flex 2, a new and improved Flex. After working with Flex 2, we were certain that this was going to revolutionize how we build applications. Running on a new virtual machine using new, streamlined metaphors, Flex 2 was light years ahead of anything we'd been working with to develop rich Internet applications. It was at that point that we got serious about writing this book.

You'll learn shortly (starting in Chapter 1) what Flex 2 is and what you can do with it. However, briefly, Flex 2 is a framework and a set of tools (e.g., compilers) for building rich Internet applications. The framework is built on Flash Player technology, and it leverages a new (and lightning-fast) virtual machine built into Flash Player 9. This means Flex 2 applications can utilize all the functionality of Flash Player, such as animation, audio, video, request/response network data communication, real-time data communication, and much more. Furthermore, the Flex 2 framework vastly simplifies the creation of Flash Platform applications over previous options (Flash authoring, Flex 1.5, etc.).

Flex 2 is huge. Although the learning curve is not steep (it's actually very easy to get started building Flex 2 applications), it is a long learning curve simply because of the massive amount of features packed into the framework. The official Flex documentation is quite good at telling you how to do something once you know what you're looking for. Therefore, we made it our goal to present to you a book that fills in the gaps and helps you to get comfortable enough with Flex that you start to quickly know what you're looking for. It is our intention in this book to provide you with practical advice from our own experiences learning Flex and drawing from our longer-term experiences building rich Internet applications using Flash Platform technologies.

We really feel that Flex 2 is a fantastic product and a great way to build applications. Although this is a technical book, we have poured our enthusiasm into our writing, and we'd like to think you will share our enthusiasm as you read this book. We feel that Flex 2 is a far better way to build rich Internet applications than any alternative currently on the market, and we feel that as you read this book and learn how to work with Flex, you'll agree. With Flex, you have few (if any) problems involving cross-browser compatibility, network data communication is a snap, and the framework is built with solid object-oriented principals and standards in mind. In short, we feel it's the fastest way to build the coolest, most stable applications.

Who This Book Is For

This book is intended for anyone looking to learn more about Flex 2. We recognize that the audience for this book represents a very diverse group of people with many different backgrounds. Some readers may have years of experience working with Flash Platform technologies, and others may be completely new to creating content that runs in Flash Player. Some readers may have computer science degrees or have worked in the software industry for years. Yet other readers may be self-taught. We have done our best to write a book that will cater to this diverse group.

However, be aware that in order to get the most from this book, it is best that you have a solid understanding of object-oriented principles, and that you are comfortable with understanding concepts such as runtime environments, byte code, and compilers. Furthermore, you will get the most from this book if you already know ActionScript, Java, C, C#, or another language that uses similar syntax. Although we do have a chapter dedicated to the basics of ActionScript (the programming language utilized by Flex applications), we don't discuss any of the core APIs in detail. If you are interested in learning more about the ActionScript language, we encourage you to find a good ActionScript 3.0 book.

How This Book Is Organized

We spent a lot of time organizing and reorganizing the content of this book. Although there is likely no one way to present the content that will seem perfect to all readers, we've done our best to present it in an order that we feel will make sense.

Chapter 1, Introducing Flex
What is Flex? What are rich Internet applications (RIAs)? This chapter answers these questions, providing a context for the rest of the book.

Chapter 2, Building Applications with the Flex Framework
In this chapter, we discuss the various elements and steps involved in building a Flex application. Topics include using the compilers, building scripts, Flash Player security, deploying applications, and more.

Chapter 3, MXML

MXML is the declarative language used by Flex. In this chapter, you'll learn the basics of MXML.

Chapter 4, ActionScript

ActionScript is the object-oriented programming language used by Flex. In this chapter, you'll learn the basics of ActionScript 3.0.

Chapter 5, Framework Fundamentals

Flex vastly simplifies many aspects of building applications. Although you don't often have to look under the hood, understanding the fundamentals of how the framework works is useful. In this chapter, you'll learn about Flex application life cycles, bootstrapping, and more.

Chapter 6, Managing Layout

Flex provides many layout containers that allow you to quickly and easily create all sorts of layouts within your applications. This chapter explains how to work with those containers.

Chapter 7, Working with UI Components

In this chapter, you'll learn about the user interface components (buttons, lists, menus, etc.) that are part of the Flex framework.

Chapter 8, Framework Utilities and Advanced Component Concepts

Once you've learned the basics of working with components, you'll likely want to know how to expand on that knowledge. In this chapter, you'll learn about such topics as tool tips, customizing lists, pop-up windows, and more.

Chapter 9, Working with Media

Flex allows you to include all sorts of assets and media in your applications, from images to animations to video and audio. In this chapter, you'll learn how to work with these elements.

Chapter 10, Managing State

Flex applications and components within those applications can change from one view to another. Flex refers to these changes as *states*. This is sometimes as simple as adding a new component to a form, and it sometimes involves changing the entire contents of the screen. How to manage states is the subject of this chapter.

Chapter 11, Using Effects and Transitions

For animated changes between states or in response to user events or system events, Flex includes features called *transitions* and *effects*. You can learn about transitions and effects in this chapter.

Chapter 12, Working with Data

In this chapter, you'll learn how to model data in Flex applications as well as how to link components so that they automatically update when data values change.

Chapter 13, Validating and Formatting Data
In this chapter, you'll learn how to validate user input and how to format data such as numbers, phone numbers, and so on.

Chapter 14, Customizing Application Appearance
Customizing the appearance of Flex applications is important because it allows you to create applications that adhere to a corporate style guide or to a creative vision. This chapter explains how to change the appearance of Flex applications.

Chapter 15, Client Data Communication
Client data communication is any transfer of data into or out of Flash Player where the data remains on the client computer. Examples of this are communication between two or more Flex applications running on the same computer and storing persistent data on the computer. These topics are discussed in this chapter.

Chapter 16, Remote Data Communication
In this chapter, you'll learn how to communicate from a Flex application running on a client computer to a remote data service. You'll learn how to use XML, SOAP, AMF, and more.

Chapter 17, Application Debugging
Debugging applications is just as important as writing them. It's unusual to build an application that has no errors, and therefore it's crucial that you can track down those errors efficiently. In this chapter, you'll learn how to work with the debugging features of Flex.

Chapter 18, Application Components
To make Flex application development manageable it's important to know how to break up the application into discrete parts. This chapter discusses strategies for this.

Chapter 19, Building Custom Components
Custom components are an important part of Flex applications because they allow you to create elements that can be used, customized, and distributed. This chapter discusses the steps necessary to create custom components using the Flex framework.

What You Need to Use This Book

In order to use this book, you should have the Flex SDK and a text editor. Our intention with this book is that anyone with the (free) SDK can follow along. However, we recommend using Flex Builder for anyone serious about developing Flex applications. If you're just starting with Flex, you might want to use the free trial version of Flex Builder initially to have the optimal experience building Flex applications.

Conventions Used in This Book

The following typographical conventions are used in this book:

Italic

 Indicates new terms, URLs, email addresses, filenames, file extensions, pathnames, directories, and Unix utilities.

`Constant width`

 Indicates commands, options, switches, variables, attributes, keys, functions, types, classes, namespaces, methods, modules, properties, parameters, values, objects, events, event handlers, XML tags, HTML tags, macros, the contents of files, or the output from commands.

`Constant width bold`

 Shows commands or other text that should be typed literally by the user.

`Constant width italic`

 Shows text that should be replaced with user-supplied values.

 This icon signifies a tip, suggestion, or general note.

Using Code Examples

This book is here to help you get your job done. In general, you may use the code in this book in your programs and documentation. You do not need to contact us for permission unless you're reproducing a significant portion of the code. For example, writing a program that uses several chunks of code from this book does not require permission. Selling or distributing a CD-ROM of examples from O'Reilly books *does* require permission. Answering a question by citing this book and quoting example code does not require permission. Incorporating a significant amount of example code from this book into your product's documentation *does* require permission.

We appreciate, but do not require, attribution. An attribution usually includes the title, author, publisher, and ISBN. For example: "*Programming Flex 2,* by Chafic Kazoun and Joey Lott. Copyright 2007 O'Reilly Media, Inc., 978-0-596-52689-4."

If you feel your use of code examples falls outside fair use or the permission given above, feel free to contact us at *permissions@oreilly.com*.

Comments and Questions

Please address comments and questions concerning this book to the publisher:

 O'Reilly Media, Inc.

1005 Gravenstein Highway North
Sebastopol, CA 95472
(800) 998-9938 (in the United States or Canada)
(707) 829-0515 (international or local)
(707) 829-0104 (fax)

We have a web page for this book, where we list errata, examples, and any additional information. You can access this page at:

http://www.oreilly.com/catalog/059652689X/

To comment or ask technical questions about this book, send email to:

bookquestions@oreilly.com

For more information about our books, conferences, Resource Centers, and the O'Reilly Network, see our web site at:

http://www.oreilly.com

Acknowledgments

This book, perhaps more than most, represents the efforts and contributions of many people. We'd like to acknowledge the following people.

Many thanks are due to the many people at O'Reilly who made this book possible. Special thanks to Steve Weiss and Audrey Doyle for their continued hard work and patience throughout the writing and editing of this book. They have each continuously gone above and beyond the call of duty, and we very much appreciate their efforts.

We'd also like to thank the many people at Adobe for not only working to create such a fantastic product as Flex 2, but also for answering our questions and helping us to see what things we might have missed. We'd especially like to thank a few select people: Matt Chotin, Alex Harui, Andrew Spaulding, and Manish Jethani, who not only answered our questions, but also took the time to review our chapters and provide valuable comments. We're also very grateful to Mark Anders from Adobe for graciously accepting our invitation to write the Foreword to this book. We're also thankful for the help of Mike Chambers throughout the planning and writing of this book.

The technical quality of this book is not just the work of the authors. The technical reviewers for this book are a fantastic group of people who have dedicated hours and hours of time to tell us when we're wrong so that we can correct it before you can read it. The technical reviewers are the reason the code in this book works. The technical reviewers for this book (in addition to the Adobe folks mentioned in the preceding paragraph) include: Darron Schall, Keith Peters, Marc Leuchner, Sam Roach, Steven Schelter, Daniel Williams, Ben Stucki, Sam Neff, Eric Cancil, Larry Davidson, and Veronique Brossier.

From Chafic

I would like to thank Joey Lott for being an excellent coauthor. His experience in both the technical realm and the publishing industry helped me get through the long process of writing this book. I would also like to thank my family, friends, and the team at Atellis for their support through this experience; I made it! Finally, I would like to thank the O'Reilly team for believing in a first-time author, and in this book.

From Joey

I would also like to thank a few people. This is Chafic's book, and I am grateful that he has trusted me enough to ask me to participate. Chafic has also pushed me to ensure that I do my very best. I'd also like to thank Robert Reinhardt for his show of faith in me all those years ago, giving me my first break in the writing business. Thanks go to all my colleagues at Schematic for their willingness to help with reviews and for asking all the right questions. Certainly I am grateful to my family and loved ones for their support and generosity of spirit.

CHAPTER 1

Introducing Flex

Flex is a collection of technologies that enables you to rapidly build applications deployed to Flash Player, a runtime environment for delivering sophisticated user interfaces and interactivity. Flex leverages existing, matured technologies and standards such as XML, web services, HTTP, Flash Player, and ActionScript. Even though Flex allows you to create complete rich Internet applications, it does so in a relatively simple and intuitive manner. While Flex does allow you to get under the hood for more granular control over all the elements, it significantly lowers the learning curve in that it allows you to compose applications rapidly by assembling off-the-shelf components, including UI controls, layout containers, data models, and data communication components.

In this chapter, we'll introduce Flex and Flex technologies in more detail so that you can better understand what Flex is and how you can best get started working with it. You'll learn what elements a Flex application uses and how they work together. We'll also compare and contrast Flex with other technologies for creating both standard and rich Internet applications.

Understanding Flex Application Technologies

If you're new to Flex, you may not yet have a clear understanding of what a Flex application is, how it works, and what benefits it has over alternative technologies and platforms. You build Flex applications utilizing the Flex framework, and you deploy them using Flash Player. In the following sections, you'll learn more about Flash Player, the Flex framework, and additional technologies that may be part of a Flex application.

Flash Player

Flex is part of the Adobe Flash Platform, which is a set of technologies with Flash Player at the core. Flex applications are intended to be deployed to Flash Player, meaning Flash Player runs all Flex applications. With nearly every computer connected to the Internet having some version of Flash Player installed, and an increasing number of mobile devices being Flash-enabled, Flash Player is one of the most ubiquitous pieces of software anywhere. Adobe estimates that each new version of Flash Player has adoption rates reaching 80% in less than 12 months (Flash Player 8 reached 86% within 9 months). The reasons for such quick adoption rates are debatable, but there are a few factors that are almost certainly causative:

- Flash Player content is potentially more compelling and engaging than static HTML content.
- Flash Player is capable of providing integrated solutions that utilize data services, interactive UI design, media elements such as audio and video, and even real-time communications.
- Well-made Flash Player content can provide a refreshing user experience that utilizes metaphors from desktop computing, such as drag-and-drop and double-click. Flash Player frees the UI design from scrolling pages of text and images.
- Flash Player is a relatively small (one-time) download. Even with the multitude of new features added with every release, the Flash Player download is less than 1 MB. And with built-in features such as Express Install, upgrading Flash Player versions is very simple.
- Stability and security are important considerations. Flash Player is a stable program that has been around for nearly a decade. Adobe is very careful with Flash Player security as well. Flash Player has very little access to the client's local system. It cannot save arbitrary files to the local system, and it cannot access Internet resources unless they meet very strict requirements.
- Flash Player is cross-platform (and cross-browser) compatible. Flash Player runs on Windows, OS X, and Linux, and on all major browsers, including Firefox, Internet Explorer, Safari, and Opera.

Flex 2 content relies on features of Flash Player 9, meaning that users must be running Flash Player 9 or higher to correctly view Flex 2 content. You can read more about deploying Flex applications and detecting player versions in Chapter 2.

Using the Flex framework you can build and compile to the *.swf* format. The compiled *.swf* file is an intermediate bytecode format that Flash Player can read. Flash Player 9 introduces a new virtual machine called AVM2. AVM2 is written from the ground up, and it functions in a fundamentally different way than previous versions of Flash Player. With AVM2, *.swf* content is no longer interpreted. Rather, it is compiled (the equivalent of just-in-time compilation) and run such that it can take advantage of lower-level computing power. This is very similar to how Java and .NET applications work.

AVM2 brings the best of both worlds. Since *.swf* content is compiled to bytecode that the ActionScript virtual machine can understand, the *.swf* format is platform-independent. That also means that Flash Player ultimately dictates the functionality allowed by a Flex application. As mentioned previously, that means that Flash Player can guarantee certain security safeguards so that you can deploy applications that users can trust. Yet at the same time, AVM2 compiles the content so that it runs significantly faster and more efficiently than previous versions of Flash Player.

The Flex Framework

The Flex framework is synonymous with the Flex class library and is a collection of ActionScript classes used by Flex applications. The Flex framework is written entirely in ActionScript classes, and defines controls, containers, and managers designed to simplify building rich Internet applications.

The Flex class library is the subject of much of this book. It consists of the following categories:

Form controls
Form controls are standard controls such as buttons, text inputs, text areas, lists, radio buttons, checkboxes, and combo boxes. In addition to the standard form controls familiar to most HTML developers, the Flex class library also includes controls such as a rich text editor, a color selector, a date selector, and more.

Menu controls
Flex provides a set of menu controls such as pop-up menus and menu bars.

Media components
One of the hallmarks of Flex applications is rich media support. The Flex class library provides a set of components for working with media such as images, audio, and video.

Layout containers
Flex applications enable highly configurable screen layout. You can use the layout containers to place contents within a screen and determine how they will change over time or when the user changes the dimensions of Flash Player. With a diverse set of container components you can create sophisticated layouts using grids, forms, boxes, canvases, and more. You can place elements with absolute or relative coordinates so that they can adjust correctly to different dimensions within Flash Player.

Data components and data binding
Flex applications are generally distributed applications that make remote procedure calls to data services residing on servers. The data components consist of connectors that simplify the procedure calls, data models to hold the data that is returned, and data binding functionality to automatically associate form control data with data models.

Formatters and validators

Data that is returned from remote procedure calls often needs to be formatted before getting displayed to the user. The Flex class library includes a robust set of formatting features (format a date in a variety of string representations, format a number with specific precision, format a number as a phone number string, etc.) to accomplish that task. Likewise, when sending data to a data service from user input, you'll frequently need to validate the data beforehand to ensure it is in the correct form. The Flex class library includes a set of validators for just that purpose.

Cursor management

Unlike traditional web applications, Flex applications are stateful, and they don't have to do a complete screen refresh each time data is sent or requested from a data service. However, since remote procedure calls often incur network and system latency, it's important to notify the user when the client is waiting on a response from the data service. Cursor management enables Flex applications to change the cursor appearance in order to notify the user of such changes.

State management

A Flex application will frequently require many state changes. For example, standard operations such as registering for a new account or making a purchase usually require several screens. The Flex class library provides classes for managing those changes in state. State management works not only at the macro level for screen changes, but also at the micro level for state changes within individual components. For example, a product display component could have several states: a base state displaying just an image and a name, and a details state that adds a description, price, and shipping availability. Furthermore, Flex provides the ability to easily apply transitions so that state changes are animated.

Effects

Flex applications aren't limited by the constraints of traditional web applications. Since Flex applications run within Flash Player, they can utilize the animation features of Flash. As such, the Flex class library enables an assortment of effects such as fades, zooms, blurs, and glows.

History management

As states change within a Flex application, the history management features of the Flex class library enable you to navigate from state to state using the back and forward buttons of the web browser.

Drag and drop management

The Flex class library simplifies adding drag and drop functionality to components with built-in drag and drop functionality on select components and a manager class that allows you to quickly add drag and drop behaviors to components.

Tool tips

Use this feature of the Flex class library to add tool tips to elements as the user moves the mouse over them.

Style management

The Flex class library enables a great deal of control over how nearly every aspect of a Flex application is styled. You can apply style changes such as color and font settings to most controls and containers directly to the objects or via CSS.

Flex Builder 2

Flex Builder 2 is the official Adobe IDE for building and debugging Flex applications. Built on the popular Eclipse IDE, Flex Builder has built-in tools for writing, debugging, and building applications using Flex technologies such as MXML and ActionScript.

The Flex framework ships as part of Flex Builder. However, Flex Builder and the Flex framework are not synonymous. You do not have to use Flex Builder to use the Flex framework. Instead, you can opt to install the free Flex SDK, which includes the compiler and the Flex framework. You can then integrate the Flex framework with a different IDE, or you can use any text editor to edit the MXML and ActionScript files, and you can run the compiler from the command line.

 Flex Builder is a commercial product. See *http://www.adobe.com/go/ flexbuilder* for more information.

Integrating with Data Services

Data services are an important aspect of most Flex applications. They are the way in which the Flex application can load and send data originating from a data tier such as a database (we discuss the concept of tiers in the section "Understanding the Differences Between Traditional (HTML) and Flex Web Applications" later in this chapter). Flash Player supports any text data, XML, a binary messaging format called AMF, and persistent socket connections, allowing for real-time data pushed from the server to the client.

Each data format Flex supports may or may not require special server resources. For example, a Flex application can request XML data from a static resource or from a dynamic resource such as a PHP page. AMF is a binary messaging format that Flash Player understands natively, but for a server to interact with Flash Player via AMF, it requires an AMF translator on the server, such as the remote object services that are part of Flex Data Services.

Flex simplifies working with data services by way of classes and components that are part of the framework. Working with data services is discussed in more detail in Chapter 14.

Integrating with Media Servers

Since Flex applications are deployed using Flash Player, they can leverage the media support for Flash video and audio. Although Flash Player can play back Flash video and MP3 audio as progressive downloads, you can benefit from true streaming media by way of a technology such as Flash Media Server.

Additional Flex Libraries and Components

At the time of this writing there is just one official add-on Flex library, the Flex Charting Components. As time goes on, it is expected that many additional Flex libraries will become available. Additional Flex libraries such as the Flex Charting Components are not part of the standard component sets that ship with the Flex framework. Rather, you must acquire the software and licenses, and add them to the Flex classpath. Add-on libraries enable more rapid application development because they provide prebuilt functionality. For example, with the addition of the charting component set, you can quickly and simply add robust charting and graphing features to Flex applications.

 You can find many extensions, such as Flex libraries and components, at the Adobe Exchange (*http://www.adobe.com/exchange*).

Using Flex Elements

The Flex framework includes a core set of languages and libraries that are the basis of any Flex application. Using MXML, ActionScript, and the Flex class library you can construct and compile *.swf* content that you can then deploy to Flash Player.

MXML

MXML is an XML-based markup language that primarily describes screen layout. In that respect it is much like HTML. Using MXML tags, you can add components such as form controls and media playback components to layout containers such as grids.

In addition to screen layout, you can use MXML to describe effects, transitions, data models, and data binding. MXML is robust enough that it is possible to build many applications entirely with MXML. Flex Builder enables you to construct MXML with a WYSIWYG approach, which allows you to build basic Flex applications without writing any code.

While the WYSIWYG approach is helpful for basic prototypes and simple applications, writing MXML code is still necessary for more complex tasks. Additionally, sophisticated Flex applications generally require both MXML and ActionScript.

MXML is a declarative way to create Flex content, but the simplicity should not fool you into thinking that MXML is not powerful. MXML provides a fast and powerful way to create layout and UI content. However, MXML documents get compiled in several steps, the first of which converts the MXML to an ActionScript class. This means that MXML documents provide you with all the power of object-oriented design, but with the convenience of a markup language. Furthermore, MXML documents are treated as ActionScript classes at runtime.

ActionScript

ActionScript is the programming language understood by Flash Player and is the fundamental engine of all Flex applications. MXML simplifies screen layout and many basic tasks, but all of what MXML does is made possible by ActionScript, and ActionScript can do many things that MXML cannot do. For example, you need ActionScript to respond to events such as mouse clicks.

Although it is possible to build an application entirely with MXML or entirely with ActionScript, it is more common and more sensible to build applications with the appropriate balance of both MXML and ActionScript. Each offers benefits, and they work well together. MXML is best suited for screen layout and basic data features. ActionScript is best suited for user interaction, complex data functionality, and any custom functionality not included in the Flex class library.

ActionScript is supported natively by Flash Player, and does not require any additional libraries to run. All the native ActionScript classes are packaged in the flash package or in the top-level package. In contrast, the Flex framework is written in ActionScript, but those classes are included in a *.swf* file at compile time. All the Flex framework classes are in the mx package.

Working with Data Services (Loading Data at Runtime)

Flex applications are generally distributed applications. That means that several computers work in conjunction to create one system. For example, all Flex applications have a client tier (discussed shortly) that runs on the user's computer in the form of a *.swf* running in Flash Player. In most cases, the client tier communicates with a server or servers in order to send and retrieve data. The servers provide what are called *data services*, which are essentially programs that have public interfaces (APIs) whereby a client can make a request to a method of that program. When a client makes such a request, it is called a *remote procedure call*, or RPC.

There are many types of data services. In its simplest form a data service could consist of a static text file or XML document served from a web server. A slightly more sophisticated data service might be a dynamic XML document generated via a server-side script or program, such as a PHP or ASPX page. Many data services require greater sophistication. One of the most common types of such a sophisticated data service is the *web service*. Web services use XML (generally in the form of SOAP) as a messaging format, and they enable RPCs using the HTTP protocol for requests and responses. Although a SOAP web service is an example of a standards-based data service, many types of data services don't necessarily conform to a particular standard set by the W3C. Many programs on the Web, for example, expose primitive data services that use arbitrary messaging formats and protocols. One such program is used by MapQuest, a popular mapping web site. For instance, you would use the following URL to view a MapQuest page with a map of Los Angeles:

http://www.mapquest.com/maps/map.adp?country=US&city=Los+Angeles&state=CA

Notice that the query string uses arbitrary parameters to determine what to map. Therefore, if you wanted to display a map of New York, you would change the city and state parameter values in the URL as follows:

http://www.mapquest.com/maps/map.adp?country=US&city=New+York&state=NY

Flash Player is capable of making RPCs to many types of data services. For example, Flash Player can make requests to any web resource using HTTP, which means it can make requests to many primitive data services such as a static or a dynamic XML document, or the MapQuest example mentioned previously. That also means it can make requests to web services. Moreover, the Flex class library simplifies requests to most data services.

In addition to the types of data services previously mentioned, Flex applications can also make calls to methods of classes on the server, using a technology called *Flash Remoting*. Flash Remoting uses the AMF binary messaging format, which is supported natively by Flash Player. AMF has all the benefits of SOAP, but since it is binary, the bandwidth overhead is greatly reduced. And since AMF is natively supported by Flash Player, no special coding is necessary to use Flash Remoting data services from the client tier. However, for a Flash Remoting data service to be available to the client tier, it must be made accessible via a piece of software that resides on the server, and can read and write AMF packets and delegate the requests to the correct services. Flex Data Services provides an implementation of Flash Remoting that integrates easily with components in the Flex framework. That means that if you use Flex Data Services, you can quickly configure applications to utilize Flash Remoting without writing ActionScript. However, you're not locked into using Flex Data Services in order to use Flash Remoting. There are many Flash Remoting server products, including open source options such as OpenAMF (*http://www.openamf.org*) and AMFPHP (*http://www.amfphp.org*).

Understanding the Differences Between Traditional (HTML) and Flex Web Applications

Many applications deployed on the Web use an HTML user interface. Flex applications are similar in many respects, but they have distinct differences. If you're used to building applications that use an HTML UI, it's important to take a few moments to shift how you approach building applications when you start working with Flex. What works for HTML-based applications may or may not work for Flex applications.

Both traditional and Flex applications are generally n-tiered. The exact number and types of tiers an application has depend on many factors. Most traditional applications have, at a minimum, a data tier, a business tier, and a presentation tier. Flex applications have a data tier and a business tier; however, as noted earlier, they also introduce a client tier, which is what strongly differentiates them from traditional web applications. The client tier of Flex applications enables clients to offload computation from the server, freeing up network latency and making for responsive and highly interactive user interfaces.

Data tiers generally consist of databases or similar resources. Business tiers consist of the core application business logic. As an example, a business tier may accept requests from a client or presentation tier, query the data tier, and return the requested data.

In traditional applications the presentation tier consists of HTML, CSS, JavaScript, JSP, ASP, PHP, or similar documents. Typically a request is made from the user's web browser for a specific presentation tier resource, and the web server runs any necessary interpreters to convert the resource to HTML and JavaScript, which is then returned to the web browser running on the client computer. Technically the HTML rendered in the browser is a client tier in a traditional web application. However, since the client tier of a traditional web application is stateless and fairly nonresponsive, it is generally not considered a full-fledged tier. (The exception to that generalization is the case of Ajax applications, which use client-side JavaScript and XML to build responsive and sophisticated client tiers.)

Flex applications generally reside embedded within the presentation tier. In addition, Flex applications can integrate with the presentation tier to create tightly coupled client-side systems. Flex applications use Flash Player to run sophisticated client-tier portions of the application. The Flex application client is *stateful*, which means that it can make changes to the view without having to make a request to the server. Furthermore, the Flex application client is responsive. For example, Flash Player can respond to user interaction such as mouse movement, mouse clicks, and keyboard presses, and it can respond to events such as notifications from the business tier when data is returned or pushed to the client. Flash Player also can respond to timer events. Since Flash Player is a smart client, it is capable of saving on network overhead and bandwidth usage by managing client-side logic without having to consult the business tier. For example, Flex applications can walk the user through a step-based or wizard-like interface, collect and validate data, and allow the user to update and edit previous steps, all without having to make requests to the business tier until the user wants to submit the data. All this makes Flex clients potentially far more compelling, responsive, and engaging than traditional web applications.

Because the Flex application client tier is so much more sophisticated than the presentation tier of a traditional web application, the Flex client tier requires significantly more time and resources to build successfully. A common mistake is to assume that Flex client tiers require the same time and resources as a traditional web application presentation tier. Successful Flex client tiers often require the same time and resources during design, implementation, and testing phases as the business tier.

Understanding How Flex Applications Work

Flex applications deployed on the Web work differently than HTML-based applications. It's important to understand how Flex applications work in order to build them most effectively. When you understand how Flex applications work, you can know what elements are necessary for an application and how to build the application for the best user experience. Figure 1-1 summarizes the basic concepts discussed in this section.

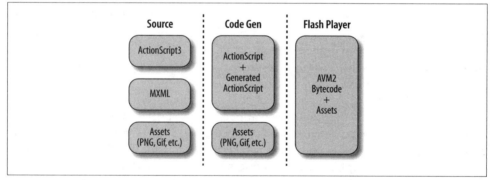

Figure 1-1. Understanding Flex application source-compile-deploy workflow

Every Flex application deployed on the Web utilizes Flash Player as the deployment platform. That means that a fundamental understanding of Flash Player is essential to understanding Flex. Additionally, all Flex applications use the Flex framework at a minimum to compile the application. As such, it's important to understand the relationship between the source code files, the compiler, and Flash Player.

All Flex applications require at least one MXML file or ActionScript class file, and most Flex applications utilize both MXML and ActionScript files. The MXML and ActionScript class files comprise the source code files for the application. Flash

Player does not know how to interpret MXML or uncompiled ActionScript class files. Instead, it is necessary to compile the source code files to the *.swf* format, which Flash Player can interpret. A typical Flex application compiles to just one *.swf* file. You then deploy that one *.swf* to the server, and when requested, it plays back in Flash Player. That means that unlike HTML-based applications, the source code files remain on the development machine, and you do not deploy them to the production server.

Asset files such as MP3s, CSS documents, and PNGs can be embedded within a *.swf*, or they can be loaded at runtime. When an asset is embedded within a *.swf*, it is not necessary to deploy the file to the production server, because it is compiled within the *.swf* file. However, since embedding assets within the *.swf* often makes for a less streamlined downloading experience and a less dynamic application, it is far more common to load such assets at runtime. That means that the asset files are not compiled into the *.swf*, and much like an HTML page, the assets are loaded into Flash Player when requested by the *.swf* at runtime. In that case, the asset files must be deployed to a valid URL when the *.swf* is deployed.

Data services are requested at runtime. That means that the services must be available at a valid URL when requested at runtime. For example, if a Flex application utilizes a web service, that web service must be accessible from the client when requested. Media servers and Flex Enterprise Services must also be accessible when used by Flex applications.

Understanding Flex and Flash Authoring

Many developers first learning about Flex 2 may still be unclear as to the relationship between Flex and Flash authoring, the traditional tool for creating content for Flash Player. First, you do not have to understand Flash authoring in order to work with Flex. In fact, you can get started with Flex without any prior knowledge of or experience in Flash authoring.

Flash authoring is a product that was first created in 1996 as a vector animation tool primarily aimed at creating animation content for the Web. In the many versions since that time, both Flash authoring and Flash Player (the deployment platform for Flash authoring content) have enabled greater and greater capabilities, and developers began to create rich Internet applications with the tools. However, while Flash authoring is a fantastic tool for creating animations, it is not the ideal tool for creating applications. The metaphors that Flash authoring uses at its core (such as timelines) are simply not applicable to application development.

Flex 2 is a product aimed primarily at creating applications. The framework includes a rich set of layout and user interface components, and the technology uses metaphors such as states and transitions that are appropriate to application development.

Both Flex and Flash authoring allow you to create *.swf* content that runs in Flash Player. In theory you can achieve the same things using both products. However, Flash is a tool that allows you to create timeline-based animations and to use drawing tools best suited for expressiveness, while Flex allows you to much more rapidly assemble screens of content with transitions and data communication behaviors. As with any craft, it is advisable to use the best tool for the job. Up until now, Flash authoring was one of the only tools for creating *.swf* content. But with Flex 2, we now have a tool with a more specific focus.

Although many people may initially try to frame the Flex and Flash authoring debate as a winner-takes-all scenario, it is rather naive to think of them as competing technologies. Rather, they are two complementary technologies that allow all Flash platform developers to utilize specialized tools when creating rich Internet content. In fact, Flex and Flash authoring can work very well together. As you'll see in this book, Flex can import content created in Flash authoring, allowing you to create rich Internet applications that use timeline-based content.

Understanding Flex 1.5 and Flex 2

If you are familiar with earlier versions of Flex (Flex 1 and Flex 1.5), you may be interested in the relationship between Flex 2 and those earlier versions. While Flex 2 continues to utilize MXML and ActionScript (both supported in earlier versions of Flex), it is vastly different from Flex 1 and Flex 1.5 in other respects. Flex 2 allows you to compile and deploy independent *.swf* files without any sort of expensive server-side services as was required by Flex 1 and 1.5 (though the ability to compile *.swf* files on the server at request time is still available in Flex Data Services). Flex 2 requires Flash Player 9, which allows for (and requires) the use of ActionScript 3. This latest ActionScript version introduces significant changes to the Flash Player API that offers a much improved way to add and remove display objects (including components) to the view.

Summary

In this chapter, we introduced the basics of what Flex is and what technologies and products are used to create Flex applications. You learned that Flex 2 consists of a framework (a class library) and a compiler that allow you to rapidly create Flex applications. These applications are *.swf* files, which you can then run in Flash Player 9.

CHAPTER 2

Building Applications with the Flex Framework

The majority of this book is dedicated to programming Flex applications, with detailed discussions of working with MXML and ActionScript. However, in order to meaningfully use most of what we discuss in the chapters that follow, you'll need to know how to create a Flex project, how to compile the project, and how to deploy that project so that you can view it.

In this chapter we'll discuss important topics such as the tools required for creating Flex applications and how to create new projects for Flex applications. We'll look at the elements comprising a Flex project and discuss compiling and deploying Flex applications.

Using Flex Tool Sets

In order to work with Flex and build Flex applications, you'll need tools. At a minimum you must have a compiler capable of converting all your source files and assets into the formats necessary to deploy the application. That means you need to be able to compile MXML and ActionScript files into a *.swf* file.

There are two primary tools you can use that include the necessary compilers:

- The Flex SDK (Software Development Kit)
- Flex Builder 2

The Flex SDK is a free product that includes the entire Flex framework as well as the `mxmlc` and `compc` compilers (see the section "Building Applications" later in this chapter, for more details on the compilers). You can download the SDK at *http://www. adobe.com/products/flex/sdk*.

Flex Builder 2 is a commercial product designed to work with Flex, and it too includes the `mxmlx` and `compc` compilers. You can download a trial version of Flex Builder 2 or purchase a license at *http://www.adobe.com/go/flexbuilder*.

Flex Builder includes the entire SDK.

You can work with Flex Builder 2 in two ways: standalone and as a plug-in for Eclipse (*http://www.eclipse.org*). The standalone version of Flex Builder 2 is built on Eclipse, so it and the plug-in version are essentially equivalent. The primary differences are:

- Flex Builder 2 standalone does not require that you already have Eclipse installed, making it an optimal solution for those who have no other use for Eclipse. On the other hand, if you already use Eclipse, or if you intend to use Eclipse for other purposes, the standalone version would essentially require you to have two installations of Eclipse—one running Flex Builder and one standard installation. If you use or plan to use Eclipse for other reasons you should definitely install the plug-in version of Flex Builder 2.

- The standalone version disables Java Development Tools (JDT), a plug-in used by some standard Eclipse features such as Ant (*http://ant.apache.org*). If you want to use JDT, you should install the plug-in version of Flex Builder 2.

Since Flex Builder is built on Eclipse, you can use any third-party Eclipse plug-ins with the standalone version of Flex Builder.

Many factors might drive your decision as to whether to use the Flex SDK or Flex Builder 2. The following is a list of just a few to consider:

Price

The Flex SDK is a free product. It includes the entire Flex framework. Flex Builder 2, on the other hand, is a commercial product. There is no difference in the price between the standalone and plug-in versions of Flex Builder 2.

Commitment to an existing IDE

If you already have a considerable investment in an IDE in terms of time and resources, and if that IDE works very well for you, you may want to integrate the Flex SDK with your existing IDE. On the other hand, if you're already using Eclipse, consider that you can install the Flex Builder 2 plug-in for an existing installation of Eclipse.

Debugging capabilities

The Flex SDK includes a command-line debugger. However, Flex Builder 2 includes an integrated debugger that allows you to set breakpoints and step through code, all from within your IDE.

Efficiency

Unless and until other IDEs have increased support for Flex (ActionScript and MXML), Flex Builder is the fastest way to build Flex applications. With its built-in code hinting, code completion, error detection, and debugging capabilities, Flex Builder is far superior to the SDK for serious Flex application developers.

The majority of the content of this book is not dependent on any one tool. Much of our focus is on working with the Flex framework and ActionScript 3.0 and will require only the Flex SDK. When there are specific topics that do have dependencies on a particular tool, we make that clear. For example, in this chapter we discuss the differences between configuring a Flex Builder project versus a Flex SDK project.

Creating Projects

A Flex application consists of potentially many files. Although it's possible that a Flex project could consist of as little as one source file, most use tens if not hundreds of files. A typical Flex project might utilize the following:

MXML files

These files contain the majority of the application view—the layout and UI components. You can read an introduction to MXML in Chapter 3. You can also learn about application and MXML components (both written in MXML) in Chapter 18.

ActionScript classes

These files contain the source code for all the custom components, data models, client-side business logic, and server proxies. You'll find an introduction to ActionScript in Chapter 4.

XML files

Although XML is frequently loaded from a server as a dynamic response to an HTTP request from Flash Player, many applications also utilize static XML files as configuration parameters.

Image files

Flex applications can embed image files or load them at runtime. Working with images is covered in Chapter 9.

Audio and video files

Flex applications can load audio and video content for playback within the application. Audio and video are almost always loaded at runtime. Audio and video are also discussed in Chapter 9.

Runtime shared libraries

Runtime shared libraries are *.swf* files that contain code libraries that are shared between two or more Flex applications deployed on the same domain. In order to utilize a runtime shared library, you need two files: a *.swf* and a *.swc*. The *.swf* file contains the libraries, and the *.swc* file is used by the compiler to determine which libraries to exclude from the application *.swf*. Runtime shared libraries are discussed in more detail later in this chapter, in the section titled "Using Runtime Shared Libraries."

HTML wrapper file

Flex applications are typically deployed on the Web. The published application is a *.swf* file. The most common way to playback a *.swf* on the Web is to embed it in an HTML page. The HTML wrapper file is the file that embeds the *.swf*.

Setting Up a New Project

How you configure a new Flex project depends in large part on what tool set you are using. If you're using the Flex SDK, that tool set generally requires the most work in order to configure a new project.

Creating an SDK project

Presumably if you are using the Flex SDK, you are integrating it with an IDE such as Eclipse (*http://www.eclipse.org*), PrimalScript (*http://www.sapien.com*), or FlashDevelop (*http://www.osflash.org/flashdevelop*). If you are indeed using an IDE, you most likely want to start a new project (or workspace or whatever particular terminology your IDE uses). If you are not using an IDE (you like to edit code using a plain-text editor), you will want to create a new directory for the project.

You'll place all the project files in the project directory, likely organizing them into subdirectories. Which subdirectory structure you use is ultimately up to you. You'll need to know where and how you're organizing all the source code and assets so that you can configure the appropriate compiler options when building the application. (Compiler options are discussed in the next section, "Building Applications.") Files typically are organized into the following directories:

src

A directory containing all the source MXML and ActionScript class files. The files are then generally organized into packages. You can organize both MXML and ActionScript files into packages in a Flex project. Packages are discussed in more detail in Chapters 3 and 4.

bin

A directory to which you save the compiled version of the application.

html

A directory in which you keep the HTML wrapper file(s).

assets
A directory in which you save all the asset files used by the application either at compile time or at runtime.

build
A directory in which you can place build scripts if using Apache Ant.

Creating a Flex Builder 2 project

Using Flex Builder 2, you can create a new project with a few clicks on the mouse. From the Flex Builder 2 menus you can select File → New → Flex Project. This opens the Flex Project dialog which walks you through a short wizard comprising the following steps:

1. The first step asks you to select how the application will access data. Unless we specify otherwise, all the examples we provide in this book will work via the Basic option. See Figure 2-1.

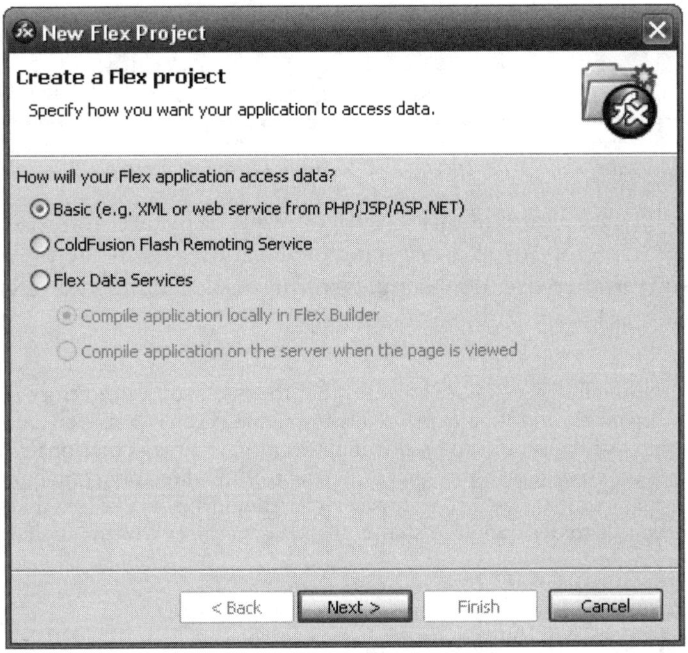

Figure 2-1. *Specifying how the application will access data*

2. The second step asks you to name the project. You can also specify a nondefault location for the new project directory. See Figure 2-2.

3. At the completion of step 2, you can click Finish. If you click Next, you'll see a third step asking you to customize the source path and library path. These set-

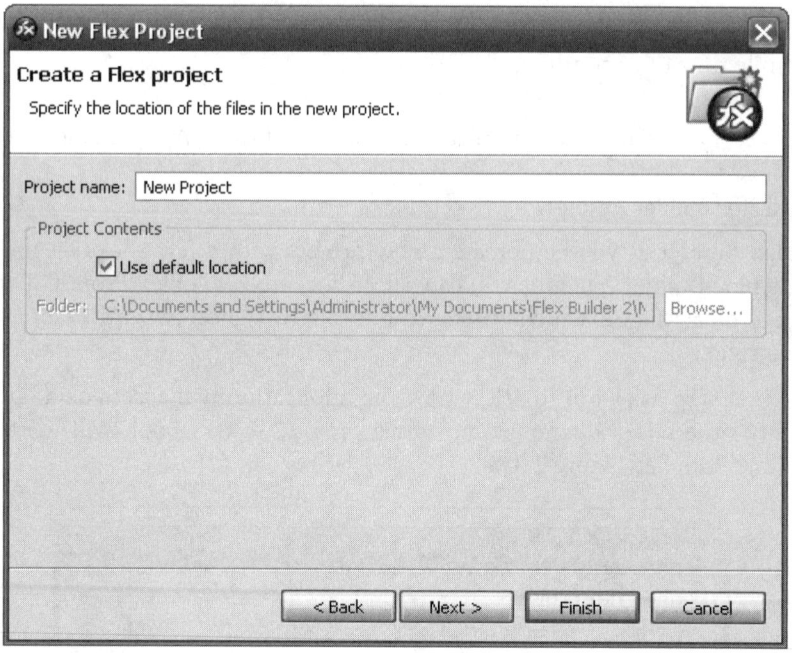

Figure 2-2. Naming the project and specifying a location for the new project directory

tings specify classes and libraries that you want to use but that reside outside of the project directory or in a nonstandard location within the project directory. Unless stated otherwise, no examples in this book require you to customize the source path or library path. See Figure 2-3.

> Normally Flex Builder assumes that the main source directory is synonymous with the project directory. However, when you create a project that points to an existing directory, you may occasionally want to point to a directory that is a parent of the directory containing the main source files. In such cases you should be sure to set the Main source folder option in step 3 of the new project wizard, as shown in Figure 2-3.

When you create a Flex Builder project, you'll see that the new directory has a *bin* directory to which Flex Builder saves the compiled application by default, as well as an *html-template* directory which stores the templates used by Flex Builder to generate the HTML wrapper file. You'll also see that new Flex Builder Flex projects automatically create an MXML document with the same name as the project.

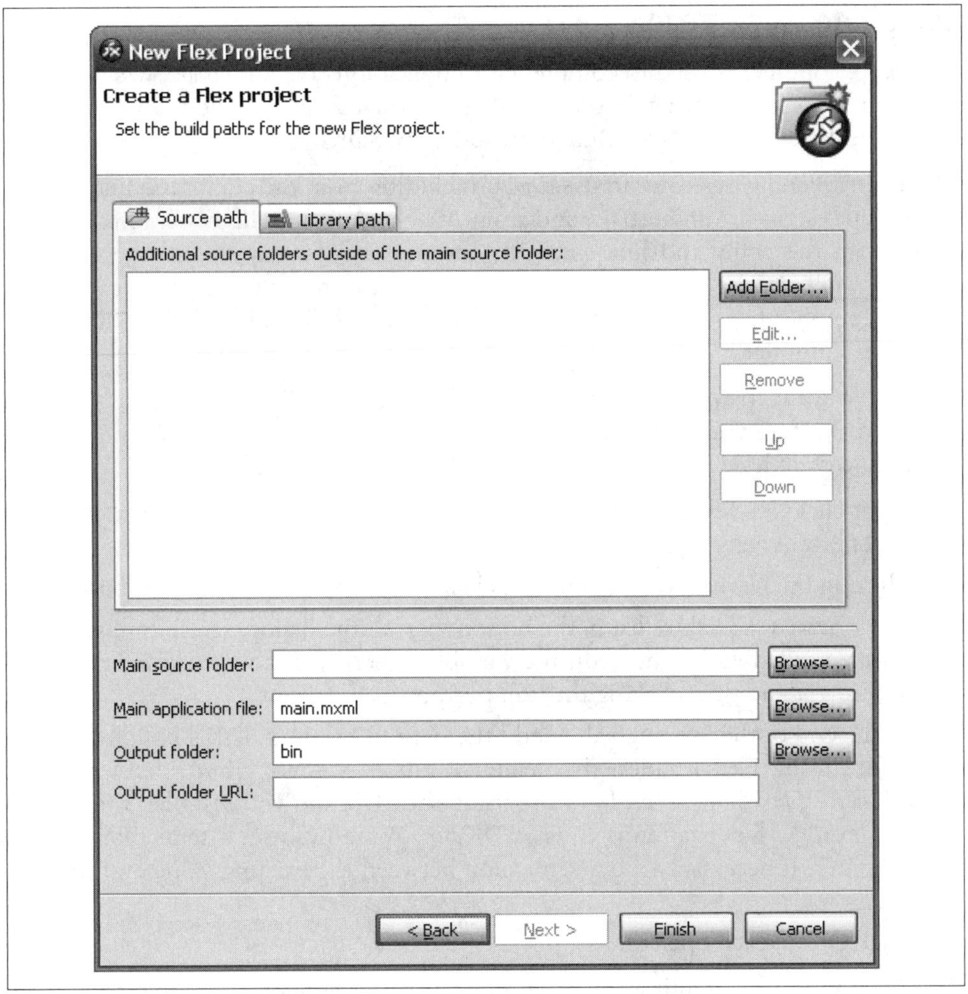

Figure 2-3. Setting the build paths for the new Flex project

Building Applications

Once you've created a project and written some code, you'll want to build the project, which means compiling it and deploying it. How you accomplish these tasks depends, in part, on what tools you're using. The following subsections discuss how to compile using the `mxmlc` compiler. If you're using Flex Builder 2, you may want to skip directly to the section "Compiling Using Flex Builder" later in this chapter.

Compiling Using mxmlc

The mxmlc compiler is used to compile Flex applications (versus compc, which is used to compile components and libraries). When you use Flex Builder to compile, it automatically calls mxmlc (Flex Builder includes the SDK).

There are several ways you can use mxmlc, including from the command line, from a *.bat* or shell script, from an IDE, and from Apache Ant. Initially we'll look at using mxmlc from the command line since it's the most basic way to use the compiler (though we'll also look at using the compiler via Apache Ant later in this chapter). All the compiler flags we'll look at from the command line also apply to any other use of the compiler.

When you want to work with mxmlc from the command line, it's generally a good idea to make sure you add it to your system path. If you're running Windows and you're uncertain how to edit your system path, follow these steps:

1. Right-click on My Computer from the desktop or from the Start menu, and select Properties.

2. Click on the Advanced tab, and then click the Environment Variables button.

3. In the System Variables list in the bottom part of the dialog, scroll until you see a variable called Path. Then edit the variable either by double-clicking on it or by selecting it and then clicking the Edit button.

4. At the end of the existing value, add the path to the Flex SDK's *bin* directory. If you're using Flex Builder, the default location is *C:\Program Files\Adobe\Flex Builder 2\Flex SDK 2\bin*. If you're using the SDK and you installed the SDK in *C:\FlexSDK*, the location is *C:\FlexSDK\bin*. Windows uses a semicolon (;) as a delimiter. If necessary, add a semicolon between the existing value and the new addition.

5. Click OK on each open dialog.

For OS X and Linux you'll want to set the PATH environment variable in your shell. If you are using *.bash* or any shell that supports *.profile* files, you will want to add a *.profile* file in your user directory (or edit the file if it already exists). You can edit the file with any text editor that you want. If you are familiar with *vi*, for example, you can simply open a Terminal and type **vi ~/.profile**. The *.profile* should contain a line such as the following:

    export PATH=$PATH:/Users/username/FlexSDK/bin

The preceding assumes that you have installed the SDK in your user directory (you'll need to change *username* to your actual username). If you've installed the SDK elsewhere you should modify the path correspondingly. Also note that the preceding assumes that you don't want to add additional directories to your path. If you have an existing *.profile* file that already contains an export PATH line, you should simply append the Flex bin path to that line using a colon (:) as a delimiter. For example:

    export PATH=$PATH:/existing/directories:/Users/username/FlexSDK/bin

Once you've edited the *.profile* you'll need to run the following command from any existing Terminal windows or command prompts:

```
source ~/.profile
```

To use the compiler from the command line you simply specify the compiler name followed by the options. The only required option is called `file-specs`, and it allows you to specify the entry point to the application you want to compile, i.e., the main MXML document (or ActionScript class):

```
mxmlc -file-specs SampleApplication.mxml
```

Notice that `file-specs` is preceded by a hyphen. All options are preceded by a hyphen.

 You can get help for the compiler by running `mxmlc` with the help option:
```
mxmlc -help
```

The `file-specs` option is the default option for `mxmlc`. That means a value that is not preceded by an option flag will be interpreted as the value for `file-specs`. The following example is equivalent to the preceding example:

```
mxmlc SampleApplication.mxml
```

Each of the following examples attempts to compile *SampleApplication.mxml* to *SampleApplication.swf*.

Specifying an output location

By default, `mxmlc` compiles the application to a *.swf* with the same name as the input file (i.e., *SampleApplication.mxml* compiles to *SampleApplication.swf*) in the same directory as the input file. However, you can specify an output path using the `output` option. The following compiles *SampleApplication.mxml* to *bin/main.swf*:

```
mxmlc SampleApplication.mxml -output bin/main.swf
```

Specifying source paths

The source path is the path in which the compiler looks for required MXML and ActionScript files. By default, the compiler looks in the same directory as the compile target (the file specified by `file-specs`). This means it will also look in subdirectories for documents and classes that are in packages. However, any files located outside the same directory structure will not be found using the default source path compiler settings.

You can use the `source-path` option to specify one or more directories in which the compiler should look for the MXML and ActionScript files. You can specify a list of directories by using spaces between directories. The following example looks for files in the current directory as well as in *C:\FlexApplicationCommonLibraries*:

```
mxmlc -source-path . C:\FlexApplicationCommonLibraries -file-specs
SampleApplication.mxml
```

Customizing application background color

The default background color is the blue color you see for most Flex applications. You can use the `default-background-color` option to customize the background value. You can specify the value using 0x-prefixed hexadecimal representation in the form of RRGGBB. The following sets the default background color of *SampleApplication* to white:

```
mxmlc -default-background-color=0xFFFFFF SampleApplication.mxml
```

Note that the background color in this case is the background color of Flash Player. Flex components including Application (the main container of a Flex application) have backgrounds as well. Therefore, you have to set the styles of a Flex application's components in most cases.

Changing script execution settings

Flash Player automatically places restrictions on script execution in an attempt to prevent applications from crashing client systems. This means that if too many levels of recursion occur, or if a script takes too long to execute, Flash Player will halt the script.

The `default-script-limits` option allows you to customize each of these settings. The option requires two values: one for the maximum level of recursion and one for the maximum script execution time. The default maximum level of recursion is 1000, and the default maximum script execution time is 60 seconds (you cannot specify a value larger than 60 for this parameter):

```
mxmlc -default-script-limits 200 15 -file-specs SampleApplication.mxml
```

While it's important to know about the existence of `default-script-limits`, it's also important to know that it should rarely be used. If you have to increase the `default-script-limits` setting for an application to avoid an error, frequently it's because there is a problem in the code or in the application logic.

Setting metadata

The *.swf* format allows you to encode metadata in the application file. The allowable metadata includes the following: `title`, `description`, `creator`, `publisher`, `language`, and `date`. You can set these values using options with the same names as the metadata elements:

```
mxmlc -title "Sample Application" -description "A Flex Sample Application" -file-
specs SampleApplication.mxml
```

Using incremental builds

By default, when you compile from the command line, mxmlc compiles a clean build every time. That means that it recompiles every source file, even if it hasn't changed since you last compiled. That is because by default, mxmlc doesn't have a way of knowing what has changed and what hasn't.

There are times when a clean build is exactly the behavior you want from mxmlc. However, in most cases you'll find that it's faster to use *incremental builds*. An incremental build is one in which the compiler recompiles only those elements that have changed since you last compiled. For all other elements it uses the previously compiled versions. Assuming not much has changed since the previous compile, an incremental build can be much faster than a clean build.

If you want to use incremental builds, you need a way to determine what things have changed between builds. When you set the -incremental option to true, mxmlc writes to a file in the same directory as the target file you are compiling, and it shares the same name. The name of the cache file is *TargetFile_#.cache*, in which the # is a number generated by the compiler. For example, the following might write to a file called *SampleApplication_302345.cache* (where the number is determined by the compiler):

```
mxmlc -incremental=true -file-specs SampleApplication.mxml
```

Storing compiler settings in configuration files

Although it is undoubtedly great fun to specify compiler options on the command line, you can also store settings in configuration files. You can then specify the configuration file as a single option from the command line. The load-config option lets you specify the file you want to load to use as the configuration file:

```
mxmlc -load-config=configuration.xml SampleApplication.mxml
```

By default, mxmlc uses a configuration file called *flex-config.xml* located in the *frameworks* directory of the SDK or Flex Builder installation. If you specify a value for the load-config option, that can override the *flex-config.xml*. Many, though not all, of the settings in *flex-config.xml* are required. That means that it's important that you do one of the following:

- Copy and modify the content of *flex-config.xml* for use in your custom configuration file. When you do so, you will likely have to modify several values in the file so that they point to absolute paths rather than relative paths. Specifically, you have to modify:
  - The <external-library-path> setting from the relative *libs/playerglobal.swc* to a valid path pointing to the actual *.swc* file
  - The <library-path> settings from libs and locale/{locale} to the valid paths pointing to those resources (you can keep the {locale} variable)

- Load your custom file in addition to the default. When you use the = operator to assign a value to the load-config option you load the file in place of the default. When you use the += operator, you load the file in addition to the default. Any values specified in the custom configuration file override the same settings in the default file:

```
mxmlc -load-config+=configuration.xml SampleApplication.mxml
```

Configuration files must have exactly one root node, and that root node must be a <flex-config> tag. The <flex-config> tag should define a namespace as in the following example:

```
<flex-config xmlns="http://www.adobe.com/2006/flex-config">
</flex-config>
```

Within the root node you can nest nodes corresponding to compiler options. You can configure any and every compiler option from a configuration file. However, the option nodes must appear in the correct hierarchy. For example, some option nodes must appear within a <compiler> tag, and others must appear within a <metadata> tag. You can determine the correct hierarchy from the compiler help. The following is a list of the options returned by mxmlc -help list:

```
-benchmark
-compiler.accessible
-compiler.actionscript-file-encoding <string>
-compiler.context-root <context-path>
-compiler.debug
-compiler.external-library-path [path-element] [...]
-compiler.fonts.max-glyphs-per-face <string>
-compiler.include-libraries [library] [...]
-compiler.incremental
-compiler.library-path [path-element] [...]
-compiler.locale <string>
-compiler.namespaces.namespace <uri> <manifest>
-compiler.optimize
-compiler.profile
-compiler.services <filename>
-compiler.show-actionscript-warnings
-compiler.show-binding-warnings
-compiler.show-deprecation-warnings
-compiler.source-path [path-element] [...]
-compiler.strict
-compiler.theme [filename] [...]
-compiler.use-resource-bundle-metadata
-file-specs [path-element] [...]
-help [keyword] [...]
-licenses.license <product> <serial-number>
-load-config <filename>
-metadata.contributor <name>
-metadata.creator <name>
-metadata.date <text>
-metadata.description <text>
-metadata.language <code>
```

```
-metadata.localized-description <text> <lang>
-metadata.localized-title <title> <lang>
-metadata.publisher <name>
-metadata.title <text>
-output <filename>
-runtime-shared-libraries [url] [...]
-use-network
-version
-warnings
```

You'll notice that some options you already know, such as incremental and title, are prefixed (e.g., compiler.incremental and metadata.title). These prefixed commands are the full commands. The compiler defines aliases that you can use from the command line. That way, the compiler knows that when you type incremental, you really mean compiler.incremental. However, when you use a configuration file, you must use the full option names. Prefixes translate to parent nodes. For example, the following sets the incremental option to true and the title option to Example:

```
<flex-config xmlns="http://www.adobe.com/2006/flex-config">
  <compiler>
    <incremental>true</incremental>
  </compiler>
  <metadata>
    <title>Example</title>
  </metadata>
</flex-config>
```

In the options list you'll notice that some options are followed by a value enclosed in <>. For example, the title option is followed by <text>. These values indicate that the option value should be a string. For example, as you can see in the preceding sample code, the <title> tag has a nested string value of Example. If an option is followed by two or more <value> values, the option node should contain child tags with the specified names. For example, the localized-title option is followed by <text> <lang>. Therefore, the following is an example of a configuration file that correctly describes the localized-title option:

```
<flex-config xmlns="http://www.adobe.com/2006/flex-config">
  <metadata>
    <localized-title>
      <text>Example</text>
      <lang>en_US</lang>
    </localized-title>
  </metadata>
</flex-config>
```

If an option is followed by [value] [...], it means the option node must contain one or more tags with the name specified. For example, file-specs is followed by [path-element] [...]. This means that the following is a valid configuration file specifying a file-specs value:

```
<flex-config xmlns="http://www.adobe.com/2006/flex-config">
  <file-specs>
```

```
    <path-element>Example.mxml</path-element>
  </file-specs>
</flex-config>
```

The following is also a valid configuration file. This time it defines several target files to compile:

```
<flex-config xmlns="http://www.adobe.com/2006/flex-config">
  <file-specs>
    <path-element>Example.mxml</path-element>
    <path-element>Example2.mxml</path-element>
    <path-element>Example3.mxml</path-element>
    <path-element>Example4.mxml</path-element>
  </file-specs>
</flex-config>
```

When an option is not followed by anything, it indicates that the value should be Boolean. For example, incremental is not followed by anything in the list.

If you want a complete list of all compiler options you can use this command:

```
mxmlc -help advanced
```

Using Ant

Using the compiler from the command line is not the best way to build applications, for the following reasons:

- It's inconvenient because you have to open a command line and type the command each time.

- Because you have to type the command each time, there's a greater chance of introducing errors.

- Not only is opening a command line and typing a command inconvenient, but it's also slow.

- Compiling from the command line doesn't allow you much in the way of features, such as copying and deploying files, testing for dependencies, and so on.

A standard tool used by application developers for scripting application builds is a program called Apache Ant. Ant (*http://ant.apache.org*) is an open source tool that runs on Java to automate the build process. This includes testing for dependencies (e.g., existence of directories), compiling, moving and copying files, and launching applications. Although you can use *.bat* files or shell scripts to achieve many of Ant's basic tasks, Ant is extremely feature-rich (it offers support for compressing and uncompressing archives, email support, and FTP support, to name just a few) and can better handle potential errors than *.bat* or shell scripts.

If you're not familiar with Ant, the first thing you should do is to download and install Ant from *http://ant.apache.org*. Once you've installed Ant, you should add a new environment variable, called ANT_HOME, as well as the Ant *bin* directory to the system path. The `ANT_HOME` environment variable should point to the root directory of the Ant installation on the computer. For example, if Ant is installed at *C:\Ant* on a Windows system, the `ANT_HOME` environment variable should point to *C:\Ant*. Additionally, you should add the Ant *bin* directory to the system path. For example, if Ant is installed at *C:\Ant*, add *C:\Ant\bin* to the system path.

Ant uses XML files named *build.xml*. The *build.xml* file for a project contains all the instructions that tell Ant how to compile and deploy all the necessary files (e.g., the application). The *build.xml* file consists of a <project> root node that contains nested target nodes. The project node allows you to define three attributes:

name
> The name of the project

default
> The name of the target to run when no other target is specified

basedir
> The directory to use for all relative directory calculations

For our sample *build.xml*, the <project> node looks like this to start:

```
<project name="FlexTest" default="compile" basedir="./">
</project>
```

This says that the base directory is the directory in which the file is stored, and the default target is called `compile`.

Within the <project> node is one or more <target> nodes. Each target node represents a named collection of tasks. Ant tasks could involve compiling an application, moving files, creating directories, launching applications, creating ZIP archives, using FTP commands, and so on. You can read all about the types of tasks available within Ant at *http://ant.apache.org/manual/tasksoverview.html*. In our discussion of using Ant with Flex applications we'll focus primarily on just a few of the core Ant tasks, such as exec and move. The following defines the `compile` target for our sample *build.xml* file:

```
<project name="FlexTest" default="compile" basedir="./">

  <target name="compile">
    <exec executable="C:\FlexSDK\bin\mxmlc.exe">
      <arg line="-file-specs FlexTest.mxml" />
    </exec>
  </target>

</project>
```

This `compile` target runs by default because it is set as the default for the project. When you run the Ant build, the `compile` target runs the exec task with an executable of `C:\FlexSDK\bin\mxmlc.exe` (you'll need to change the value to point to `mxmlc.exe` on your system as necessary). Nested within the <exec> tag you can place one or more <arg> tags that allow you to add arguments to the command. In this case we're simply adding the file-specs option when calling the compiler.

Within a *build.xml* document you can also use property elements to define variables that you can use in your document. Once you've defined a property you can reference it using ${*property*}, where *property* is the name of the property. This can be useful for several reasons:

- Properties allow you to define a value once but use the property many times.
- Properties allow you to define key values in a group, making it easier to read and edit the file.

In this next version of the *build.xml* file, we define a few properties and then use them in the target tasks. This version also adds an output option, which outputs the file to a specific path:

```
<project name="FlexTest" default="compile" basedir="./">

  <property name="deployDirectory" value="C:\www\FlexProjects\FlexTest\bin" />
  <property name="compiler" value="C:\FlexSDK\bin\mxmlc.exe"/>

  <target name="compile">
    <exec executable="${compiler}">
      <arg line="-file-specs FlexTest.mxml" />
      <arg line="-output='${deployDirectory}\application.swf'" />
    </exec>
  </target>

</project>
```

Ant targets can have dependencies. This allows you to write several targets that you can chain together in order. This is useful when there are several distinct groups of tasks, some of which you want to run independently, but some of which you want to run together with others. You can create dependencies using the depends attribute for a <target> node. The depends value should be the name of the target that must run before the current target. The following build file adds two new targets called initialize and run. The initialize target runs the mkdir task to ensure that the deploy directory exists. The run task in this example runs a web browser (Firefox), passing it the URL to the deployed application. This version of the *build.xml* file sets the run target as the default, and it uses dependencies to ensure that when the run target is executed, it first calls the compile target which, in turn, calls the initialize target. The effect is that running the run target makes sure the deploy directory exists, compiles the application, and launches the application in a web browser.

```
<project name="FlexTest" default="run" basedir="./">

  <property name="deployDirectory"
            value="C:\Program Files\xampp\htdocs\FlexProjects\FlexTest\bin" />
  <property name="compiler" value="C:\FlexSDK\bin\mxmlc.exe"/>
  <property name="testApplication"
            value="C:\Program Files\Mozilla Firefox\Firefox.exe"/>
```

```
<target name="intialize">
  <mkdir dir="${deployDirectory}" />
</target>

<target name="compile" depends="initialize">
  <exec executable="${compiler}">
    <arg line="-file-specs FlexTest.mxml" />
    <arg line="-output='${deployDirectory}\application.swf'" />
  </exec>
</target>

<target name="run" depends="compile">
  <exec executable="${testApplication}" spawn="yes">
    <arg line="'http://localhost/FlexProjects/FlexTest/bin/application.swf'" />
  </exec>
</target>
</project>
```

Once you have a valid *build.xml* file you can run it from the command line by running the ant command from the same directory as the file:

```
ant
```

This runs the default target in the *build.xml* file located in the same directory. To run a nondefault target, you can specify the target name after the command. To run several targets, specify each target in a list, separated by spaces:

```
ant target1 target2
```

Ant integrates well with most IDEs, including Eclipse, PrimalScript, FlashDevelop, and jEdit. You can read more about integrating Ant with your IDE at *http://ant. apache.org/manual/ide.html*.

Compiling Using Flex Builder

If you work with Flex Builder, you can use the built-in options for building. By default, all Flex Builder projects get built automatically whenever you save changes to source code. For most projects this automatic build option will be appropriate. All you then need to do is run the application to test it. You can run the application by selecting Run → Run *Application Name* (Ctrl-F11), or by clicking the Run button from the Flex menu bar.

> Flex Builder runs the application in your default web browser unless you configure it to do otherwise. You can configure what web browser Flex Builder uses by selecting Window → Preferences → General → Web Browser.

Flex Builder builds all projects incrementally by default. That means that it compiles only the elements that have changed since the last build. If you need to recompile all the source code, you need to clean the project, meaning that you instruct the compiler to recompile every necessary class, not just those that have changed since the last compile. You can do that by selecting Project → Clean.... This opens the Clean dialog. The Clean dialog has two options: "Clean all projects" and "Clean projects selected below." If you select "Clean projects selected below" it cleans only the projects that you have selected in the list that appears in the dialog. Flex Builder then builds the project or projects the next time it is prompted, either by automatic triggers (saving a file) or when explicitly directed to run a build.

If you want to manually control a build, you must disable the automatic build feature by deselecting Project → Build Automatically. You can then select the Build All, Build Project, or Build Working Set option from the Project menu to manually run a build. The automatic build option is convenient for smaller projects that compile quickly. However, it's frequently helpful to disable automatic build for larger projects that require more time to compile. In such cases, the automatic build feature causes long delays every time you save a file rather than allowing you to build on demand.

Publishing Source Code

Since Flex applications are compiled, the source code for the application is not available by default. This is in contrast with traditional HTML applications in which the user has the option to view the source code from the browser. Although not appropriate for all applications, you do have the option to publish the source code for Flex applications using a Flex Builder feature. When you publish the source code, the user can select a View Source context menu item from Flash Player. The menu option will launch a new browser window that allows the user to view the published source code.

From Flex Builder you can select Project → Publish Application Source. The Publish Application Source dialog will open, prompting you to select which source elements you want to publish. By default, all project source code and assets are selected. You can also specify the subdirectory to which to publish the source code files. All the selected ActionScript and MXML files are saved as HTML files.

If the main application entry point is an MXML file, Flex Builder automatically adds the necessary code to enable the View Source context menu item. If you want to manually enable the View Source context menu for an MXML document, you should add the viewSourceURL attribute to the <mx:Application> tag such that it points to the *index.html* page in the published source code directory.

If you are publishing the source code for an application that uses an ActionScript class as the main entry point, you will have to enable the context menu item using ActionScript code. This step requires the com.adobe.viewsource.ViewSource class. You should then call the static addMenuItem( ) method, passing it a reference to the main class instance and the URL for the source code, like so:

ViewSource.addMenuItem(this, "sourcecode/index.html");

Deploying Applications

Once you've compiled a Flex application, you next need to deploy the application. Most Flex applications are deployed to the Web, and therefore that will be our primary focus in our discussion of deploying Flex applications in this chapter.

Every Flex application consists of at least one main *.swf* file. Therefore, at a minimum you will always need to copy at least this one file to the deployment location (typically a web server). However, in addition to the main *.swf*, a Flex application may consist of the following deployable elements:

- An HTML wrapper file
- Data services (web services, Flash Remoting services, etc.)
- Text and XML assets loaded at runtime
- Images loaded at runtime
- Audio and video assets loaded at runtime
- Additional *.swf* files loaded at runtime
- Runtime shared libraries

When you deploy an application you need to make sure that you copy all the necessary files to the deployment locations.

If you are using Ant, you can easily write a *build.xml* file that copies the necessary files to the deployment directories. Ant natively supports filesystem tasks such as copy and move. It also supports FTP tasks for deploying applications to remote servers.

Flash Player Security

Flash Player enforces security rules for what and how applications can access data. Flex applications can access all data resources in the same domain as the *.swf*. For example, if the *.swf* is deployed to *www.example.com*, it can access a web service that is also deployed at *www.example.com*. However, access to data resources at different domains is disallowed by Flash Player unless that domain explicitly gives permission. The Flash Player security rules disallow access to data resources unless the domains match exactly, including subdomains and even if the domain names resolve to the same physical address. That means that a *.swf* deployed at *www.example.com* cannot access data from *test.example.com* or even *example.com* unless the server explicitly allows access. The way that the domain can give permission is by way of a cross-domain policy file.

A *cross-domain policy file* is an XML file that resides on the server that hosts the data resources. The format for a cross-domain policy file is as follows:

```
<?xml version="1.0"?>
<!DOCTYPE cross-domain-policy SYSTEM
        "http://www.adobe.com/xml/dtds/cross-domain-policy.dtd">
<cross-domain-policy>
    <allow-access-from domain="www.example.com" />
</cross-domain-policy>
```

The root <cross-domain-policy> node can contain one or more <allow-access-from> elements. The <allow-access-from> elements specify the domains that can access the resources on the server. You can use an * wildcard in place of the subdomain, which means that any subdomain can access the data resources. For example, the following policy allows access from *www.example.com*, *beta.example.com*, *test.example.com*, and so on:

```
<?xml version="1.0"?>
<!DOCTYPE cross-domain-policy SYSTEM
        "http://www.adobe.com/xml/dtds/cross-domain-policy.dtd">
<cross-domain-policy>
    <allow-access-from domain="*.example.com" />
</cross-domain-policy>
```

You can also use the * wildcard in place of the entire domain to allow access from all domains:

```
<?xml version="1.0"?>
<!DOCTYPE cross-domain-policy SYSTEM
        "http://www.adobe.com/xml/dtds/cross-domain-policy.dtd">
<cross-domain-policy>
    <allow-access-from domain="*" />
</cross-domain-policy>
```

If the server uses HTTPS and wants to allow access to *.swf* files deployed on non-secure domains, it must specify a value for the secure attribute. The following allows access to *.swf* files deployed at *http://www.example.com*:

```
<?xml version="1.0"?>
<!DOCTYPE cross-domain-policy SYSTEM
        "http://www.adobe.com/xml/dtds/cross-domain-policy.dtd">
<cross-domain-policy>
    <allow-access-from domain="www.example.com" secure="false" />
</cross-domain-policy>
```

By default, Flash Player looks for a policy file named *crossdomain.xml* at the root of the web server from which it is requesting the data resources. For example, if Flash Player attempts to load an XML document from *http://www.example.com/data/xml/data.xml*, it will look for *http://www.example.com/crossdomain.xml*. If you want to set different permissions for different resources on a server, you can optionally deploy different policy files in different locations on the server. For example, a policy file located at *http://www.example.com/data/xml* would apply only to the resources in that directory. However, when you place policy files in nondefault locations, you must use ActionScript to load the policy file in your Flex application. The ActionScript code uses the static loadPolicyFile( ) method of the flash.system. Security class. The following loads a policy file:

```
Security.loadPolicyFile("http://www.example.com/data/xml/policy.xml");
```

Deploying a cross-domain policy file presupposes that you have access to the server with the data resources—or that you can persuade those with the server to deploy the policy file. In the few cases where you cannot deploy a policy file on a server whose data resources you need to utilize, you have the option of deploying a *proxy file* on your server. A proxy file is a file that exists on your server (a *.jsp*, an ASP.NET page, a ColdFusion page, a PHP page, etc.) to which your Flex application can make requests. The proxy file then makes the requests to the remote resource and relays the data back to Flash Player.

Understanding HTML Wrappers

Flex applications run in Flash Player, and therefore they don't require any additional wrappers. However, most Flex applications embed Flash Player in an HTML page for the following reasons:

- Many Flex applications exist as part of a larger application that is based in HTML.
- Embedding Flash Player in an HTML page enables greater interaction with the web browser.

Assuming that you want to embed your Flex application within an HTML page, there are many ways you can go about that task. The most complex approach is to write the necessary HTML and/or JavaScript code by hand. On the other end of the spectrum, you can use a template or a tool that embeds Flash Player in an HTML page. Since templates and tools capable of embedding Flash Player are so prevalent, we won't focus on writing the HTML code, though we'll review the basics.

Flash Player runs as an ActiveX control in Internet Explorer and as a plug-in on all other browsers. You can add a Flash Player ActiveX control using the <object> HTML tag, and you can add a plug-in instance using the <embed> HTML tag. The basic code to add Flash Player to a page for any browser is as follows:

```
<object id='application' classid='clsid:D27CDB6E-AE6D-11cf-96B8-444553540000'
codebase='http://download.macromedia.com/pub/shockwave/cabs/flash/
swflash.cab#version=9,0,0,0' height='100%' width='100%'>
  <param name='src' value='application.swf'/>
  <embed name='application' pluginspage='http://www.macromedia.com/
shockwave/download/index.cgi?P1_Prod_Version=ShockwaveFlash' src='application.swf'
height='100%'
width='100%'/>
</object>
```

While the preceding code will embed Flash Player playing *application.swf*, it is a fairly rudimentary implementation that does not take into account issues such as Flash Player detection. In order to detect that the user has the required version of Flash Player you need a more complex implementation that generally uses JavaScript. You can also utilize something called Express Install that transparently upgrades the user's Flash Player version if he already has a version of Flash Player installed that is Version 6.0.65.0 or higher.

Templates for Flash Player detection and Express Install are included with the Flex SDK and with Flex Builder in the Flex SDK resources directory. You can customize any of the templates for your application. The templates use ${variable} to indicate variables that you'll need to replace with values:

${title}
> The title of the HTML page.

${swf}
> The path to the *.swf* file.

${width}
> The width of the Flash Player instance.

${height}
> The height of the Flash Player instance.

${application}
> The name of the Flash Player instance. This is an arbitrary value, but it is the way in which you can address the application from JavaScript.

${bgcolor}
> The background color of the application.

If you use a Flash Player detection or Express Install template, you'll need to deploy the *.js* file and, in the case of Express Install, the additional *.swf* file along with your Flex application.

Using SWFObject

An alternative to using the HTML templates or writing custom HTML/JavaScript to embed Flex applications is to use *SWFObject*. SWFObject is a JavaScript file that enables you to quickly and simply embed Flex (and/or Flash) content in a web page. SWFObject not only simplifies your work, but it also makes the pages friendly for search engines and outputs valid HTML that can be used in HTML or XHTML 1.0 pages.

To work with SWFObject, you first need to download the JavaScript file from *http://blog.deconcept.com/swfobject*. You can find detailed descriptions and instructions at that same page. Briefly, here's how it works.

1. First you must deploy the *swfobject.js* file with your HTML page. In the HTML you must include the *.js* file:

```
<script type="text/javascript" src="swfobject.js"></script>
```

2. Then you should create a div into which you'll write the *.swf* content:

```
<div id="flexApplication">
   This text will be replaced with the Flex application.
</div>
```

3. Now you construct a new SWFObject instance and tell it to write to the div:

```
<script type="text/javascript">
   var so = new SWFObject("flexApplication.swf", "exampleApplication",
                   "600", "400", "9", "#000000");
   so.write("flexApplication");
</script>
```

The parameters for the constructor are as follows: path to *.swf* file, identifier to use for the embedded content, width, height, minimum Flash Player version required, and background color.

Using Runtime Shared Libraries

Runtime shared libraries are a way to share assets and libraries among multiple *.swf* files on the same domain. This is useful when you have several *.swf* files that comprise an application or span several applications deployed in the same domain in which each of the *.swf* files utilizes many common assets and/or libraries. For example, if *a.swf* and *b.swf* both utilize the same subset of 25 classes and embedded images that add up to 100 KB, the user has to download the same 100 KB twice, once for each *.swf*.

The theory behind runtime shared libraries involves a concept called *linking*. All *.swf* files employ one or both forms of linking: static and dynamic. By default, all linking is static. When an asset or source file is statically linked with a *.swf*, that means that it is compiled into the *.swf*. Dynamic linking means that the asset or source file is not compiled into the *.swf*, but the *.swf* has a reference to a *.swf* into which it has been compiled. Through dynamic linking you can specify certain elements that should not be compiled into a *.swf* in order to reduce the total file size of the *.swf*. The *.swf* is then linked to another *.swf* where the elements have been compiled. This allows you to extract common elements from two or more *.swf* files and place them into another *.swf* to which all the *.swf* files are linked dynamically. This new *.swf* is called a *runtime shared library*.

We can understand the benefit of runtime shared libraries by looking at the *a.swf* and *b.swf* example in more detail. In this example, *a.swf* is 200 KB, and *b.swf* is 400 KB. Both *.swf* files are deployed on the same domain. The two *.swf* files happen to use 100 KB of common elements. That means that if a user uses both *a.swf* and *b.swf*, she downloads 600 KB, of which 100 KB is duplicate content. Using a runtime shared library, you can introduce a new *.swf*, *library.swf*, which contains the 100 KB of common content. Although there's some overhead in creating a runtime shared library for our purposes, we'll keep the numbers simple: *a.swf* will now be 100 KB, and *b.swf* will now be 300 KB. Each will be dynamically linked to *library.swf*, which also has to download. However, the second time that the user requests *library.swf*, it will be retrieved from client cache rather than from the server, effectively saving 100 KB.

Although it's theoretically possible to use the Flex framework as a runtime shared library, in most cases it does not work to your advantage to do so. All Flex applications use the Flex framework, which is composed of ActionScript classes that add to the *.swf* file's size. It would seem logical to use the runtime shared library concept to create a framework runtime shared library that is shared by all Flex applications on a domain. However, it's important to understand a significant difference between static and dynamic linking: when you statically link an element from a library only that element is compiled into the *.swf*, but when you use dynamic linking the entire library containing the element must be compiled into the runtime shared library. That means only applications using most or all of the Flex framework would benefit from runtime shared libraries. Generally runtime shared libraries work best for custom class libraries, custom components, and assets you want to embed, such as fonts and images.

The underlying manner in which you create and use runtime shared libraries is always the same. However, if you are working with the compiler from a command line or from a custom build script using Ant, the workflow is different from using Flex Builder, which automates a lot of the work involved with runtime shared libraries.

Creating Runtime Shared Libraries with the Command-Line Compilers

When you want to create a runtime shared library with the command-line compilers you need to use both the mxmlc application compiler and the compc component compiler. First you must use the compc compiler to compile all the common elements into a *.swc* file. A *.swc* is an archive format, and in the case of a runtime shared library it contains two files: *library.swf* and *catalog.xml*. The *.swf* file contained within the *.swc* is the runtime shared library file. You then use the mxmlc compiler to compile the application as usual, but this time you notify the compiler to dynamically link to the runtime shared libraries.

Creating runtime shared libraries is an advanced feature. You may want to return to this section only after you're comfortable creating Flex applications, and you want to optimize an application or applications that would benefit from runtime shared libraries.

Using compc

Like the mxmlc compiler, the compc compiler has options that you can use to determine what gets compiled and how. The first option you'll need to specify is source-path, which tells the compiler where to look for the files you want to compile. If you are compiling classes in packages, the source-path should be the root directory of the packages. If you want to use the current directory you must still specify a value, using a dot. If you want to use more than one directory, you can list the directories delimited by spaces.

You must compile one or more classes into a runtime shared library. You have to list each class using the include-classes option. There is no option to simply include all the classes in a directory. You must list each class individually. You must list each class using the fully qualified class name, and you can list multiple classes by separating them with spaces.

You must also specify an output file when calling compc. Use the output option, and specify the path to a *.swc* file that you want to export. The following example compiles the class com.oreilly.programmingflex.A into a *.swc* file called *example.swc*:

```
compc -source-path . -include-classes com.oreilly.programmingflex.A
-output example.swc
```

Compiling many classes into a runtime shared library can result in a very long command. To simplify this you can use either configuration files or manifest files.

Like mxmlc, you can use configuration files with compc by specifying a load-config option. Also like mxmlx, the compc compiler automatically loads a default configuration file called *flex-config.xml*, and unless you want to duplicate all the contents of *flex-config.xml* (much of which is required), it is generally better to specify a configuration file in addition to the default by using the += operator, as in the following example:

```
compc -load-config+=configuration.xml
```

The following example configuration file is the equivalent of the earlier command, which specified the source path and output, and included classes from the command line:

```
<flex-config>
  <compiler>
    <source-path>
      <path-element>.</path-element>
    </source-path>
  </compiler>
  <output>example.swc</output>
  <include-classes>
    <class>com.oreilly.programmingflex.A</class>
  </include-classes>
</flex-config>
```

If you want to include many classes, you can simply add more <class> nodes, as in the following example:

```
<flex-config>
  <compiler>
    <source-path>
      <path-element>.</path-element>
    </source-path>
  </compiler>
  <output>example.swc</output>
  <include-classes>
    <class>com.oreilly.programmingflex.A</class>
    <class>com.oreilly.programmingflex.B</class>
    <class>com.oreilly.programmingflex.C</class>
    <class>com.oreilly.programmingflex.D</class>
  </include-classes>
</flex-config>
```

You can use manifest files to achieve the same result of simplifying the compiler command. However, manifest files also have an added benefit in that they allow you to create a namespace for components that you compile into the runtime shared library. This is more useful when the runtime shared library contains user interface components that you want to be able to add to an application using MXML tags. However, using a manifest file is not hurtful in any case, because it lets you simplify the compiler command.

A manifest file is an XML file in the following format:

```
<?xml version="1.0"?>
<componentPackage>
    <component id="Identifier" class="ClassName"/>
</componentPackage>
```

The following example will tell the compiler to add classes A, B, C, and D to the library:

```
<?xml version="1.0"?>
<componentPackage>
    <component id="A" class="com.oreilly.programmingflex.A"/>
    <component id="B" class="com.oreilly.programmingflex.B"/>
    <component id="C" class="com.oreilly.programmingflex.C"/>
    <component id="D" class="com.oreilly.programmingflex.D"/>
</componentPackage>
```

Once you've defined a manifest file you need to tell the compiler to use the file. You can achieve that with the namespace and include-namespaces options. A *namespace* is an identifier that you can use within your MXML documents that will map to the manifest file contents. The namespace option requires that you specify two values: first the namespace identifier and then the manifest file to which the identifier corresponds. The include-namespaces option requires that you list all the identifiers for which you want to compile the contents into the *.swc* file. The following example compiles the classes specified in *manifest.xml* into the *.swc*:

```
compc -namespace http://oreilly.com/programmingflex manifest.xml
-include-namespaces http://oreilly.com/programmingflex -output example.swc
```

You can also combine the use of a manifest file with a configuration file. The following configuration file uses the manifest file:

```
<flex-config xmlns="http://www.adobe.com/2006/flex-config">
  <compiler>
    <source-path>
      <path-element>.</path-element>
    </source-path>
    <namespaces>
      <namespace>
        <uri>http://oreilly.com/programmingflex</uri>
        <manifest>manifest.xml</manifest>
      </namespace>
    </namespaces>
  </compiler>
  <output>example.swc</output>
  <include-namespaces>
    <uri>http://oreilly.com/programmingflex</uri>
  </include-namespaces>
</flex-config>
```

When you use a runtime shared library you'll need two files: the *.swc* and the library *.swf* file contained within the *.swc* file. You need the *.swc* file because the mxmlc compiler uses the *.swc* file to determine which classes to dynamically link. You need the *.swf* file because it's the file you deploy with the application and from which the application loads the libraries. The SWC format is an archive format—essentially a ZIP format. You can use any standard unzip utility to extract the *.swf* file from the *.swc*. The *.swc* always contains a file called *library.swf* that you should extract and place in the deploy directory for the application. If you plan to use several runtime shared libraries with an application, you need to either place the *library.swf* files in different subdirectories or rename the files.

Compiling an application using a runtime shared library

Once you've compiled an *.swc* file containing a runtime shared library and extracted the *.swf* file, you next need to compile the application that uses the library. In order to accomplish that you'll use mxmlc in much the same way as you'd compile an application that uses only static linking. However, when you use a runtime shared library you need to dynamically link the relevant classes in the main application and tell the application where to find the runtime shared library *.swf* file at runtime. The external-library-path option specifies the *.swc* file or files that tell the compiler which classes to dynamically link. Use the runtime-shared-libraries option to tell the compiler where it can find the runtime shared library file(s) at runtime. The following tells the compiler to compile the application using *example.swc* for dynamic linking and *example.swf* as the URL for the shared library:

```
mxmlc -external-library-path=example.swc
```

```
-runtime-shared-libraries=example.swf Example.mxml
```

You can use configuration files for these purposes as well. The following configuration file achieves the same result as the preceding command:

```
<flex-config>
  <compiler>
    <external-library-path>
      <path-element>example.swc</path-element>
    </external-library-path>
  </compiler>
  <file-specs>
    <path-element>RSLClientTest.mxml</path-element>
  </file-specs>
  <runtime-shared-libraries>
    <url>example.swf</url>
  </runtime-shared-libraries>
</flex-config>
```

When you deploy the application, you must also deploy the runtime shared library *.swf* file. You do not need to deploy the *.swc* file along with the rest of your application.

Using Ant to build runtime shared library applications

As you've seen, there are quite a few steps to building an application that uses a runtime shared library. To summarize:

1. Compile the *.swc*.

2. Extract the *.swf*.

3. Move the *.swf*.

4. Compile the application.

Using Ant can simplify things because you can write just one script that will run all the tasks. The following is an example of such a script:

```
<?xml version="1.0"?>
<project name="RSLExample" basedir="./">

    <property name="mxmlc" value="C:\FlexSDK\bin\mxmlc.exe"/>
    <property name="compc" value="C:\FlexSDK\bin\compc.exe"/>

    <target name="compileRSL">
      <exec executable="${compc}">
        <arg line="-load-config+=rsl/configuration.xml" />
      </exec>
      <mkdir dir="application/rsl" />
      <move file="example.swc" todir="application/rsl" />
      <unzip src="application/rsl/example.swc" dest="application/rsl/" />
    </target>

    <target name="compileApplication">
```

```
    <exec executable="${mxmlc}">
      <arg line="-load-config+=application/configuration.xml" />
    </exec>
  </target>

  <target name="compileAll" depends="compileRSL,compileApplication">
  </target>

</project>
```

Using Flex Builder to Build Runtime Shared Libraries

Flex Builder automates a lot of the tasks and provides dialog boxes for steps in order to create and use runtime shared libraries. Working with runtime shared libraries in Flex Builder comprises two basic steps: creating a Flex Library Project and linking your main application to the library project.

Creating a Flex Library Project

The first step in creating a Flex Library Project is to create the project by selecting File → New → Flex Library Project. Every Flex Library Project needs to have at least one element—generally a class. You can add classes to the project as you would any standard Flex project. Once you've defined all the files for the project, you'll next need to tell Flex Builder which of those classes to compile into the *.swc* file. You can do that by way of the project properties. You can access the properties by selecting Project → Properties. Then select the Flex Library Build Path option from the menu on the left of the dialog. In the Classes tab you should select every class that you want to compile into the library. This is all that is necessary to create a Flex Library Project.

Linking an application to a library

When you want to use a library from a Flex application, you need to tell Flex Builder to link to the corresponding Flex Library Project. You can accomplish this by selecting Project → Properties for the Flex project. Then select the Flex Build Path option from the menu in the dialog, and select the Library path tab. Within the Library path tab you click on the Add Project button. This opens a new dialog that prompts you to select the Flex Library Project you want to link to your application. When you select the library project and click OK, the project will show up in the Library path tab list. By default, libraries are statically linked rather than dynamically linked. You must tell Flex Builder to dynamically link the library by expanding the library project icon in the list, selecting the Link Type option, and then selecting the Runtime Shared Library (RSL) option from the menu.

When you add a library project to the library path for a Flex project, the application can use any of the classes defined in the library project.

Adding Nonclass Assets to Runtime Shared Libraries

Runtime shared libraries do not directly allow you to dynamically link anything other than classes. That means you cannot directly add a dynamic link to an asset such as an image, a sound, or a font. However, if you can embed an asset in an ActionScript class, you can add indirect dynamic linking. (See Chapter 9 for more details on general embedding.) The following example embeds an image using a class constant:

```
package com.oreilly.programmingflex {
  public class Images {

    [Embed(source="image.jpg")]
      public static const IMAGE_A:Class;

  }
}
```

You can compile such a class into a runtime shared library, and the asset (an image in this case) is also embedded into the runtime shared library. The following example illustrates how you could use the dynamically linked image from an application:

```
<?xml version="1.0" encoding="utf-8"?>
<mx:Application xmlns:mx="http://www.adobe.com/2006/mxml" layout="absolute">

  <mx:Script>
    <![CDATA[

      import com.oreilly.programmingflex.Images;

    ]]>
  </mx:Script>
  <mx:VBox>
    <mx:Image source="{Images.IMAGE_A}" scaleContent="true"
              width="100" height="100" />
  </mx:VBox>
</mx:Application>
```

Summary

This chapter discussed the tool sets and the techniques that you need to create, configure, compile, and deploy Flex applications. You learned how to use the command-line compilers and well as how to use build tools such as Apache Ant. You also learned about the elements of a Flex application, how to deploy those elements, and how to optimize applications by using runtime shared libraries.

CHAPTER 3

MXML

MXML is a declarative markup language used to create the user interface and to view portions of Flex applications. As the name implies, MXML is an XML-based language. If you're familiar with XML or even HTML, many of the basic MXML concepts we discuss in this chapter will already be familiar to you in a general sense. In this chapter, we'll look at all the basics of working with MXML, including the syntax and structure of the language, the elements that comprise MXML, creating interactivity in MXML, and how you can use MXML to build applications.

Understanding MXML Syntax and Structure

If you've ever worked with XML or HTML, the structure of MXML will be familiar to you. MXML uses tags to create components such as user interface controls (buttons, menus, etc.), and to specify how those components interact with one another and with the rest of the application, including data sources. In the following sections we'll look at how to write MXML code.

Creating MXML Documents

All MXML must appear within MXML documents, which are plain-text documents. You can use any text editor, XML editor, or IDE that can work with text or XML in order to write MXML, including those listed in the preceding chapter. In order to create a new MXML document, you can create a new file with the *.mxml* file extension. If you are using Flex Builder, you can use the program's menus to add either a new MXML application or a new MXML component. Both are MXML documents, differing only in the root element added to the document.

XML encoding

Every document can and should have an XML declaration. Many IDEs and XML editors automatically add an XML declaration. Flex Builder adds an XML declaration by default using UTF-8 as the encoding. You must place the declaration as the first line of code in the MXML document, and unless you have a compelling reason to use a different encoding, you should use UTF-8 for the best compatibility:

```
<?xml version="1.0" encoding="utf-8"?>
```

Note that an XML declaration is not strictly required by the Flex compilers. However, for well-formed MXML, you should always include the XML declaration as it is recommended by the XML 1.0 specification.

Applications and components

All MXML documents can have just one root node. There are two types of MXML documents, and they are defined by the type of root node they have. The first type of MXML document is an application document. Application documents use Application nodes as the root node. All Flex applications must have one application document that is the only type of document you can compile into an application. The following is an example of a basic application document that Flex Builder creates by default:

```
<?xml version="1.0" encoding="utf-8"?>
<mx:Application xmlns:mx="http://www.adobe.com/2006/mxml" layout="absolute">

</mx:Application>
```

Note that the layout attribute is not strictly required, but it is shown here because this is the default tag Flex Builder creates.

There are a few items to notice about this example:

- The Application node has matching opening and closing tags. The closing tag is prefixed by a forward slash (/). All MXML nodes must be closed.

- The tag name uses an mx namespace. You can identify a namespace because the tag name is prefixed with the namespace identifier followed by a colon. We'll talk more about namespaces in the next section.

- The Application tag in this example has two attributes, called xmlns and layout. You use attributes to set values for a node. In this case, the xmlns attribute defines the mx namespace prefix (more about this in the next section), and the layout attribute defines the way in which the contents of the document will be positioned. The layout attribute is optional (we discuss this attribute in more detail in Chapter 6). For now, you can define application documents with an absolute layout or with no explicit layout attribute value. We'll talk more about attributes in the section titled "Setting component properties" later in this chapter.

Component documents are used to define *MXML components*, which are encapsulated elements of your application that you can abstract and isolate into their own documents to make your applications more manageable. We'll talk more about custom components in Chapters 18 and 19. The structure of component documents is similar to that of application documents in all respects except that the root node is not an Application tag. Rather, a component document uses an existing component as the root node (which is the superclass for the new MXML document/class). Again, we'll discuss this in much more detail later in this chapter and later in the book. However, for illustrative purposes here we'll look at a simple example of a component document that is based on a standard Flex framework component called Canvas:

```
<?xml version="1.0" encoding="utf-8"?>
<mx:Canvas xmlns:mx="http://www.adobe.com/2006/mxml">

</mx:Canvas>
```

As you can see in this example, the structure of the document is much the same as that of the application document, but with a difference: the root node is a Canvas tag rather than an Application tag.

All other MXML code appears within the root node of a document. For example, if you want to add a button to an application, the document might look like this.

```
<?xml version="1.0" encoding="utf-8"?>
<mx:Application xmlns:mx="http://www.adobe.com/2006/mxml" layout="absolute">
  <mx:Button label="Example Button"></mx:Button>
</mx:Application>
```

Although we haven't yet discussed the button component, you can see quite clearly that the tag that adds the component is nested within the opening and closing tags of the root node. You'll also see that the syntax for the tag that adds the button is similar to that of the Application tag. It uses < and > characters to demarcate the tag, and it uses the same syntax for attributes. The Button tag in this example also has an opening and closing tag. If you omitted the closing tag, the compiler would not be able to compile the application. However, in the case of the button component, you would not typically nest any tags within it. Therefore, it is sometimes convenient to be able to open and close a node with just one tag. There is a shortcut to achieve this goal. You can simply add a forward slash immediately prior to the > character of the opening tag. That means you can rewrite the preceding example in the following way:

```
<?xml version="1.0" encoding="utf-8"?>
<mx:Application xmlns:mx="http://www.adobe.com/2006/mxml" layout="absolute">
  <mx:Button label="Example Button" />
</mx:Application>
```

That covers the fundamentals of MXML structure. We'll be elaborating on how to work with specific components and specialized tags throughout the remainder of the book.

Understanding namespaces

As shown in the preceding section, MXML uses something called a *namespace*. Simply put, a namespace is a unique grouping for elements—in this case, Flex libraries. The entire Flex framework is written in ActionScript classes and a few MXML component documents that are stored in external libraries within *.swc* files. These external libraries contain tens if not hundreds of classes (and MXML components). Using these elements from ActionScript is not difficult. However, in order to use the elements from MXML you have to be able to map the library classes and MXML components to tags. You do this through manifest files and namespaces.

As shown in Chapter 2, a manifest file maps an ActionScript class to an identifier: the MXML tag name. A manifest file in and of itself would be enough to enable access to ActionScript classes and MXML components by way of MXML tags. However, the difficulty is that you need a way to ensure uniqueness of scope for the mappings. For example, the Flex framework defines a mapping called Button that points to a class called mx.controls.Button—a component that creates a simple user interface button. Yet what if you wanted to create your own class that maps to a Button identifier? This poses a problem because you cannot meaningfully have two Button identifiers within the same scope. If you did, how would the application know which button you are referencing? This highlights the utility of namespaces.

A namespace allows you to create a unique uniform resource identifier (URI) that corresponds to a particular manifest document. In the case of the Flex framework, the namespace is called http://www.adobe.com/2006/mxml. This namespace URI is set when the *.swc* file is compiled, as described in Chapter 2. You may recognize this particular URI from the MXML examples shown in the previous section. Within the MXML document you must tell Flex which namespaces you want the document to use. You can do that using the xmlns attribute. If you use the xmlns attribute by itself, it defines the default namespace for the document. Therefore, the following is a valid MXML application document that adds a button component:

```
<?xml version="1.0" encoding="utf-8"?>
<Application xmlns="http://www.adobe.com/2006/mxml" layout="absolute">
  <Button label="Example Button" />
</Application>
```

This example says to use the Flex framework namespace as the default namespace for the document. This means that every tag used in the document is assumed to correspond to one of the mappings in the Flex framework manifest file. Therefore, the Application tag maps to the class that corresponds to the Application identifier in the manifest file. This is perfectly valid. However, this is not the way in which MXML documents typically utilize the Flex framework namespace; an MXML document may contain tags that shouldn't map to the Flex framework namespace by default. Therefore, it is better not to define that namespace as the default, but rather to use a namespace prefix. By convention we use the mx prefix for the Flex framework namespace. You can use a namespace prefix by following `xmlns` with a colon and the prefix before assigning the value, as in the following example:

```
<?xml version="1.0" encoding="utf-8"?>
<mx:Application xmlns:mx="http://www.adobe.com/2006/mxml" layout="absolute">
  <mx:Button label="Example Button" />
</mx:Application>
```

This example, exactly the same as an earlier example, adds the `mx` prefix for the Flex framework namespace. That means you must then prefix all tags that are part of that namespace with the `mx` prefix (e.g., `<mx:Button>`).

By using namespace prefixes, you can create additional namespaces and utilize them within Flex applications. Each namespace can use a different prefix within the MXML document, ensuring that even if two namespaces use the same mapping identifiers, they will not be in conflict. The following example illustrates this:

```
<?xml version="1.0" encoding="utf-8"?>
<mx:Application xmlns:mx="http://www.adobe.com/2006/mxml"
                xmlns:example="http://www.example.com" layout="absolute">
  <mx:Button label="Example Button" />
  <example:Button />
</mx:Application>
```

This example presupposes that there is a valid external library already compiled with the namespace URI of *http://www.example.com* and that the library's manifest file contains a mapping identifier of `Button`. In this example, the application creates one button from the Flex framework and one button from the example library. We'll see more examples of creating custom namespaces for custom libraries in Chapter 17. Although there's no rule stating that you must use the `mx` prefix for the Flex framework namespace, it is the standard convention, and we use that convention in this book.

Components

Flex applications are largely composed of *components*, or modular elements. Technically, a component is an ActionScript class or an MXML component document that has been mapped to an identifier via a manifest file so that it can be instantiated via MXML. There are many different types of components, but in terms of the Flex framework components, there are two basic categories: visual and nonvisual. The visual components consist of the following:

- Containers
- User interface controls

The nonvisual components consist of the following:

- Data components
- Utility components

Containers

Containers are types of components that can contain other components. Every application must use containers. At a minimum, the Application element itself is a container because you can place other components within it. You use containers for layout. There are containers for vertical layout, horizontal layout, grids, tiles, and all sorts of layout configurations. When you use layout containers, you place other components within them using nested tags. The following uses a VBox (a container that automatically arranges the child elements so they are stacked vertically) to stack two buttons:

```
<?xml version="1.0" encoding="utf-8"?>
<mx:Application xmlns:mx="http://www.adobe.com/2006/mxml" layout="absolute">
  <mx:VBox>
    <mx:Button label="Example Button 1" />
    <mx:Button label="Example Button 2" />
  </mx:VBox>
</mx:Application>
```

You can nest containers within containers, as the following example shows, by placing an HBox (a container that automatically arranges the child elements so they are placed side-by-side horizontally) inside a VBox:

```
<?xml version="1.0" encoding="utf-8"?>
<mx:Application xmlns:mx="http://www.adobe.com/2006/mxml" layout="absolute">
  <mx:VBox>
    <mx:Button label="Example Button 1" />
    <mx:Button label="Example Button 2" />
    <mx:HBox>
      <mx:Button label="Example Button 3" />
      <mx:Button label="Example Button 4" />
    </mx:HBox>
  </mx:VBox>
</mx:Application>
```

You can read more about layout containers in Chapter 7.

UI controls

User interface controls are visible interface elements such as buttons, text inputs, lists, and data grids. There are many types of UI controls, and we discuss them in more detail in Chapter 5. You've already had a chance to see several examples with a button control.

Setting component properties

When you work with components, you often need to configure them by setting properties. For example, a button component allows you to apply a label by setting a property. Every component type has its own unique set of properties that you can set. For example, a button and a VBox clearly have different properties because they do different things. However, despite the difference in the specific properties available for components, you can set the properties using the same techniques. You can set properties of components in several ways:

- Using tag attributes
- Using nested tags
- Using ActionScript

The simplest and most common way to set properties for a component is to use the tag attributes. We've already shown several examples of this technique in earlier code examples. For instance, the Application tag allows you to set a layout property using a tag attribute as in the following example:

```
<?xml version="1.0" encoding="utf-8"?>
<mx:Application xmlns:mx="http://www.adobe.com/2006/mxml" layout="absolute">

</mx:Application>
```

You'll notice that tag attributes always appear in the opening tag following the tag name. A tag can have many attributes, each separated by spaces. The attributes themselves consist of the attribute name, an equals sign, and the value enclosed in quotation marks.

Almost all components (all visible components) have an id property. In almost all cases of containers and UI controls, you should set the id property, because that is how to reference the instance using data binding or ActionScript. The id property is the name of the component instance, and it must be unique within the document. The value must also follow a few naming rules. Specifically, the id property for a component should consist only of letters, numbers, and underscores, and it should start with either an underscore or a letter, but not a number. The following assigns an id value to a button:

```
<mx:Button id="exampleButton" label="Example Button" />
```

You can set most properties (though not the id property) using nested tags as an alternative to tag attributes. The nested tags use the same name as the property/attribute, but they must be prefixed with the correct namespace prefix. The following example assigns a button label using a nested tag:

```
<mx:Button id="exampleButton">
  <mx:label>Example Button</mx:label>
</mx:Button>
```

In most cases, it's preferable to set properties using attributes rather than nested tags because attributes are a more compact and more readable format. However, there are legitimate use cases that justify using nested tags. For example, some properties require complex values that cannot be represented by a string value placed within quotation marks. One such example is the dataProvider property for a combo box (a drop-down menu component). The dataProvider property of a combo box must be some sort of collection of values. The following example creates a combo box and uses a nested `dataProvider` tag to populate it with values:

```
<mx:ComboBox id="exampleComboBox">
  <mx:dataProvider>
    <mx:ArrayCollection>
      <mx:String>A</mx:String>
      <mx:String>B</mx:String>
      <mx:String>C</mx:String>
      <mx:String>D</mx:String>
    </mx:ArrayCollection>
  </mx:dataProvider>
</mx:ComboBox>
```

Note that you can also set the `dataProvider` property using Action-Script, which would not require nested tags. However, when you want to use MXML to set the `dataProvider` property, you must use nested tags, as in this example.

You can also set properties using ActionScript. When you set an `id` property for a component you can reference it using that name as an ActionScript object. Most (though not all) component properties have the same names as attributes and as ActionScript properties. We'll look at working with ActionScript in the next chapter.

Nonvisual components

As mentioned earlier, there are two types of nonvisual components: data components and utility components. *Data components* are used to create data structures, such as arrays and collections, and for making remote procedure calls with protocols such as SOAP for web services or AMF for Flash Remoting. You can read more about data components in Chapter 15.

Utility components are components used to achieve functionality. Examples of utility components are those used for creating repeating components and for creating data binding between components. Since utility components are responsible for varied, generally unrelated tasks, we haven't grouped them all in one chapter. Rather, you'll find discussions of utility components in the context of the topics when you'd most likely use the components. For example, the data binding component is discussed in Chapter 12, and the repeater component is discussed in Chapter 6.

Making MXML Interactive

MXML is useful for creating user interfaces—layout and controls. However, static content is not the hallmark of rich Internet applications. Users expect to be able to interact with Flex applications. There are two basic ways to create interactivity in MXML: handling events and data binding.

Handling Events

Every component does certain things. For example, at a minimum, all visual components can initialize themselves and resize. Most components can do things specific to that component type. For example, a button can respond to a user click. All of these things translate into something called an *event*. An event is a way that a component can notify other parts of the application when some action occurs. When a component sends out this notification we say that it *dispatches an event*.

 The Flex event model is based on the W3C specification (see *http:// www.w3.org/TR/DOM-Level-3-Events*).

Every type of component has set events that it dispatches. For example, a button component will always dispatch a click event when the user clicks on it (assuming the button is enabled). However, just because a component dispatches an event doesn't mean that anything is receiving a notification. If you want your application to respond to an event you must tell it to handle the event.

There are several ways you can handle events. One way is to use ActionScript to register listeners. We'll talk about that solution in Chapter 4, when we talk about ActionScript in more detail. In this chapter, we're more interested in the MXML solutions. Within MXML, you can add inline event handler attributes within a component tag. The event handler attribute name always matches the event name. For example, to handle a click event for a button you use the `click` attribute within the component tag. The value that you assign to an event attribute gets interpreted as ActionScript. The following example handles a button click event and launches an alert window:

```
<?xml version="1.0" encoding="utf-8"?>
<mx:Application xmlns:mx="http://www.adobe.com/2006/mxml" layout="absolute">
  <mx:Button id="alertButton" label="Show Alert"
             click="mx.controls.Alert.show('Example')" />
</mx:Application>
```

Even though we haven't yet talked about ActionScript or the Alert component, you can see that in this example, the click event attribute is defined to call `mx.controls.Alert.show('Example')`. If you test this example you will find that when you click on the button, an alert dialog opens with the message that says `Example`.

In this section, our goal was simply to explain the concept of MXML event handling and to show the basic syntax. We'll discuss specific events throughout the book when talking about the components that dispatch the events.

Using Data Binding

Data binding is a feature you can use to link a component to another component or an ActionScript object. Data binding automates changing the value of one object when the value of another object changes. Data binding is an important concept for building Flex applications, and we've dedicated much of Chapter 12 to a detailed discussion of the topic. However, you'll need to understand data binding basics for some of the examples in the intervening chapters.

there are several syntaxes you can employ to enable data binding, but the simplest is a syntax that uses curly braces ({}) to evaluate a statement inline within an MXML tag. In Chapter 12, we'll discuss the additional ways to enable data binding, but before that point, we'll use the curly brace syntax. The following example uses a text control and a text input control stacked vertically. Each of these controls is a standard Flex framework UI control. The text property of each of these controls allows you to read and write the value displayed in the control. In this first example, the text control displays the value Example:

```
<mx:VBox>
  <mx:Text id="output" text="Example" width="200" height="200"  />
  <mx:TextInput id="input" />
</mx:VBox>
```

Now we'll use data binding to link the two controls so that as the user changes the value in the text input, the value displayed in the text control also changes:

```
<mx:VBox>
  <mx:Text id="output" text="{input.text}" width="200" height="200" />
  <mx:TextInput id="input" />
</mx:VBox>
```

You can see that this example uses curly braces to surround an expression. The expression in this case points to the text input control (with an id of input)—specifically, the text property of that control. This data binding statement tells the Flex application that the text value for the text control should always use the value of the text property of the text input control, even when that value changes.

The preceding example was extremely simple and fairly impractical. However, it does illustrate the basic concept and syntax for data binding. We'll be using data binding to link components in a similar fashion in the following chapters.

Summary

This chapter discussed the fundamentals of the MXML language, including its purpose and syntax. We showed how to create MXML documents, add containers and UI components, and how to make the elements of an MXML document interactive.

CHAPTER 4

ActionScript

ActionScript is the programming language that you can use along with MXML to create sophisticated Flex applications. While MXML is an important part of a Flex application, it is mostly used for creating the user interface, and it can go only so far in creating a complete application. For data models and sophisticated client-side business logic, you'll need to use ActionScript as well.

Flex applications require ActionScript 3.0, which represents a significant maturation from earlier versions of the language. ActionScript 3.0 is compliant with the ECMA-262 specification and leverages parts of the pending ECMAScript Edition 4 specification. ActionScript 3.0 supports a wide range of features including formalized classes, interfaces, and packages, runtime exception handling, runtime data types, reflection, regular expressions, E4X (XML), and more.

ActionScript is a standards-based, object-oriented language. Since ActionScript is an object-oriented language it can be viewed as a collection of APIs generally in the form of classes. There are three tiers of ActionScript APIs:

Flash Player APIs

These APIs are part of the Flash Player itself, and they run natively in that runtime environment. Flash Player APIs consist of core classes such as `String`, `Number`, `Date`, and `Array` as well as Flash Player-specific classes such as `DisplayObject`, `URLLoader`, `NetConnection`, `Video`, and `Sound`.

Flex framework APIs

These are the APIs that make up the Flex framework itself. The Flex framework is written in ActionScript, so it leverages the lower-level Flash Player APIs. The Flex framework is effectively a layer on top of the Flash Player APIs. The Flex framework APIs consist of all the Flex containers (`Application`, `VBox`, etc.), controls (`Button`, `TextInput`, etc.), and other assorted data, manager, and utility classes that are discussed throughout much of this book.

Custom APIs

These APIs are for the classes you build for use in custom applications. Custom classes can use Flash Player APIs as well as the Flex framework APIs.

The APIs that comprise the Flash Player are far too large a category to attempt to discuss in this chapter, and in fact there are books spanning many hundreds of pages that still can't cover all of the Flash Player APIs. Our assumption in this book is that you are either already basically familiar with the Flash Player APIs or you are also reading a companion reference specific to Flash Player APIs. Most ActionScript 3.0 books focus primarily on the Flash Player APIs. You will most likely find that the Flex documentation API reference is quite helpful in this regard.

Much of this book is dedicated to the Flex framework APIs, via either ActionScript or MXML. For that reason, this chapter doesn't focus on the Flex framework APIs.

ActionScript 3.0 is an object-oriented language, which means that in one form or another, the ActionScript code you write is part of a class. This book assumes you are already familiar with basic object-oriented programming concepts. It is not our intention to attempt to teach object-oriented theory in this chapter. Yet you will need to have a fundamental understanding of object-oriented concepts to make the most of this chapter. You can find a good introduction to object-oriented concepts at *http://en.wikipedia.org/wiki/Object-oriented*.

ActionScript is an important and essential part of Flex applications. In fact, ActionScript is the foundation upon which the entire Flex framework is written. This chapter teaches you the important fundamental concepts about ActionScript, including the relationship between MXML and ActionScript, ActionScript syntax, events, error handling, XML, and reflection.

Using ActionScript

When you want to use ActionScript within Flex, you have four basic options for where to place the code:

- Inline within MXML tags
- Nested within MXML tags
- In MXML scripts
- Within ActionScript classes

The preceding lists the techniques for working with ActionScript code, from the simplest to the most complex form. We'll look at each of these techniques in the following sections.

Inline ActionScript

Inline ActionScript appears within MXML tags. Believe it or not, you've already seen several examples of this in Chapter 3. Inline event handling and data binding using curly brace syntax necessarily uses basic ActionScript. The following example uses ActionScript to display an alert dialog box when the user clicks on a button:

```
<mx:Button id="alertButton" label="Show Alert"
        click="mx.controls.Alert.show('Example')" />
```

In this example, the text assigned to the `click` event handler attribute is ActionScript code, which calls a `show( )` method of an ActionScript class called `Alert`.

The next example uses data binding:

```
<mx:VBox>
  <mx:TextInput id="input" />
  <mx:Text id="output" text="{input.text}" />
</mx:VBox>
```

This example uses the ActionScript expression `input.text` to evaluate the text property value for the `input` object (the text input control).

Inline data binding represents the most limited use of ActionScript, because it can evaluate only one expression. For instance, the preceding example evaluates the expression `input.text`. You could use a more complex expression, such as the following:

```
<mx:VBox>
  <mx:TextInput id="input" />
  <mx:Text id="output" text="{'User input: ' + input.text}" />
</mx:VBox>
```

This example concatenates the string `User input:` with the user input from the text input control. You can also create even more complex expressions using inline data binding.

Inline event handlers allow you to write more complex ActionScript that can consist of several statements. ActionScript statements generally end with semicolons. The following example illustrates a button with slightly more complex event handler code, consisting of two expressions:

```
<mx:Button id="alertButton" label="Show Alert" click="mx.controls.Alert.
show('Example');alertButton.x += 40;" />
```

This example first displays an alert dialog box. It then moves the button to the right by 40 pixels. Although you can string together many statements (as in this example), it is very uncommon. It's not difficult to understand why this would be. Rather simply: the code is difficult to read and manage when you try to use several inline statements in that fashion. If an event handler needs to run several statements, it is far more common to simply call a function. We'll look more at functions in the next section, and then later in the chapter, in the "Methods" section.

Nested ActionScript

You also can nest ActionScript code within MXML tags. Just as you can nest values for most properties you can nest the values (ActionScript) for event handlers. You must place the code within a CDATA block. Here's an example:

```
<mx:Button>
  <mx:click>
    <![CDATA[
      mx.controls.Alert.show("Example");
    ]]>
  </mx:click>
</mx:Button>
```

MXML Scripts

The second way to add ActionScript code to an application is to place it within an MXML script. An MXML script appears in an MXML document within a Script element:

```
<mx:Script>
</mx:Script>
```

Since ActionScript code may use special characters otherwise interpreted by the MXML compiler, you must place ActionScript code within Script tags and also within a CDATA block, as in the following example:

```
<mx:Script>
<![CDATA[

  import mx.controls.Alert;

  private function example():void {
    Alert.show("Example");
  }

]]>
</mx:Script>
```

You can optionally place ActionScript code blocks in separate files, and you can embed them in a script block using the source attribute of a Script tag:

```
<mx:Script source="code.as" />
```

Within MXML scripts, you can import classes and declare properties and methods. We discuss each of these in more detail in the "Understanding ActionScript Syntax" section, later in this chapter.

Classes

Classes are the most sophisticated and powerful use of ActionScript. Although it's not wrong to use inline code and MXML scripts, it's generally advisable to place the majority of ActionScript code within ActionScript classes.

ActionScript class code exists within separate documents, apart from the MXML application and component documents. ActionScript class files are text files that use the file extension *.as*. We'll talk more about creating classes later in this chapter, in the "Declaring Classes" section.

MXML and ActionScript Correlations

MXML is a powerful way to simplify the creation of user interfaces. In most cases, it is far better to use MXML for layout than to attempt the same thing with Action-Script. ActionScript is far better suited for business logic and data models. However, MXML and ActionScript are not really so different. In fact, MXML actually gets converted to ActionScript during compilation, and the MXML structure can be understood in terms of an ActionScript class. This can be useful because it allows you to better understand how MXML works and how it relates to ActionScript.

When you use an MXML tag to create a component instance, it is the equivalent to calling the component class's constructor as part of a new statement. For example, the following MXML tag creates a new button:

```
<mx:Button id="button" />
```

That is equivalent to the following piece of ActionScript code:

```
var button:Button = new Button();
```

If you assign property values using MXML tag attributes, that's equivalent to setting the object properties via ActionScript. For example, the following creates a `button` and sets the `label`:

```
<mx:Button id="button" label="Click" />
```

The following code is the ActionScript equivalent:

```
var button:Button = new Button();
button.label = "Click";
```

This demonstrates that MXML component tags correspond to ActionScript classes. Furthermore, MXML documents themselves are essentially ActionScript classes, simply authored in a different syntax. This is an extremely important point to understand. An application document is a class that extends the `mx.core.Application`, and component documents are classes that extend the corresponding component class (e.g., `mx.containers.VBox`).

MXML simplifies writing these classes because the MXML tags automatically translate into many lines of ActionScript code that handle important Flex framework tasks such as initialization, layout rules, and so forth.

When you create components with IDs in an MXML document, those are really *properties* of the class formed by the document. For example, the following creates a new class that extends $mx.core.Application$ and creates one property called Button of type $mx.controls.Button$:

```
<?xml version="1.0" encoding="utf-8"?>
<mx:Application xmlns:mx="http://www.adobe.com/2006/mxml" layout="absolute">
  <mx:Button id="Button" />
</mx:Application>
```

The preceding example is essentially the same as the following ActionScript class:

```
package {
  import mx.core.Application;
  import mx.controls.Button;
  public class Example extends Application {
    internal var button:Button;
    public function Example( ) {
      super( );
      button = new Button( );
      addChild(button);
    }
  }
}
```

 The preceding example is an over-simplification. The actual equivalent ActionScript class would be more complex due to initialization requirements of Flex framework components. However, it illustrates the basic relationship between MXML and ActionScript.

When code is placed in an MXML script, it is equivalent to placing code within a class body. Variable declarations within MXML scripts are treated as properties of the class, and functions are methods of the class. This means that the rules that apply to writing pure ActionScript classes also apply to MXML scripts. For this reason, we'll focus almost exclusively on writing pure ActionScript class code throughout the remainder of this chapter. However, note that you can apply what you learn to MXML scripts as well.

Understanding ActionScript Syntax

Whether you're writing ActionScript code inline, in an MXML script, or in a class, you'll need to understand its basic syntax. The following sections look at the basic elements of ActionScript, such as class syntax, variables, statements, expressions, functions, and objects.

Understanding Packages

The majority of classes are organized into structures called *packages*. To understand most of ActionScript, you must understand what packages are and how you can work with them.

A package groups together classes so that you can ensure uniqueness of scope. For example, you can have only one `Button` class within a scope. If you tried to declare two `Button` classes in the same scope, there would be a conflict; the compiler wouldn't know which one to use.

A package allows you to create several classes with the same name by placing them in different scopes. For example, the `Button` class that's part of the Flex framework (i.e., the button UI component) exists within a package called `mx.controls`. When a class is placed within a package, it has what's called a *fully qualified class name*. Therefore, the fully qualified class name for `Button` is `mx.controls.Button`. That ensures that if you want to create another `Button` class in a different package, you can do so without conflicting with `mx.controls.Button`. For example, `mx.controls.Button` and `com.example.ui.Button` (a fictitious class) could exist within the same application without causing a problem.

When classes are in packages, it can be quite cumbersome to have to refer to a class by its fully qualified name. For example, if you want to declare a `Button` variable, you have to use the following code if you wish to use the fully qualified class name:

```
var button:mx.controls.Button;
```

And if you wanted to use the constructor, you'd have to use the following code:

```
button = new mx.controls.Button();
```

Obviously, it's much more convenient to use the shorthand form of a class name (i.e., `Button`). ActionScript allows you to reference a class by the shorthand notation if you first add an `import` statement. An `import` statement tells the compiler that you can refer to the class by its shorthand notation from that point forward. The following is an `import` statement for the `Button` class:

```
import mx.controls.Button;
```

You can simply refer to `Button` as such from that point forward.

 If you import two `Button` classes (from different packages) in the same class, you must still refer to them using their fully qualified class names within that class.

Declaring Classes

Next, let's look at the basic syntax and structure of a class. At a minimum, all ActionScript 3.0 classes consist of the following elements:

- Class package declaration
- Class declaration

Additionally, classes almost always also have `import` statements.

Creating class files

Each class must be defined in its own file. (There are a few unique exceptions, but in most practical cases, a class must be defined in its own file.) The name of the file must be the same as the name of the class it contains, and the file must use the *.as* file extension. For instance, if you want to define an `Example` class, you must create a file named *Example.as*.

Package declarations

The syntax for all ActionScript 3.0 classes begins with a package declaration. As discussed earlier in this chapter, packages are used to organize classes. A package name in ActionScript corresponds to the directory structure within which the ActionScript file is stored. Each directory and subdirectory is delimited by a dot (.) in a package name. For example, if a class is stored in the *example* subdirectory of a *com* directory, the package name would be `com.example`. A class's package declaration uses the `package` keyword followed by the package name. Opening and closing curly braces, which contain any `import` statements and class declarations, follow the package declaration. The following `package` declaration says that the enclosed class exists within the `com.example` package. This also means that the file must exist within a *com/ example* directory relative to one of the source path directories:

```
package com.example {
  // Import statements go here.
  // Class declaration goes here.
}
```

 It's considered a best practice to place all class files within packages with the possible exception of main class files when creating Action-Script 3.0-only (non-Flex) applications.

Import statements

As noted earlier, `import` statements should appear within the package declaration, but not within the class declaration. (Technically, `import` statements can be placed anywhere, but by convention, they should be placed within the package declaration, but not in the class declaration.) You must `import` any and all classes you intend to use.

ActionScript 3.0 classes don't automatically import classes. The following example imports the URLLoader and URLRequest classes from the Flash Player API:

```
package com.example {
  import flash.net.URLLoader;
  import flash.net.URLRequest;
  // Class declaration goes here.
}
```

Class declaration

All public ActionScript 3.0 classes placed within package declarations must be declared using the public keyword, followed by the class keyword and the name of the class. Opening and closing curly braces then follow, within which you place the class definition. Class names always start with initial capital letters by convention. The following example declares an Example class in the com.example package:

```
package com.example {
  import flash.net.URLLoader;
  import flash.net.URLRequest;
  public class Example {
    // Class code goes here.
  }
}
```

Variables and Properties

A *variable* is a named element you can use to store data or a reference to data. You can assign values to and read values from a variable.

When you want to work with a variable, the first thing you'll need to do is declare it. Declaring a variable allocates memory for it and tells the application that the variable exists. You can declare a variable using the var keyword as follows:

```
var variableName;
```

The var keyword is followed by the name of the variable. Variable names in Action-Script are arbitrary, but they must follow a few simple rules:

- The variable name can consist only of letters, numbers, dollar signs, and underscores.
- The variable name must not start with a number.

By convention, all ActionScript variables use initial lowercase characters rather than initial uppercase characters. The following declares a variable called userName:

```
var userName;
```

Although you can declare a variable without a data type, it's always recommended that you declare a variable *with* a data type. You can add a data type to the variable declaration using post-colon syntax as follows:

```
var variableName:DataType;
```

The data type determines the kind of data you can store in the variable. There are many data types, ranging from simple strings and numbers to reference types (such as arrays), and all the types defined by the Flex framework (e.g., TextInput, Button, etc.). There are far too many data types to list comprehensively here (especially since you can define custom data types). However, some of the most common core data types are String, Number, int, uint, Boolean, Date, and Array, as defined in Table 4-1.

Table 4-1. Common data types and their descriptions

Data type	Description
String	One or more characters, including all Unicode characters
Number	Any numeric value, including floating-point numbers
int	Positive and negative integers and 0
uint	Positive integers and 0
Boolean	True or false
Date	The date and time
Array	An index-ordered collection of data

When a variable is declared with a data type, you'll receive errors if you attempt to assign an invalid value to the variable. Flex applications provide both compile-time and runtime type checking.

The following example declares the userName variable with the data type String:

```
var userName:String;
```

Once you've declared a variable, the next thing to do is assign values using an *assignment operator* (an equals sign), as in the following example:

```
userName = "Flex User";
```

You can also combine a declaration and assignment into one line:

```
var userName:String = "Flex User";
```

When you want to retrieve a value from a variable, you simply reference the variable in a statement or expression that expects that type of value. The following example assigns the value from the userName variable to the text property of a text input component:

```
textInput.text = userName;
```

Variables are placed within class methods (find more on method syntax in the "Methods section, later in this chapter). Variables declared outside of methods are called *properties*, and they are scoped to the entire class. In most respects, variables and properties are the same. However, there is one key difference that shows up syntactically, which is simply a matter of scope. Here we describe the contrast between variable and property scope:

- All variables declared within methods are scoped exclusively to those methods. That means you cannot reference a variable outside the method in which it is declared.
- Properties, on the other hand, have much greater scope. At a minimum, a property is accessible within the entire class. However, you can also opt to allow the property to be accessible outside the class with various settings called *modifiers*.

Classes define properties using quite a few possible modifiers. A property can be one of the following:

public
> The public modifier means the property is accessible outside the class (e.g., from an instance of the class).

private
> The private modifier makes the property accessible only within the class.

protected
> The protected modifier makes the property accessible only within the class and its subclasses.

internal
> The internal modifier makes the property accessible only within the package.

Practically, you should always declare properties as private or protected. It is not a good idea to declare public properties because a class should always manage its state (the values of its properties). internal properties are a bad idea for the same reason.

You can declare properties in much the same way as you would declare variables: using the var keyword. In addition, a property name must follow the same rules as variable names. A common convention (and one used by this book) names private and protected properties with an initial underscore (_) to help distinguish them from local variables declared within methods. The following example declares a private property called _loader of type URLLoader:

```
package com.example {
  import flash.net.URLLoader;
  import flash.net.URLRequest;
  public class Example {
    private var _loader:URLLoader;
  }
}
```

In addition to the public, private, protected, and internal modifiers, you can also combine these modifiers with the static modifier. The static modifier says that the property is directly accessible from the class rather than from instances. Static modifiers are used for many purposes, including design patterns such as the

Singleton pattern. The following example adds a static private property called _
instance of type Example:

```
package com.example {
  import flash.net.URLLoader;
  import flash.net.URLRequest;
  public class Example {
    private var _loader:URLLoader;
    static private var _instance:Example;
  }
}
```

A concept related to properties is that of the *constant*. A constant is a container for
data, much like a variable/property except that once it has a value, you cannot
change the value (hence the name, *constant*). You've likely seen constants in the
Flash Player and Flex framework API. A few examples of constants are Event.
COMPLETE, MouseEvent.CLICK, TimerEvent.TIMER, and Math.PI. Although not a requirement, most constants are declared as static, and most are also declared as public
(unlike properties, constants aren't part of a class's state and can therefore be
declared public). To declare a constant, use the const keyword rather than var. By
convention, constant names are all uppercase, as shown here:

```
package com.example {
  import flash.net.URLLoader;
  import flash.net.URLRequest;
  public class Example {
    private var _loader:URLLoader;
    static private var _instance:Example;
    static public const TEST:String = "test constant";
  }
}
```

Methods

A *method* is a way to group together statements, give that group a name, and defer
the execution of those statements until the method is called by its name. All method
definitions must be placed within a class body, and they use the function keyword
followed by the name of the method. Following the method name is a pair of parentheses enclosing any parameters that the method might accept. That is followed by a
colon and the return type of the method. If the function does not return a value, the
return type is declared as *void*. Following the return type declaration is the function
definition enclosed in opening and closing curly braces. The following is a declaration for a function called test( ):

```
function test( ):void {
}
```

The test( ) method is declared so that it does not expect any parameters, and it does not expect to return a value. Currently, the test( ) method doesn't do anything either. Next, add a few statements inside the function so that it does something:

```
function test():void {
  var message:String = "function message";
  trace(message);
}
```

The trace( ) function writes text to an output such as a console or log-file. Chapter 17 discusses trace( ) in more detail.

Now the test( ) method declares a variable called message, assigns a value to it (function message), and then uses trace( ) to output the value to the console (if debugging).

To call a method, use the method name followed by the function call operator (the parentheses). For example, if you want to call the test( ) method, you would use the following statement:

```
test();
```

If you want to declare a method so that you can pass it parameters, you must declare the parameters within the parentheses as a comma-delimited list. The parameter declarations consist of the parameter name and post-colon data typing. The following example rewrites test( ) so that it expects two parameters (a and b):

```
function test(a:String, b:String):void {
  trace("Your message is " + a + " and " + b);
}
```

When you want to call a method with parameters, simply pass the values within the function call operator, as in the following example:

```
test("one", "two");
```

ActionScript does not allow *overloading*. That means you cannot have two methods with the same name but different signatures (different parameter lists). However, ActionScript does allow for *rest parameters*. Rest parameters allow you to pass zero or more additional parameters of unknown types to a function. You declare a rest parameter using a parameter name preceded immediately by three dots. Within the method you can access the rest parameter values as an array.

Currently, the test( ) example requires exactly two parameters (a and b). You cannot pass fewer or more than two parameters. If you want to pass just one parameter (or five parameters), you need a solution that rest parameters provide. The following code rewrites test( ) so that it always requires at least one parameter, but it also allows for zero or more additional parameters. By convention, the rest parameter is called rest (though you may use arbitrary names for the parameter):

```
function test(a:String, ...rest):void {
  var message:String = "Your message is";
  for(var i:uint = 0; i < rest.length; i++) {
    message += " " + rest[i];
  }
  trace(message);
}
```

If you want to return a value from a method you need to do two things: specify the correct return type, and add a return statement. When you specify a return type, you'll get both compile-time and runtime checking. A function set to return a String value must return a string, not a number, date, array, or any other type. A return statement immediately exits the function and returns the specified value to the expression or statement from which the function was called. The following rewrite of test( ) returns a string:

```
function test(a:String, ...rest):String {
  var message:String = "Your message is";
  for(var i:uint = 0; i < rest.length; i++) {
    message += " " + rest[i];
  }
  return message;
}
```

Methods use the same public, private, protected, internal, and static modifiers as properties. If you omit the modifiers (as in the preceding examples), Flex assumes the methods are internal. The following declares two methods, one public and one public and static:

```
package com.example {
  import flash.net.URLLoader;
  import flash.net.URLRequest;
  public class Example {
    private var _loader:URLLoader;
    static private var _instance:Example;
    static public const TEST:String = "test constant";
    public function traceMessage(message:String):void {
      trace("Your message is " + message):
    }
    static public function getInstance( ):Example {
      if(_instance == null) {
        _instance = new Example( );
      }
      return _instance;
    }
  }
}
```

Unlike properties, it is common and acceptable to declare public methods.

Classes also can and should have a special type of method called a *constructor*. The constructor method has the following rules:

- The method name must be the same as that of the class.
- The method must be declared as public.
- The method must not declare a return type or return a value.

The following constructor assigns a new value to the _loader property:

```
package com.example {
  import flash.net.URLLoader;
  import flash.net.URLRequest;
  public class Example {
    private var _loader:URLLoader;
    static private var _instance:Example;
    static public const TEST:String = "test constant";
    public function Example() {
      _loader = new URLLoader();
    }
    public function traceMessage(message:String):void {
      trace("Your message is " + message);
    }
    static public function getInstance():Example {
      if(_instance == null) {
        _instance = new Example();
      }
      return _instance;
    }
  }
}
```

There are two additional special method types called: *implicit getter* and *setter* methods. These are declared as methods, but they are accessible as though they were public properties. The method declarations are identical to normal method declarations, except for the following:

- Getter methods use the get keyword.
- Setter methods use the set keyword.
- Getter methods must not expect any parameters and must return a value.
- Setter methods must expect exactly one parameter and must be declared with a void return type.

The following example declares a getter and a setter method, each called sampleProperty. In this example, a new private property is declared using the getter and setter methods as *accessors*. This is not a requirement for getter and setter methods, but it is a common use case:

```
package com.example {
  import flash.net.URLLoader;
  import flash.net.URLRequest;
  public class Example {
    private var _loader:URLLoader;
    static private var _instance:Example;
    private var _sampleProperty:String;
    public function get sampleProperty():String {
      return _sampleProperty;
    }
    public function set sampleProperty(value:String):void {
      _sampleProperty = value;
    }
    static public const TEST:String = "test constant";
    public function Example() {
      _loader = new URLLoader();
    }
    public function traceMessage(message:String):void {
      trace("Your message is " + message);
    }
    static public function getInstance():Example {
      if(_instance == null) {
        _instance = new Example();
      }
      return _instance;
    }
  }
}
```

You can call the getter method by using the method name as a property in a context that attempts to read the value. You can call the setter method by using the method name as a property in a context that attempts to write a value. The following example creates an instance of the Example class, then writes and reads a value to and from the instance using the getter and setter methods:

```
var example:Example = new Example();
example.sampleProperty = "A";   // Call the setter, passing it A as a parameter
trace(example.sampleProperty);  // Call the getter
```

Expressions

An *expression* is any ActionScript that can be evaluated. At its simplest, an expression might consist of just one literal value or one variable. More complex expressions combine several values and/or variables using *operators*. There are many types of operators in ActionScript, ranging from mathematical operators to Boolean operators to bitwise operators. Most operators operate on two operands. For example, the following uses variables as operands in conjunction with a multiplication operator:

```
unitValue * quantity
```

Generally, expressions are not used in isolation. For example, the preceding code multiplies the values from two variables, but it does not do anything with that product. That value would typically be used in an assignment statement or as part of a larger expression. Boolean expressions are often used in `if` and `for` statements, which we'll look at next.

Statements

Statements are the building blocks of an application. They define the actions and program flow. Statements tell the application to do something. They can consist of variable declarations, assignments, function calls, loops, and conditionals.

You've already seen examples of variable declaration statements, as in the following:

```
var total:Number;
```

An assignment statement uses the equals sign (=) to apply the value on the right side to the variable on the left. For example, the following code assigns the product of `unitValue` and `quantity` to a variable called `total`:

```
total = unitValue * quantity;
```

A statement can also be a call to a function. The following example calls a `trace( )` function, which is a built-in Flash Player function that writes to the console when running a debug version of an application in the debug player:

```
trace("This is a simple statement.");
```

So far, you'll notice that each of the statements ends with a semicolon. All statements of these types should end with semicolons in ActionScript. These types of statements comprise the majority of ActionScript statements. However, there are some statements that do not end in semicolons. Those statements are looping and conditional statements including `while`, `for`, and `if` statements.

Looping statements, such as `while` and `for`, allow you to loop the execution of a group of statements as long as a condition is met. The following is an example of a `while` statement in ActionScript. This statement increments `total` as long as `total` is less than `maxTotal`:

```
while(total < maxTotal) {
   total += 5;
}
```

You can use `for` statements as a compact way to write common loops. The `for` statement syntax is similar to that of the `while` statement, except that in place of the one conditional expression, a `for` statement uses three expressions: initialization, condition, and update. The following `for` statement calls `trace( )` five times:

```
for(var i:int = 0; i < 5; i++) {
   trace(i);
}
```

Conditional statements use Boolean expressions to make the execution of some statement or statements conditional. The following example adds five to total if total is less than maxTotal:

```
if(total < maxTotal) {
   total += 5;
}
```

You can use if statements on their own as in the preceding example. You can also use if statements in conjunction with else clauses. You can use these clauses only as part of an if statement. If the if statement conditional expression evaluates to false, else clauses that follow are run until one of the conditions evaluates to true. It is possible to nest conditionals, and by convention the nested if statement starts on the same line as the else clause within which it is nested, creating what are often thought of as else if clauses (though they are technically else clauses with nested if statements). The following example adds five to total if total is less than maxTotal; otherwise, the code subtracts five:

```
if(total < maxTotal) {
   total += 5;
}
else {
   total -= 5;
}
```

The following interjects an else if clause that tests whether the total is 20 more than maxTotal. If so, it subtracts 10; otherwise, it goes to the else clause:

```
if(total < maxTotal) {
   total += 5;
}
else if(total > maxTotal + 20) {
   total -= 10;
}
else {
   total -= 5;
}
```

Arrays

Arrays are sets of data organized by integer indices or keys. ActionScript defines an Array type. New arrays are defined using an Array constructor as part of a new statement (which we'll talk about in the next section, "Objects"), or using *literal notation*. The literal notation uses square brackets to create an array. The following creates a new empty array and assigns it to a variable:

```
var books:Array = [];
```

You can also populate an array by adding a comma-delimited list of values between the square brackets:

```
var books:Array = ["Programming Flex 2", "ActionScript 3.0 Cookbook"];
```

You can access specific elements of the array using *array access notation*. The following example retrieves the first element from the array (ActionScript arrays are 0-indexed) and displays it in the console (again, if you are debugging the application):

```
trace(book[0]);
```

You can also assign values to elements using array access notation, as follows:

```
book[2] = "Web Services Essentials";
```

Arrays are objects in ActionScript, and they have methods and properties like most objects. It's beyond the scope of this book to delve into the Array API in depth. However, of the Array API, the length property and push( ) method are the most commonly used. The length property returns the number of elements in the array, and it is commonly used with a for statement to loop through all the elements of an array. The push( ) method allows you to append elements to an array.

ActionScript arrays are not strongly typed. That means you can store any sort of data in an array, even mixed types. Theoretically, you could store numbers, strings, dates, and even other arrays in an array.

ActionScript does not have any formal *hashmaps* or similar types. ActionScript does have an Object type, which is the most basic of all object types. Unlike the majority of ActionScript classes the Object class is dynamic, which means you can add arbitrary properties to Object instances. Although it is generally better to write data model classes than to store data in Object instances using arbitrary properties, there are cases when it is useful to use an Object instance as a hashmap/associative array. The following example creates an Object instance and assigns several keys and values:

```
var authorsByBook:Object = new Object();
authorsByBook["Programming Flex 2"] = "Chafic Kazoun,Joey Lott";
authorsByBook["ActionScript 3.0 Cookbook"] = "Joey Lott,Keith Peters,Darron Schall";
```

Objects

Objects are composites of state and functionality that you can use as elements within ActionScript code. There are potentially an infinite range of object types, including those from the built-in Flash Player types to Flex framework types to custom types.

An object is an instance of a class, which is a blueprint of sorts. Although there are other mechanisms for creating objects, the most common is to use a new statement with a constructor. The constructor for a class is a special function that shares the same name as the class. For example, the constructor for the Array class is called Array. Like any other functions a constructor may or may not expect parameters. The only way to know whether a particular constructor expects parameters is to consult the API documentation. However, unlike most functions, a constructor must be used as part of a new statement, and it always creates a new instance of the class. The following example creates a new array using a new statement:

```
var books:Array = new Array();
```

Objects may have properties and methods depending on the type. Properties are essentially variables associated with an object, and methods are essentially functions associated with the object. You can reference properties and methods of an object in ActionScript using *dot-syntax*. Dot-syntax uses a dot between the name of the object and the property of the method. The following example uses dot-syntax to call the push( ) method of the array object (the push( ) method appends the value as an array element):

```
books.push("Programming Flex 2");
```

The next example uses dot-syntax to reference the length property of the array object:

```
trace(books.length);
```

Inheritance

You can create new classes (called *subclasses*) that inherit from existing classes (called *superclasses*). You achieve this using the extends keyword when declaring the class. The extends keyword should follow the class name and be followed by the class from which you want to inherit. The following defines class B, so it inherits from a fictional class, A:

```
package com.example {
    import com.example.A;
    public class B extends A {
    }
}
```

ActionScript 3.0 allows a class to inherit from just one superclass. The subclass inherits the entire implementation of the superclass, but it can access only properties and methods declared as public or protected. Properties that are declared as private and methods are never accessible outside a class—not even to subclasses. Classes in the same package can access properties declared as internal. Consider the class A and class B example, if A is defined as follows:

```
package com.example {
    public class A {
        private var _one:String;
        protected var _two:String;
        public function A() {
            initialize();
        }
        private function initialize():void {
            _one = "one";
            _two = "two";
        }
        public function run():void {
            trace("A");
        }
    }
}
```

In this example, B (which is defined as a subclass of A) can access _two and run( ), but it cannot access _one or initialize( ).

If a subclass wants to create its own implementation for a method that it inherits from a superclass, it can do so by overriding it. Normally, a subclass blindly inherits all of the superclass implementation. However, when you override a method, you tell the subclass that it should disregard the inherited implementation and use the overridden implementation instead. To override a method, you must use the override keyword in the method declaration; the following overrides the run( ) method:

```
package com.example {
  import com.example.A;
  public class B extends A {
    override public function run( ):void {
      trace("B");
    }
  }
}
```

When a subclass overrides a superclass method, the subclass method's signature must be identical to the superclass method's signature, i.e., the parameters, return type, and access modifier must be the same.

Interfaces

ActionScript 3.0 also allows you to define *interfaces*. Interfaces allow you to separate the interface from the implementation, which enables greater application flexibility.

Much of what you learned about declaring classes applies to declaring interfaces as well. In fact, it's easier to list the differences:

- Interfaces use the interface keyword rather than the class keyword.
- Interfaces cannot declare properties.
- Interface methods declare the method signature but not the implementation.
- Interfaces declare only the public interface for implementing classes, and therefore method signature declarations do not allow for modifiers.

By convention, interface names start with an uppercase I. The following is an example of an interface:

```
package com.example {
  public interface IExample {
    function a( ):String;
    function b(one:String, two:uint):void;
  }
}
```

In the preceding example, interface says that any implementing class must declare methods a( ) and b( ) using the specified signatures.

You can declare a class so that it implements an interface using the `implements` keyword, following the class name or following the superclass name if the class extends a superclass. The following example implements `IExample`:

```
package com.example {
  import com.example.IExample;
  public class Example implements IExample {
    public function Example() {
    }
    public function a():String {
      return "a";
    }
    public function b(one:String, two:uint):void {
      trace(one + " " + two);
    }
  }
}
```

When a class implements an interface, the compiler verifies that it implements all the required methods. If it doesn't, the compiler throws an error. A class can implement methods beyond those specified by an interface, but it must always implement at least those methods. A class can also implement more than one interface with a comma-delimited list of interfaces following the `implements` keyword.

Handling Events

ActionScript 3.0 and the Flex framework use *events* to notify and receive notification when things occur. Events occur in response to the user (for example, the user clicks on something), time (timer events), and asynchronous messaging (such as remote procedure calls). Regardless of the cause of an event, nearly all ActionScript events use the same event model.

In MXML (Chapter 3), you saw how to use event handler attributes. In Action-Script, you can handle events by registering *listeners*. A listener is a function or method that should receive notifications when an event is dispatched. For example, you can register a method to receive a notification when the user clicks a button.

You need at least two elements to register a listener: an object that dispatches events, and a function that listens for events. Objects capable of dispatching events either extend the `flash.events.EventDispatcher` class or implement the `flash.events.IEventDispatcher` interface. When an object can dispatch events, it has a public `addEventListener()` method that requires at least two parameters; the name of the event for which you want to listen and the function/method that should listen for the event:

```
object.addEventListener("eventName", listenerFunction);
```

In most cases, the event names are stored in *constants* of the corresponding event type class. For example, the click event name is stored in the `MouseEvent.CLICK` constant.

The listener function must expect one parameter of type mx.events.Event or the relevant subclass of Event. For example, if the object dispatches an event of type MouseEvent, the listener should accept a MouseEvent parameter. The event parameter contains information about the event that occurred, including a reference to the object dispatching the event (the target property of the event object) and the object that most recently bubbled (relayed) the event (the currentTarget property). (In many cases, the target and currentTarget properties reference the same object.) The following example adds an event listener using ActionScript, and when the user clicks the button, the listener displays the event object in an alert dialog box:

```
<?xml version="1.0" encoding="utf-8"?>
<mx:Application xmlns:mx="http://www.adobe.com/2006/mxml" layout="absolute"
initialize="initializeHandler(event)">
  <mx:Script>
    <![CDATA[

      import mx.controls.Alert;

      private function initializeHandler(event:Event):void {
        button.addEventListener(MouseEvent.CLICK, clickHandler);
      }

      private function clickHandler(event:MouseEvent):void {
        Alert.show(event.toString());
      }

    ]]>
  </mx:Script>

  <mx:Button id="button" />

</mx:Application>
```

You can also unregister an event listener using the removeEventListener() method. This method requires the same parameters as addEventListener(). The method unregisters the specified listener function as a listener for the specified event. It is extremely important that you remove event listeners when they are no longer necessary. This includes all cases where you want to remove from memory the object listening for the events. Flash Player will not garbage-collect an object if there are any references to it still in memory. That means that even if an object is no longer used anywhere in the application, except for a reference held by an event dispatcher, it will not be garbage-collected.

The following example removes the event listener added in the previous example:

```
button.removeEventListener(MouseEvent.CLICK, onClick);
```

Error Handling

ActionScript 3.0 supports *runtime error handling*. That means that if and when an error occurs, the application can respond to the error in an elegant fashion rather than simply fail to work without any notification to the user. ActionScript 3.0 uses two types of runtime errors: *synchronous* and *asynchronous*.

Handling Synchronous Errors

Synchronous errors occur immediately when trying to execute a statement. You can use try/catch/finally to handle synchronous errors.

When you have some code that may throw runtime errors, surround it with a try statement:

```
try {
  // Code that might throw errors
}
```

You must then include one or more catch blocks following a try. If the code in the try block throws an error, the application attempts to match the error to the catch blocks in the order in which they appear. Every catch block must specify the specific type of error that it handles. The application runs the first catch block that it encounters to see if it matches the type of error thrown. All error types are either flash.errors.Error types or subclasses of Error. Therefore, you should try to catch more specific error types first, and more generic types (e.g., Error) later; for example:

```
try {
  // Code that might throw errors
}
catch (error:IOError) {
  // Code in case the specific error occurs
}
catch (error:Error) {
  // Code in case a non-specific error occurs
}
```

In addition, you can add a finally clause that runs regardless of whether the try statement is successful:

```
try {
  // Code that might throw errors
}
catch (error:IOError) {
  // Code in case the specific error occurs
}
catch (error:Error) {
  // Code in case a non-specific error occurs
}
finally {
  // Code to run in any case
}
```

Most Flash Player and Flex framework classes use *asynchronous errors* rather than synchronous errors, so the following example may seem impractical, but it does illustrate the syntax for using try/catch. The browse( ) method for a FileReference object opens a browse dialog box that lets the user select a file from his local filesystem. However, Flash Player can display only one browse dialog box at a time. If you call browse( ) while a browse dialog box is already open, it throws a flash.errors.IOError type of error. If you don't handle the error, the user receives a notification in a default error dialog box:

```
<?xml version="1.0" encoding="utf-8"?>
<mx:Application xmlns:mx="http://www.adobe.com/2006/mxml" layout="absolute"
initialize="initializeHandler(event)">
  <mx:Script>
    <![CDATA[

      import flash.net.FileReference;

      private function initializeHandler(event:Event):void {
        var file:FileReference = new FileReference( );
        file.browse( );
        file.browse( );
      }

    ]]>
  </mx:Script>

</mx:Application>
```

The following example rewrites the preceding code using error handling:

```
<?xml version="1.0" encoding="utf-8"?>
<mx:Application xmlns:mx="http://www.adobe.com/2006/mxml" layout="absolute"
initialize="initializeHandler(event)">
  <mx:Script>
    <![CDATA[

      import flash.net.FileReference;

      private function initializeHandler(event:Event):void {
        var file:FileReference = new FileReference( );
        try {
          file.browse( );
          file.browse( );
        }
        catch(error:Error) {
          errors.text += error + "\n";
        }
      }

    ]]>
  </mx:Script>

  <mx:TextArea id="errors" />

</mx:Application>
```

Handling Asynchronous Errors

Many objects in ActionScript can potentially throw *asynchronous errors*. Asynchronous errors are those that occur in response to network operations. For example, if a requested file is not found, the network operation fails asynchronously, and an asynchronous error is thrown. All asynchronous errors are in the form of events, and they use the same event model as standard events. For example, if a URLLoader object attempts to load data outside the Flash Player security sandbox, it dispatches a securityError event. The following example illustrates how to handle error events:

```
<?xml version="1.0" encoding="utf-8"?>
<mx:Application xmlns:mx="http://www.adobe.com/2006/mxml" layout="absolute"
initialize="initializeHandler(event)">
  <mx:Script>
    <![CDATA[

      private function initializeHandler(event:Event):void {
        var loader:URLLoader = new URLLoader();

        // In order to test this you'll need to specify a URL of a file that
        // exists outside of the security sandbox.
        loader.load(new URLRequest("data.xml"));
        loader.addEventListener(SecurityErrorEvent.SECURITY_ERROR,
securityErrorHandler);
      }

      private function securityErrorHandler(event:SecurityErrorEvent):void {
        errors.text += event + "\n";
      }

    ]]>
  </mx:Script>

  <mx:TextArea id="errors" />

</mx:Application>
```

Using XML

XML is a standard protocol for transferring, storing, and reading data for a variety of purposes, including application initialization parameters, data sets, and remote procedure calls. Flex applications can work with XML by using Flash Player's native support.

Flash Player 9 supports two mechanisms for working with XML: a legacy XMLDocument class and the new XML class that implements the ECMAScript for XML (E4X) standard. All XML examples in this book use E4X unless otherwise noted.

Creating XML Objects

There are two ways to create XML objects in ActionScript: using XML literals or with the XML constructor. XML literals are useful when you want to define the XML data directly in the code and you know the exact XML data you want to use. The following example defines an XML literal and assigns it to a variable:

```
var xml:XML = <books>
              <book>
                <title>Programming Flex 2</title>
                <authors>
                  <author first="Chafic" last="Kazoun" />
                  <author first="Joey" last="Lott" />
                </authors>
              </book>
              <book>
                <title>ActionScript 3.0 Cookbook</title>
                <authors>
                  <author first="Joey" last="Lott" />
                  <author first="Keith" last="Peters" />
                  <author first="Darron" last="Schall" />
                </authors>
              </book>
            </books>;
```

 We'll assume that this is the XML object referenced by the remainder of the XML examples in this chapter.

If you aren't able to define the XML data directly in ActionScript, you can load the data as a string and pass it to the XML constructor. In the following example, loadedXMLData is a variable containing XML data loaded from an external source at runtime:

```
var xml:XML = new XML(loadedXMLData);
```

When you use the XML constructor, any string data you pass to the constructor is parsed into the XML object as XML nodes. By default, Flash Player attempts to interpret all string data as XML. That means it interprets whitespace (carriage returns, tabs, etc.) as XML nodes. That can cause unexpected results. Therefore, if the XML string data you pass to an XML constructor contains extra whitespace (for formatting purposes) that you don't want interpreted as XML nodes, you should first set the static ignoreWhitespace property to true for the XML class, as shown here:

```
XML.ignoreWhitespace = true;
var xml:XML = new XML(loadedXMLData);
```

Reading XML Data

Once you have an XML object, you can read from the object. There are two basic ways in which you can read the data: by traversing the document object model (DOM) or by accessing the data using E4X syntax. The two techniques are not exclusive of one another: you can use them in conjunction with one another.

 In each case that outputs an XML node, the following examples use the toXMLString( ) method to format the XML node as a string.

When viewing the XML data in light of the DOM, treat it simply as a hierarchical structure of data consisting of parent and child nodes. When looking at the DOM, focus primarily on the structure rather than the content. You can retrieve all the content from an XML object by treating it in this manner, but you access the data by structure by stepping into the XML one node at a time. The XML class defines a host of methods for retrieving DOM structure information, including the following:

children( )
> The children( ) method returns an XMLList object with all the child nodes of an XML object. The XMLList class implements a very similar interface to that of XML, and all of the methods discussed in this section apply to both XML and XMLList. An XMLList object is essentially an array of XML or XMLList objects. You can even retrieve elements from an XMLList object using array access notation. For example, the following code retrieves the book nodes as an XMLList. It then displays the first element from that list:
> ```
> var bookNodes:XMLList = xml.children( );
> trace(bookNodes[0].toXMLString( ));
> ```

length( )
> The length( ) method returns the number of elements. For XML objects, this always returns 1. For XMLList objects, it may return more than 1. The following example illustrates the children( ) and length( ) methods used in conjunction. This example displays the titles of each of the books:
> ```
> var bookNodes:XMLList = xml.children( );
> for(var i:uint = 0; i < bookNodes.length( ); i++) {
>   trace(bookNodes[i].children()[0].toXMLString( ));
> }
> ```

parent( )
> You can retrieve the parent of an XML or XMLList object using the parent( ) method. For example, the following displays the first book node by accessing the title node first, and then it retrieves the parent of that node:
> ```
> trace(xml.children()[0].children()[0].parent().toXMLString( ));
> ```

attributes()

The attributes() method returns an XMLList object with all the data from the attributes contained within an XML object. You can call the name() method for each attribute in the XMLList to retrieve the name of the attribute as a string. You can then use that value as a parameter, which you can pass to the attribute() method of the XML object to retrieve the value of the attribute. The following example illustrates how this works:

```
var author0:XML = xml.children()[0].children()[1].children()[0];
var attributes:XMLList = author0.attributes();
var attributeName:String;
for(var i:uint = 0; i < attributes.length(); i++) {
  attributeName = attributes[i].name();
  trace(attributeName + " " + author0.attribute(attributeName));
}
```

As you can see, traversing the XML DOM is effective but laborious. Often, it's far more effective to use E4X syntax, particularly when you already know the structure. E4X syntax allows you to access child nodes by name as properties of parent nodes. For example, the following accesses the first book node:

```
trace(xml.book[0]);
```

You can chain together this simple E4X syntax as in the following example, which retrieves the first author node of the first book node:

```
trace(xml.book[0].authors.author[0].toXMLString());
```

E4X also allows you to easily access attributes using the @ symbol. The following uses this syntax to retrieve the value of the first attribute of the author node:

```
trace(xml.book[0].authors.author[0].@first);
```

You can also use E4X filters. Filters are enclosed in parentheses within which you specify conditions. The following example retrieves all the author nodes in which the last attribute is Kazoun:

```
var authors:XMLList = xml.book.authors.author.(@last == "Kazoun");
for(var i:uint = 0; i < authors.length(); i++) {
  trace(authors[i].parent().parent().toXMLString());
}
```

Writing to and Editing XML Objects

You can also write to and edit XML objects using ActionScript. There are three things you can do in this category:

- Modify existing data.
- Add new data.
- Remove existing data.

You can modify existing data using the same E4X syntax you use to read the data on the left side of an assignment statement. For example, the following changes the title of the first book:

```
xml.book[0].title = "Programming Flex 2: Edition 1";
```

The following example changes the name of the second author of the first book:

```
xml.book[0].authors.author[1].@first = "Joseph";
```

If you want to add new data, you can use the appendChild( ), prependChild( ), insertChildBefore( ), and insertChildAfter( ) methods. Each method inserts a new XML node into an XML or XMLList structure. The appendChild( ) and prependChild( ) methods each accept one parameter and insert the node at the end and at the beginning of the structure, respectively. The following adds a new publisher node to each book:

```
xml.book[0].appendChild(<publisher>O'Reilly</publisher>);
xml.book[1].appendChild(<publisher>O'Reilly</publisher>);
```

You can use the insertChildBefore( ) and insertChildAfter( ) methods to add a new node before or after an existing node. The methods each require two parameters: the new node to add, and a reference to the existing node. The following adds a new publication date node (publicationDate) between the authors and publisher nodes of the books:

```
xml.book[0].insertChildAfter(xml.book[0].authors, <publicationDate>2006</
publicationDate>);
xml.book[1].insertChildAfter(xml.book[1].authors, <publicationDate>2006</
publicationDate>);
```

You can remove elements using the delete operator. The following example first adds a new middle attribute to an author node and then removes it:

```
xml.book[0].authors.author[1] = <author first="Joey" middle="Persnippity" last="Lott"
/>;
trace(xml.book[0].authors);
delete xml.book[0].authors.author[1].@middle;
trace(xml.book[0].authors);
```

Reflection

ActionScript 3.0 supports class reflection using the following functions in the flash.utils package:

- getQualifiedClassName
- getQualifiedSuperclassName
- getDefinitionByName
- describeType

We'll next discuss each of these functions in more detail.

Getting the Class Name

You can retrieve the name of the class for which an object is an instance using the getQualifiedClassName( ) function. The function requires that you pass it a reference to an object; it then returns the fully qualified class name:

```
var loader:URLLoader = new URLLoader( );
var className:String = getQualifiedClassName(loader);
trace(className); // Displays flash.net.URLLoader
```

If you want to retrieve the fully qualified superclass name for an object, you can use the getQualifiedSuperclassName( ) function:

```
var loader:URLLoader = new URLLoader( );
var className:String = getQualifiedSuperclassName(loader);
trace(className); // Displays flash.events.EventDispatcher
```

Getting the Class by Name

If you have a class name, you can retrieve a reference to the class using the getDefinitionByName( ) function. The function requires a string parameter specifying a class name, and it returns an Object type. The function returns an Object type rather than a Class type because it could also theoretically return a reference to a function if you pass it a fully qualified function name (e.g., flash.util.getTimer). If you're certain that you're retrieving a class reference, you can cast the return value to Class, as in the following example:

```
var classReference:Class = Class(getDefinitionByName("flash.net.URLLoader"));
```

Once you've retrieved a reference to a class, you can create a new instance, as follows:

```
var instance:Object = new classReference( );
```

Obviously you can use the return value from getQualifiedClassName( ) or getQualifiedSuperclassName( ) in conjunction with getDefinitionByName(), as in the following example:

```
var loader:URLLoader = new URLLoader( );
var className:String = getQualifiedClassName(loader);
var classReference:Class = Class(getDefinitionByName(className));
var instance:Object = new classReference( );
```

Class Introspection

You can use describeType( ) to return a description of all the events, public properties, and public methods of an object. Simply pass the method a reference to the object you want to introspect. The method returns an XML object that details the class name, superclass, various class settings, implemented interfaces, constructor signature, public method signatures, and public properties descriptions.

The following example retrieves the description for a URLLoader object:

```
var loader:URLLoader = new URLLoader( );
var description:XML = describeType(loader);
trace(description);
```

The preceding example outputs the following:

```
<type name="flash.net::URLLoader" base="flash.events::EventDispatcher"
isDynamic="false" isFinal="false" isStatic="false">
  <metadata name="Event">
    <arg key="name" value="httpStatus"/>
    <arg key="type" value="flash.events.HTTPStatusEvent"/>
  </metadata>
  <metadata name="Event">
    <arg key="name" value="securityError"/>
    <arg key="type" value="flash.events.SecurityErrorEvent"/>
  </metadata>
  <metadata name="Event">
    <arg key="name" value="ioError"/>
    <arg key="type" value="flash.events.IOErrorEvent"/>
  </metadata>
  <metadata name="Event">
    <arg key="name" value="progress"/>
    <arg key="type" value="flash.events.ProgressEvent"/>
  </metadata>
  <metadata name="Event">
    <arg key="name" value="complete"/>
    <arg key="type" value="flash.events.Event"/>
  </metadata>
  <metadata name="Event">
    <arg key="name" value="open"/>
    <arg key="type" value="flash.events.Event"/>
  </metadata>
  <extendsClass type="flash.events::EventDispatcher"/>
  <extendsClass type="Object"/>
  <implementsInterface type="flash.events::IEventDispatcher"/>
  <constructor>
    <parameter index="1" type="flash.net::URLRequest" optional="true"/>
  </constructor>
  <variable name="bytesTotal" type="uint"/>
  <variable name="data" type="*"/>
  <method name="load" declaredBy="flash.net::URLLoader" returnType="void">
    <parameter index="1" type="flash.net::URLRequest" optional="false"/>
  </method>
  <method name="close" declaredBy="flash.net::URLLoader" returnType="void"/>
  <variable name="dataFormat" type="String"/>
  <variable name="bytesLoaded" type="uint"/>
  <method name="dispatchEvent" declaredBy="flash.events::EventDispatcher"
returnType="Boolean">
    <parameter index="1" type="flash.events::Event" optional="false"/>
  </method>
  <method name="toString" declaredBy="flash.events::EventDispatcher"
returnType="String"/>
```

```
  <method name="willTrigger" declaredBy="flash.events::EventDispatcher"
returnType="Boolean">
    <parameter index="1" type="String" optional="false"/>
  </method>
  <method name="addEventListener" declaredBy="flash.events::EventDispatcher"
returnType="void">
    <parameter index="1" type="String" optional="false"/>
    <parameter index="2" type="Function" optional="false"/>
    <parameter index="3" type="Boolean" optional="true"/>
    <parameter index="4" type="int" optional="true"/>
    <parameter index="5" type="Boolean" optional="true"/>
  </method>
  <method name="hasEventListener" declaredBy="flash.events::EventDispatcher"
returnType="Boolean">
    <parameter index="1" type="String" optional="false"/>
  </method>
  <method name="removeEventListener" declaredBy="flash.events::EventDispatcher"
returnType="void">
    <parameter index="1" type="String" optional="false"/>
    <parameter index="2" type="Function" optional="false"/>
    <parameter index="3" type="Boolean" optional="true"/>
  </method>
</type>
```

With some work, you can create complex systems that use objects to create sophisticated and dynamic applications.

Summary

In this chapter, we discussed the fundamentals of ActionScript 3.0. ActionScript is the ECMAScript-standard-based programming language used by Flex applications. Although the topic of ActionScript is far too complex to discuss comprehensively in one chapter, we have covered many of the basics you'll need to get started writing ActionScript code, including where to place the code, basic syntax, common data types, how to write classes, the event model, error handling, working with XML, and reflection.

CHAPTER 5
Framework Fundamentals

Much of what Flex does is to simplify application development. In order to do that, Flex does a lot behind the scenes. In many cases, you don't need to know about these things in order to build applications with Flex. However, as you try to achieve more complex and sophisticated goals using Flex, you'll likely find that it is important to understand how Flex works at a more fundamental level. This chapter is all about these behind-the-scenes low-level functionalities and behaviors. You'll learn about the life cycle for Flex applications, differentiating between Flash Player and Flex class libraries, bootstrapping Flex applications, partitioning loaded applications into application domains, and more.

Understanding the Flex Application Life Cycle

Although it's possible to build some Flex applications without having an understanding of the application life cycle, it will behoove you to know the basic mechanics: the order in which things occur. This will help you configure features such as customized preloaders, do things such as load other Flex applications at runtime, and manage the process of loading and unloading class libraries and assets at runtime. Furthermore, a good understanding of the Flex application life cycle will enable you to build better applications because you will know where to optimally run code. For example, if you need to ensure that some code runs during a preloader, you need to know where to place the code for that event. An understanding of the application life cycle helps you to create applications that will deliver an optimal user experience.

As shown in Chapter 1, Flex applications are essentially Flash applications that use the Flex framework (which is written in ActionScript). That means everything in a Flex application can be reconciled to something that is available to Flash applications. The root of a Flex application is typically SystemManager, which is a subclass of flash.display.MovieClip, a Flash Player display object type. A movie clip is a display object type that supports frames, which are units of a timeline. SystemManager has two frames. The *.swf* format is a progressive download format, which means that

Flash Player can access content on frames as they download without having to wait for the entire file to download. The first frame is used to display a progress indicator while the application loads. This frame is lightweight in terms of file size so that it can download and run almost immediately, and it does not house much of the Flex framework. The second frame is the one in which the application itself (along with the majority of the Flex framework utilized by the application) is actually housed. (You can read more about how an application is started and managed in the "Bootstrapping Flex Applications" section, later in this chapter.) Understanding how SystemManager works is essential for customizing preloaders and for effectively loading Flex applications at runtime. Figure 5-1 illustrates the basic application startup event flow.

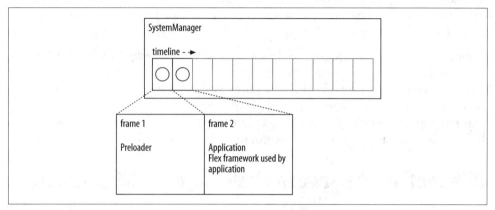

Figure 5-1. Basic application startup event flow

Once the SystemManager instance for a Flex application has advanced to the second frame, it creates an instance of the main application class for the Flex application. The SystemManager instance for the Flex application has an application property that is null until it creates the application object on frame 2. At that point, the application instance is initialized and runs through its own startup procedure. That means that all the application object's internal life cycle events occur. The internal life cycle events are as follows:

preinitialize
: The application has been instantiated but has not yet created any child components.

initialize
: The application has created child components but has not yet laid out those components.

creationComplete
: The application has been completely instantiated and has laid out all components.

Once an application has completed its internal startup procedure, it notifies `SystemManager`, which dispatches an `applicationComplete` event. From that point forward, the application is ready to run.

`SystemManager` also manages all things that are displayed in front of the application content. This means that all pop ups, cursors, and tool tips are placed within the `SystemManager` instance.

`SystemManager` has a property called `topLevelSystemManager`. This is a reference to the `SystemManager` instance that is at the root of everything running in Flash Player at that time. For a Flex application loaded as the main application within Flash Player, this property will always be self-referencing. However, a Flex application loaded into another Flex application also has its own `SystemManager`, and that `SystemManager` object's `topLevelSystemManager` will reference the `SystemManager` object of the parent Flex application rather than itself.

Although you don't frequently need to reference `SystemManager` for an application, you can do so if necessary. All subclasses of `UIComponents` (including `Application`) have a `systemManager` property that references `SystemManager` for the application. The primary way in which developers are likely to use `SystemManager` is to listen for events that are dispatched by any display object in the application. When those events bubble up, the last object to have an opportunity to handle the event is `SystemManager`.

Differentiating Between Flash Player and Framework

One of the most important concepts to understand about Flex is the relationship between the Flex framework and Flash Player. Distinguishing between these things is not difficult once you have an understanding of the basic differentiators. Furthermore, understanding the difference between the framework and Flash Player will enable you to have a much greater mastery of Flex overall.

Flash Player is a runtime environment for Flash and Flex applications. It can run *.swf* files, which contain bytecode that can communicate with Flash Player, instructing it to perform operations such as loading images, drawing graphics, making HTTP requests, and so on. Flash and Flex applications can do only what Flash Player allows them to do. Flash Player provides an API for all the operations it can perform.

Flex applications run in the same Flash Player as Flash applications. That means the *.swf* files for Flex applications cannot contain anything that a standard Flash application can't contain, and therefore, both applications have the same behaviors. This is because the applications contain only the instructions, and Flash Player is what runs the instructions. Therefore, what differentiates Flash and Flex applications is not the content, but how you create that content.

Flex consists of a compiler that is capable of compiling MXML and ActionScript. The entire Flex framework is written in ActionScript and MXML. It provides a layer of abstraction. The Flex framework consists of many thousands of lines of code, all of which ultimately run instructions that Flash Player can understand. This means that when you utilize the Flex framework, the compiler will include the necessary libraries in the *.swf* files. As a result, you can much more rapidly develop applications. For example, although you could write your own custom grid layout container or combo box UI control, doing so takes a lot longer than simply using the components that are part of the Flex framework.

The trade-off of using the framework is that the file size of the *.swf* increases. This is in contrast with ActionScript 3.0-only projects that use none of the Flex framework. If you don't use the framework, increases in *.swf* file size are in pace with the amount of code you write and the assets you compile into the file. This is because when you do not use the Flex framework, you are likely referencing primarily Flash Player classes. Because the classes already exist within Flash Player itself, they don't have to be compiled into the *.swf*. Yet when you work with the Flex framework, a single line of code that adds a framework component can add a nontrivial amount to the file size because it requires the compiler to include a class or a library of classes that aren't part of Flash Player.

You must determine on a case-by-case basis whether the trade-off in added file size is worth the benefits of using the Flex framework. It is a very subjective issue. However, noting that Flex applications are rich Internet applications targeted at broadband audiences, the few hundred kilobytes added by the framework in the typical application are often viewed as inconsequential.

You can easily differentiate between Flash Player and Flex framework classes using these guidelines:

- If the class is in a package starting with the word *flash* (e.g., `flash.net.URLLoader`), it is part of Flash Player.
- If the class is in a package starting with the letters *mx* (e.g., `mx.controls.Button`), it is part of the Flex framework.
- MXML tags almost always (with few exceptions) correspond to Flex framework classes.

Bootstrapping Flex Applications

Although it would be natural enough to assume that the root of a Flex application is an `Application` object (because the root tag of the runnable application is an `Application` tag), it turns out that the default root object is, in fact, of type `mx.managers.SystemManager`.

In order to understand `SystemManager` and the bootstrapping process, you have to understand just a little about a Flash Player class called `flash.display.MovieClip`. The `MovieClip` class is a display object type which allows you to programmatically work with timelines. Timelines are a feature often used in Flash applications because

Flash authoring allows developers to work with timelines through the program interface. Timelines are not used frequently in Flex applications because there is no programmatic way to add frames (the basic units of a timeline) to a timeline. However, timelines and frames are an essential part of SystemManager, and in order to understand how Flex applications work, you must understand a few things about timelines.

A timeline is composed of frames. A frame represents a point in time during the playback of a timeline. This is similar to timeline concepts used in any sort of animation or video program. Because there's no way to programmatically add frames, almost all display objects in Flex applications consist of just one frame. However, SystemManager is the one exception to this rule. SystemManager consists of two frames. This is essential because it enables the Flex application to have a preloader that indicates download progress to the user. The preloader must exist on the first frame, and the Flex application (the Application object) must exist on the second frame.

Most of the time, this information about two frames and SystemManager will be fairly unimportant to you while you're building Flex applications because Flex automatically handles all the bootstrapping and initialization, including creation of the SystemManager object and the default preloader. However, there are at least two instances when you'll want to know this information: when loading a Flex application into another Flex application and when customizing the preloader.

Loading One Flex Application into Another Flex Application

Loading one Flex application into another Flex application is actually remarkably simple. You need only to create an SWFLoader instance and set the source property, as in this example:

```
<mx:SWFLoader source="application.swf" />
```

However, it gets slightly more challenging when you want to interact with the content you are loading. For example, if you want to call a public method defined in the loaded application, you must know two important things:

- What is the path to the loaded application relative to the SWFLoader used to load the application?
- When has the loaded application actually initialized?

The answers to these questions are as follows. When an SWFLoader loads a Flex application, the SWFLoader object's content property provides a reference to the root of the loaded Flex application. As we've already discussed, that root is a SystemManager object. The SystemManager class defines an application property that references the Application object. However, it's important to understand that the application property of a SystemManager object for a Flex application that has just loaded will be null because the loaded content will still be on its first frame, and the Application instance isn't constructed until the second frame. This might seem to pose a problem, but there is a relatively elegant solution.

When an SWFLoader loads and initializes the content, it dispatches an init event. You should first handle the init event. This tells you when you can reference the SystemManager for the loaded content. You must then add an event listener for the applicationComplete event for the SystemManager. When the applicationComplete event occurs, you can reference the Application object for the loaded content.

Let's look at an example that illustrates the proper way to load one Flex application into another and use events to wait until the application has actually initialized before trying to communicate with the loaded content. In this example, we'll first look at the code for the Flex application that will load into another. This is the code for a runnable MXML application file called *B.mxml*. This application creates a canvas with a background color of white. It also adds a public method that allows loading applications to set the background color.

```
<?xml version="1.0" encoding="utf-8"?>
<mx:Application xmlns:mx="http://www.adobe.com/2006/mxml" layout="absolute">
    <mx:Script>
        <![CDATA[

            public function setBackground(color:Number):void {
                canvas.setStyle("backgroundColor", color);
            }

        ]]>
    </mx:Script>
    <mx:Canvas id="canvas" backgroundColor="#FFFFFF" width="100" height="100" />
</mx:Application>
```

Here's the runnable MXML application file for the Flex application that loads *B.swf*. Note that we first listen for the init event. Once the init event occurs, you add a listener to the SystemManager object for applicationComplete. Then, once applicationComplete occurs, you can call the public method of the loaded content.

```
<?xml version="1.0" encoding="utf-8"?>
<mx:Application xmlns:mx="http://www.adobe.com/2006/mxml" layout="absolute">
    <mx:Script>
        <![CDATA[
            import mx.managers.SystemManager;
            import mx.events.FlexEvent;

            private function initHandler(event:Event):void {
                event.target.content.addEventListener(FlexEvent.APPLICATION_COMPLETE,
applicationCompleteHandler);
            }

            private function applicationCompleteHandler(event:Event):void {
                event.target.application.setBackground(0xFFFF00);
            }

        ]]>
    </mx:Script>
    <mx:SWFLoader source="B.swf" init="initHandler(event)" />
</mx:Application>
```

With this simple example, you can see how to load one application into another application.

 Note that Flex 2.0.1 has a built-in feature for building modular applications that use several *.swf* files stitched together at runtime. In many cases, using modules is a much simpler way to achieve the same goals as loading one *.swf* into another. See Chapter 18 for more information on modules.

Understanding Application Domains

Application domains are critically important to how Flex applications function, but in most cases, you don't even know they are there. An application domain is the partition within which an application runs in Flash Player. In many cases, just one application is running in Flash Player, and in such cases, there is just one application domain. However, when you load additional *.swf* files into an existing application, you can create additional application domains for some or all of those additional applications.

When you load a *.swf* file, three possible things can occur:

- The loaded *.swf* runs in a new application domain that is completely partitioned from all other application domains.
- The loaded *.swf* runs in a new application domain that is a child of an existing application domain.
- The loaded *.swf* runs in an existing application domain.

Each scenario is subtly different. However, subtle differences can have a big effect, and it's important to understand these differences so that you can understand what choices to make in each case.

All Flex and Flash applications are composed of collections of classes. An application domain holds the collections of classes for an application or applications. When just one application is running in Flash Player, the concept of an application domain is practically a formality because you are guaranteed that an *.swf* will never contain more than one definition for a class. However, when you load an additional *.swf* file, there is a possibility that it will contain a definition for a class by the same name as one that is already loaded from another *.swf* file. An application domain ensures that within the domain there is only one definition for each class. Therefore, it has a set of rules for determining how to choose between conflicting definitions if such a scenario presents itself.

If an application is loaded into an application domain with a parent, it essentially inherits all the class definitions from the parent application domain. The result is that the child application domain cannot have class definitions for classes that are otherwise defined in the parent application domain. For example, if you load one

Flex application *.swf* into another Flex application *.swf* with the default settings, there would be two application domains but one would be a child of the other, and all duplicate Flex framework classes from the child would be disregarded in favor of the same classes from the parent application domain. This is often appropriate, and it has several possible benefits:

- It uses less memory. If the duplicate classes were not disregarded, memory usage would increase.

- Singleton manager classes are accessible to both the parent and the child applications (meaning that just one instance of the class is shared by parent and child applications).

- Theoretically, it is possible to compile the child *.swf* files by excluding any duplicate classes the child *.swf* would inherit at runtime from the parent application domain. This would reduce the file size overhead in child *.swf* files.

Just as there are cases in which this default child domain behavior is useful, sometimes it works at cross purposes with the needs or requirements of a project. For example, consider the scenario in which two applications are built using two classes with the same name but very different implementations. If one is loaded into the other, the child will not work as intended because that class will be discarded in the child, and the parent version will be used in both applications. In such a case, it is clear that there is a need to be able to completely partition the applications into separate application domains. Separate application domains ensure that the sorts of conflicts just described don't occur. However, it is important to use these sorts of exclusive application domains only when necessary because they will increase memory usage.

The third scenario is one in which an *.swf* is loaded into the same application domain as the loading/requesting application. This is the behavior utilized by runtime shared libraries. It is also useful when you want to load libraries of fonts and other assets at runtime for use in the requesting application.

You create each scenario (exclusive application domains, parent/child application domains, and same application domains) by specifying a `flash.system.LoaderContext` with the appropriate setting when calling the `load()` method of a `flash.display.Loader` or a `flash.net.URLLoader` object. The `LoaderContext` class defines an `applicationDomain` property. Setting the value of this property determines the application domain for the loaded content. The `applicationDomain` property is of type `flash.system.ApplicationDomain`. The `ApplicationDomain` class has a static property called `currentDomain` that is a reference to the application domain of the requesting code. We'll next look at how to use a `LoaderContext` and an `ApplicationDomain` object (in conjunction with the `currentDomain` property) to achieve the necessary behavior for each of the aforementioned scenarios.

You can achieve the default behavior (the content is loaded into a child domain) by passing no second parameter to the load( ) method. You can achieve the same behavior when passing a LoaderContext object with the applicationDomain set to a new ApplicationDomain object that uses ApplicationDomain.currentDomain as the parent application domain. You do this by passing ApplicationDomain.currentDomain to the constructor of the constructor, as shown here:

```
var context:LoaderContext = new LoaderContext( );
context.applicationDomain = new ApplicationDomain(ApplicationDomain.currentDomain);
var request:URLRequest = new URLRequest("RuntimeLoadingExample.swf");
var loader:Loader = new Loader( );
loader.load(request, context);
```

You can achieve an exclusive, separate application domain for loaded content by constructing an ApplicationDomain object with no parameter passed to the constructor:

```
var context:LoaderContext = new LoaderContext( );
context.applicationDomain = new ApplicationDomain( );
var request:URLRequest = new URLRequest("RuntimeLoadingExample.swf");
var loader:Loader = new Loader( );
loader.load(request, context);
```

If you want to load the content into the same application domain, you can simply use ApplicationDomain.currentDomain:

```
var context:LoaderContext = new LoaderContext( );
context.applicationDomain = ApplicationDomain.currentDomain;
var request:URLRequest = new URLRequest("RuntimeLoadingExample.swf");
var loader:Loader = new Loader( );
loader.load(request, context);
```

 You can read more about ApplicationDomain in the Flex documentation and at *http://mannu.livejournal.com/372662.html*.

Understanding the Preloader

By default, all Flex applications have a preloader with a progress bar that indicates progress as the application loads and initializes. This preloader is a lightweight class that is created on the first frame of the system manager. The preloader dispatches a series of events that the progress bar then handles. Typically the progress bar registers one or more listeners for events dispatched by the preloader object. The following are valid events for preloaders:

progress
    Indicates download progress

complete
    Indicates that the download is complete

`rslError`
    Indicates that a runtime shared library could not load

`rslProgress`
    Indicates the download progress for a runtime shared library

`rslComplete`
    Indicates that the download is complete for runtime shared libraries

`initProgress`
    Indicates that the application is initializing

`initComplete`
    Indicates that the application has initialized

Once the `complete` event occurs, the system manager advances to the second frame where the application itself is created and initialized. The application runs through its initial events, and it then notifies the system manager which in turn notifies the preloader about initialization progress. The preloader then notifies the system manager when it is ready to have the system manager remove it from the display.

You can read more about customizing preloaders in Chapter 14.

Summary

In this chapter, you learned about the low-level workings of the Flex framework. Although it's not always necessary to work directly with these aspects of a Flex application, an understanding of these topics can help you when building applications that might require lower-level changes. We also discussed the Flex application life cycle, differentiating between the Flex framework and Flash Player API, bootstrapping a Flex application, application domains, and preloader events.

CHAPTER 6
Managing Layout

One of the key features of Flex is its ability to simplify application layout. Traditional application development requires writing layout code, or working with layout components in a nonintuitive manner. With MXML and Flex's layout containers, you can produce most applications without having to write a single line of custom layout code.

In this chapter, we will provide an overview of Flex layout containers and discuss the layout rules used by containers. We will also cover how to work with containers and children, nesting containers, and building fluid interfaces.

Flex Layout Overview

Container components are the basis of how Flex provides layout logic. At the most basic level, the `Application` class is a container, and subitems within the `Application` class (tag) are called *children*. In MXML, placing nodes within a container declaration signifies that the objects are instantiated and added to the container as container children, and the container automatically handles their positioning and sizing.

For example, in the following code two children are added to the `Application` container—a `TextInput` instance and a `Button` instance:

```
<?xml version="1.0" encoding="utf-8"?>
<mx:Application xmlns:mx="http://www.adobe.com/2006/mxml">
    <mx:TextInput/>
    <mx:Button label="Submit"/>
</mx:Application>
```

If you are using Flex Builder, the default MXML template sets the layout property of the root `Application` instance to absolute. The layout property of the `Application` container controls how children are positioned and sized, and if the value is set, the examples may not work as expected.

96

In the preceding code, you added two children to the Application container by simply placing the children as subnodes of the container using MXML. This adds the children to the container's display list, which is very similar to Flash Player 9's display list. Also, notice that you didn't have to explicitly place the children at a specific position within the container in the code. That is because some containers by default automatically position children for you using their layout rules, rather than requiring you to provide the exact coordinates of each child's position. Although this may seem like a limitation, it is not a requirement, and you have the option of setting your own values, using different containers to achieve the layout you want, or even specifying an exact fixed pixel position and size, as we will discuss throughout this chapter.

Containers and user interface components have many things in common regarding the inheritance chain, which makes containers easier to work with if you are familiar with Flex components in general. The main difference is that containers are not meant to receive user input, as most user interface components are; instead, their purpose is to house child controls or other layout containers. Because of this, their tabChildren property is set to true, and their tabEnabled property is set to false.

The tabEnabled property built into Flash Player is part of the InteractiveObject class, from which containers inherit. The property controls whether an object can receive user focus, which is not the purpose of containers. So, by default, the tabEnabled property is usually set to false. The tabChildren property, inherited from DisplayObjectContainer, is what instructs Flash Player to allow children of a container to receive user focus.

In the previous code sample, we added children to a container using MXML. You can also do this using ActionScript, as shown in Example 6-1. Understanding the code in Example 6-1 will give you insight into how MXML works.

Example 6-1. Adding children to a container using ActionScript

```
<?xml version="1.0" encoding="utf-8"?>
<mx:Application xmlns:mx="http://www.adobe.com/2006/mxml" initialize="addItems()">
    <mx:Script>
        <![CDATA[
            import mx.controls.Button;
            import mx.controls.TextInput;
            private function addItems():void
            {
                var ti:TextInput = new TextInput();
                this.addChild(ti);
                var btn:Button = new Button();
                btn.label = "Submit";
                this.addChild(btn);
            }
        ]]>
```

Example 6-1. Adding children to a container using ActionScript (continued)

```
    </mx:Script>
</mx:Application>
```

As you can see in Example 6-1, the ActionScript code is much more verbose than the MXML code. This is a prime example of how MXML is ideal for rapidly developing application user interfaces. In general, you should write application layout in MXML whenever possible, and choose ActionScript only when you want to do more at run-time, such as add an arbitrary number of children, or in cases where MXML doesn't provide enough control to achieve the desired layout. Keep in mind that you can mix both ActionScript and MXML in an application's layout, so it's important to learn how to code in both ways. If you find that a portion of your layout requires dynamic control over child instantiation, you may opt to handle that with ActionScript and the display list API, and handle the rest of the layout using MXML.

Working with Children

In addition to adding children, you also have the ability to remove, reorder, and retrieve the children of a container. In Flex, container children are synonymous with children that inherit from the UIComponent class.

> Container children must implement the IUIComponent interface. Because the UIComponent class implements this interface, we typically will refer to UIComponent-based components as *valid container children*. If you plan to implement a custom child, you need to ensure that you implement IUIComponent for containers to handle the child properly.

Setting up the initial state of a container via MXML is simple enough, but managing change afterward requires a better understanding of the ActionScript display list API. The methods addChild( ), addChildAt( ), getChildAt( ), getChildByName( ), getChildIndex( ), getChildren( ), removeAllChildren( ), contains( ), and setChildIndex( ), as well as the numChildren property, are the Container class members related to working with Children. Most of them are self-explanatory. Example 6-2 takes the last child and moves it to the first position in a container's children when the button is pressed.

Example 6-2. Reordering children using the display list API

```
<?xml version="1.0" encoding="utf-8"?>
<mx:Application xmlns:mx="http://www.adobe.com/2006/mxml">
    <mx:Script>
        <![CDATA[
        private function moveToTheBeginning( ):void
        {
```

Example 6-2. Reordering children using the display list API (continued)

```
            // Retrieve the index of the last child, child indices are zero-based
            var lastChildIndex:int = tileOfLabels.numChildren - 1;

            // Get a reference to the last child
            var child:DisplayObject = tileOfLabels.getChildAt(lastChildIndex);

            // Change the index of the child
            tileOfLabels.setChildIndex(child,0);
        }
      ]]>
  </mx:Script>
  <mx:Tile id="tileOfLabels">
      <mx:Label text="1"/>
      <mx:Label text="2"/>
      <mx:Label text="3"/>
      <mx:Label text="4"/>
      <mx:Label text="5"/>
      <mx:Label text="6"/>
  </mx:Tile>
  <mx:Button label="Move to the beginning" click="moveToTheBeginning()"/>
</mx:Application>
```

This basic example covers a few important concepts. First, the initial layout contains six buttons within a Tile container, each labeled according to its order within the Tile. A button at the bottom is used to call a function to move the last child to the beginning of the Tile container. In moveToTheBeginning( ), the index of the last child is retrieved, which is zero-based. Next, a reference to the last child in the display list is obtained using getChildAt( ). After the last child index is retrieved, setChildIndex( ) is called and passes a reference to the button instance and a new index.

 A good thing to keep in mind is that although MXML is ideal for laying out an application, you have full control of that layout at runtime using ActionScript. For instance, in ActionScript you can achieve tasks such as hiding containers depending on user interaction, as well as reordering containers and changing their sizes.

If you are familiar with how Flash Player handles display objects, handling children within containers should already look familiar, because Flex implements the same API for handling child objects that Flash Player does. Note, however, that although the API between Flash Player and Flex is the same, there is a subtle difference. Flex containers, unlike Flash Player, *do not* return at runtime a reference to all children that are actually part of a container. Children in Flex are divided into two types: content and chrome. Children used to draw the outline, header, or other unique rendered items related to the container are hidden from the display list API in Flex and are referred to as *chrome children*. Children added to a container, such as Button or

Label, are *content children*. Flex does this to simplify the process of dealing with children, because typically a developer is more interested in the content children.

 Although Flex hides the chrome-related children, you still can gain access to the complete display list and manipulate its children using the container property, rawChildren. Flex provides this property to grant access to the entire display list. Typically you won't need to work with this, although when working on custom containers you may find this very useful.

Container Types

Every container provided by the Flex framework has a set of rules by which it lays out its children. Flex uses these rules to measure the available space for children, and to decide where children are positioned. A VBox container, for example, arranges its children vertically, placing only one item per row. Similarly, an HBox container arranges its children horizontally. Every container in Flex was designed with a purpose (see Figure 6-1). Knowing when to use a particular container is important as you build your Flex applications.

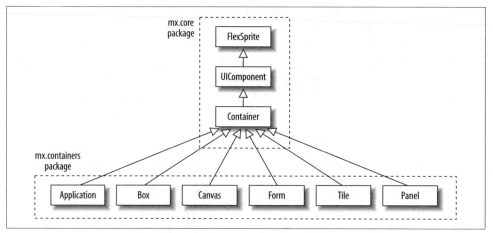

Figure 6-1. Class diagram of container components

Table 6-1 lists the different container types in Flex, and describes how each is used.

Table 6-1. The different Flex container types

Container type	Description
Application	This special container is the root of a Flex application. By default, it behaves like a VBox container. The layout property controls how children are laid out. The possible values are ContainerLayout. ABSOLUTE, ContainerLayout.VERTICAL, and ContainerLayout.HORIZONTAL. Setting the layout property to ABSOLUTE causes this container to behave as a Canvas container, and allows you to specify absolute positions for each child. Setting the value to HORIZONTAL or VERTICAL causes the layout to behave like an HBox or VBox, respectively.
Box	Typically, you will not use this container directly, but it is an important container to understand because many containers base their layout rules on it. This container lays out its children, one after the other, in a single column (or row), depending on the direction of the property value. By default, the contents are laid out vertically. Possible values for the direction property are BoxDirection.VERTICAL and BoxDirection.HORIZONTAL. Box is the base implementation for the Application, VBox, HBox, ControlBar, HDividedBox, VDividedBox, NavBar, Panel, and TitleWindow containers.
Canvas	This container is for absolute positioning and constraint-based layout. Children are laid out using the x and y properties, and the top, bottom, right, left, verticalCenter, and horizontalCenter properties are used for achieving a constraint-based layout.
ControlBar	This container is used to provide a reserved region at the bottom of a Panel or TitleWindow container for placing children. This container lays out its content in the same way that HBox does.
DividedBox	This container lays out children in the same way that Box does, except it places an interactive divider bar between each child. This container is ideal for separating regions of an application and allowing a user to resize regions by dragging a divider. As with Box, children can be laid out horizontally or vertically.
Form	This special container is designed specifically for laying out forms. It allows you to easily position form labels, headings, and input controls.
Grid	This container allows you to position children within columns and rows. This container's behavior is very similar to that of HTML tables.
HBox	This container is derived from Box with the direction property set to BoxDirection. HORIZONTAL. Otherwise, it behaves as Box does.
HDividedBox	This container is derived from DividedBox with the direction property set to BoxDirection. HORIZONTAL by default.
Panel	This is a layout container that contains a chrome border with a title bar area. The content area by default behaves like a VBox. The layout property controls how children are laid out and the default value is ContainerLayout.VERTICAL. Additional possible values are ContainerLayout.ABSOLUTE and ContainerLayout.HORIZONTAL. Setting the layout property to ABSOLUTE causes this container to behave as a Canvas container. Setting the value to HORIZONTAL or VERTICAL causes the layout to behave like an HBox or VBox, respectively.
Tile	This container tiles children, and by default it tries to keep the number of rows and columns equal to each other. If the width or height properties of the container are specified, the container will try to satisfy the available area. If no width or height is specified, it tries its best to keep the number of rows and columns equal to each other. The Tile container contains a direction property, which by default is set to VERTICAL. Possible values are TileDirection.VERTICAL and TileDirection. HORIZONTAL.
TitleWindow	Ideal for pop-up windows, TitleWindow inherits from Panel, with the addition of a button in the title bar to allow users to close the window.
VBox	This container is derived from Box with the direction property set to BoxDirection.VERTICAL. Otherwise, it behaves as Box does.
VDividedBox	This container is derived from DividedBox, with the direction property set to BoxDirection. VERTICAL by default.

Layout Rules

Many containers internally make use of two main layout rules: box and canvas. These rules define how containers internally implement child positioning and sizing. Understanding the different layout rules will help you to understand how layout containers work, and to develop application layouts more effectively.

Layout rules are executed when children containers are initially instantiated, anytime children are added or removed, and whenever a container is resized. The only time that is not the case is when the autoLayout property is set to false. In this case, the layout rules execute only on initialization, and when children are added or removed.

Setting the autoLayout property to false still causes the container to measure and position children on initial rendering, and when children are added or removed. However, this won't cause the container to lay out its children again when the container is resized. This is beneficial in cases when you do not want to implement a liquid interface that automatically resizes, or when the exact layout needs to remain the same when the container is resized.

It is also important to note that measuring and positioning a container can sometimes be a processor-intensive process, so you may opt to set autoLayout to false to handle such cases.

When layout rules are executing, they go through two steps. First, the container measures the space needed for each child. This allows the container to decide how much space it needs in order to best fit all of its children, and it allows the container to decide where everything should be positioned if it is responsible for positioning the children. During this process, if a child's includeInLayout property is set to false, the child will be ignored and won't be factored into the positioning of children. In the second step, the container repositions and sizes the children as needed.

Box-based layout

Now that you understand a bit about how layout rules work, let's discuss each type of layout rule in more detail. The containers HBox, VBox, HDividedBox, VDividedBox, ApplicationControlBar, and ControlBar all base their layout rules on those of the Box container. For this reason, you will often find they are often referred to as *box-based layout containers*.

The box layout rule dictates that each child occupies its own row or column, depending on the direction under which the rule is operating. The two directions supported are vertical and horizontal. All box-based layout containers implement the direction property, and the default value of the direction property depends on the container. You can set the value of the direction property to horizontal or vertical using the constant values BoxDirection.HORIZONTAL and BoxDirection.VERTICAL.

In Box, the default direction is set to vertical, as shown in Figure 6-2. Each child occupies its own row, and the children are stacked one on top of the other.

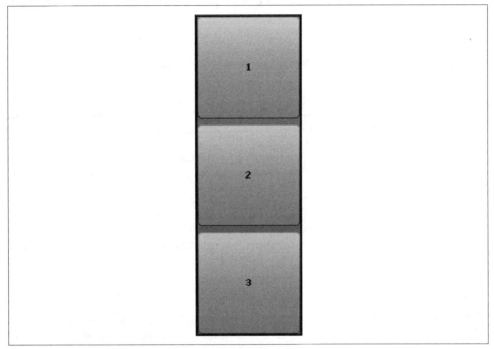

Figure 6-2. A VBox container with three child objects

If the width of the container is not specified, the container determines it by identifying the child with the largest width and adjusting its own width so that it can display the child with little or no clipping. If an explicit width is set, the container will adhere to the specified width, and if the width of the child objects exceeds the set width, by default the child objects will be clipped and a scrollbar will be displayed. In the same manner, the height of the container expands to allow all children to fit accordingly, unless an explicit height for the box-based container is set, at which point a scrollbar is used by the container to allow the user access to all the children. Changing the number of children or their width or height at runtime causes the container to be marked for invalidation, which will cause the layout rule to be reevaluated and the children to be automatically repositioned and sized as required.

In an attempt to minimize unnecessary redraws, which can cause severe performance degradation, Flex components mark parts of a component that need to be redrawn as *invalid*. We discuss invalidation in Chapter 19.

When the box layout rule is operating with the direction property set to horizontal, the rules apply in the same way as when the direction property is set to vertical, except the box attempts to grow and lay out children horizontally rather than vertically.

In this layout rule, the size of the container depends on a few factors:

- If the container has a target width and height, those values are used to set the size.

- If the size that is set is smaller than the area needed for the children to be displayed, a scrollbar is automatically displayed unless scrollPolicy is set to ScrollPolicy.OFF.

- If no size is explicitly set, the container attempts to expand as needed within the available space. If enough space is not available, a scrollbar is used to allow the user access to the content.

It's important to note here that typically you will not be using the Box container directly. Instead, you will be using a container such as VBox or HBox, which sets the default direction property depending on the container chosen. Technically, there is no reason not to use the Box container other than convenience and consistency.

Canvas-based layout

The Canvas container is the base implementer of the canvas-based layout rule. Though simple, it is an important layout container to discuss because its rules are used by other containers (discussed in the next section). *The canvas layout rule* provides a lot of flexibility in attaining sophisticated layout while attempting to ensure that application layout routines perform well. That's because you must provide all the positioning logic, which means that Flex doesn't have to do all the work of measuring the Canvas container's children and calculating optimal positions.

Canvas-based layout allows you to position children using explicit x and y coordinates. This allows you to accurately control the position of each child. Example 6-3 shows two children positioned using exact x and y positions, relative to the position of the Canvas itself.

Example 6-3. Absolute positioning using a Canvas container

```
<?xml version="1.0" encoding="utf-8"?>
<mx:Application xmlns:mx="http://www.adobe.com/2006/mxml">
    <mx:Canvas>
        <mx:Label x="0" y="50" text="Enter your name:"/>
        <mx:TextInput x="110" y="50"/>
    </mx:Canvas>
</mx:Application>
```

As you can see, the Canvas container is most suitable for reproducing a pixel-perfect layout. Unlike other containers, where layout rules set the positions of children, the Canvas container doesn't prevent you from overlapping children. If the positions of the children need to change, you can handle it on your own by setting the x and y values at runtime.

Constraint-based layout. Canvas also supports the ability to lay out children using what is called *constraint-based layout*. Constraint-based layout lets you lay out children at predefined positions relative to their parent. This gives you the flexibility of positioning children in a predefined position while at the same time repositioning them as needed to satisfy the constraints set. This tends to be a more practical method of accurately positioning children than simply supplying a specific location, because it allows the container to resize according to the maximum available real estate.

To position children using the constraint-based layout method, you set one or several child style properties—top, bottom, left, right, horizontalCenter, and verticalCenter—with a value based on the parent's position in relation to the child. For example, when you set the right style to 10, you are positioning the child 10 pixels away from the right edge of the parent container. When the container is resized, the child automatically repositions itself 10 pixels from the right edge.

Example 6-4 shows two buttons positioned using container-based layout. One is positioned 10 pixels from the bottom right, and the other is positioned 10 pixels from the right. Both buttons will automatically be repositioned whenever the browser is resized.

Example 6-4. Positioning children using constraint-based layout

```
<?xml version="1.0" encoding="utf-8"?>
<mx:Application xmlns:mx="http://www.adobe.com/2006/mxml">
    <mx:Canvas width="100%" height="100%">
        <mx:Button right="10" label="Right Most Button"/>
        <mx:Button right="10" bottom="10" label="Right Bottom Most Button"/>
    </mx:Canvas>
</mx:Application>
```

Figure 6-3 shows the results.

In Example 6-4, two buttons are positioned within a Canvas. The first button is positioned 10 pixels away from the right edge, with the default y value of 0 (if a child doesn't have its position set in a Canvas container, the default x and y values are 0, 0). The second button is positioned to the bottom right of the Canvas container. This is accomplished by setting the first button's right style property to 10. The second button's right and bottom style properties also are set to 10, thus resulting in the button being offset 10 pixels from the bottom-right edge of the parent container. Also note that the width and height properties of the Canvas container are set to 100 percent.

Right Most Button

Right Bottom Most Button

Figure 6-3. Result from Example 6-4, in which children are positioned using constraint-based layout

This is to ensure that the canvas automatically resizes to occupy as much space as possible.

Like all style properties, you can set constraint-based layout styles directly inline within MXML tags, via ActionScript using the setStyle( ) method, or any other method that style properties support.

Here are some additional things to remember concerning constraint-based layouts:

- Setting the top style property causes the child's y value to be set to that many pixels away from the parent container's top edge.
- Setting the bottom style property causes the y property of the child to be set to the height of the container, minus the child's height.
- You can set both the bottom and the top values of a child, which automatically resizes the child height and remains within the top and bottom constraints.
- Setting the left style property sets the x value of the child at runtime to that many pixels away from the parent's edge.
- Setting the right style property at runtime sets the x value to the total width of the container minus the right value and the width of the child.

- Setting both the `right` and `left` style properties causes the child to be resized to satisfy the constraint rules.
- Setting the values `top`, `bottom`, `left`, and `right` causes the child to be resized and positioned to satisfy the constraint rules.
- As with explicitly positioning items in a `Canvas` container, children you position using constraint-based layout rules can overlap each other.
- You can set a child's `width` and `height` to a percentage; the canvas positions and sizes them appropriately.
- You can mix constraint-based layout with absolute positioning within the same `Canvas` container.

Hybrid layout containers

The containers `Application`, `Panel`, and `TitleWindow` are based on both Box and Canvas layout rules; that's why they are called *hybrid layout containers*. The rules by which these children are laid out depend on the value of the `layout` property. The `layout` property accepts three valid values: `ContainerLayout.ABSOLUTE`, `ContainerLayout.HORIZONTAL`, and `ContainerLayout.VERTICAL`.

When you set the `layout` property value to `absolute`, the container behaves as a `Canvas`-based container. Setting the value to `horizontal` or `vertical` causes the container to act as a Box-based container with the appropriate direction (either a horizontal or a vertical layout, respectively).

Additional layout rules

Flex provides three other layout rules you can use in your application: Tile, Grid, and Form. These don't serve a general purpose like the others do, and they are not shared across containers. Instead, they are embedded within specific containers, as discussed in the following sections.

Tile layout rule. The Tile layout rule is found in the `Tile` container. Its purpose is to lay out children in a grid form, while optimally keeping the number of rows and columns equal. If Tile cannot keep them equal, it creates an extra row or column, depending on the `direction` property of the `Tile` container instance.

The `direction` property for the `Tile` container can accept two values: `TileDirection.HORIZONTAL` and `TileDirection.VERTICAL`. The default is for children to be laid out horizontally first (see Figure 6-4). This means that each child is instantiated one next to the other, horizontally, starting from left to right. When the intended number of children per row is reached depending on the optimal number of rows versus columns, it places the next child on the row below. Vertical orientation, of course, works the same way, except it begins laying children out next to each other from the top left and moving down until it reaches the current number of rows before continuing on to the next column.

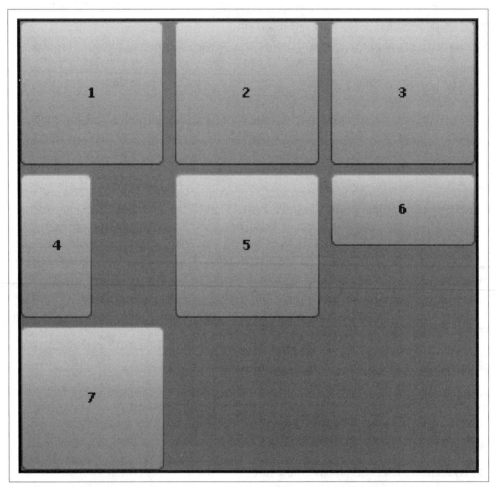

Figure 6-4. Results from having a Tile container with seven children, using the default horizontal direction

The width and height properties, when set, play a key role in how a Tile container lays out children. A Tile with a set width and height is forced to satisfy those limits, thus causing the rule of rows to columns to be adjusted. Under such cases, the direction property still behaves the same.

Grid layout rule. The Grid layout rule is used by the Grid container component. This layout rule/container replicates how an HTML table works in Flex, as shown in Example 6-5.

Example 6-5. Grid container example

```
<?xml version="1.0" encoding="utf-8"?>
<mx:Application xmlns:mx="http://www.adobe.com/2006/mxml">
    <mx:Grid>
        <mx:GridRow>
            <mx:GridItem width="100">
                <mx:Label text="Select a Color:"/>
            </mx:GridItem>
            <mx:GridItem>
                <mx:ColorPicker/>
            </mx:GridItem>
        </mx:GridRow>
        <mx:GridRow>
            <mx:GridItem colSpan="2" horizontalAlign="right">
                <mx:Button label="Submit"/>
            </mx:GridItem>
        </mx:GridRow>
    </mx:Grid>
</mx:Application>
```

Example 6-5 contains two rows: the first row contains a Label and a ColorPicker. The second contains a submit button, which is aligned to the right of the table. To understand this example, it is helpful to take a look at how Grid-related classes relate to traditional HTML tables:

- An HTML <table> is synonymous with a Grid.
- An HTML <tr> (table row) is synonymous with a GridRow.
- An HTML <td> (table data) is synonymous with a GridItem.
- The colspan and rowspan properties in HTML are properties of the GridItem as colSpan and rowSpan.
- The HTML align attribute is a style called horizontalAlign.
- The HTML valign property is a style called verticalAlign.

If you are familiar with HTML, you may feel more comfortable using the Grid container over others.

Although the Grid container is a good representation of a familiar layout model, you should use the Grid container only as a last resort when laying out an application. Other containers such as Canvas and box-based containers are easier to maintain, provide better performance, and offer most of what Grid provides.

Form layout rule. The best way to introduce the Form layout rule is to show an example of it in use (see Figure 6-5).

The Form layout rule is found in the Form container. This container is used to lay out forms such as those you'd see on a web page, which typically include headings and input controls in a Flex application. The Form container, like the Grid container, has

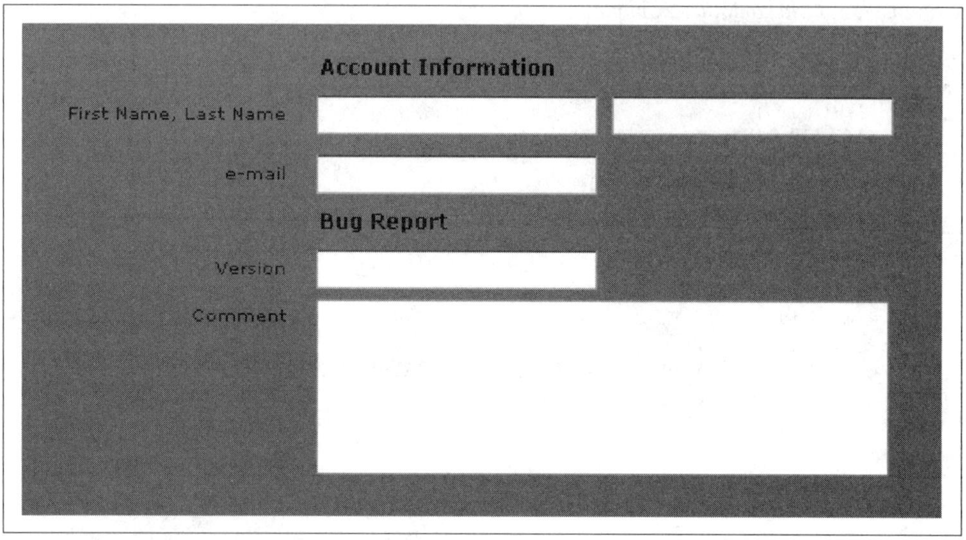

Figure 6-5. A typical form using the Form layout rule

associated components and exists for convenience. You can reproduce the same layout using other containers, but for traditional forms, you may find this container ideal.

Although you can reproduce the same layout a Form container can using other containers, you may find using the Form container more convenient. The Form container's related components are FormHeading and FormItem:

FormHeading

You use this to place a heading over a group of multiple FormItems within a Form by setting the label property. You can use multiple FormHeading controls within a form; you should place them before the group of form items the FormHeading represents. The label text is positioned and aligned to the body of the form items. You can control spacing between FormHeading children using the paddingTop, paddingLeft, and paddingRight style properties.

FormItem

You use this when a form container needs to contain items such as input boxes and combo boxes. Multiple instances of FormItem can be placed within a single form. FormItem implements the box-based layout rule, which allows you to place multiple children within a FormItem and exposes a direction property in the same way that other box-based containers do. Finally, FormItem exposes a label property that allows you to place text to the left of a row in a form.

Example 6-6 shows the code you would use to reproduce Figure 6-6 using the Form container.

Example 6-6. Example of using the Form container

```xml
<?xml version="1.0" encoding="utf-8"?>
<mx:Application xmlns:mx="http://www.adobe.com/2006/mxml">
    <mx:Form>
        <mx:FormHeading label="Account Information"/>
        <mx:FormItem label="First Name, Last Name" direction="horizontal">
            <mx:TextInput id="firstName"/>
            <mx:TextInput id="lastName"/>
        </mx:FormItem>
        <mx:FormItem label="e-mail">
            <mx:TextInput id="email"/>
        </mx:FormItem>
        <mx:FormHeading label="Bug Report"/>
        <mx:FormItem label="Version">
            <mx:TextInput id="version"/>
        </mx:FormItem>
        <mx:FormItem label="Comment">
            <mx:TextArea id="comment" editable="true" width="326" height="100"/>
        </mx:FormItem>
    </mx:Form>
</mx:Application>
```

Notice how the form neatly positions and sizes all the children. This is the convenience of using a Form container.

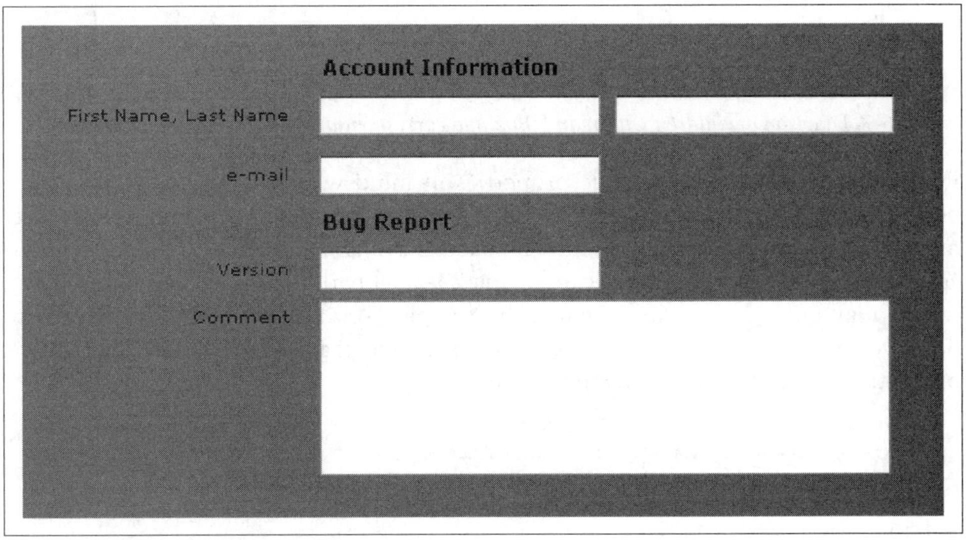

Figure 6-6. Application output from Example 6-6

Padding, Borders, and Gaps

Thus far, we have worked with containers using many of their default behaviors. In this section, we will discuss the important issue of style properties for padding, borders, and gaps.

Padding, borders, and gaps are style properties that control how children are positioned. Padding controls the space between a child and the container and is typically seen in box-, tile-, and grid-based layout containers. Borders are found in most containers and they control the border surrounding the containers' bounding box. Finally, gaps control the space between each child when working with box-, tile-, and grid-based layout containers. To better understand how these style properties work, look at Figure 6-7, which shows some of the style properties and their purposes.

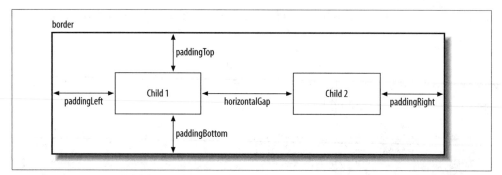

Figure 6-7. Diagram of children within an HBox and corresponding padding, border, and gaps

It's important to keep these style properties in mind when laying out applications, because properties are taken into account when a container performs its measurement routines to determine how much space is available. Some containers, such as Application, for example, default to having 24-pixel padding on all four sides. If you want to lay out an application that truly occupies 100 percent of the browser window, you would set the paddingTop, paddingBottom, paddingLeft, and paddingRight properties to 0. Let's take a look at such an example:

```
<?xml version="1.0" encoding="utf-8"?>
<mx:Application xmlns:mx="http://www.adobe.com/2006/mxml"
paddingBottom="0" paddingLeft="0" paddingRight="0" paddingTop="0">
    <mx:Button label="Max sized button" width="100%" height="100%"/>
</mx:Application>
```

The preceding code results in an application with one large button that occupies truly 100 percent of the available space in the browser, as shown in Figure 6-8.

Figure 6-8. Application with zero padding

Nesting Containers

Most applications will require more than just one container to achieve the layout you desire. In such cases, you'll want to use multiple containers, and perhaps mix Box- and Canvas-based containers in the same application. Flex allows you to easily nest containers within other containers, and although you may not have realized it earlier, you have been nesting containers all along, because Application is itself a container. When you nest containers, children of containers will act like any other children. Example 6-7 shows how to nest containers; Figure 6-9 shows the result.

Example 6-7. Example of nesting containers

```
<?xml version="1.0" encoding="utf-8"?>
<mx:Application xmlns:mx="http://www.adobe.com/2006/mxml" layout="absolute">
    <mx:HBox width="100%" height="100%">
        <mx:Canvas width="50%" height="100%">
            <mx:Button label="Button 1" bottom="10" right="10"/>
            <mx:Button label="Button 2" bottom="40" right="10"/>
        </mx:Canvas>
        <mx:Panel width="50%" height="100%" layout="absolute">
        </mx:Panel>
    </mx:HBox>
</mx:Application>
```

Figure 6-9. Result of Example 6-7

Example 6-7 combines multiple container types to achieve a layout that you could not easily attain with just one container. In this example, two areas in the application have been separated. To do this, we used an HBox container and placed two containers, one Panel and one Canvas, within, each occupying 50 percent of the total area. In this example, HBox is managing the positioning and layout of the two subcontainers. Also, each child container has its own area where the children rely on its layout rules and not on those of HBox.

Although this is a simple example, nested containers provide a powerful and easy way to lay out complex Flex applications. It is good to keep in mind, however, that excessive container nesting can lead to poor performance, and generating the layout you desire using constraint- or Canvas-based layout may lead to a better overall application experience for the user.

Nested containers are ideal in another scenario as well. At times, you may want to use a container because of its chrome appearance. For example, a Panel container does not implement the form layout rule, but it does provide a chrome appearance that you might be interested in using. For such a case, you can nest a Form container (or any other container) within a Panel to obtain the chrome appearance of the Panel and the layout rules of the nested container.

Handling Scrolling and Clipping

Containers can't always fit their children within the available viewing area. This can occur because, for example, screen resolutions are different among end users, the children need more space than what's available, or the canvas was resized. As a result, sooner or later you will have to deal with containers that have a scrollbar. Thankfully, Flex makes the process of dealing with this problem simple.

If a container doesn't have enough available space, a scrollbar (shown in Figure 6-10) appears by default, which allows the user to reach the content he desires.

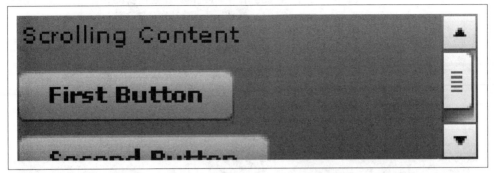

Figure 6-10. The scrollbar that appears when clipping occurs by default in containers

You can override this default behavior and have a container always display a scrollbar, or none at all even if one is needed. Each container has the properties horizontalScrollPolicy and verticalScrollPolicy. These properties accept the values ScrollPolicy.ON, ScrollPolicy.OFF, and ScrollPolicy.AUTO, which is the default for containers.

Clipping is another function that containers perform on children when they exceed the available area. Using clipping, a container can clip (hide) the parts that exceed its viewable area. In the preceding example, the content was clipped but a scrollbar was provided to allow the user to scroll. Flex containers allow you to disable clipping, if needed, using the clipContent property. By default, the clipContent property is set to true; if it is set to false, the content will not be clipped. Disabling clipping also causes the children to extend beyond the container's boundaries. This can adversely effect your application layout, because the container boundaries are not adhered to when clipping is disabled.

The Spacer Component

The Spacer component is a component that can assist in handling layout within Flex. It is a commonly used with containers when you need to reposition a child when using a container that does not give you precise control, like the Canvas container. The Spacer component is treated like any other container child component. It can be added to a container, and given a width and height. Once added to a component, it does not render on the user's screen. Instead, it will just occupy the space a regular component would.

Figure 6-11 shows a simple application where three buttons are displayed. The buttons are placed within an HBox component, and the first and second buttons, unlike the second and third, require extra space in between. To achieve this, a Spacer component is used in between the first and second buttons.

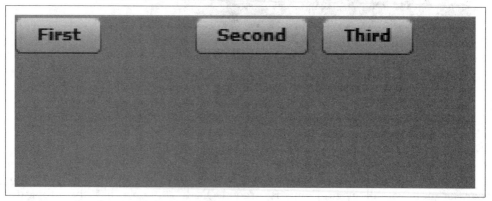

Figure 6-11. Three buttons within an HBox, with a spacer separating the first and second buttons

Here is the code used to create Figure 6-11:

```
<?xml version="1.0" encoding="utf-8"?>
<mx:Application xmlns:mx="http://www.adobe.com/2006/mxml" layout="absolute">
    <mx:HBox>
        <mx:Button label="First"/>
        <mx:Spacer width="40"/>
        <mx:Button label="Second"/>
        <mx:Button label="Third"/>
    </mx:HBox>
</mx:Application>
```

Spacers are a useful way to adjust child positioning rules easily. Although you may be tempted to use Spacer everywhere, it is recommended that you first review why you need spacers instead of assuming spacers may be the ideal solution, because often you may find that your layout could be handled in a more ideal manner.

Making Fluid Interfaces

Another benefit of using Flex is the ability to build *fluid interfaces* (i.e., interfaces that expand or contract when their available real estate changes). For applications deployed to the Web, this usually occurs when the browser window is resized. Without Flex, you would need to handle the resize event of the Flash Player manually and adjust all containers and their children sizes to handle the change in available space.

In Flex, all layout containers and controls support the ability to set some values as percentages, the most basic of which are the width and height properties that set the available real estate for the container. Setting the width and height properties to a percentage value causes the container to occupy a percentage of the container of which it is currently a child. Example 6-8 has a Panel container that occupies 70 percent of the width and 40 percent of the height of the Application container.

Example 6-8. A panel that occupies 70 percent of the width and 40 percent of the height of the available area

```
<?xml version="1.0" encoding="utf-8"?>
<mx:Application xmlns:mx="http://www.adobe.com/2006/mxml">
    <mx:Panel width="70%" height="40%">
    </mx:Panel>
</mx:Application>
```

The Application container's width and height values are set by default to occupy all the space available to it. As such, in Example 6-8, the Panel automatically adjusts to changes in the browser's size during runtime, as Application automatically grows to satisfy its size.

 You can use percentage values in MXML for the width and height properties of any UI control in Flex, but percentage values are not valid in ActionScript. Instead, you have to use the percentWidth and percentHeight properties of a component. This is actually how the Flex compiler translates the percentage values from MXML to Action-Script at compile time.

Putting It All Together

Now that we have covered the many concepts related to managing layout within Flex, let's dig a bit deeper and learn how to put it all together. The layout shown in Figure 6-12 contains a fixed left region for two List components that are stacked with a draggable divider, and a Canvas region that expands and repositions the Save button as needed to keep it at the bottom right.

In Figure 6-12, the application is contained within a Panel and the width and height properties are set to resize to maximize the application area. When resizing occurs, the left DividedBox continues to have the same width, but it expands to fill up the maximum vertical space. The Canvas on the right expands to fill the entire region, which allows the children to be laid out with the Canvas using constraint-based layout techniques (discussed earlier). Example 6-9 shows the code used to produce Figure 6-12.

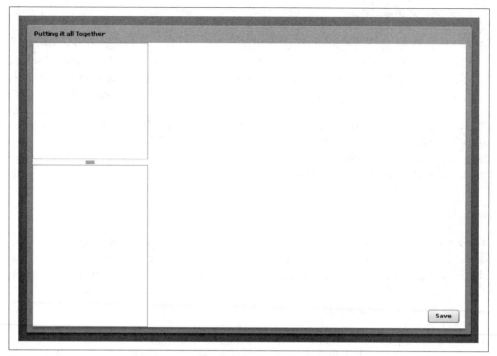

Putting it all Together

Save

Figure 6-12. Layout example that contains different nested container types and controls

Example 6-9. Code used to produce the layout in Figure 6-12

```
<?xml version="1.0" encoding="utf-8"?>
<mx:Application xmlns:mx="http://www.adobe.com/2006/mxml">
    <mx:Panel layout="horizontal" width="100%" height="100%" title="Putting it
all Together">
        <mx:DividedBox direction="vertical" width="200" height="100%">
            <mx:List width="100%" height="200">
            </mx:List>
            <mx:List width="100%">
            </mx:List>
        </mx:DividedBox>
        <mx:Canvas width="100%" height="100%">
            <mx:Button bottom="10" right="10" label="Save"/>
        </mx:Canvas>
    </mx:Panel>
</mx:Application>
```

Now let's walk through the code. First, we declared the application, as seen in Example 6-10. Our intent is not to use the Application layout rules because the entire application is contained within a Panel which will serve as the root container.

Example 6-10. Adding the application

```
<?xml version="1.0" encoding="utf-8"?>
<mx:Application xmlns:mx="http://www.adobe.com/2006/mxml">

</mx:Application>
```

Next, we added the `Panel` container and set the `width` and `height` to 100 percent to ensure that the interface expands as needed. This also ensures that the interface's children get the maximum possible real estate available to the application. As shown in Example 6-11, the layout value of `Panel` is set to `horizontal`, because you want the children to be positioned vertically, one next to the other, using the box layout rule.

Example 6-11. Adding the Panel container

```
<?xml version="1.0" encoding="utf-8"?>
<mx:Application xmlns:mx="http://www.adobe.com/2006/mxml">
    <mx:Panel layout="horizontal" width="100%" height="100%" title="Putting it
all Together"/>
</mx:Application>
```

Next, we added the two `List` controls within a `VDividedBox`, as seen in Example 6-12.

Example 6-12. Adding the VDividedBox

```
<?xml version="1.0" encoding="utf-8"?>
<mx:Application xmlns:mx="http://www.adobe.com/2006/mxml">
    <mx:Panel layout="horizontal" width="100%" height="100%" title="Putting it
all Together">
        <mx:VDividedBox width="200" height="100%">
            <mx:List width="100%" height="200">
            </mx:List>
            <mx:List width="100%">
            </mx:List>
        </mx:VDividedBox>
    </mx:Panel>
</mx:Application>
```

The `VDividedBox`'s direction is set to `vertical` by default, so there is no need to set a direction value. The `VDividedBox`'s `width` property is set to a fixed pixel value of 200. This ensures that the `VDividedBox` always has a 200-pixel width—no more and no less. The `height` is set to 100 percent to ensure that the panel expands as the canvas is resized. The `VDividedBox` expands too, and its children get to take advantage of the extra space.

Next, we placed two `List` controls. Each `List` control has a `width` of 100 percent. You could achieve the same result by setting the `List` controls to occupy 200 pixels rather than 100 percent. However, we've found that setting the value to 100 percent makes it easier in the future to resize the parent container (in this case, the `VDividedBox`) without having to change the behavior of the children. The height of the first `List` control is set to an explicit 200 pixels to ensure that on initial load, the top `List` control is given at least 200 pixels of real estate, both in height and in width for displaying content to the user. (You can omit this if you don't have a preference on its size.) After the initial load, if the user decides there is no need for the space, he can resize the DividedBox children interactively.

Finally, we added the Canvas container with a Button, as shown in Example 6-13.

Example 6-13. Adding the Canvas to complete the example

```
<?xml version="1.0" encoding="utf-8"?>
<mx:Application xmlns:mx="http://www.adobe.com/2006/mxml">
    <mx:Panel layout="horizontal" width="100%" height="100%" title="Putting it
all Together">
        <mx:VDividedBox direction="vertical" width="200" height="100%">
            <mx:List width="100%" height="200">
            </mx:List>
            <mx:List width="100%">
            </mx:List>
        </mx:VDividedBox>
        <mx:Canvas width="100%" height="100%">
            <mx:Button bottom="10" right="10" label="Save"/>
        </mx:Canvas>
    </mx:Panel>
</mx:Application>
```

The Canvas container's width and height properties are set to 100 percent to ensure that the Canvas container grows as needed. The container's x and y properties aren't set, so x and y both take the default value of 0. The Canvas container is a child of the Panel, which uses the horizontal BoxLayout rule. This ensures that the canvas is positioned to the right of the DividedBox.

Within the Canvas container, the Button is positioned using constraint-based layout rules to anchor it to the bottom right. To achieve that, the bottom and right style properties are set to 10. That ensures that the Button is always 10 pixels away from the bottom-right corner of the Canvas container, even when the user resizes the Canvas container.

Summary

In this chapter, we covered the many mechanisms for performing application layout rapidly and efficiently in Flex. Flex has powerful layout containers that allow you to combine different layout containers. As you've seen, Flex offers many layout containers that can greatly assist you in rapidly laying out applications.

Working with UI Components

The Flex framework consists, in large part, of components. Within the framework there are many types of components, from data components to layout components to user interface (UI) components. You can read about each type of component in the appropriate chapters throughout this book. In this chapter, we focus on UI components. UI components are visual components that display something to the user and/or prompt the user to interact with the application.

Although there's no formal classification for the majority of the UI components in the Flex framework, it is useful to categorize them just for the purposes of discussion. We've organized our discussion of the UI components based on the categories listed in Table 7-1.

Table 7-1. UI component categories

Category	Components
Buttons	Button, LinkButton, RadioButton, CheckBox
Value selectors	HSlider, VSlider, NumericStepper, ColorPicker, DateField, DateChooser
Text components	Label, Text, TextInput, TextArea, RichTextEditor
List-based controls	List, ComboBox, DataGrid, HorizontalList, TileList, Tree
Pop-up controls	PopUpButton, PopUpMenuButton
Windows	Panel, TitleWindow
Navigators	ViewStack, Accordion, ButtonBar, LinkBar, MenuBar, TabBar, TabNavigator, ToggleButtonBar
Control bars	ControlBar, ApplicationControlBar
Media and progress indicators	Image, SWFLoader, VideoDisplay, ProgressBar

Layout containers are not included in the preceding table because they are discussed entirely within their own chapter (Chapter 6).

In this chapter, we will discuss each category of component listed in Table 7-1, with the exception of the windows and media components, which are discussed in Chapters 6 and 9, respectively. However, we will discuss the components in a generalized sense rather than focusing on every individual component. This book is not intended to be an API reference. You can find a thorough API reference in the Flex help documentation at *http://livedocs.adobe.com/flex/2/langref/*.

Understanding UI Components

All UI components (and all layout components) are related because they inherit from a common superclass called `mx.core.UIComponent`. This `UIComponent` class is part of the Flex framework. The class is abstract, meaning you would never create a `UIComponent` instance directly. However, it's important to understand `UIComponent` because it will tell you a lot about all the components that inherit from it.

The `UIComponent` class itself inherits from `mx.core.FlexSprite`, which directly inherits from `flash.display.Sprite`, which is part of the Flash Player API. This means that all Flex UI components behave very much like standard Flash display objects because they inherit from the display object inheritance chain. Figure 7-1 illustrates the inheritance relationship of UI components, showing only a partial list of the UI components (`Button`, `ComboBox`, `DateField`, etc.) in the interest of brevity.

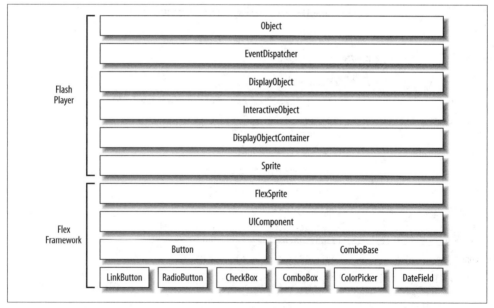

Figure 7-1. A partial list of the UI components and the inheritance relationship of UI components and Flash Player classes

Creating Component Instances

You can create UI component instances either with MXML or with ActionScript. If you use MXML you should use the tag that has the same name as the component. For example, the following code creates a button instance:

```
<mx:Button />
```

When you want to use ActionScript, you should use the constructor of the component class in a new statement. The following code creates a button instance using ActionScript:

```
var button:Button = new Button();
```

When you create a component using ActionScript the component is not automatically added to the display list as it is when you use MXML. If you want to add the component to the display list so that it is visible, you must use the addChild() method of a container:

```
addChild(button);
```

You can read more about adding components to containers in Chapter 6.

Common UI Component Properties

When you work with UI components, you can always count on certain properties being implemented. Those properties are as follows:

x The x coordinate of the component relative to its parent container's content area. You can set the property to move the component, and you can read the property to get the current x coordinate of the component.

y The y coordinate of the component relative to its parent container. Like the x property, you can both read and write the y property.

width
    The width of the component in pixels. You can read the property to retrieve the current width, and you can set the property to change the width of the component.

height
    The height of the component in pixels. Like the width property, you can both read and write the height property.

scaleX
    The scale of the component in the horizontal direction relative to its original width. The scaleX and width properties are linked. When you change the scaleX, the width changes as well, yet the opposite is not true. You can both read and write the scaleX property.

scaleY

The scale of the component in the vertical direction relative to its original height. The scaleY and height properties are linked just as the scaleX and width properties are linked. The values for scaleY are on the same range as are those for scaleX. And you can both read and write the scaleY property.

rotation

The number of degrees of rotation of the component relative to its original orientation. Rotation is always clockwise and is always relative to the origin point of the component's internal coordinate system. In almost all cases, a component's origin exists at the upper-left corner. You can both read and write the rotation property.

alpha

The opacity of the component. The default value is 1, which means the component is fully opaque. The effective range for alpha is from 0 (transparent) to 1 (opaque). You can read and write the alpha property.

visible

The visibility of the component. The default value is true, meaning the component is visible. A value of false means the component is not visible. You can both read and write the visible property.

enabled

Whether a component is interactive. For example, if a button is enabled, it can accept mouse clicks. The default value is true. A value of false disables the component. You can both read and write the enabled property.

parent

A reference to the parent container for the component. The parent property is read-only. If you want to change the parent of a component, you must use the removeChild( ) method of the parent container to remove the component or use addChild( ) to add the component to a new container.

The preceding list is not intended to be comprehensive by any means. However, it does represent some of the most commonly used properties of all UI components.

You can work with most of these properties both in MXML and in ActionScript (except when a property is read-only, in which case you must use ActionScript to read the value). The following example sets several properties of a button instance using MXML:

```
<mx:Button id="button" label="Example Button"
    width="200" height="50" enabled="false" />
```

Here's the equivalent ActionScript code:

```
var button:Button = new Button( );
button.label = "Example Button";
button.width = 200;
button.height = 50;
```

```
button.enabled = false;
addChild(button);
```

Handling Events

Events are the way in which objects (such as Flex UI components) can communicate with the rest of the application. There are two basic types of events: *user events* and *system events*. User events are events that occur directly because of user interaction with the application. For example, when the user clicks on a button, a click event occurs, and when the user expands a drop-down menu (a combo box component), an open event occurs. On the other hand, a system event occurs because something happens within the application in response to initialization, asynchronous operations, or other such nonuser-driven behavior. For example, when a component is created, several events occur during the stages of creation indicating that various aspects of the component are accessible.

When an event occurs, we say that the event is *dispatched* (or *broadcasted*). The object that dispatches an event is called the *target*. All Flex UI components are potential event targets, meaning all UI components dispatch events. The event that gets dispatched is in the form of an object of type flash.events.Event (or a subtype). The Event instance provides information about the event, including the type of event (click, open, etc.) and the target that dispatched the event.

When a component dispatches an event, nothing occurs in response unless something (called a listener) is configured to receive notifications. There are two ways that you can handle events in a Flex application: one uses MXML attributes and the other uses ActionScript.

 As you saw in Figure 7-1, all UI components inherit from the Flash Player EventDispatcher class, meaning that all UI components can dispatch events to listeners.

Handling events with MXML

When you create a component using MXML, you can add an event handler using an attribute that has the same name as the event you want to handle. For example, buttons dispatch click events when the user clicks on them. Therefore, you can add a click attribute to the Button tag to handle the click event. You also can assign ActionScript to the attribute. For example, the following code lowers the alpha by .1 of the button each time the user clicks on it:

```
<mx:Button id="button" label="Alpha Button" click="button.alpha -= .1" />
```

Although you can assign ActionScript expressions to event handler attributes, as in the preceding example, it is more common (and useful) to assign a function call to the event handler attribute. This allows you to define more complex functionality in response to the event. When you call a function/method from an event handler attribute, you should pass a parameter called event to the function. In MXML, the event parameter will automatically pass along the event object that the component dispatches:

```
<mx:Button id="button" label="Alpha Button" click="clickHandler(event)" />
```

You then need to define the method that is intended to handle the event. The method should accept a parameter of type Event (or the appropriate subtype). The following example accomplishes the same thing as the inline expression did previously. However, in addition, it resets the alpha to 1 if and when the alpha is less than 0:

```
private function clickHandler(event:Event):void {
  var target:Button = Button(event.target);
  target.alpha -= .1;
  if(target.alpha < 0) {
    target.alpha = 1;
  }
}
```

Handling events with ActionScript

You can use ActionScript to add event listeners to a component as an alternative to using MXML event attributes. This is advantageous for several reasons. First, it is useful to add event listeners with ActionScript when you are creating the component instance using ActionScript as opposed to MXML. Second, when you add event listeners using ActionScript, you can also remove the event listeners later. This is handy if you want to temporarily or permanently stop listening for a specific event for a component.

In order to register a listener for an event using ActionScript you should employ the addEventListener( ) method. This method requires that you pass it at least two parameters: the name of the event for which you want to listen and the function to use as the listener. Typically, you should use constants for event names rather than quoted strings to avoid typos that would introduce bugs that would not be caught by the compiler. The event name constants are members of the associated event class. For example, the Event class defines OPEN, CLOSE, SCROLL, SELECT, and many other constants. The MouseEvent class defines CLICK, MOUSE_OVER, and other mouse-related event constants. The FlexEvent class defines constants for many of the Flex-specific events such as ADD, REMOVE, CREATION_COMPLETE, and INITIALIZE. The following code creates a button and then adds a listener for the click event:

```
var button:Button = new Button( );
button.addEventListener(MouseEvent.CLICK, clickHandler);
addChild(button);
```

The event listener function is automatically passed an Event object as a parameter:

```
private function clickHandler(event:MouseEvent):void {
  var target:Button = Button(event.target);
  target.alpha -= .1;
  if(target.alpha < 0) {
```

```
        target.alpha = 1;
    }
}
```

Event objects

The `flash.events.Event` class is the base class for all events in Flex applications. However, many event objects are instances of event subtypes. For example, events related to mouse behavior (`click`, `mouseOver`, etc.) are of type `MouseEvent`.

Event objects always have a type property that indicates the type of event the object represents. For example, a click event dispatches an object with a type property of `click`. Event objects also have target properties that reference the actual object which dispatched the event. In some cases, the target may not be the object for which you have registered a listener. This can occur when the object for which you have registered a listener contains a child component that also dispatches the same event (and the event bubbles). If you want to ensure that you are getting a reference to the object for which the listener is registered to listen for the event, use the `currentTarget` property.

Standard Flex component events

Each UI component type may have events that are specific to that type. For example, combo boxes dispatch open events when the menu is expanded. However, all UI components have a set of events in common. Table 7-2 lists these common events.

Table 7-2. Common UI component events

Event	Constant	Description
add	FlexEvent.ADD	The component has been added to a container.
remove	FlexEvent.REMOVE	The component has been removed from a container.
show	FlexEvent.SHOW	The component has been made visible (the visible property is now true).
hide	FlexEvent.HIDE	The component has been made nonvisible (the visible property is now false).
resize	FlexEvent.RESIZE	The component dimensions have changed.
preinitialize	FlexEvent.PREINITIALIZE	The component has started to initialize, but children haven't yet been created.
initialize	FlexEvent.INITIALIZE	The component has been constructed, but it has not yet been measured and laid out.
creationComplete	FlexEvent.CREATION_COMPLETE	The component is completely created, measured, and laid out.

The list of common events in Table 7-2 is not comprehensive. The `UIComponent` class (from which all UI components inherit) defines many more events. For a comprehensive list, look at the Flex documentation listing for `mx.core.UIComponent`. We'll also discuss many of the events in this book in the sections for which they are most appropriate (e.g., we discuss drag and drop events in the drag and drop section of Chapter 10).

Buttons

There are four basic button types of controls: Button, LinkButton, RadioButton, and CheckBox. Although each type behaves similarly, they have different intended uses. Figure 7-2 shows instances of each type.

Figure 7-2. Button components

Of the four types, Button and LinkButton are the most similar in use. In fact, the primary difference between Button and LinkButton is purely cosmetic: buttons have borders and backgrounds, and link buttons do not. However, you'll typically use both types for similar purposes—generally to initiate some behavior when the user clicks on the button or link button. Buttons are typically more common than link buttons.

With buttons and link buttons, the default behavior is that they respond to every click in the same way. However, you can set the toggle property of a button or link button to true, in which case the button will have two states—selected and deselected—and it will toggle between those states each time the user clicks it.

Radio buttons are quite different in use from standard buttons. Radio buttons are typically used in groups. Radio buttons can be selected or deselected, and only one button can be selected per group. For this reason, radio buttons are often used when you want to allow the user to select just one from a group of options. You should typically first create a RadioButtonGroup instance when using radio buttons. Then, assign the ID of the group to the groupName property of each radio button in the group, as shown here:

```
<mx:RadioButtonGroup id="exampleGroup" />
<mx:RadioButton groupName="exampleGroup" label="A" value="a" />
<mx:RadioButton groupName="exampleGroup" label="B" value="b" />
```

Checkboxes are also buttons. They are most similar to standard buttons that have been set to toggle. When a user clicks a checkbox, it toggles the selected state of the component.

Value Selectors

Value selectors are components that allow the user to select a value. This is a fairly diverse category of components because the types of values they allow the user to select and the ways in which they allow the user to select the values are quite different. Figure 7-3 shows the basic value selector components (except for VSlider, because it is the vertical version of HSlider, which is shown).

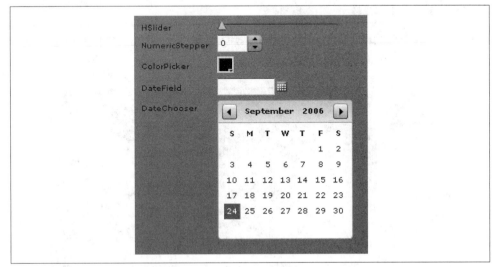

Figure 7-3. Value selector components

The slider components (HSlider and VSlider) differ only in that one is horizontal and one is vertical. Otherwise, they behave identically. The slider components allow the user to select a numeric value along a range from a minimum to a maximum value. The default range is 0 to 10, but you can adjust the range using the minimum and maximum properties. The slider components allow the user to drag a thumb along that range. Optionally, you can add more than one thumb and allow the user to select a range of values.

The numeric stepper control allows the user to select a numeric value as well. However, the interface for a numeric stepper is quite different from that of a slider interface. Where a slider interface is very graphical, the numeric stepper interface actually displays the current numeric value in digits, allowing the user to scroll through the list of possible values in the range.

The color picker component is very useful for allowing the user to select a color value from an expandable/collapsible grid of color swatches.

The date field and date chooser components are useful because they allow the user to select date values. The date field component enables the user to select a single date in a compact form. Although the date field component expands to display a calendar while the user is selecting a date, it again collapses to a compact form once the user has selected a value. The date chooser component, on the other hand, is an expanded format component that always displays the calendar from which the user can select a date. The date chooser component also allows the user to select multiple dates and ranges of dates.

Text Components

There are five basic text components that we can further categorize into display and input components. Figure 7-4 shows these components.

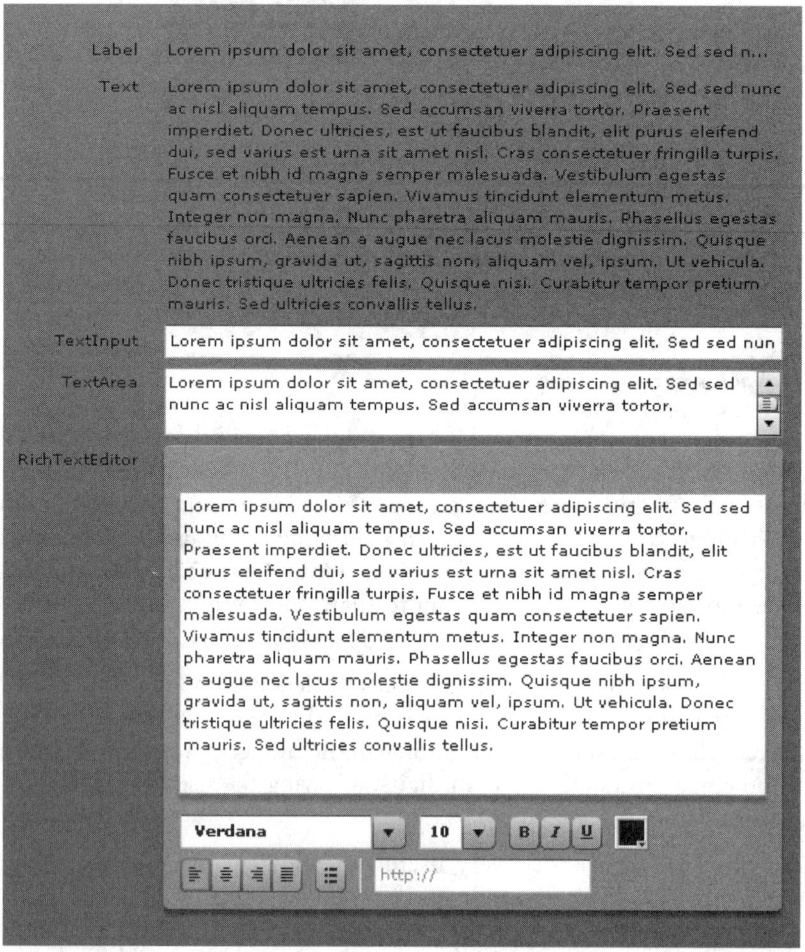

Figure 7-4. Text components

The label and text components are display-only components. The user cannot edit the contents of either of these types. The label component is useful for displaying one line of text, whereas the text component is useful for displaying multiple lines of text.

The text input, text area, and rich text editor components are user input text controls. The text input component allows the user to input one line of text. The text area component allows the user to input multiple lines of text, and it automatically adds scrollbars when necessary. The rich text editor component not only allows the user to input multiple lines of text, but it also allows her to apply formatting styles such as bold, italic, underline, text align, etc.

List-Based Controls

List-based controls are some of the most sophisticated of the standard controls. These are the components that allow the user to select an item or items from a list of options. In the simplest form, a list might be a vertical, scrollable list of text labels from which the user can select. However, list-based controls can be increasingly complex from there, supporting columns, horizontal and grid-based layout, hierarchical and collapsible structures, and even icons, images, and more. Figure 7-5 shows the list-based controls.

The most fundamental of all the list-based controls is the *list*. Such lists are vertically scrolling, single-column controls.

Horizontal lists are identical to standard lists except that they scroll horizontally rather than vertically. Horizontal lists are typically useful for scrolling icons and/or images (thumbnails), though you could also use a horizontal list for simple text.

Combo boxes are lists that collapse to a single line when not activated. These types of controls are often referred to by users as *drop-down menus*, and they allow the user to select from a vertically scrolling list of options when in an expanded state. Once a value has been selected, the control returns to the collapsed state.

Tile lists are scrollable lists in which the contents are arranged in a grid. Tile lists are useful when you want to display contents in a grid, but you need the grid to scroll.

Data grids are vertically scrolling, multicolumn lists. Data grids are good for displaying data that consists of records of multiple values that a user might need to see at the same time. For example, a data grid would be a good choice for displaying the details of a user's phone use history in which each row displays the time, the duration, and the destination phone number, each in a different column (see Figure 7-5).

Tree controls are hierarchical types of lists. They are very similar to standard lists because they vertically scroll. However, where standard lists have linear data models, trees have hierarchical data models in which individual elements can expand and collapse to reveal and hide nested elements.

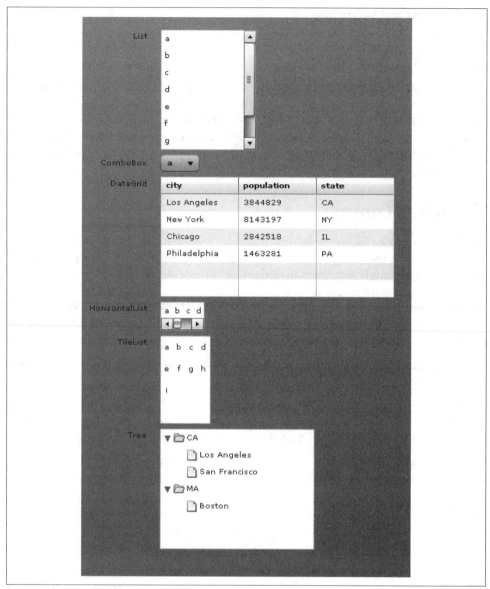

Figure 7-5. List-based controls

When you work with a list you always need a *data provider*. A data provider is the data model for which the list is the view. All list-based components have a dataProvider property you can use to assign the data model or retrieve a reference to the current data model.

UI components have a data property as well as a `dataProvider` property. Although it is easy enough to initially confuse the two, they are different properties with different purposes. The `dataProvider` property allows you to set the data model for a component. The `data` property is used only when using a component as an item renderer for a list-based component, as discussed in Chapter 8.

Data Models

Flex controls use model-view-controller, a software pattern that differentiates between the display of data and the data itself. This is very evident in the list-based controls. All list-based controls utilize data models. In the language used by these components, the data models are called *data providers* are independent objects which you can associate with a control. The control then uses that object's data to render its view.

Data providers always implement the `mx.collections.ICollectonView` interface. Although you can assign an array or an XML object to the `dataProvider` property of most list-based components, Flex converts the object behind the scenes to a type that implements `ICollectionView`. That means that arrays get converted to a type called `mx.collections.ArrayCollection` and XML and `XMLList` objects get converted to `mx.collections.XMLListCollection`. It's generally best to always explicitly wrap the object as a collection first before assigning it as the data provider. That way you are assured of having a reference to the actual data provider collection rather than the object wrapped by the collection.

Creating a Collection Object

There are two basic ways to create collections: using ActionScript and using MXML. The ActionScript solution involves creating a new collection type, typically with the constructor. The following ActionScript example creates a new `ArrayCollection` object that wraps an array:

```
var collection:ICollectionView = new ArrayCollection(["a", "b", "c", "d"]);
```

Note that the variables in these examples are typed as ICollectionView rather than the concrete types (e.g., ArrayCollection) so that polymorphism can be utilized in later examples. In the case of the preceding example, you could technically type the variable as ArrayCollection.

Likewise, this ActionScript example creates an `XMLListCollection` that wraps an `XMLList` object:

```
var xmlList:XMLList = <items><item>a</item><item>b</item>
                        <item>c</item><item>d</item></items>;
var collection:ICollectionView = new XMLListCollection(xmlList);
```

You can create the same collections using MXML. The following example creates an ArrayCollection object using MXML:

```
<mx:ArrayCollection>
    <mx:Array>
        <mx:String>a</mx:String>
        <mx:String>b</mx:String>
        <mx:String>c</mx:String>
        <mx:String>d</mx:String>
    </mx:Array>
</mx:ArrayCollection>
```

This creates an XMLListCollection using MXML:

```
<mx:XMLListCollection>
    <mx:XML id="example">
        <items>
            <item>a</item>
            <item>b</item>
            <item>c</item>
            <item>d</item>
        </items>
    </mx:XML>
</mx:XMLListCollection>
```

Setting the Data Provider

You can use any sort of collection (as long as it implements ICollectionView) with any sort of list-based control, allowing for versatile data structures. All you have to do is set the dataProvider property of the list-based control to be equal to the collection. For example, the following uses an ArrayCollection to populate a list:

```
var collection:ICollectionView = new ArrayCollection(["a", "b", "c", "d"]);
list.dataProvider = collection;
```

On the other hand, if the data happens to be in XML format, you can easily use an XMLListCollection instead:

```
var xmlList:XMLList = <items><item>a</item><item>b</item>
                            <item>c</item><item>d</item></items>;
var collection:ICollectionView = new XMLListCollection(xmlList);
list.dataProvider = collection;
```

If you're using MXML to set the data provider, you can simply nest the collection within the list-based control tag. Because the dataProvider property is the default property for list-based controls, you don't need to explicitly state that the value should be assigned to the dataProvider property. The following example assigns an ArrayCollection to the dataProvider for a list:

```
<mx:List id="list" width="100">
    <mx:ArrayCollection>
        <mx:Array>
            <mx:String>a</mx:String>
            <mx:String>b</mx:String>
```

```
        <mx:String>c</mx:String>
        <mx:String>d</mx:String>
    </mx:Array>
  </mx:ArrayCollection>
</mx:List>
```

Using Data Grids

The preceding examples illustrated how to work with simple list-based controls such as lists, combo boxes, tile lists, and horizontal lists. Data grids inherit from standard lists, and therefore they function in much the same way. However, because data grids are more complex than standard lists, they have behavior that is specific to them. In the following sections, we'll look at working with data grids.

Using data providers

Data grid data providers are quite similar to standard data providers except that each element of a data grid data provider should consist of an object whose properties correspond to the columns of the data grid. The following example creates a data grid with columns named *city*, *state*, and *population*:

```
<mx:DataGrid>
    <mx:ArrayCollection>
        <mx:Array>
            <mx:Object city="Los Angeles" state="CA" population="3844829" />
            <mx:Object city="New York" state="NY" population="8143197" />
            <mx:Object city="Chicago" state="IL" population="2842518" />
            <mx:Object city="Philadelphia" state="PA" population="1463281" />
        </mx:Array>
    </mx:ArrayCollection>
</mx:DataGrid>
```

You can, of course, achieve the same result using ActionScript. Here's an example that displays the same content using ActionScript:

```
<?xml version="1.0"?>
<mx:Application xmlns:mx="http://www.adobe.com/2006/mxml"
creationComplete="creationCompleteHandler(event)">
    <mx:Script>
        <![CDATA[
            import mx.collections.ArrayCollection;

            private function creationCompleteHandler(event:Event):void {
                var array:Array = new Array({city: "Los Angeles",
state: "CA", population: 3844829},
                                    {city: "New York", state: "NY",
population: 8143197},
                                    {city: "Chicago", state: "IL",
population: 2842518},
                                    {city: "Philadelphia", state: "PA",
population: 1463281});
                var collection:ArrayCollection = new ArrayCollection(array);
                grid.dataProvider = collection;
```

```
            }

        ]]>
    </mx:Script>
    <mx:DataGrid id="grid" width="500" />

</mx:Application>
```

Working with data grid columns

By default, data grids automatically display columns corresponding to all the properties of the data provider elements. The code in the preceding section creates a data
grid with three columns with the headings city, state, and population. Although
this may be the intended behavior, in many cases it is not very versatile. For this reason, it is possible to explicitly control the columns of a data grid.

You can specify which columns will display within a data grid by setting the columns
property of the data grid to an array of DataGridColumn objects. Using these column
objects, you can filter which columns get displayed, the widths of the columns, the
editability of the columns, the heading text for the columns, and more. Here's an
example that displays the city and population values with custom labels, but does
not display the state data:

```
<mx:DataGrid width="500">
    <mx:columns>
        <mx:DataGridColumn headerText="City" dataField="city" />
        <mx:DataGridColumn headerText="Population (within city limits)"
                           dataField="population" />
    </mx:columns>
    <mx:ArrayCollection>
        <mx:Array>
            <mx:Object city="Los Angeles" state="CA" population="3844829" />
            <mx:Object city="New York" state="NY" population="8143197" />
            <mx:Object city="Chicago" state="IL" population="2842518" />
            <mx:Object city="Philadelphia" state="PA" population="1463281" />
        </mx:Array>
    </mx:ArrayCollection>
</mx:DataGrid>
```

Using Tree Controls

Like data grids, tree controls inherit from standard lists but have specialized behavior. In the case of trees, the specialized behavior is that trees can render hierarchical
data providers.

Although most lists display a linear list of elements (whether vertically, horizontally,
or in grid format), tree controls allow you to render elements that themselves have
nested child elements. These sorts of data providers are called *hierarchical data
providers*. The following simple XML snippet demonstrates a hierarchical relationship in which the cities are child elements of states:

```
<state label="CA">
   <city label="Los Angeles" />
   <city label="San Francisco" />
</state>
<state label="MA">
   <city label="Boston" />
</state>
```

A tree control can represent this sort of data. Tree controls have two types of elements: branch elements and leaf nodes. When a data provider element has child elements it is automatically treated as a branch element, meaning it is expandable within the tree. Here's an example that uses a tree to display state and city data:

```
<mx:Tree labelField="@label" width="200">
    <mx:XMLListCollection>
        <mx:XMLList>
                <state label="CA">
                    <city label="Los Angeles" />
                    <city label="San Francisco" />
                </state>
                <state label="MA">
                    <city label="Boston" />
                </state>
        </mx:XMLList>
    </mx:XMLListCollection>
</mx:Tree>
```

You'll notice that in this example, the tree requires a labelField property value indicating what to use as the label for the elements. The @label value uses E4X (see Chapter 4) syntax to indicate that the tree should use the label attributes of each XML node for the label of the corresponding tree element.

Although it's easiest to visualize hierarchical relationships with XML, you are not restricted to using XML-based data providers for trees. You can use any sort of collection. For example, you can use an ArrayCollection object as a data provider. However, when you want to establish hierarchical relationships using collection types that aren't intrinsically hierarchical, you must follow certain rules. Specifically, in order to add children to an element, you must add them as an array for a property called children. The following example illustrates this using the city/state example from before:

```
<mx:Tree labelField="label" width="200">
    <mx:ArrayCollection>
        <mx:Array>
                <mx:Object label="CA">
                    <mx:children>
                        <mx:Object label="Los Angeles" />
                        <mx:Object label="San Francisco" />
                    </mx:children>
                </mx:Object>
                <mx:Object label="MA">
                    <mx:children>
```

```
                <mx:Object label="Boston" />
            </mx:children>
        </mx:Object>
    </mx:Array>
</mx:ArrayCollection>
</mx:Tree>
```

Of course, you can achieve the same result using ActionScript in every case. First, here's an example that populates a tree using XML data:

```
<?xml version="1.0"?>
<mx:Application xmlns:mx="http://www.adobe.com/2006/mxml"
creationComplete="creationCompleteHandler(event)">
    <mx:Script>
        <![CDATA[
            import mx.collections.XMLListCollection;
            import mx.controls.List;

            private function creationCompleteHandler(event:Event):void {
                var xmlList:XMLList = <items>
                                        <item label="CA">
                                            <item label="Los Angeles" />
                                            <item label="San Francisco" />
                                        </item>
                                        <item label="MA">
                                            <item label="Boston" />
                                        </item>
                                     </items>;
                var collection:XMLListCollection = new XMLListCollection(xmlList);
                tree.dataProvider = collection;
            }

        ]]>
    </mx:Script>
    <mx:Tree id="tree" labelField="@label" width="200" />
</mx:Application>
```

And here's an example that achieves the same goal using an array:

```
<?xml version="1.0"?>
<mx:Application xmlns:mx="http://www.adobe.com/2006/mxml"
creationComplete="creationCompleteHandler(event)">
    <mx:Script>
        <![CDATA[
            import mx.collections.ArrayCollection;
            import mx.controls.List;

            private function creationCompleteHandler(event:Event):void {
                var array:Array = new Array({label: "CA", children: new Array(
                                    {label: "Los Angeles"},
                                    {label: "San Francisco"})},
                                {label: "MA", children: new Array(
                                    {label: "Boston"})});
                var collection:ArrayCollection = new ArrayCollection(array);
                tree.dataProvider = collection;
```

```
                }

        ]]>
    </mx:Script>
    <mx:Tree id="tree" labelField="label" width="200" />
</mx:Application>
```

Working with Selected Values and Items

List-based controls allow for programmatic and user selection of elements. An application may frequently need to be able to detect which item the user has selected. For this purpose, list-based controls have the following properties:

allowMultipleSelection
> By default, lists allow for one selected item at a time. By setting allowMultipleSelection to true, a user can select more than one item at a time.

value
> The value of the selected item. The value of the value property depends on the structure of the data provider. Because it has very strict requirements, in order to get predictable results, it is frequently better not to rely on the value property.

selectedItem
> The element from the data provider corresponding to the selected item in the list. This is a very predictable property because it will always be a reference rather than an interpretation. That means that if the data provider is a collection of strings, the selectedItem will be a string, but if the data provider is a collection of XML elements, the selectedItem will be an XML element.

selectedItems
> An array of elements. This is the multiselect equivalent to selectedItem.

selectedIndex
> The integer index of the selected item. For all controls using linear data providers, this is a predictable and useful property. If the selectedIndex property of a standard list is 0, the first element is selected. This property is complicated only when using hierarchical data providers because the relationship of the index of a visible element and the data provider depends on the expanded/collapsed state of the rest of the control's elements.

selectedIndices
> An array of the indices of the selected items. This is the multiselect equivalent of selectedIndex.

Now let's look at a few examples using these properties. First, here's an example that sets the selected index of a list based on an index from a numeric stepper:

```
<mx:VBox>
    <mx:List id="list" width="100">
        <mx:ArrayCollection>
            <mx:Array>
```

```
                <mx:String>a</mx:String>
                <mx:String>b</mx:String>
                <mx:String>c</mx:String>
                <mx:String>d</mx:String>
            </mx:Array>
        </mx:ArrayCollection>
    </mx:List>
    <mx:NumericStepper id="stepper" minimum="0" maximum="3"
                        change="list.selectedIndex = stepper.value" />
</mx:VBox>
```

Here's an example that displays the selected values from a data grid when the user
selects them:

```
<mx:VBox>
    <mx:DataGrid id="grid" width="500" change="output.text =
grid.selectedItem.city">
        <mx:columns>
            <mx:DataGridColumn headerText="City" dataField="city" />
            <mx:DataGridColumn headerText="Population (within city limits)"
dataField="population" />
        </mx:columns>
        <mx:ArrayCollection>
            <mx:Array>
                <mx:Object city="Los Angeles" state="CA" population="3844829" />
                <mx:Object city="New York" state="NY" population="8143197" />
                <mx:Object city="Chicago" state="IL" population="2842518" />
                <mx:Object city="Philadelphia" state="PA" population="1463281" />
            </mx:Array>
        </mx:ArrayCollection>
    </mx:DataGrid>
    <mx:TextInput id="output" width="200" />
</mx:VBox>
```

Pop-Up Controls

Apart from the ability to programmatically create menus and the menu bar navigator (discussed in the next section), there are two Flex framework controls that you
can use to create pop-up controls: PopUpButton and PopUpMenuButton. Both controls
are very similar, and they each may require an understanding of menus.

Understanding Menus

Menus are an instance of mx.controls.Menu. Like tree controls, menu controls require
hierarchical data providers. The following code creates a menu and populates it with
an XMLListCollection data provider. It also sets the labelField property just like
when using a hierarchical data provider for a tree control.

```
var menu:Menu = new Menu( );
var xmlList:XMLList = <items>
                        <item label="ActionScript">
                          <item label="Class" />
```

```
                              <item label="Interface" />
                           </item>
                           <item label="MXML">
                             <item label="Application" />
                             <item label="Component" />
                           </item>
                        </items>;
   menu.dataProvider = new XMLListCollection(xmlList);
   menu.labelField = "@label";
```

Using PopUpButton

The PopUpButton control allows you to associate the button with a pop up, such as a menu. Here's an example:

```
<?xml version="1.0"?>
<mx:Application xmlns:mx="http://www.adobe.com/2006/mxml" layout="absolute"
creationComplete="creationCompleteHandler(event)">

    <mx:Script>
        <![CDATA[
            import mx.controls.Menu;
            import mx.collections.XMLListCollection;

            private var _menu:Menu;

            private function creationCompleteHandler(event:Event):void {
                _menu = new Menu( );
                var xmlList:XMLList = <items>
                                       <item label="ActionScript">
                                         <item label="Class" />
                                         <item label="Interface" />
                                       </item>
                                       <item label="MXML">
                                         <item label="Application" />
                                         <item label="Component" />
                                       </item>
                                     </items>;
                _menu.dataProvider = new XMLListCollection(xmlList);
                _menu.labelField = "@label";
                button.popUp = _menu;
            }

        ]]>
    </mx:Script>
    <mx:PopUpButton id="button" label="New File" />

</mx:Application>
```

If you test this example, you'll see the menu appear when you click on the button, as shown in Figure 7-6.

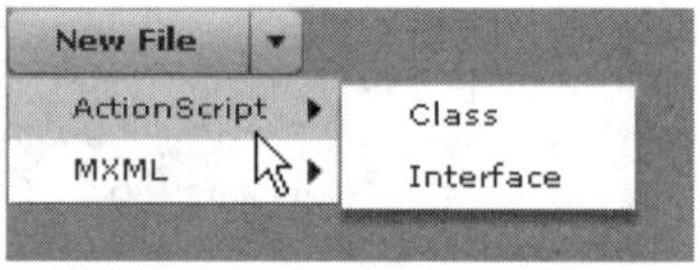

Figure 7-6. PopUpButton

Using PopUpMenuButton

The PopUpMenuButton control simplifies associating a menu with a button by automatically creating the menu when assigning a data provider to the button, as illustrated in this example:

```
<mx:PopUpMenuButton labelField="@label">
    <mx:dataProvider>
        <mx:XMLListCollection>
            <mx:XMLList>
                <item label="ActionScript">
                    <item label="Class" />
                    <item label="Interface" />
                </item>
                <item label="MXML">
                    <item label="Application" />
                    <item label="Component" />
                </item>
            </mx:XMLList>
        </mx:XMLListCollection>
    </mx:dataProvider>
</mx:PopUpMenuButton>
```

Figure 7-7 shows what this example looks like.

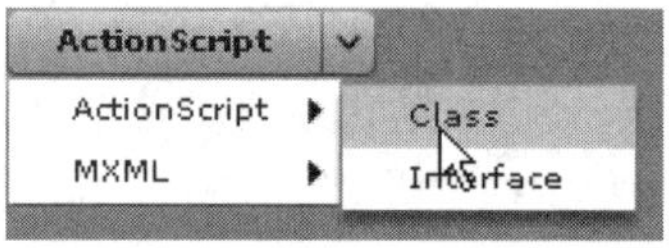

Figure 7-7. PopUpMenuButton

Listening to Menu Events

Menu controls dispatch itemClick events of type mx.events.MenuEvent every time the user selects a menu item. You can listen for the event directly from the menu using ActionScript and addEventListener. If using PopUpMenuButton, you can listen for the itemClick event directly from the button, and you can even use MXML to listen for the event, as illustrated in this example which changes the button label each time the user selects a menu item:

```
<mx:PopUpMenuButton id="button" labelField="@label"
                    itemClick="button.label = event.label">
    <mx:dataProvider>
        <mx:XMLListCollection>
            <mx:XMLList>
                <item label="ActionScript">
                    <item label="Class" />
                    <item label="Interface" />
                </item>
                <item label="MXML">
                    <item label="Application" />
                    <item label="Component" />
                </item>
            </mx:XMLList>
        </mx:XMLListCollection>
    </mx:dataProvider>
</mx:PopUpMenuButton>
```

Navigators

Navigators are controls that allow users to navigate from screen to screen, page to page, section to section, or option to option within a Flex application. We can further categorize navigator controls as follows: accordion, divided boxes, option bars, and view stacks.

Accordion Controls

The accordion control consists of two or more collapsible containers. Only one element within an accordion can be visible at a time. The other elements in the accordion are collapsed so that only a title bar is visible. Accordions are often good for processes that require several steps and allow the user to return to previous steps. For example, an accordion is useful when a user input form contains many sections. Rather than try to present all the sections at once, an accordion allows the user to view just one section at a time, making for a more manageable experience. Figure 7-8 shows an example of an accordion.

Creating accordions, like most other components in Flex, is quite simple. Accordions act just like all standard containers in that you can nest child elements in MXML or use addChild( ) to add child elements using ActionScript. In the case of accordions all child elements should be containers themselves, and you should add a label property to all accordion children. Accordions use the label properties of child elements for the title bar, and also have the ability to display icons when the icon property is set. Here's an example :

```
<mx:Accordion>
    <mx:Form label="Name" icon="@Embed(source='/firstStep.png')">
        <mx:FormItem label="First Name">
            <mx:TextInput id="first" />
        </mx:FormItem>
```

```
    <mx:FormItem label="Middle Name">
        <mx:TextInput id="middle" />
    </mx:FormItem>
    <mx:FormItem label="Last Name">
        <mx:TextInput id="last" />
    </mx:FormItem>
</mx:Form>
<mx:Form label="Comments">
    <mx:FormItem label="Comments">
        <mx:TextArea id="comments" />
    </mx:FormItem>
</mx:Form>
</mx:Accordion>
```

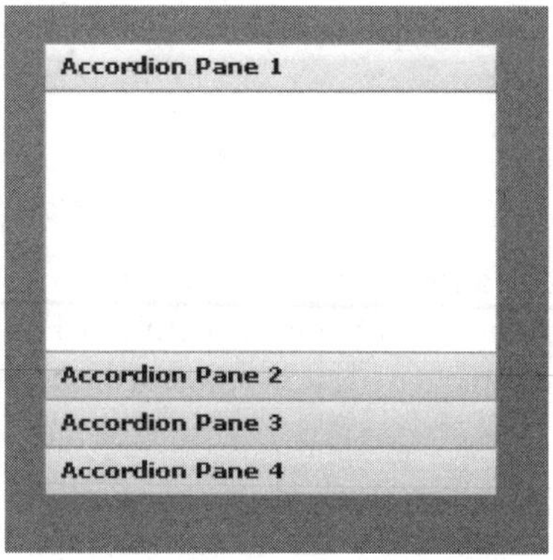

Figure 7-8. An accordion component

Option Bars

Option bars consist of the following: ButtonBar, LinkBar, MenuBar, and
ToggleButtonBar. Each option bar type is similar in that they provide a convenient
way in which to create groups of controls, whether buttons, link buttons, menus,
and so on. Furthermore (and perhaps more important), you can use option bars in
conjunction with view stacks, as discussed in the next section. Figure 7-9 shows
examples of each of the option bar types.

Button bars, link bars, and toggle button bars are ways to create horizontal or vertical groups of buttons. These controls provide a convenient way to group buttons
together. Furthermore, in the case of toggle button bars, you have the added behavior that only one of the toggle buttons can be selected at a time. All button, link, and
toggle button bars use data providers. Here's an example that creates a toggle button
bar:

```
<mx:ToggleButtonBar>
    <mx:ArrayCollection>
        <mx:Array>
```

```
            <mx:Object label="A" />
            <mx:Object label="B" />
            <mx:Object label="C" />
            <mx:Object label="D" />
        </mx:Array>
    </mx:ArrayCollection>
</mx:ToggleButtonBar>
```

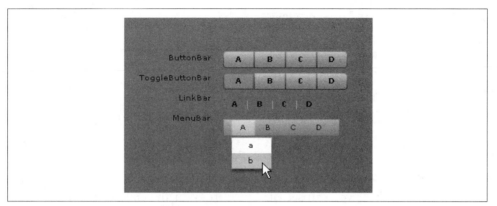

Figure 7-9. Option bars

Menu bars provide a convenient way to group together menus with a single data provider. Here's an example:

```
<mx:MenuBar labelField="@label">
    <mx:XMLListCollection>
        <mx:XMLList>
            <item label="File">
                <item label="New" />
                <item label="Open" />
                <item label="Close" />
                <item label="Properties" />
            </item>
            <item label="Edit">
                <item label="Select All" />
                <item label="Copy" />
                <item label="Cut" />
                <item label="Paste" />
            </item>
        </mx:XMLList>
    </mx:XMLListCollection>
</mx:MenuBar>
```

View Stacks

View stacks allow you to group together a set of containers and display just one at a time. This is useful when you want to use a page/screen/section metaphor. The easiest way to work with a view stack is to use the tab navigator control, which has view stack behavior built in. Here's an example of a tab navigator with nearly the same form contents used earlier in the accordion example:

```
<mx:TabNavigator>
    <mx:Form label="Name">
        <mx:FormItem label="First Name">
            <mx:TextInput id="first" />
        </mx:FormItem>
        <mx:FormItem label="Middle Name">
            <mx:TextInput id="middle" />
        </mx:FormItem>
        <mx:FormItem label="Last Name">
            <mx:TextInput id="last" />
        </mx:FormItem>
    </mx:Form>
    <mx:Form label="Comments">
        <mx:FormItem label="Comments">
            <mx:TextArea id="comments" />
        </mx:FormItem>
    </mx:Form>
</mx:TabNavigator>
```

As with the accordion, you can set label properties for the child containers of a tab navigator to determine what the tab labels should be. Figure 7-10 shows what this tab navigator looks like.

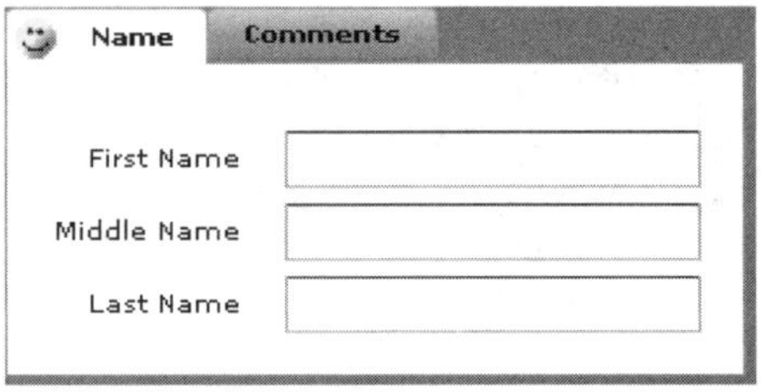

Figure 7-10. A tab navigator

You can use a view stack without having to use the tab navigator. It simply requires that you first create the view stack with the child containers. Then, assuming you use a button bar, link bar, or toggle button bar, you can simply assign the view stack as the data provider of the bar:

```
<mx:VBox>
    <mx:ToggleButtonBar dataProvider="{viewStack}" />
    <mx:ViewStack id="viewStack">
        <mx:Form label="Name">
            <mx:FormItem label="First Name">
                <mx:TextInput id="first" />
            </mx:FormItem>
            <mx:FormItem label="Middle Name">
                <mx:TextInput id="middle" />
            </mx:FormItem>
```

```
            <mx:FormItem label="Last Name">
                <mx:TextInput id="last" />
            </mx:FormItem>
        </mx:Form>
        <mx:Form label="Comments">
            <mx:FormItem label="Comments">
                <mx:TextArea id="comments" />
            </mx:FormItem>
        </mx:Form>
    </mx:ViewStack>
</mx:VBox>
```

Otherwise, you have to set the selectedIndex property of the view stack programmatically to change the view:

```
viewStack.selectedIndex = 1;
```

Control Bars

Control bars allow you to group together all the controls for a panel or title window. Application control bars are the application-wide analogs to control bars. Each allows you to group together all the controls for that container, even if they are nonuniform (not all buttons, etc.).

Control bars work with title window and panel components, and you should add them as the last child for a title window or panel. You can then place controls within the control bar. Here's an example:

```
<mx:Panel id="panel" width="250" height="200">
    <mx:TextArea id="textArea" width="80%" height="80%" text="Example" />
    <mx:ControlBar>
        <mx:Button label="Random Font Size"
            click="textArea.setStyle('fontSize', Math.random( ) * 20 + 8)" />
        <mx:ColorPicker id="color"
            change="panel.setStyle('backgroundColor', color.value)" />
    </mx:ControlBar>
</mx:Panel>
```

Figure 7-11 shows what this looks like. Clicking on the button changes the font size, and changing the value of the color selector changes the background of the panel.

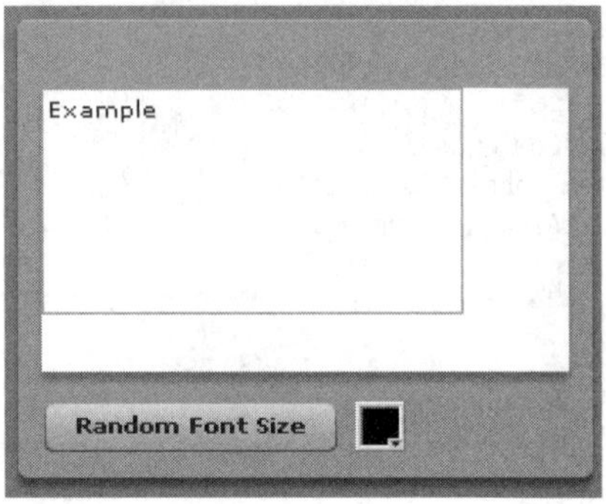

Figure 7-11. A panel with a control bar

The application control bar works similarly, but it is applied only to an application container. By default, the application control bar scrolls with the rest of the content. However, it is possible to set the dock property to true to dock the control panel such that it does not scroll. Here's how you would do that:

```
<?xml version="1.0"?>
<mx:Application xmlns:mx="http://www.adobe.com/2006/mxml" layout="absolute">
    <mx:Canvas x="0" y="0" width="200" height="2000" />
    <mx:ApplicationControlBar dock="true">
        <mx:Label text="Jump To Section:"/>
        <mx:ComboBox>
            <mx:dataProvider>
                <mx:ArrayCollection>
                    <mx:Array>
                        <mx:String>A</mx:String>
                        <mx:String>B</mx:String>
                        <mx:String>C</mx:String>
                        <mx:String>D</mx:String>
                    </mx:Array>
                </mx:ArrayCollection>
            </mx:dataProvider>
        </mx:ComboBox>
        <mx:VRule width="20" height="28"/>
        <mx:TextInput/>
        <mx:Button label="Search"/>
    </mx:ApplicationControlBar>
</mx:Application>
```

Figure 7-12 shows what this looks like.

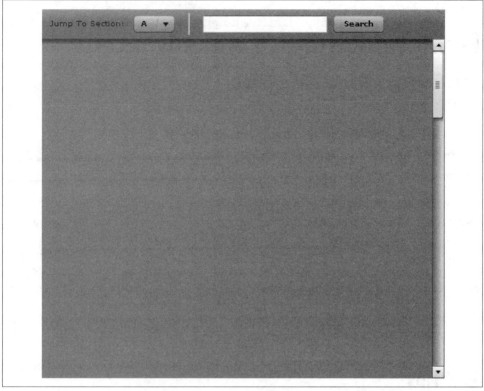

Figure 7-12. Application control bars docked so that they don't scroll with the rest of the content

Summary

In this chapter, you learned everything you need to know to get started working with user interface controls in Flex 2. We discussed event handling with controls, and we provided an overview of all the major types of standard UI controls, from buttons to lists to control bars.

CHAPTER 8

Framework Utilities and Advanced Component Concepts

As you've already learned in earlier chapters, the Flex framework provides a large library of components, including layout containers and UI controls. However, in addition to the components themselves, the framework also provides libraries that offer you advanced features and functionality when working with those components. In this chapter, we'll look at the features and functionality these libraries provide. Specifically, we'll discuss tool tips, pop ups, cursor management, drag and drop, the ability to customize list-based items, and focus management and keyboard control.

Tool Tips

When an application contains graphics, it can often be helpful to users if you provide text-based descriptions to accompany the graphics. This is especially beneficial when the meaning of a particular graphic is not immediately obvious. It can also be useful for low-sighted and non-sighted users who rely on screen readers. Rather than cluttering the user interface with many text-based descriptions of graphics, however, many applications use *tool tips*, which are blocks of text that appear when the user moves the mouse over a graphic. In the following sections you'll learn how to work with Flex tool tips.

Adding Tool Tips

All components that inherit from UIComponent (which includes all UI controls and layout containers) implement a toolTip getter/setter property that allows you to assign a string to the object that it will use to display tool tips. You can set the property inline using MXML, as in the following example:

```
<mx:Button id="button" label="Tool Tip Example" toolTip="Display Tool Tip" />
```

You can also set the toolTip property in ActionScript:

```
button.toolTip = "Example of Tool Tips";
```

By default, the toolTip property value for a component is null. When the value is null, no tool tip will appear. When you assign the property a non-null value, the tool tip will appear after a short delay once the user moves the mouse over the object and holds it there. The tool tip then disappears after a delay or after the user moves the mouse outside the object, whichever occurs first.

You can also use data binding to set the value of a tool tip for an object. The following example uses data binding to update the value of the tool tip text for a button based on the text input value:

```
<mx:VBox>
  <mx:Button id="button" label="Button" toolTip="{textInput.text}" />
  <mx:TextInput id="textInput" />
</mx:VBox>
```

There are rules that determine the tool-tip behavior for containers and child components. The innermost component always takes highest precedence. If the innermost component has a valid tool-tip text value, the tool tip for that component is triggered. If not, the trigger bubbles up to the container until either a valid tool-tip text value is found, or no more containers exist. The following simple example illustrates this behavior. Because the button has a tool-tip text value, moving the mouse over the button triggers that component's tool tip. And because the text input has no tool-tip text setting, the trigger will bubble up to the VBox container, displaying the container's tool tip:

```
<mx:VBox toolTip="This is the VBox tool tip.">
  <mx:Button id="button" label="Button" toolTip="This is the button tool tip." />
  <mx:TextInput id="textInput" />
</mx:VBox>
```

Navigator components such as accordions and tab navigators have a different default behavior in this regard. Whereas most container children will trigger the parent container tool tip, the children of navigator components do not. The only trigger for the container tool tips are the navigator elements corresponding to the containers. For example, in a tab navigator, the tabs will trigger the tool tips for the corresponding containers. The following example illustrates this behavior. The accordion has two elements, each a VBox container. Each VBox specifies a toolTip value. Each VBox instance contains one button. The button within the first VBox does not specify a toolTip value, while the second does. If you test this code, you'll see that the tool tips for the VBox containers are never triggered by the child buttons:

```
<mx:Accordion height="200" width="200">
  <mx:VBox toolTip="A">
    <mx:Button />
  </mx:VBox>
  <mx:VBox toolTip="B">
    <mx:Button toolTip="Button" />
  </mx:VBox>
</mx:Accordion>
```

Controlling Tool Tip Width and Line Formatting

By default, tool tips have a maximum width of 300 pixels, and the text automatically wraps at that width. You can see the default behavior with the following example:

```
<mx:Button id="button" label="Tool Tip" toolTip="Lorem ipsum dolor sit amet,
consectetuer adipiscing elit. Integer commodo lacus sed dui. Pellentesque
est nisi, semper sit amet, feugiat eu, pellentesque id, erat." />
```

This example creates a button that has a tool tip with the default maximum width so that the text automatically wraps to form three lines.

You can control the maximum width of the tool tip using the static `mx.controls.ToolTip.maxWidth` property. The default value is 300, which accounts for the default width of 300 pixels. If you set the value of the property, it will affect the width of all tool tips within the application that are displayed from that point forward, unless and until you assign a new value to the property. There is no API for controlling the maximum width of an individual tool tip. The following example uses a button with a tool tip. Initially the maximum width of the tool tip is set to the default. However, when the user clicks on the button, it sets the maximum width to 500. Mousing over the button again displays the tool tip text on just two lines.

```
<mx:Button id="button" label="Tool Tip" toolTip="Lorem ipsum dolor sit amet,
consectetuer adipiscing elit. Integer commodo lacus sed dui. Pellentesque
est nisi, semper sit amet, feugiat eu, pellentesque id, erat."
click="mx.controls.ToolTip.maxWidth = 500" />
```

Tool tips use automatic word wrap to add soft line breaks when the text reaches the maximum width. If you want to add a hard line break, you can do so by inserting a newline character (\n), carriage return (\r), or form feed (\f) character in the tool-tip text when assigning the text using ActionScript. When using an MXML attribute, you should use the  XML entity, as in the following example:

```
<mx:Button id="button" label="Tool Tip" toolTip="Lorem ipsum dolor sit amet,
consectetuer adipiscing elit.&#13;Integer commodo lacus sed dui.&#13;Pellentesque
est nisi, semper sit amet, feugiat eu, pellentesque id, erat." />
```

Applying Styles to Tool Tips

You can customize the look of tool tips using styles. The Flex framework doesn't provide a way to set the styles of individual tool tips; you must set the tool-tip style globally for all instances. You can do so by changing the `ToolTip` style definition. The following illustrates how to change the style definition using a `Style` tag:

```
<mx:Style>
  ToolTip {
    fontFamily: "_typewriter";
    backgroundColor: #FFFFFF;
  }
</mx:Style>
```

You can also use ActionScript to set the style using the StyleManager.getStyleDeclaration( ) method to retrieve the ToolTip declaration. You can then use setStyle( ) to change individual styles:

```
var toolTipDeclaration:CSSStyleDeclaration =
    StyleManager.getStyleDeclaration("ToolTip");
toolTipDeclaration.setStyle("fontFamily", "_typewriter");
```

If you want to use a specific font, and you want to ensure that the user will be able to view the tool tip with that specific font, you can embed the font. Embedding the font for tool tips works just as it would for any other text for which you use styles. The following example embeds a font called *Georgia*:

```
<mx:Style>
  @font-face {
    src: local("Georgia");
    fontFamily: GeorgiaEmbedded;
  }
  ToolTip {
    fontFamily: GeorgiaEmbedded;
    backgroundColor: #FFFFFF;
  }
</mx:Style>
```

Customizing Tool-Tip Settings

You can customize several global tool-tip settings using the mx.managers.ToolTipManager class. Using the static enabled property, you can enable and disable tool tips globally. This can be useful if, for example, you want to temporarily disable tool tips while the application is awaiting a response to a remote procedure call. The default value of the enabled property is true, which means that if you want tool tips enabled, you don't have to do anything. If you want to disable tool tips, you can set the value to false:

```
ToolTipManager.enabled = false;
```

Of course, you'll need to set the property to true again if you want to reenable tool tips:

```
ToolTipManager.enabled = true;
```

The showDelay, hideDelay, and scrubDelay static properties allow you to control the amount of delay before showing and hiding tool tips. The showDelay property controls the amount of time before a tool tip displays after a user moves the mouse over the object. The value is specified in milliseconds. The default value is 500, which means the tool tip displays half a second after the user moves the mouse over the object. The following sets the delay to one second:

```
ToolTipManager.showDelay = 1000;
```

Tool tips disappear after the user moves the mouse off an object. However, they can also disappear after a delay even while the mouse is still over the object. The `hideDelay` property determines the number of milliseconds before the tool tip disappears. The default value is 10000, which means the tool tip disappears after 10 seconds. Setting the value to 0 is the same as telling the tool tips to disappear as soon as they appear, so they are never shown. You can use a value of `Infinity` (a global constant) if you want the tool tips to remain visible as long as the mouse is over the object:

```
ToolTipManager.hideDelay = Infinity;
```

The `scrubDelay` property allows you to specify the amount of allowable delay between mousing out of one object and mousing over another object to omit the show delay on the second object. This is especially important if there is a long show delay. For example, if you have a line of buttons, each with tool tips, you may want the user to be able to scroll across the buttons quickly and read the tool tips. Without the scrub delay setting, the user would have to pause over each button for the show delay duration before he could see the tool tip. The scrub delay setting says that if the amount of time between mousing out of one object and mousing over a second object is less than a specified number of milliseconds, the application should display the tool tip for the second object immediately. The default value for `scrubDelay` is 100. The greater the value for `scrubDelay`, the more likely it is that the user will have to delay before showing the tool tip on objects after mousing over them in succession.

> The `ToolTipManager` class also allows you to use a custom class as a tool tip. This is a very rare use case, and for that reason, we won't discuss it in detail. However, you can assign a `DisplayObject` class reference to the static `toolTipClass` property to use that class as the tool-tip blueprint:
>
> ```
> ToolTipManager.toolTipClass = CustomClass;
> ```
>
> Note that if you want to use the custom class in the same way as a standard tool tip (e.g., set the tool tip text), the custom class must also implement `mx.core.IToolTip`. Because `IToolTip` extends `IUIComponent`, the most practical way to implement `IToolTip` is to first extend `mx.core.UIComponent` and then to implement just the specific interface defined by `IToolTip`.

Applying Effects

You can apply effects such as blurs, motion, and so on, to the showing and hiding of tool tips. You can use any effect that you can use with any Flex component. As with almost all other tool-tip settings, the effect settings apply globally to all tool tips. You can set the effect that gets applied when showing the tool tips by way of the `ToolTipManager.showEffect` property, and you can set the effect that gets applied when hiding the tool tips using the `ToolTipManager.hideEffect` property. Example 8-1 illustrates how this works, and it demonstrates that you can use not only single effects, but also composite effects.

Example 8-1. Applying composite effects

```
<?xml version="1.0" encoding="utf-8"?>
<mx:Application xmlns:mx=http://www.adobe.com/2006/mxml
 initialize="initializeHandler(event)">

  <mx:Style>
  @font-face {
    src: local("Georgia");
    fontFamily: GeorgiaEmbedded;
  }
  ToolTip {
    fontSize: 16;
    fontFamily: GeorgiaEmbedded;
    backgroundColor: #FFFFFF;
  }
  </mx:Style>

  <mx:Script>
  <![CDATA[

    import mx.managers.ToolTipManager;

    private function initializeHandler(event:Event):void {
      ToolTipManager.showEffect = toolTipShowEffect;
      ToolTipManager.hideEffect = toolTipHideEffect;
    }

  ]]>
  </mx:Script>

  <mx:Parallel id="toolTipShowEffect">
    <mx:Fade alphaFrom="0" alphaTo="1" duration="1000" />
    <mx:Blur blurXFrom="10" blurYFrom="10" blurXTo="0"
            blurYTo="0" duration="1000" />
  </mx:Parallel>

  <mx:Parallel id="toolTipHideEffect">
    <mx:Fade alphaFrom="1" alphaTo="0" duration="1000" />
    <mx:Blur blurXFrom="0" blurYFrom="0" blurXTo="10"
            blurYTo="10" duration="1000" />
  </mx:Parallel>

  <mx:Button id="button" toolTip="Tool Tip Effect Example" />

</mx:Application>
```

You'll notice that Example 8-1 embeds the font for the tool tips. This is because the font must be embedded to properly animate the alpha of text. In this particular example, the blur portion of the effect causes the tool tips to be rendered as bitmap surfaces, lessening the need to embed the font. However, even with the bitmap surfaces enabled, the text can still quickly flash before fading in unless the font is embedded.

Pop-Ups

The Flex framework has built-in support for pop-up windows and alerts. Pop ups can be useful for many reasons, including notifying the user of messages or news and displaying simple forms such as login forms or mailing-list sign-up forms. Unlike HTML pop ups, Flex pop ups do not open new browser windows. Flex application pop ups appear within the same Flash Player instance. This means that Flex application pop ups are never subject to the same restrictions as some types of HTML pop ups.

There are two basic sorts of pop ups you can use in Flex applications: alerts and custom pop-up windows. Alerts are quite similar to the pop ups that appear in HTML applications when using the JavaScript alert( ) function. They display text messages to the user in a modal window, and prompt the user to click a button. However, as we'll see in the next section, Flex alerts are more sophisticated than HTML alerts. Custom pop ups allow you to create more complex pop-up content. For example, using a custom pop-up you can display a mailing list email form.

Using Alerts

Flex alerts are instances of the mx.controls.Alert component. Unlike many of the other Flex components, you cannot create an alert using MXML tags. You must use the static show( ) method of the Alert class. The show( ) method requires at least one parameter: a string specifying the message to display. The show( ) method returns a reference to the new Alert instance that you can use to manipulate the Alert instance if needed. Example 8-2 displays an alert with a message and an OK button (the default behavior) when the user clicks a button.

Example 8-2. Using alerts

```
<?xml version="1.0" encoding="utf-8"?>
<mx:Application xmlns:mx="http://www.adobe.com/2006/mxml">

  <mx:Script>
  <![CDATA[

    import mx.controls.Alert;

    private function showAlert(event:Event):void {
      var alert:Alert = Alert.show("You have clicked a button to
display an alert.");
    }

  ]]>
  </mx:Script>

  <mx:Button id="button" label="Show Alert" click="showAlert(event)" />

</mx:Application>
```

The show( ) method also allows you to specify a value to display in a title bar, as in the following example:

```
var alert:Alert = Alert.show("You have clicked a button to display an alert.",
                             "Important Message");
```

As already noted, the default behavior for an alert is to display an OK button. However, alerts can display from one to four buttons, including the following: OK, Cancel, Yes, and No. You can control which button is displayed by specifying a third parameter value using the OK, CANCEL, YES, and NO constants of the Alert class. The following displays a Cancel button rather than the default OK button:

```
var alert:Alert = Alert.show("You have clicked a button to display an alert.",
                             "Important Message",
                             Alert.CANCEL);
```

If you want to display several buttons, you can combine the constants using the bitwise OR operator (|). This example displays both an OK and a Cancel button:

```
var alert:Alert = Alert.show("You have clicked a button to display an alert.",
                             "Important Message",
                             Alert.OK | Alert.CANCEL);
```

The next optional parameter allows you to specify the parent container of the alert. This determines what parts of the application are affected by the alert's modality, and it affects where the alert is centered. By default, the application container is used. In most cases, the application container is the appropriate parent, and you generally need to set the value only when passing additional parameters.

You may want to add listeners for click events dispatched by the alert. By default, alerts close when the user clicks a button. However, your application may still want to receive a notification that the user clicked a button. Furthermore, when an alert has several buttons, it is often particularly important to know which button the user clicked. You can add a listener to an alert by passing a listener function reference to the show( ) method as the fifth parameter. The listener will receive a parameter of type mx.events.CloseEvent. The detail property of that event object will have the value of the Alert constant corresponding to the button that the user clicked. Example 8-3 uses a listener to display which button the user clicked.

Example 8-3. Customizing alerts

```
<?xml version="1.0" encoding="utf-8"?>
<mx:Application xmlns:mx="http://www.adobe.com/2006/mxml">

  <mx:Script>
  <![CDATA[

    import mx.controls.Alert;
    import mx.events.CloseEvent;

    private function showAlert(event:Event):void {
      var alert:Alert = Alert.show("You have clicked a button to display
an alert.",
```

Example 8-3. Customizing alerts (continued)

```
                                "Important Message",
                                Alert.OK | Alert.CANCEL,
                                this,
                                alertClickHandler);
    }

    private function alertClickHandler(event:CloseEvent):void {
      var buttonType:String;
      if(event.detail == Alert.OK) {
        buttonType = "OK";
      }
      else {
        buttonType = "Cancel";
      }
      textInput.text = buttonType;
    }

  ]]>
  </mx:Script>

  <mx:VBox>
    <mx:Button id="button" label="Show Alert" click="showAlert(event)" />
    <mx:TextInput id="textInput" />
  </mx:VBox>
</mx:Application>
```

You can use embedded images as icons within alerts as well. Alert icons always appear to the left of the message text. You can specify any valid embedded image resource (see Chapter 9 for information regarding embedding images) as the sixth parameter, as in the following example:

```
    <?xml version="1.0" encoding="utf-8"?>
    <mx:Application xmlns:mx="http://www.adobe.com/2006/mxml">

      <mx:Script>
      <![CDATA[

        import mx.controls.Alert;

        [Embed(source="icon.png")]
        private var sampleIcon:Class;

        private function showAlert(event:Event):void {
          var alert:Alert = Alert.show("You have clicked a button
    to display an alert.",
                                    "Important Message",
                                    Alert.OK,
                                    this,
                                    null,
                                    sampleIcon);

        }
```

```
    ]]>
    </mx:Script>

    <mx:Button id="button" label="Show Alert" click="showAlert(event)" />

</mx:Application>
```

Creating a Pop-Up Window

Custom pop ups are different from alerts in a few important ways:

- Custom pop ups allow you to create many distinct types of content, from images to forms to audio and video players.
- Custom pop ups don't have built-in buttons and button event handling.
- Custom pop ups can be modal or nonmodal.

You can create custom pop ups using the static method mx.managers.PopUpManager. createPopUp( ). The createPopUp( ) method requires at least two parameters: the parent container for the pop up and the class from which to create the new pop up. The method returns a reference to the new pop-up instance. The return type for createPopUp( ) is mx.core.IFlexDisplayObject, which means in almost all cases, you'll want to cast the return value to the correct type.

You can theoretically make a new pop up based on any sort of visual component, but most frequently you'll use mx.containers.TitleWindow as the class for the new pop up. Example 8-4 uses a button to display a new window with a text area as a pop up.

Example 8-4. Using a pop-up window

```
<?xml version="1.0" encoding="utf-8"?>
<mx:Application xmlns:mx="http://www.adobe.com/2006/mxml">

  <mx:Script>
  <![CDATA[

    import mx.managers.PopUpManager
    import mx.containers.TitleWindow;
    import mx.controls.TextArea;

    private var _window:TitleWindow;

    private function showWindow(event:MouseEvent):void {
      var textArea:TextArea = new TextArea( );
      textArea.text = "Lorem ipsum dolor sit amet, consectetuer adipiscing elit.
Sed eget massa iaculis metus interdum accumsan. Mauris pellentesque pulvinar
orci. Etiam suscipit tellus a nisl. Mauris elit risus, blandit non, varius vitae,
laoreet ac, ipsum. Fusce erat libero, imperdiet id, suscipit lacinia, nonummy
quis, metus. Ut sit amet est quis velit ullamcorper congue. Etiam in nunc id
mauris porta volutpat. Sed vitae metus. Integer lacinia. Maecenas a tortor.
Fusce mauris arcu, ullamcorper ac, sagittis id, condimentum in, dolor.
Praesent eros tortor, tincidunt in, blandit a, luctus quis, est.";
```

Example 8-4. Using a pop-up window (continued)

```
      textArea.height = 200;
      _window = TitleWindow(PopUpManager.createPopUp(this, TitleWindow));
      _window.addChild(textArea);
   }

]]>
</mx:Script>

<mx:Button id="button" label="Show Window" click="showWindow(event)" />

</mx:Application>
```

Removing a Pop-Up Window

You can remove a pop-up window using the `PopUpManager.removePopUp( )` method. The method requires one parameter—the pop up you want to remove:

```
   PopUpManager.removePopUp(_window);
```

Windows don't display close buttons by default. Nor do they handle close events automatically even when the close button is displayed. You can enable the close button by setting the `displayCloseButton` property to `true` for the window, and you can add a close event listener to handle the close button event, as shown in Example 8-5.

Example 8-5. Removing pop-up windows

```
<?xml version="1.0" encoding="utf-8"?>
<mx:Application xmlns:mx="http://www.adobe.com/2006/mxml">

  <mx:Script>
  <![CDATA[

    import mx.managers.PopUpManager
    import mx.containers.TitleWindow;
    import mx.controls.TextArea;
    import mx.events.CloseEvent;

    private var _window:TitleWindow;

    private function showWindow(event:Event):void {
      var textArea:TextArea = new TextArea( );
      textArea.text = "Lorem ipsum dolor sit amet, consectetuer adipiscing elit.
Sed eget massa iaculis metus interdum accumsan. Mauris pellentesque pulvinar
orci. Etiam suscipit tellus a nisl. Mauris elit risus, blandit non, varius
vitae, laoreet ac, ipsum. Fusce erat libero, imperdiet id, suscipit lacinia,
nonummy quis, metus. Ut sit amet est quis velit ullamcorper congue.
Etiam in nunc id mauris porta volutpat. Sed vitae metus. Integer lacinia.
Maecenas a tortor. Fusce mauris arcu, ullamcorper ac, sagittis id,
condimentum in, dolor. Praesent eros tortor, tincidunt in, blandit a,
luctus quis, est.";
      textArea.height = 200;
```

Example 8-5. Removing pop-up windows (continued)

```
      _window = TitleWindow(PopUpManager.createPopUp(this, TitleWindow));
      _window.addChild(textArea);
      _window.showCloseButton = true;
      _window.addEventListener(CloseEvent.CLOSE, closeHandler);
    }

    private function closeHandler(event:CloseEvent):void {
      PopUpManager.removePopUp(_window);
    }

  ]]>
  </mx:Script>

  <mx:Button id="button" label="Show Window" click="showWindow(event)" />

</mx:Application>
```

Custom Pop-Up Component Types

Although the preceding examples are valid use cases for a pop up, more often than not custom pop ups use custom components written in ActionScript or MXML. (See Chapters 17 and 18 for more information regarding how to create custom components.) For example, the following MXML component is a `TitleWindow` subclass with a text area that automatically handles the close event:

```
<?xml version="1.0" encoding="utf-8"?>
<mx:TitleWindow xmlns:mx="http://www.adobe.com/2006/mxml" showCloseButton="true"
close="closeWindow(event)">
  <mx:Script>
  <![CDATA[

    import mx.managers.PopUpManager;
    import mx.events.CloseEvent;

    private function closeWindow(event:CloseEvent):void {
      PopUpManager.removePopUp(this);
    }

  ]]>
  </mx:Script>
  <mx:TextArea height="200" width="200" text="Lorem ipsum dolor sit amet,
consectetuer adipiscing elit. Sed eget massa iaculis metus interdum accumsan.
Mauris pellentesque pulvinar orci. Etiam suscipit tellus a nisl.
Mauris elit risus, blandit non, varius vitae, laoreet ac, ipsum. Fusce erat
libero, imperdiet id, suscipit lacinia, nonummy quis, metus. Ut sit amet
est quis velit ullamcorper congue. Etiam in nunc id mauris porta volutpat.
Sed vitae metus. Integer lacinia. Maecenas a tortor. Fusce mauris arcu,
ullamcorper ac, sagittis id, condimentum in, dolor. Praesent eros
tortor, tincidunt in, blandit a, luctus quis, est." />
</mx:TitleWindow>
```

You can then create pop ups based on this component using the following code. Assume that the preceding component is saved in a file called *TextAreaWindow.mxml*.

```
<?xml version="1.0" encoding="utf-8"?>
<mx:Application xmlns:mx="http://www.adobe.com/2006/mxml">

  <mx:Script>
  <![CDATA[

    import mx.managers.PopUpManager;

    private function showWindow(event:Event):void {
      PopUpManager.createPopUp(this, TextAreaWindow);
    }

  ]]>
  </mx:Script>

  <mx:Button id="button" label="Show Window" click="showWindow(event)" />

</mx:Application>
```

Adding Modality

Pop-up windows are not modal by default. However, you can easily make a pop up modal by passing a third parameter to the createPopUp( ) method. The default value is false, meaning the pop up should not be modal. If you specify a value of true, the new pop up will be modal, meaning nothing else within the parent container can receive focus as long as the pop up is visible:

```
PopUpManager.createPopUp(this, TextAreaWindow, true);
```

Cursor Management

By default, the Flex application cursor is an arrow except when a selectable/editable text element has focus, when the cursor becomes a text-selection cursor. Using the mx.managers.CursorManager class, you can control the cursor that gets displayed in the application. This can be useful for giving the user a visual cue of the status of the application.

The CursorManager class has a handful of static methods that allow you to control the cursor by doing the following: showing and removing busy cursors, and showing and removing custom cursors.

The Flex framework has just one built-in cursor apart from the default system cursors. The one built-in cursor is a busy cursor that displays a small clock face with a spinning hand to let the user know that something is being processed. The CursorManager class has two static methods for displaying and removing the busy cursor: setBusyCursor( ) and removeBusyCursor( ). The following demonstrates a very simple example that sets and removes the busy cursor when the user clicks two buttons:

```
<?xml version="1.0" encoding="utf-8"?>
<mx:Application xmlns:mx="http://www.adobe.com/2006/mxml">

  <mx:Script>
  <![CDATA[

    import mx.managers.CursorManager;

  ]]>
  </mx:Script>

  <mx:VBox>
    <mx:Button label="Show Busy Cursor" click="CursorManager.setBusyCursor()" />
    <mx:Button label="Hide Busy Cursor" click="CursorManager.removeBusyCursor()"
/>
  </mx:VBox>

</mx:Application>
```

Typically you use the busy cursor for asynchronous operations such as remote procedure calls. You can use the setBusyCursor( ) method just prior to starting such an operation, and you can call removeBusyCursor( ) when the operation completes. To simplify things, several components have a built-in feature that automatically does this. The SWFLoader, WebService, HttpService, and RemoteObject components all allow you to set a showBusyCursor property. When the showBusyCursor property is set to true for any of these components, the component automatically displays the busy cursor when initiating the request; it hides the busy cursor when the response is complete.

For customized cursors you can use any standard embedded graphic or SWF as a cursor using the CursorManager.setCursor( ) method. You can remove custom cursors using the removeCursor( ) method.

The setCursor( ) method requires at least one parameter: the Class object representing the embedded graphic. Example 8-6 uses a PNG as the cursor.

Example 8-6. Customizing the cursor

```
<?xml version="1.0" encoding="utf-8"?>
<mx:Application xmlns:mx="http://www.adobe.com/2006/mxml"
               initialize="initializeHandler(event)">

  <mx:Script>
  <![CDATA[

    import mx.managers.CursorManager;

    [Embed(source="cursor.png")]
    private var customCursor:Class;
```

Example 8-6. Customizing the cursor (continued)

```
  private function initializeHandler(event:Event):void {
    CursorManager.setCursor(customCursor);
  }

]]>
</mx:Script>

</mx:Application>
```

The setCursor( ) method returns an integer ID that you need in order to remove the cursor. You can pass the ID to the removeCursor( ) method, as the following example illustrates:

```
<?xml version="1.0" encoding="utf-8"?>
<mx:Application xmlns:mx="http://www.adobe.com/2006/mxml"
                initialize="initializeHandler(event)">

  <mx:Script>
  <![CDATA[

    import mx.managers.CursorManager;

    [Embed(source="cursor.png")]
    private var customCursor:Class;

    private var cursorId:int;

    private function initializeHandler(event:Event):void {
      cursorId = CursorManager.setCursor(customCursor);
    }

  ]]>
  </mx:Script>

  <mx:Button label="Reset Cursor" click="CursorManager.removeCursor(cursorId)" />

</mx:Application>
```

In this example, the custom cursor is applied when the application initializes using an initialize event handler. When the user clicks the button, it calls the removeCursor( ) method to remove the cursor. Note that the cursor ID returned by setCursor( ) is saved in a property so that it is accessible throughout the document.

Drag and Drop

Drag and drop functionality is one of the many features that set Flex applications apart from other types of applications. As you'll see in the next few sections, it is extremely simple to enable drag-and-drop functionality for some standard components, and with a little additional work you can enable drag and drop functionality to any type of component.

Using Built-In Drag and Drop Features

The simplest way to implement drag and drop functionality is to use the built-in features of many of the components, including List, Tree, DataGrid, Menu, HorizontalList, PrintDataGrid, and TileList. Each component enables drag and drop in the same way. They each have a dragEnabled property and a dropEnabled property. The two properties are false by default. When you set the dragEnabled property to true for a component, the user can click and drag items. Of course, in most cases enabling a component so that a user can click and drag an item is not very useful until the user can also drop the item somewhere in the application. Typically this is accomplished by setting the dropEnabled property of another component to true. When the dropEnabled property is set to true for a component, the user can drop an item on the component that he dragged from another component. This adds the data from that item to the drop target component. Example 8-7 illustrates both a dragEnabled and a dropEnabled component working in conjunction. The first data grid contains data about the user's music collection. The user can drag items from the music collection to the second data grid to create a playlist.

Example 8-7. A simple drag and drop application

```
<?xml version="1.0"?>
<mx:Application xmlns:mx="http://www.adobe.com/2006/mxml">
  <mx:HBox width="100%">
    <mx:VBox height="100%">
      <mx:Label text="My Music"/>
      <mx:DataGrid dragEnabled="true">
        <mx:columns>
          <mx:DataGridColumn headerText="Song Title" dataField="title"/>
          <mx:DataGridColumn headerText="Artist" dataField="artist"/>
        </mx:columns>
        <mx:dataProvider>
          <mx:ArrayCollection>
            <mx:Object songId="0" title="Astronaut" artist="David Byrne" />
            <mx:Object songId="1" title="Rio" artist="Duran Duran" />
            <mx:Object songId="2" title="Enjoy the Silence" artist="Depeche
Mode" />
            <mx:Object songId="3" title="Mesopotamia" artist="B-52s" />
          </mx:ArrayCollection>
        </mx:dataProvider>
      </mx:DataGrid>
    </mx:VBox>
    <mx:VBox height="100%">
      <mx:Label text="Playlist"/>
      <mx:DataGrid dropEnabled="true">
        <mx:columns>
          <mx:DataGridColumn headerText="Song Title" dataField="title"/>
```

Example 8-7. A simple drag and drop application (continued)

```
            <mx:DataGridColumn headerText="Artist" dataField="artist"/>
          </mx:columns>
        </mx:DataGrid>
      </mx:VBox>
    </mx:HBox>

</mx:Application>
```

When you test this, you'll see two data grids side by side. You can click and drag an element in the My Music data grid, and you'll see that it creates a copy of that element that moves with the mouse. A small red circle with a white X appears next to the mouse cursor until the mouse is over a drop-enabled component, at which point the red circle becomes a green circle with a white +. If you drop the item anywhere in the application that is not drop-enabled, no further action occurs. However, if you drop the item on a drop-enabled component, the item is added to the drop target at the location where you dropped the object.

The default behavior for drag-enabled components is to allow the user to copy elements from the component. However, you can also allow the user to move elements rather than copy them by setting the dragMoveEnabled property to true. By itself, the dragMoveEnabled property will not have any effect. You must also ensure that dragEnabled is set to true for the component. Example 8-8 uses dragMoveEnabled to create a simple application that allows the user to move an email message from her inbox to the trash.

Example 8-8. A drag and drop example that moves items

```
<?xml version="1.0"?>
<mx:Application xmlns:mx="http://www.adobe.com/2006/mxml">
  <mx:HBox width="100%">
    <mx:VBox height="100%">
      <mx:Label text="Inbox"/>
      <mx:DataGrid dragEnabled="true" dragMoveEnabled="true">
        <mx:columns>
          <mx:DataGridColumn headerText="From" dataField="from"/>
          <mx:DataGridColumn headerText="To" dataField="to"/>
          <mx:DataGridColumn headerText="Subject" dataField="subject"/>
          <mx:DataGridColumn headerText="Date" dataField="date"/>
        </mx:columns>
        <mx:dataProvider>
          <mx:ArrayCollection>
            <mx:Object emailId="0" from="a@a.com" to="joey@person13.com"
                       subject="Important New Message" date="10/1/2010" />
            <mx:Object emailId="1" from="b@b.com" to="joey@person13.com"
                       subject="All Items On Sale" date="10/1/2010" />
            <mx:Object emailId="2" from="c@c.com" to="joey@person13.com"
                       subject="Amazing New Stock" date="10/1/2010" />
            <mx:Object emailId="3" from="d@d.com" to="joey@person13.com"
                       subject="Blatant Chain Letter" date="10/1/2010" />
```

Example 8-8. A drag and drop example that moves items (continued)

```
          </mx:ArrayCollection>
        </mx:dataProvider>
      </mx:DataGrid>
    </mx:VBox>
    <mx:VBox height="100%">
      <mx:Label text="Trash"/>
      <mx:DataGrid dropEnabled="true">
        <mx:columns>
          <mx:DataGridColumn headerText="From" dataField="from"/>
          <mx:DataGridColumn headerText="To" dataField="to"/>
          <mx:DataGridColumn headerText="Subject" dataField="subject"/>
          <mx:DataGridColumn headerText="Date" dataField="date"/>
        </mx:columns>
      </mx:DataGrid>
    </mx:VBox>
  </mx:HBox>

</mx:Application>
```

In this example, you can move items only one way: from the inbox to the trash. In a real email application, you'd probably want to allow users to move messages back to the inbox from the trash if they wanted. In such a case, you can simply set dragEnabled and dropEnabled to true for both components.

When you set dragMoveEnabled to true for a component, it makes moving the default behavior. However, if the user holds down the Ctrl key while dragging and dropping, the item is copied rather than moved. In some cases, that is acceptable behavior. In other cases, you want to ensure that the items always are moved rather than copied. You cannot make such a change via MXML. As shown in the next section, you can use ActionScript and event listeners to handle that behavior.

Understanding Drag and Drop Events

When using drag and drop functionality, the framework utilizes a handful of events behind the scenes. Understanding those events can be very helpful when you want to modify the default behavior or write completely customized drag and drop elements.

Table 8-1 lists all the events, the targets of the events, and what those events mean.

Table 8-1. Drag and drop events

Event	Target	Description
mouseDown	Drag initiator	This is usually the event that triggers the start of a drag and drop operation.
mouseMove	Drag initiator	In some cases, the drag and drop operation does not occur until a mouseMove event.
dragEnter	Drop target	The mouse has entered the drop target while still dragging an object.

Table 8-1. Drag and drop events (continued)

Event	Target	Description
dragMove	Drop target	The mouse is moving within the drop target. This is analogous to a mouseMove event, except that it is specific to the drop target while still dragging an object.
dragExit	Drop target	The mouse has moved outside the drop target while still dragging the object.
dragDrop	Drop target	The user has dropped an object on the target.
dragComplete	Drag initiator	This occurs anytime the user drops the object, whether over a drop target or not. You can use the dragComplete event to clean up whatever is necessary for the drag initiator.

The mouseDown and mouseMove events are standard Flash Player events of type flash.events.MouseEvent. The rest of the events are part of the Flex framework, and they are of type mx.events.DragEvent. DragEvent objects have a dragInitiator property that references the component that originated the drag and drop behavior. They also have a dragSource property that is of type mx.core.DragSource, and it contains data copied from the initiator.

DragSource objects have a dataForFormat() method that requires a string parameter and returns the data that was stored for the format specified by the string parameter. We'll look more at DragSource formats in the next section. For now, all you need to know is that list-based drag initiators always create DragSource objects with one format called *items*, and the data returned for that format is an array of all the elements from the data provider of the drag initiator corresponding to the selected items. For example, if the user drags one element from a data grid, the DragSource object will contain an array with just one element.

DragSource objects also have an action property that reports a value of copy, move, or none. You can use the mx.managers.DragManager COPY, MOVE, and NONE constants for comparison tests. The action property tells you what the expected action is for the drag and drop operation. This value is automatically set when using the built-in drag and drop behavior of list-based components.

In the preceding section, you saw how there's no simple MXML-based way to ensure that the user cannot copy elements rather than move them. Using events and Action-Script, you can put such safeguards into place, as illustrated in Example 8-9.

Example 8-9. Using ActionScript for drag and drop behavior

```
<?xml version="1.0"?>
<mx:Application xmlns:mx="http://www.adobe.com/2006/mxml">
  <mx:Script>
    <![CDATA[
      import mx.collections.ArrayCollection;
      import mx.controls.DataGrid;
      import mx.events.DragEvent;
      import mx.managers.DragManager;
```

Example 8-9. Using ActionScript for drag and drop behavior (continued)

```
      private function dragCompleteHandler(event:DragEvent):void {
        if(event.action != DragManager.NONE) {
          var grid:DataGrid = DataGrid(event.dragInitiator);
          var data:ArrayCollection = ArrayCollection(grid.dataProvider);
          var item:Object = event.dragSource.dataForFormat("items")[0];
          for(var i:uint = 0; i < data.length; i++) {
            if(data.getItemAt(i).emailId == item.emailId) {
              data.removeItemAt(i);
              break;
            }
          }
        }
      }

    ]]>
  </mx:Script>
  <mx:HBox width="100%">
    <mx:VBox height="100%">
      <mx:Label text="Inbox"/>
      <mx:DataGrid dropEnabled="true" dragEnabled="true"
dragComplete="dragCompleteHandler(event)">
        <mx:columns>
          <mx:DataGridColumn headerText="From" dataField="from"/>
          <mx:DataGridColumn headerText="To" dataField="to"/>
          <mx:DataGridColumn headerText="Subject" dataField="subject"/>
          <mx:DataGridColumn headerText="Date" dataField="date"/>
        </mx:columns>
        <mx:dataProvider>
          <mx:ArrayCollection>
            <mx:Object emailId="0" from="a@a.com" to="joey@person13.com"
subject="Important New Message" date="10/1/2010" />
            <mx:Object emailId="1" from="b@b.com" to="joey@person13.com"
subject="All Items On Sale" date="10/1/2010" />
            <mx:Object emailId="2" from="c@c.com" to="joey@person13.com"
subject="Amazing New Stock" date="10/1/2010" />
            <mx:Object emailId="3" from="d@d.com" to="joey@person13.com"
subject="Blatant Chain Letter" date="10/1/2010" />
          </mx:ArrayCollection>
        </mx:dataProvider>
      </mx:DataGrid>
    </mx:VBox>
    <mx:VBox height="100%">
      <mx:Label text="Trash"/>
      <mx:DataGrid dropEnabled="true" dragEnabled="true"
dragComplete="dragCompleteHandler(event)">
        <mx:columns>
          <mx:DataGridColumn headerText="From" dataField="from"/>
          <mx:DataGridColumn headerText="To" dataField="to"/>
          <mx:DataGridColumn headerText="Subject" dataField="subject"/>
          <mx:DataGridColumn headerText="Date" dataField="date"/>
        </mx:columns>
      </mx:DataGrid>
```

Example 8-9. Using ActionScript for drag and drop behavior (continued)

```
        </mx:VBox>
    </mx:HBox>

</mx:Application>
```

You'll notice that in this example, both data grids have dropEnabled and dragEnabled set to true. This in and of itself allows the user to copy contents from one data grid to the other. However, as shown in Example 8-8, this does not ensure the type of behavior required in this case. To achieve the move-only behavior, each data grid also listens for dragComplete events. The dragCompleteHandler( ) method handles the events by either dismissing the event if the event action is set to none, or deleting the element from the drag initiator's data provider.

Custom Drag and Drop Operations

The built-in drag and drop functionality will work for many use cases. However, there are also many use cases in which you will want to employ drag and drop functionality not supported by the standard, built-in features of the handful of drag and drop-enabled components. For these cases, you can create custom drag and drop elements.

You can create custom drag and drop elements using the events discussed in the preceding section in conjunction with mx.managers.DragManager. The DragManager class has several static methods you can use to handle drag and drop functionality.

The doDrag( ) method allows you to start a drag and drop operation. The doDrag( ) method requires that you specify the following parameters: the drag initiator, a DragSource object specifying the data to copy from the initiator, and the mouse event used to start the drag operation. In addition, in most cases you'll need to pass it a reference to an object to use as the drag proxy image (the object that actually drags).

Before we look at an example using doDrag( ) let's first discuss the details of working with DragSource. The DragSource object you pass to doDrag( ) is what is passed along to event handlers for drag events. This object contains data that you can use when copying, moving, or comparing. That means you should generally store whatever data you want to pass along to the drag event handlers in the DragSource object. DragSource objects allow you to save many groups of data, each with a unique key (a string value) called a *format*. You can use the addData( ) method to add data to a DragSource object. The first parameter is the data to store, and the second parameter is the format, which is an arbitrary string:

```
    var dragSource:DragSource = new DragSource();
    dragSource.addData(initiator.dataProvider.getItemAt(index), "item");
```

The DragManager class also dictates the behavior of the drag proxy image when the user moves it over the drop target and when the user drops the object. Normally the proxy indicates that it cannot be dropped successfully by displaying a small red circle with a white X. You can remove that icon by calling DragManager.acceptDragDrop() and passing it a reference to the drop target on which the user can drop the object. Typically you call this method in response to a dragEnter event.

Example 8-10 illustrates how to create custom drag and drop elements. This simple application uses a column of colored canvases and a grid of canvases with the same colors. The canvases from the column are draggable. When the user drops one canvas over the other with the same color in the grid, the canvas is removed from the column, and the canvas in the grid is lowered in opacity.

Example 8-10. A customized drag and drop application

```
<?xml version="1.0"?>
<mx:Application xmlns:mx="http://www.adobe.com/2006/mxml">
  <mx:Script>
    <![CDATA[
      import mx.core.DragSource;
      import mx.containers.Canvas;
      import mx.events.DragEvent;
      import mx.managers.DragManager;

      private function beginDragAndDrop(event:MouseEvent):void {
        var canvas:Canvas = Canvas(event.currentTarget);
        var dragSource:DragSource = new DragSource();
        var color:uint = canvas.getStyle("backgroundColor");
        dragSource.addData(color, "backgroundColor");
        var proxy:Canvas = new Canvas();
        proxy.width = 50;
        proxy.height = 50;
        proxy.setStyle("backgroundColor", color);
        DragManager.doDrag(canvas, dragSource, event, proxy);
      }

      private function dragEnterHandler(event:DragEvent):void {
        var target:Canvas = Canvas(event.currentTarget);
        var initiator:Canvas = Canvas(event.dragInitiator);
        if(matches(target, initiator)) {
          DragManager.acceptDragDrop(target);
        }
      }

      private function dragDropHandler(event:DragEvent):void {
        var target:Canvas = Canvas(event.currentTarget);
        var initiator:Canvas = Canvas(event.dragInitiator);
        if(matches(target, initiator)) {
          vbox.removeChild(initiator);
          target.alpha = .25;
        }
      }

      private function matches(a:Canvas, b:Canvas):Boolean {
```

Example 8-10. A customized drag and drop application (continued)

```
          return a.getStyle("backgroundColor") == b.getStyle("backgroundColor");
      }

    ]]>
  </mx:Script>
  <mx:HBox width="100%">
    <mx:VBox id="vbox" height="100%">
      <mx:Canvas width="50" height="50" backgroundColor="#00ff80"
mouseDown="beginDragAndDrop(event)" />
      <mx:Canvas width="50" height="50" backgroundColor="#ff8040"
mouseDown="beginDragAndDrop(event)" />
      <mx:Canvas width="50" height="50" backgroundColor="#80ffff"
mouseDown="beginDragAndDrop(event)" />
      <mx:Canvas width="50" height="50" backgroundColor="#ffff80"
mouseDown="beginDragAndDrop(event)" />
    </mx:VBox>
    <mx:VRule height="213"/>
    <mx:Grid>
      <mx:GridRow width="100%" height="100%">
        <mx:GridItem width="100%" height="100%">
          <mx:Canvas width="50" height="50" backgroundColor="#00ff80"
dragEnter="dragEnterHandler(event)" dragDrop="dragDropHandler(event)" />
        </mx:GridItem>
        <mx:GridItem width="100%" height="100%">
          <mx:Canvas width="50" height="50" backgroundColor="#ff8040"
dragEnter="dragEnterHandler(event)" dragDrop="dragDropHandler(event)" />
        </mx:GridItem>
      </mx:GridRow>
      <mx:GridRow width="100%" height="100%">
        <mx:GridItem width="100%" height="100%">
          <mx:Canvas width="50" height="50" backgroundColor="#80ffff"
dragEnter="dragEnterHandler(event)" dragDrop="dragDropHandler(event)" />
        </mx:GridItem>
        <mx:GridItem width="100%" height="100%">
          <mx:Canvas width="50" height="50" backgroundColor="#ffff80"
dragEnter="dragEnterHandler(event)" dragDrop="dragDropHandler(event)" />
        </mx:GridItem>
      </mx:GridRow>
    </mx:Grid>
  </mx:HBox>


</mx:Application>
```

Customizing List-Based Controls

List-based controls such as lists, data grids, and trees have standard ways in which they display data. For example, a list displays one column of text, data grids display one or more columns of text, and trees display a hierarchical view of data. For many if not most applications, the default ways in which these controls display data are perfectly sufficient. However, there are cases in which you need to alter the displays in one way or another. For example, you may want to display a checkbox in a data grid column rather than standard text.

When you want to customize the way in which a list-based component displays elements, you can use what is called an *item renderer*. Item renderers allow you to specify what component to use in place of the standard text or text and icon that appear in the component, thus customizing the appearance of the elements in the component. The following components support custom item renderers: List, HorizontalList, DataGrid, Menu, TileList, and Tree.

There are two basic ways to use custom item renderers:

Drop-in item renderers
These are the simplest types of item renderers to implement. With a drop-in item renderer, you simply specify a standard UI component to use in a particular column. For example, you can use a checkbox as a drop-in item renderer.

Inline item renderers
These types of item renderers are still rather simple to implement, but they allow you to exert more control over the component. For example, with a drop-in item renderer, you cannot specify the property settings for the component, but with an inline item renderer you can.

You can use standard or custom components as item renderers with either of these approaches.

Drop-In Item Renderers

Drop-in item renderers are extremely simple to implement. All you need to do is set the itemRenderer property of the component for which you want to customize the item views. The itemRenderer property should be a reference to a component class you want to use. For example, the following creates a list component that uses a date field component for each item:

```
<mx:Script>
<![CDATA[
  import mx.collections.ArrayCollection;
  [Bindable]
  private var dataSet:ArrayCollection =
          new ArrayCollection([new Date(2010, 1, 1), new Date(2010, 4, 15)]);
]]>
</mx:Script>

<mx:List itemRenderer="mx.controls.DateField" dataProvider="{dataSet}" />
```

The results of this are shown in Figure 8-1.

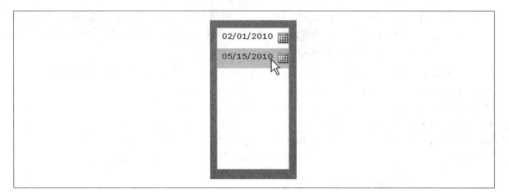

Figure 8-1. A date field used as an item renderer in a list component

All the list-based components that allow you to use item renderers allow you to set the itemRenderer property for the component itself, except in the case of the data grid, which requires that you set the itemRenderer property at the column level. Example 8-11 sets one of the columns of a data grid to display a checkbox.

Example 8-11. Using a drop-in item renderer

```
<?xml version="1.0"?>
<mx:Application xmlns:mx="http://www.adobe.com/2006/mxml">
  <mx:VBox>
     <mx:DataGrid editable="false">
       <mx:columns>
         <mx:DataGridColumn headerText="Song Title" dataField="title"/>
         <mx:DataGridColumn headerText="Artist" dataField="artist"/>
         <mx:DataGridColumn headerText="In Favorites" dataField="inFavorites"
itemRenderer="mx.controls.CheckBox" />
       </mx:columns>
       <mx:dataProvider>
         <mx:ArrayCollection>
           <mx:Array>
             <mx:Object songId="0" title="Astronaut" artist="David Byrne"
rating="5" inFavorites="true" />
             <mx:Object songId="1" title="Rio" artist="Duran Duran"
rating="3" />
             <mx:Object songId="2" title="Enjoy the Silence"
artist="Depeche Mode" rating="4" />
             <mx:Object songId="3" title="Mesopotamia"
artist="B-52s" rating="5" inFavorites="true" />
           </mx:Array>
         </mx:ArrayCollection>
       </mx:dataProvider>
     </mx:DataGrid>
  </mx:VBox>

</mx:Application>
```

Drop-in item renderers are ideal when you want to use a simple type of item renderer. However, they have several major limitations:

- You can use only a handful of standard UI components as drop-in item renderers. Those components you can use are listed in Table 8-2.
- The data value for an item always corresponds to one property of the item renderer. In other words, a list-based component is a view for the data model assigned to the dataProvider property. For example, the item value is always assigned to the value of a numeric stepper used as an item renderer. You cannot specify that the item value should be assigned to the maximum property of the numeric stepper.
- You cannot customize the components used as item renderers.

Table 8-2. Drop-in components

Component	Property set by the item value
Button	selected
CheckBox	selected
DateField	selectedDate
Image	source
Label	text
NumericStepper	value
Text	text
TextArea	text
TextInput	text

Inline Item Renderers

Although drop-in item renderers are extremely simple to implement, they are also quite limited in terms of how you can configure them. For instance, in Example 8-11 you can display the checkbox in the data grid columns, but you cannot change any of the properties of the components used as item renderers.

Inline item renderers are a slight step up from drop-in item renderers in that you can configure the settings of the component used as the item renderer. For example, you can use an inline item renderer to set the enabled property of the checkbox to disable it so that the user cannot check or uncheck the box.

Inline item renderers require that you specify the itemRenderer value using nested MXML tags rather than attributes. You must then nest within the itemRenderer tag a Component tag with a nested tag to create the type of component you want to use as an item renderer. Example 8-12 specifies the checkbox item renderer as an inline item renderer. It also applies a label to the checkbox, and it disables the checkbox so that the user cannot select or deselect it.

Example 8-12. Using inline item renderers

```
<?xml version="1.0"?>
<mx:Application xmlns:mx="http://www.adobe.com/2006/mxml">
  <mx:VBox>
      <mx:DataGrid editable="false">
        <mx:columns>
          <mx:DataGridColumn headerText="Song Title" dataField="title"/>
          <mx:DataGridColumn headerText="Artist" dataField="artist"/>
          <mx:DataGridColumn headerText="In Favorites" dataField="inFavorites">
            <mx:itemRenderer>
              <mx:Component>
                <mx:CheckBox label="Song in favorites" enabled="false" />
              </mx:Component>
            </mx:itemRenderer>
          </mx:DataGridColumn>
        </mx:columns>
        <mx:dataProvider>
          <mx:ArrayCollection>
            <mx:Array>
              <mx:Object songId="0" title="Astronaut" artist="David Byrne"
rating="5" inFavorites="true" />
              <mx:Object songId="1" title="Rio" artist="Duran Duran" rating="3" />
              <mx:Object songId="2" title="Enjoy the Silence"
                         artist="Depeche Mode" rating="4" />
              <mx:Object songId="3" title="Mesopotamia"
                         artist="B-52s" rating="5" inFavorites="true" />
            </mx:Array>
          </mx:ArrayCollection>
        </mx:dataProvider>
      </mx:DataGrid>
  </mx:VBox>
</mx:Application>
```

The Component tag is a powerful MXML tag. It creates an entirely new scope within the MXML document. The code within the Component tag is essentially an MXML component, and the rules that apply to MXML components generally apply to the code within the Component tag. You can have just one root node, and within that root node you can use Style, Script, and all standard MXML tags used in an MXML component document. Because the Component tag creates its own scope, you don't have to worry about conflicts within the Component tag and the document within which the Component tag exists. However, this also means that you cannot reference data from the MXML document within the Component tag. For example, the following will cause a compile error:

```
<mx:Script>
<![CDATA[
  private var maximumCount:uint = 5;
]]>
</mx:Script>
<mx:List>
  <mx:itemRenderer>
```

```
<mx:Component>
  <mx:NumericStepper maximum="{maximumCount}" />
</mx:Component>
    </mx:itemRenderer>
  </mx:List>
```

The error occurs because maximumCount is defined in the MXML document, but it is referenced within the Component tag, which has a different scope.

Although the Component tag is powerful, we strongly recommend that you use it only to the extent illustrated by Example 8-12 which sets the label and enabled properties of the checkbox. If you need to create more sophisticated item renderers, it is far better to define them as MXML or ActionScript components. We'll look at how to do that in the next section.

You can use a property called outerDocument within a Component tag to reference the MXML document containing the Component tag. You can then reference any public or internal properties, as in the following example:

```
<?xml version="1.0"?>
<mx:Application xmlns:mx="http://www.adobe.com/2006/mxml">
  <mx:Script>
  <![CDATA[
    internal var maximumCount:uint = 5;
  ]]>
  </mx:Script>
  <mx:List>
    <mx:itemRenderer>
      <mx:Component>
        <mx:NumericStepper maximum=
            "{outerDocument.maximumCount}" />
      </mx:Component>
    </mx:itemRenderer>
  </mx:List>
</mx:Application>
```

However, while this is possible, it is generally not recommended because it is much clearer to break out sophisticated item renderers into new custom components, as discussed next.

Custom Components as Item Renderers

In order to exert the most control over item renderers you can use a custom component. Using a custom component (either MXML or ActionScript) you can create extremely sophisticated item renderers. For example, you can create an item renderer that displays a rating using colored shapes, as we'll do in this section.

A component must implement certain interfaces to work as an item renderer. There are three basic interfaces for item renderers: IListItemRenderer, IDropInListItemRenderer, and IDataRenderer. All item renderers must implement

`IListItemRenderer` and `IDataRenderer`. Because `IListItemRenderer` extends `IDataRenderer`, you simply need to implement `IListItemRenderer` in most cases. The `IListItemRenderer` interface requires many getter/setter methods and public methods, and the best way to implement the interface is simply to extend a class that already implements the interface. The following classes already implement the interface: `Button`, `ComboBox`, `Container`, `DataGridItemRenderer`, `DateField`, `Image`, `Label`, `ListBase`, `ListItemRenderer`, `MenuBarItem`, `MenuItemRenderer`, `NumericStepper`, `TextArea`, `TextInput`, `TileListItemRenderer`, and `TreeItemRenderer`. Because `Container` implements the interface, you can extend any type of container.

The `IDataRenderer` interface requires that the implementing class defines a data getter and setter of type `Object`. The data setter is automatically called every time the data provider is updated and the item renderer needs to update. The data setter is always passed the data provider element corresponding to the item. For example, in a data grid the data is the object representing the row. Even though your custom item renderer component is likely to inherit the data implementation, you'll generally want to override that implementation.

Example 8-13 is saved in an MXML document called *Rating.mxml*, and it draws five squares using 10-by-10 canvases. The squares are blue by default, and they are colored red if they are activated by the value of the rating property from the data passed to the component. Notice that this component overrides the data getter and setter. The setter retrieves the rating value, and it draws the canvases with the appropriate colors based on the rating value.

Example 8-13. A custom component for use as an item renderer

```
<?xml version="1.0" encoding="utf-8"?>
<mx:HBox xmlns:mx="http://www.adobe.com/2006/mxml">

  <mx:Script>
    <![CDATA[

      import mx.containers.Canvas;

      private var _data:Object;

      override public function set data(value:Object):void {
        _data = value;
        var rating:uint = uint(value.rating);
        removeAllChildren();
        var canvas:Canvas;
        for(var i:uint = 0; i < 5; i++) {
          canvas = new Canvas();
          canvas.setStyle("backgroundColor", i < rating ? 0xFF0000 : 0x0000FF);
          canvas.width = 10;
          canvas.height = 10;
          addChild(canvas);
        }
```

Example 8-13. A custom component for use as an item renderer (continued)

```
      }

      override public function get data( ):Object {
        return _data;
      }

    ]]>
  </mx:Script>

</mx:HBox>
```

The MXML application document in Example 8-14 uses the custom component as an item renderer in a data grid using drop-in syntax.

Example 8-14. Using a custom component as an item renderer

```
<?xml version="1.0"?>
<mx:Application xmlns:mx="http://www.adobe.com/2006/mxml">
  <mx:VBox>
      <mx:DataGrid editable="false">
        <mx:columns>
          <mx:DataGridColumn headerText="Song Title" dataField="title"/>
          <mx:DataGridColumn headerText="Artist" dataField="artist"/>
          <mx:DataGridColumn headerText="Rating" dataField="rating"
itemRenderer="Rating" />
        </mx:columns>
        <mx:dataProvider>
          <mx:ArrayCollection>
            <mx:Array>
              <mx:Object songId="0" title="Astronaut" artist="David Byrne"
rating="5" inFavorites="true" />
              <mx:Object songId="1" title="Rio" artist="Duran Duran" rating="3" />
              <mx:Object songId="2" title="Enjoy the Silence" artist="Depeche
Mode" rating="4" />
              <mx:Object songId="3" title="Mesopotamia" artist="B-52s" rating="5"
inFavorites="true" />
            </mx:Array>
          </mx:ArrayCollection>
        </mx:dataProvider>
      </mx:DataGrid>
  </mx:VBox>
</mx:Application>
```

 Note that if the item renderer MXML or ActionScript class is in a package, you would specify the fully qualified path to the MXML document or class in the itemRenderer property value.

Creating Item Editors

When components are editable, they use standard text inputs when the user is editing a value. For example, the following code creates a list with editable values simply by setting the editable property to true. But the user can edit the values only by using the standard text input when she clicks on an item:

```
<mx:List editable="true" width="200" labelField="rating">
  <mx:dataProvider>
    <mx:ArrayCollection>
      <mx:Array>
        <mx:Object songId="0" title="Astronaut" artist="David Byrne"
                   rating="5" inFavorites="true" />
        <mx:Object songId="1" title="Rio" artist="Duran Duran" rating="3" />
        <mx:Object songId="2" title="Enjoy the Silence" artist="Depeche Mode"
                   rating="4" />
        <mx:Object songId="3" title="Mesopotamia" artist="B-52s" rating="5"
                   inFavorites="true" />
      </mx:Array>
    </mx:ArrayCollection>
  </mx:dataProvider>
</mx:List>
```

You can customize the way in which a user can edit data using an item editor. You assign an item editor using the itemEditor property in exactly the same ways you can set an item renderer using the itemRenderer property. You must also specify a value for the editorDataField property that tells the component which property of the item renderer should be bound to the data provider. The following illustrates how to rewrite the List tag from the preceding example so that it uses a numeric stepper rather than a standard text input to edit the value. Note that it specifies value as the editorDataField because value is the name of the numeric stepper property that should be linked to the data provider.

```
<mx:List editable="true" width="200" labelField="rating"
         itemEditor="mx.controls.NumericStepper" editorDataField="value">
  <mx:dataProvider>
    <mx:ArrayCollection>
      <mx:Array>
        <mx:Object songId="0" title="Astronaut" artist="David Byrne" rating="5"
                   inFavorites="true" />
        <mx:Object songId="1" title="Rio" artist="Duran Duran" rating="3" />
        <mx:Object songId="2" title="Enjoy the Silence" artist="Depeche Mode"
                   rating="4" />
        <mx:Object songId="3" title="Mesopotamia" artist="B-52s" rating="5"
                   inFavorites="true" />
      </mx:Array>
    </mx:ArrayCollection>
  </mx:dataProvider>
</mx:List>
```

One question that you might ask when working with the item editor is why you couldn't simply use an item renderer. For example, it's possible to list a numeric stepper as the item renderer in the preceding example. The user could update the numeric stepper value used as an item renderer. However, item renderers simply render the data. They do not create data binding with the data provider. Therefore, changing a value in a numeric stepper used as an item renderer will not affect the data provider, whereas it will update the data provider when used as an item renderer. However, you can tell a component to use the item renderer as the item editor by setting the `rendererIsEditor` property to true:

```
<mx:List editable="true" width="200" labelField="rating"
         itemRenderer="mx.controls.NumericStepper"
         rendererIsEditor="true" editorDataField="value">
  <mx:dataProvider>
    <mx:ArrayCollection>
      <mx:Array>
        <mx:Object songId="0" title="Astronaut" artist="David Byrne" rating="5"
                   inFavorites="true" />
        <mx:Object songId="1" title="Rio" artist="Duran Duran" rating="3" />
        <mx:Object songId="2" title="Enjoy the Silence" artist="Depeche Mode"
                   rating="4" />
        <mx:Object songId="3" title="Mesopotamia" artist="B-52s" rating="5"
                   inFavorites="true" />
      </mx:Array>
    </mx:ArrayCollection>
  </mx:dataProvider>
</mx:List>
```

Any custom component you can use as an item renderer you, can also use as an item editor. The only additional rule is that the component must set a public getter/setter method pair as bindable, and you must specify that as the `editorDataField` value for the component using the custom editor. Example 8-15 modifies `Rating` so that it can be used as an editor.

Example 8-15. A custom item editor

```
<?xml version="1.0" encoding="utf-8"?>
<mx:HBox xmlns:mx="http://www.adobe.com/2006/mxml">

  <mx:Script>
    <![CDATA[

      import mx.containers.Canvas;
      import flash.events.MouseEvent;

      private var _data:Object;

    [Bindable]
      override public function set data(value:Object):void {
        _data = value;
      draw();
      }

      override public function get data():Object {
```

Example 8-15. A custom item editor (continued)

```
      return _data;
    }

    public function onClick(event:MouseEvent):void {
      _data.rating = uint(event.currentTarget.name);
      draw();
    }

    private function draw():void {
      var rating:uint = uint(_data.rating);
      removeAllChildren();
      var canvas:Canvas;
      for(var i:uint = 0; i < 5; i++) {
        canvas = new Canvas();
        canvas.setStyle("backgroundColor", i < rating ? 0xFF0000 : 0x0000FF);
        canvas.width = 10;
        canvas.height = 10;
        canvas.name = String(i + 1);
        canvas.addEventListener(MouseEvent.CLICK, onClick);
        addChild(canvas);
      }
    }

    ]]>
  </mx:Script>

</mx:HBox>
```

Example 8-16 uses Rating as both the item renderer and the item editor.

Example 8-16. Using a custom item editor

```
<?xml version="1.0"?>
<mx:Application xmlns:mx="http://www.adobe.com/2006/mxml">
  <mx:VBox>
    <mx:DataGrid editable="false">
      <mx:columns>
        <mx:DataGridColumn headerText="Song Title" dataField="title"/>
        <mx:DataGridColumn headerText="Artist" dataField="artist"/>
        <mx:DataGridColumn headerText="Rating" dataField="rating"
                        itemRenderer="Rating" rendererIsEditor="true"
                        editorDataField="data" />
      </mx:columns>
      <mx:dataProvider>
        <mx:ArrayCollection>
          <mx:Array>
            <mx:Object songId="0" title="Astronaut" artist="David Byrne"
                    rating="5" inFavorites="true" />
              <mx:Object songId="1" title="Rio" artist="Duran Duran" rating="3" />
              <mx:Object songId="2" title="Enjoy the Silence"
artist="Depeche Mode"
                        rating="4" />
```

Example 8-16. Using a custom item editor (continued)

```
                <mx:Object songId="3" title="Mesopotamia" artist="B-52s"
                           rating="5" inFavorites="true" />
            </mx:Array>
          </mx:ArrayCollection>
        </mx:dataProvider>
      </mx:DataGrid>
  </mx:VBox>
</mx:Application>
```

Focus Management and Keyboard Control

Focus management and keyboard control are two related topics in Flex. An object has *focus* when it can respond to keyboard events. For example, when a text input control has focus, the user can enter text into the field. When a component has focus, it generally indicates that focus with a colored border. You can use the keyboard to control focus within a Flex application, and you can also respond to key presses. We'll look at all of these topics in the next few sections.

Controlling Tab Order

A standard application convention is that pressing the Tab key advances the focus to the next element, and Shift-Tab moves focus to the preceding element. This is true of most desktop applications. It is true of most HTML applications. And it is also true of Flex applications.

Many (though certainly not all) Flex components are capable of receiving focus. For example, text inputs, combo boxes, and buttons are all capable of receiving focus. Clearly there are other types of components that cannot receive focus. For example, a VBox container, a label, or a spacer cannot receive focus because none of these components can respond to keyboard input.

When several focus-enabled components exist on the screen at the same time, there exists a default order by which the user can move focus by pressing the Tab key. The order always moves from left to right, top to bottom. The following code creates a form with three text inputs and a button. The first two text inputs are side by side on the same line, the next text input follows on the next line, and that is followed by the button on the next line. In this example, if the user places focus in the firstName text input and presses Tab, the focus next moves to the lastName text field. Another press of the Tab key, and focus shifts to the email text input on the next line. Finally, one more Tab key press, and focus moves to the button.

```
<mx:Form>
  <mx:FormItem label="Name">
    <mx:HBox>
      <mx:TextInput id="firstName" />
      <mx:TextInput id="lastName" />
```

```
        </mx:HBox>
      </mx:FormItem>
      <mx:FormItem label="Email">
        <mx:TextInput id="email" />
      </mx:FormItem>
      <mx:FormItem label="">
        <mx:Button label="Submit" />
      </mx:FormItem>
    </mx:Form>
```

If the user presses Tab again with focus on the button, focus returns to the first item: the firstName text input. This is known as a *tab loop*, because pressing the Tab key shifts focus from component to component in a circular or looping fashion.

Although the default order of elements in a tab loop is generally what you would want and what a user of the application would expect, there are exceptions. For those exceptions, you can control the order of the elements in a tab loop by specifying tabIndex property values. Every focus-enabled component has a tabIndex property. By default, the properties are null, and Flex applications use the default tab order. However, you can explicitly define the order of the elements in a tab loop by specifying integer values starting with 1 for the tabIndex properties of all the components in a tab loop. The following example illustrates how this works with text inputs arranged in a grid. By default, the order would go from left to right, top to bottom. In this case, we're setting the tabIndex properties so that the order is from top to bottom, left to right.

```
    <mx:Grid>
      <mx:GridRow width="100%" height="100%">
        <mx:GridItem width="100%" height="100%">
          <mx:TextInput id="a" tabIndex="1" />
        </mx:GridItem>
        <mx:GridItem width="100%" height="100%">
          <mx:TextInput id="c" tabIndex="3" />
        </mx:GridItem>
        <mx:GridItem width="100%" height="100%">
          <mx:TextInput id="e" tabIndex="5" />
        </mx:GridItem>
        <mx:GridItem width="100%" height="100%">
          <mx:TextInput id="g" tabIndex="7" />
        </mx:GridItem>
      </mx:GridRow>
      <mx:GridRow width="100%" height="100%">
        <mx:GridItem width="100%" height="100%">
          <mx:TextInput id="b" tabIndex="2" />
        </mx:GridItem>
        <mx:GridItem width="100%" height="100%">
          <mx:TextInput id="d" tabIndex="4" />
        </mx:GridItem>
        <mx:GridItem width="100%" height="100%">
          <mx:TextInput id="f" tabIndex="6" />
        </mx:GridItem>
        <mx:GridItem width="100%" height="100%">
```

```
    <mx:TextInput id="h" tabIndex="8" />
  </mx:GridItem>
 </mx:GridRow>
</mx:Grid>
```

Note that the behavior of tab order can be unpredictable if you set one or more, but not all, of the tabIndex properties for the components in a tab loop. Generally you should either use the default tab order or set the tabIndex for all the components in a tab loop.

Although focus-enabled components are included in the tab order by default, you can explicitly exclude them by setting their tabEnabled property to false. Setting tabEnabled to false does not mean the component cannot receive focus programmatically or when the user clicks on it with the mouse. However, it does mean that it will not be included in the tab loop.

If you want to exclude all the child components of a container from a tab loop, simply set the tabChildren property of the container to false. That has the same effect as setting tabEnabled to false for each of the child controls.

Programmatically Controlling Focus

You can control focus programmatically using an mx.managers.FocusManager instance. A FocusManager instance controls one tab loop, and at one point there may exist multiple tab loops per application. This is so that some containers are capable of creating their own tab loops. For example, a pop-up window might have its own tab loop, distinct from the tab loop in a form behind the window. Because several tab loops might contain elements visible at the same time, a Flex application can have more than one FocusManager in use at any one time.

You never have to construct a new FocusManager instance. Every component has a focusManager property that references the FocusManager instance that controls the tab loop to which the component belongs.

You can programmatically retrieve the focused item using the getFocus() method of a FocusManager instance. The getFocus() method returns the component that currently has focus typed as IFocusManagerComponent. You should cast the return of getFocus() when necessary. Unlike lower-level Flash Player APIs for focus management, the getFocus() method of a FocusManager instance always returns a reference to the actual component that has focus, not a raw child object of the component. For example, from a Flash Player perspective, when a text input control has focus, it is really the nested lower-level text field that has focus. Yet from a practical standpoint, you are usually interested in the component that has focus, not its subelements.

You can set focus using the setFocus() method of a FocusManager object. You can pass setFocus() a reference to any focus-enabled component. For example, the

following code resets the values of the text input controls and then moves focus to
the first text input when the user clicks the button.

```
<mx:Script>
  <![CDATA[

    private function reset(event:Event):void {
      a.text = "";
      b.text = "";
      c.text = "";
      d.text = "";
      focusManager.setFocus(a);
    }

  ]]>
</mx:Script>
<mx:VBox height="100%">
  <mx:Grid>
    <mx:GridRow width="100%" height="100%">
      <mx:GridItem width="100%" height="100%">
        <mx:TextInput id="a" tabIndex="1" />
      </mx:GridItem>
      <mx:GridItem width="100%" height="100%">
        <mx:TextInput id="c" tabIndex="3" />
      </mx:GridItem>
    </mx:GridRow>
    <mx:GridRow width="100%" height="100%">
      <mx:GridItem width="100%" height="100%">
        <mx:TextInput id="b" tabIndex="2" />
      </mx:GridItem>
      <mx:GridItem width="100%" height="100%">
        <mx:TextInput id="d" tabIndex="4" />
      </mx:GridItem>
    </mx:GridRow>
  </mx:Grid>
  <mx:Button label="Reset" click="reset(event)"/>
</mx:VBox>
```

Responding to Keyboard Events

You can listen for keyboard events much like you can listen for any other sort of
event using inline MXML attributes and/or ActionScript. All display objects,
including all controls, containers, and the stage itself, dispatch events of type flash.
events.KeyboardEvent when the user presses a key on the keyboard. There are two
distinct events with each key press: keyUp and keyDown, which are represented by the
KeyboardEvent.KEY_UP and KeyboardEvent.KEY_DOWN constants.

The KeyboardEvent type defines several properties specific to the event. Among those
properties is the keyCode property, which contains the code of the key that was
pressed, and the charCode property, which contains the code of the specific character. The keyCode and charCode properties are the same for all alphanumeric keys

when they are not Shifted, Ctrl'd, or Alt'd. For alphanumeric keys, the key and character codes are the ASCII codes.

The flash.ui.Keyboard class defines constants that you can use for comparisons with key codes for nonalphanumeric keys. For example, Keyboard.ENTER and Keyboard.SHIFT contain the key code values for the Enter and Shift keys.

Components dispatch keyboard events only when they have focus. Example 8-17 uses this fact to create a simple context-based help system for a form in an application.

Example 8-17. A simple keyboard event example

```
<?xml version="1.0"?>
<mx:Application xmlns:mx="http://www.adobe.com/2006/mxml">

  <mx:Script>
    <![CDATA[
      import mx.controls.TextArea;
      import mx.managers.PopUpManager;
      import mx.containers.TitleWindow;
      import mx.events.CloseEvent;

      private var _helpWindow:TitleWindow;

      private function keyUpHandler(event:KeyboardEvent):void {
        if(_helpWindow != null) {
          return;
        }
        if(event.keyCode == Keyboard.F1) {
          _helpWindow = TitleWindow(PopUpManager.createPopUp(this,
TitleWindow, true));
          _helpWindow.title = "Application Help";
          _helpWindow.width = 400;
          _helpWindow.height = 400;
          _helpWindow.showCloseButton = true;
          _helpWindow.addEventListener(CloseEvent.CLOSE, closeHandler);
          var textArea:TextArea = new TextArea( );
          textArea.percentWidth = 100;
          textArea.percentHeight = 100;
          _helpWindow.addChild(textArea);
          if(event.currentTarget == firstName) {
            textArea.text = "Specify your first name, e.g. Bob";
          }
          else if(event.currentTarget == lastName) {
            textArea.text = "Specify your last name, e.g. Smith";
          }
          else if(event.currentTarget == email) {
            textArea.text = "Specify your email address, e.g. bob@yahoo.com";
          }
          else if(event.currentTarget == accountType) {
            textArea.text = "Select an account type from the drop-down";
          }
          else {
            textArea.text = "Generic application help";
          }
```

Example 8-17. A simple keyboard event example (continued)

```
      }
    }

    private function closeHandler(event:CloseEvent):void {
      PopUpManager.removePopUp(_helpWindow);
      _helpWindow = null;
    }

  ]]>
  </mx:Script>

  <mx:Form>
    <mx:FormItem label="First Name">
      <mx:TextInput id="firstName" keyUp="keyUpHandler(event)" />
    </mx:FormItem>
    <mx:FormItem label="Last Name">
      <mx:TextInput id="lastName" keyUp="keyUpHandler(event)" />
    </mx:FormItem>
    <mx:FormItem label="Email">
      <mx:TextInput id="email" keyUp="keyUpHandler(event)" />
    </mx:FormItem>
    <mx:FormItem label="Account Type">
      <mx:ComboBox id="accountType" dataProvider="[bronze,silver,gold,platinum]"
keyUp="keyUpHandler(event)" ></mx:ComboBox>
    </mx:FormItem>
  </mx:Form>

</mx:Application>
```

In Example 8-17, the user can press F1, and a help window will appear with help specific to the control that has focus.

The KeyboardEvent class also defines the Boolean properties ctrlKey, altKey, and shiftKey, which tell you whether the user is pressing the Ctrl, Alt, or Shift keys. The following rewrite to the if statement for Example 8-17 causes the help to appear only when the user presses Ctrl-F1:

```
    if(event.keyCode == Keyboard.F1 && event.ctrlKey) {
```

If you want to listen to events globally within an application, add listeners to the application container:

```
    this.addEventListener(KeyboardEvent.KEY_DOWN, keyUpHandler);
```

Summary

In this chapter, we discussed a variety of topics spanning the gamut of framework utilities and advanced component concepts. These topics included working with Flex tool tips, adding pop ups, managing the cursor, adding drag and drop behavior, customizing list-based components, and focus management and keyboard control.

Working with Media

A picture is worth a thousand words, and with Flex you have the ability to add pictures as well as animation, audio, and video. Flash Player started its roots in graphics and animation, and over time it has grown into a strong development runtime for interactive custom user interfaces. Flash Player has a long history in handling rich media on the Web, and Flex can leverage that strength and provide a truly engaging user experience. Flash Player not only handles many of the bitmap graphics formats traditional web browsers do, but it also has native support for vector-based graphics, animation, audio, and video.

This chapter covers loading and embedding assets, streaming media, supported media types, and working with the different media types.

Overview

In an application, media can be incorporated in two ways: at runtime or at compile time. Adding media at compile time is called *embedding*, because the content is compiled into the SWF. Adding media at runtime is called *loading* because the content exists as separate files that must be loaded into the Flex application when they are requested.

 One other method of loading media is called *streaming*. We will discuss streaming in the section "Working with Audio and Video" later in this chapter, because streaming applies only to those media types.

There are benefits to both methods. Which one you choose is important, because each one can impact the loading time of your application, the file size of the resulting SWF, the ability to change the media after an application is compiled, and the ability to dynamically change content.

For example, it's beneficial to embed content within a SWF file; doing so makes the media asset available to the application as soon as it is initialized, since it is packaged within the SWF file that is used to load the application. It is a good idea to embed small assets, such as button icons and application skins that often don't need to be redefined at runtime. You will typically want such graphics to be available immediately, as they can negatively impact the perceived performance of your application if each item requires a separate download.

 You also can embed assets using runtime shared libraries. Because runtime shared libraries are loaded when an application is initialized, they are treated in the same manner as embedding assets within the main application SWF. We covered working with shared libraries in Chapter 2.

It's beneficial to load content because the content won't be embedded as a constant (resource) within your application. For example, when building an application to manage images, you cannot embed the images within your application; instead, you need to load the images because the content will change often as new images are added to the image repository. Also, not having to embed the content within the application SWF will allow your application to be downloaded quickly, and once it is initialized, the application can load the media that is needed on demand without having to reload the application SWF.

Supported Media Types in Flex

As mentioned earlier, Flex's support for media is based on the capabilities of Flash Player. Flash Player natively supports SWF, GIF, JPEG, PNG, MP3, and FLV media.

 Flex 2 requires Flash Player 9 or newer. Our discussion of supported media and methods of dealing with media will assume you are targeting Flash Player 9 or newer. Although Flex 2 requires Flash Player 9, embedded and loaded SWF media do not have to be Flash Player 9 content.

In addition to formats supported natively by the player, with the help of the Flex compiler, you also can handle SVG content and Flash library items within SWF files. For example, the Flash Player does not natively support SVG content, but it has the technical capability to render basic SVG content with the help of the Flex compiler. The Flex compiler achieves this by processing SVG files and embedding the graphics definition data within a compiled SWF as native Flash bytecode. This means that at runtime, the developer cannot distinguish between SVG content and native Flash vector data. This allows you to embed SVG content seamlessly without needing to manually convert SVG files to Flash. Because SVG support is provided by the Flex compiler, SVG content can not be loaded dynamically at runtime.

Table 9-1 lists Flex-supported media types.

Table 9-1. *Flex-supported media types*

Format	Media type	Compiler required	Notes
SWF	Graphics and animation	No	Flex 2 requires Flash Player 9, but it can load any SWF content. You will be limited by what type of interoperability you can have with the content based on the version of the SWF content. Flash Player 9 content that uses ActionScript 3.0 is the most compatible.
SWF library item	Graphics and animation	Yes	SWF files that contain a library of multiple graphics and animation can be embedded. This requires the Flex compiler, and only the referenced library item will be embedded within the final SWF file.
GIF	Graphics	No	Standard GIF is supported, including transparency. Animated GIF files are not supported.
JPEG	Graphics	No	Baseline JPEG files as well as progressive JPEG files are supported.
PNG	Graphics	No	Both PNG8 and PNG24 are supported. Alpha transparency is fully supported as well.
SVG	Graphics	Yes	The Flex compiler supports the SVG 1.1 basic specifications. SMIL, animations, filters, pattern fills, advanced gradients, interactivity, and scripting are not supported.
MP3	Audio	No	MP3 files can be loaded, embedded, and streamed using an RTMP server.
FLV	Video	No	FLV is Flash's video file format. Files can be loaded, embedded, and streamed using an RTMP server.

Adding Media

As mentioned before, you can add media to an application by either loading it or embedding it. In this section, we will discuss the different syntax for loading and embedding media. This will serve as a good foundation for understanding the methods you have available to you when adding media to a Flex application. In the Flex framework, watch for component properties that accept a variable of type Class. These properties usually indicate the ability to accept a media type as a value.

If you have experience with developing Flash applications, you may be accustomed to creating classes for symbols such as images for when you want to access them in ActionScript. In Flex this is no longer required as such classes are generated automatically for you by the compiler.

Loading Media

Many of the Flex framework components are designed to enable you to easily load media into your application. Often this is possible with one MXML tag. Internally Flex ultimately makes use of Flash Player's Loader class. You typically will not make use of the Loader class directly as Flex framework abstracts away the details, but it is good to know it exists, and if you ever need to implement loading of custom file types not supported by Flex, you could easily do so. Here is an example that uses an Image tag to load a *.jpg* file:

```
<?xml version="1.0" encoding="utf-8"?>
<mx:Application xmlns:mx="http://www.adobe.com/2006/mxml">
    <mx:Image source="assets/sun.jpg"/>
</mx:Application>
```

This simple code loads an image file called *sun.jpg* at runtime and displays it in an Image component. The JPEG file format is native to Flash Player; as such, you are able to load it at runtime. Also important to note is that the application SWF does not contain the image; rather, it begins loading after the application is initialized. This behavior is very similar to how web browsers load images that are referenced in an HTML document.

 Loaded assets are referenced at runtime based on the location of the . *swf* file by default. You can reference assets both using absolute and relative paths.

This example uses the Image component, which is is a Flex component built to help you easily load images. The Image component loads the image provided by the source attribute and sizes it according to the width and height properties of the Image component instance, if any are provided. If no size is specified, the component expands to the dimensions of the image. Also, the Image component by default loads whatever you set in the source property. If you want to load the image based on user input or an event, you can call the load( ) method of the Image instance at runtime. Here is an updated example of the preceding code that provides users with a button to load the image when they want to view it, with no explicit width or height properties set:

```
<?xml version="1.0" encoding="utf-8"?>
<mx:Application xmlns:mx="http://www.adobe.com/2006/mxml">
    <mx:Image id="sun" autoLoad="false"/>
    <mx:Button label="Load Image" click="sun.load('assets/sun.jpg')"/>
</mx:Application>
```

This version of the application does not automatically load the image, as before. The Image component instance exists, but it loads the image only after the application is initialized. Also, the source property has no value in this example. When you do not specify the source property for an Image instance, the component will not load an image automatically. When a user clicks on the button, the load( ) method is called, along with the value of the image to load as a parameter. Using this method also has other benefits.

 The Flash Player security sandbox applies to loading media in the same way as loading data. If you plan to load media from a server other than the server where the application is loaded, you will need to keep these restrictions in mind. Refer back to Chapter 2 for more information on Flash Player security.

The Flex framework is designed to simplify many common tasks, such as loading media. However, as already shown, the Flex framework is written in ActionScript, and as such, it leverages lower-level Flash Player APIs. Although it is not necessary to learn the Flash Player APIs in many cases, doing so almost always provides greater insight into how the Flex framework operates, and it enables you to create more complex applications. When loading content using MXML tags such as Image, the components are using an ActionScript Loader object behind the scenes. The Loader class also exposes an instance, LoaderInfo, which allows you to gain insight on the status of the loaded content. This can be desirable if you wish to ensure that there are no errors attempting to load the content, or when you would like to know the progress of the loading process. The LoaderInfo class dispatches the following events to indicate progress: complete, ioError, open, httpStatus, and init. These events are typically mapped by the Flex components, so you don't have to worry about the LoaderInfo instance as well.

 The Flex framework components use the underlying Flash Player API to load media. To learn the internal details about the underlying mechanism that Flex uses to load images, review the documentation on the Loader class in the flash.display package.

The events you'll be most interested in are progress, complete, and ioError. The progress event is dispatched while an asset is being loaded. This allows you to provide the user with a progress bar or some other indication that something is loading. This is especially useful when loading a lot of content or large content. The complete event allows you to determine when an asset has finished loading. This can be useful if you want to provide some sort of notification to the user, or have another process begin after the content is loaded. The ioError event is important when having to deal with content that may or may not exist, especially if the user is asked to enter his own URL, for example. The ioError event is dispatched when Flash Player is unable to find the referenced file, allowing you to provide the user with the option of reentering the URL. An error is usually reported immediately if the client receives a response from the server that shows an error such as File Not Found, but if you reference a server that cannot be reached the response will not be returned in a timely manner, if ever.

The following code allows a user to enter a URL of an image to be loaded and notifies the user if he has entered an invalid URL:

```
<?xml version="1.0" encoding="utf-8"?>
<mx:Application xmlns:mx="http://www.adobe.com/2006/mxml">
    <mx:Script>
        <![CDATA[
            import mx.controls.Alert;
            private function ioErrorHandler( ):void
            {
             Alert.show("There was an error loading: "+imageUrl.text+",
please enter a new URL");
            }
        ]]>
    </mx:Script>
    <mx:Image id="imageView" ioError="ioErrorHandler( )"/>
    <!--when compiled and run locally, you can load remote images without security
    restriction that are typically encountered with an application running in the
    browser sandbox -->
    <mx:TextInput id="imageUrl" text="http://www.google.com/intl/en/images/logo.gif"/
>
    <mx:Button label="Load image" click="imageView.load(imageUrl.text)"/>
</mx:Application>
```

Embedding Media

When embedding media, you instruct the compiler to package the asset within the resulting SWF rather than just referencing it externally, as you saw in the preceding section. In other platforms, such as Java and .NET, this is sometimes referred to as compiling the asset as a resource. You can embed media with the following:

- MXML
- ActionScript
- CSS

You embed media by using the Embed( ) directive. This directive accepts the source, mimeType, scaleGridTop, scaleGridBottom, scaleGridLeft, scaleGridRight, and symbol parameters. The only required parameter is source. This parameter identifies to the compiler the asset it needs to process and embed within the final SWF.

Embedding media with MXML

The embed syntax when used in MXML begins with an @Embed( ) directive. The @ instructs the compiler that it will be receiving a directive—in this case, the Embed( ) directive.

Here is the earlier code snippet, but with the media embedded in MXML:

```
<?xml version="1.0" encoding="utf-8"?>
<mx:Application xmlns:mx="http://www.adobe.com/2006/mxml">
    <mx:Image source="@Embed(source='assets/sun.jpg')"/>
</mx:Application>
```

This example should look very similar to the earlier example, except for the additional syntax within the value of the source attribute. This syntax, when used within MXML, instructs the compiler to embed an asset rather than load it.

 When embedding an asset, the compiler will not resize or recompress the media contained with the resulting SWF. It will embed the asset as is in its original form. If you intend to use an asset only at a specific size, you should match in the source the final size that will be used in the application.

Embedding media with ActionScript

Sometimes you will want to embed your assets in ActionScript. This allows you to reference them directly within ActionScript, or even reference the embedded asset from MXML. Embedding media in ActionScript has the same result as doing so in MXML; the only difference is that the compiler instructions for embedding are in ActionScript code. Here's the earlier example in ActionScript:

```
<?xml version="1.0" encoding="utf-8"?>
<mx:Application xmlns:mx="http://www.adobe.com/2006/mxml" initialize="init()">
    <mx:Script>
        <![CDATA[
            [Embed(source="assets/sun.jpg")]
            private var sunAsset:Class;
            //This method is called when the application is initialized
            private function init():void
            {
                sunImage.source = sunAsset;
            }
        ]]>
    </mx:Script>
    <mx:Image id="sunImage"/>
</mx:Application>
```

The main difference in this example is that a change in the value of the source property for the Image instance is being set through ActionScript. When embedding content you must assign data of type Class to the source property. You don't typically specify a class yourself; instead, the Flex compiler automatically generates such a type for you when you embed an asset. When embedding content, you will need to reference a variable declared with the [Embed()] metadata syntax. The contents of the Embed() directive are the same as in the MXML example. In ActionScript, Embed() must be surrounded by []. This is called a *metadata tag*, and it instructs the compiler that it needs special handling. The Embed metadata tag must preceed the variable declaration, as shown in the preceeding example. Once done, the value of the variable will be the reference asset in the Embed() directive.

The declared variable of an asset must be of type Class. Placing an Embed metadata tag before the variable will cause the compiler to define the variable's class definition and allow you to instantiate it or reference it when needing to work with the asset.

Although the variable is declared as a generic Class datatype, each type of media asset maps to a more specific class definition, depending on the type of media embedded. All asset class types implement a common interface, IFlexAsset.

The different types of asset classes are as follows:

- BitmapAsset, which represents bitmap images (JPEG, GIF, PNG).
- MovieClipAsset, which represents Flash library items within a SWF. Typically, such an asset is an animated graphic. For static SWF library items, SpriteClass is used.
- MovieClipLoaderAsset, which represents SWF files.
- SoundAsset, which represents an embedded MP3 file.
- SpriteClass, which represents a static vector graphic from a SWF library item or SVG file.
- ButtonAsset, which is rarely used but is provided to ensure full compatibility with Flash Authoring content.
- TextFieldAsset, which will never be produced by Flex, but is produced by some other tools.

One of the strenths of using ActionScript for part of an application is the added flexibility it gives you when handling application logic at runtime. In that spirit, let's take a look at an example that allows us to change an embedded image at runtime:

```
<?xml version="1.0" encoding="utf-8"?>
<mx:Application xmlns:mx="http://www.adobe.com/2006/mxml" initialize="init( )">
    <mx:Script>
        <![CDATA[
            [Embed(source="assets/sun.jpg")]
            private var sunAsset:Class;
            [Embed(source="assets/moon.jpg")]
            private var moonAsset:Class;
            private function init( ):void
            {
                sunImage.source = sunAsset;
            }

            private function showMoon( ):void
            {
                sunImage.source = moonAsset;
            }
        ]]>
    </mx:Script>
    <mx:Image id="sunImage"/>
    <mx:Button label="Show the Moon!" click="showMoon( )"/>
</mx:Application>
```

In this example, the sun image asset is initially displayed, and the user is presented with a button to display the moon image. The button's click event is set up to call the showMoon( ) function, which will set the source property of the Image instance to the `moonAsset` that contains the embedded image. When you declare an asset to be embedded, that asset is included within the final SWF regardless of whether it is used.

Embedding media with CSS

Typically you embed assets when stylizing and skinning components. So far, we have discussed using the `Image` component to load and embed images. The `Image` component is ideal for loading and displaying images and animations. With CSS, though, you can easily specify component skins.

Here's an example of embedding assets to reskin a button component using CSS:

```
<?xml version="1.0" encoding="utf-8"?>
<mx:Application xmlns:mx="http://www.adobe.com/2006/mxml">
    <mx:Style>
    Button
    {
        down-skin:Embed(source="assets/btnDown.PNG");
        over-skin:Embed(source="assets/btnOver.PNG");
        up-skin:Embed(source="assets/btnUp.PNG");
    }
    </mx:Style>
    <mx:Button label="Hello World!"/>
</mx:Application>
```

This example showcases the power of Flex in terms of handling CSS and embedding assets. In this example, we redefined the base skin for all instances of the `Button` component within three lines (you can find more information on skinning components in Chapter 14). We did this by setting the values of the CSS properties to images that we embedded. The syntax is similar to that used in the previous two examples. In CSS, though, you don't need to use identifier characters as you do with the other two forms of syntax. In CSS, you just use the `Embed()` directive directly inline.

Working with the Different Media Types

So far, we have explored how to load media and the different syntax used for embedding media. Although the general approach is very similar across the different media types, there are some subtle differences that you need to be aware of to best use media in your Flex applications.

Working with Graphics

Graphics are static images, either bitmap or vector, and are typically the most used media asset of all. You will use such assets to reskin a UI control, to load pictures, and pretty much whenever you want to display a graphic that you do not want to reproduce using ActionScript. Graphics are an important part of Flex. The strength of using such a rich UI framework as Flex can't be completely maximized without including custom user interfaces and engaging interaction.

 Vector graphics differ from bitmap graphics in that they are represented through polygon shape definition rather than pixels. Because they're represented via polygon data rather than pixels, vector graphics have higher resolutions and smaller file sizes than bitmap graphics do. Flash Player also exposes vector drawing capability through the ActionScript drawing API.

Adding graphics

The Flex framework simplifies working with graphics. One way to work with graphics in Flex is via the Image component. All Flex components that use graphics work in a similar manner, but each serves its own purpose. For example, the Button component has an icon property. This property, like the source property of an Image component, can accept an embedded or loaded graphic. Becoming familiar with the component you are working with, and its capability to work with graphics, can help you maximize how effectively you use the Flex framework.

So far, we have looked at using JPEG files. The Flex framework also supports GIF, PNG, and SWF graphics files. When loading a media asset, the component takes care of loading the asset and displaying it. This traditionally requires writing code to load the asset, and then displaying it and sizing it appropriately.

Static (nonanimated) graphics are implemented in the same manner. When adding such content, though, it is good to understand the goals and the benefits of each file format:

GIF
> This lossless image format is for simple, nonphoto bitmaps. Flash Player can handle transparent GIF files but not animated GIF files. Thus, if animation is important, you will need to use a SWF file instead.

JPEG
> The JPEG file format is a lossy graphics format ideal for photolike content. This file format does not support any type of animation.

PNG
> This lossless bitmap graphics file format supports multiple levels of transparency. It is ideal when you need high-quality bitmap graphics. Usually, PNG files produce a file size comparable to GIF and JPEG files, although often PNG files are larger. You should compare the output quality and file size of the three different bitmap formats when trying to decide which format to use.

SVG

SVG is a vector-based format that is supported only at compile time. This format can be useful in cases where vector data can only be obtained in this format.

SWF

This is the ideal vector graphics format. Many existing tools produce SWF files that can be easily integrated into Flex applications.

Here is an example that uses a SWF file as a button icon:

```
<?xml version="1.0"?>
<mx:Application xmlns:mx="http://www.adobe.com/2006/mxml">
    <mx:Button label="Logout" icon="@Embed(assets/logoutIcon.swf)"/>
</mx:Application>
```

This example sets the icon property of the Button instance to the embedded asset. As you can see, the asset here functions similarily to the way it was used with the Image component.

So far, you've set the value of a component property to a media asset. Although this is a common usage, sometimes you might want to display an arbitrary number of images. Without Flex, the only way to do this is to manually write ActionScript code to load, position, size, and display the images. With Flex, though, you can easily display a set of images that are stored in an array using a Repeater component. Here is an example of using the Repeater component with loaded images:

```
<?xml version="1.0" encoding="utf-8"?>
<mx:Application xmlns:mx="http://www.adobe.com/2006/mxml">
    <mx:Repeater id="images" dataProvider="['assets/image1.png','assets/image2.
png']">
        <mx:Image source="{images.currentItem}"/>
    </mx:Repeater>
</mx:Application>
```

This example uses the same Image component, but this time you are using a Repeater component to instantiate an arbitrary number of Image component instances depending on how many images need to be displayed. You do this by setting the Repeater component's dataProvider property to an array of images (in this example, it is specified inline, but it could have been a list from a server), and through data binding, you set the source property of the Image component to the current item that needs to be rendered.

Scaling graphics using a scaling grid (a.k.a. Scale-9)

Another unique capability of Flash Player is the Scale-9 feature, which helps scale graphics so that the corners don't stretch. It's common when working with graphics that need to scale the content while keeping the corners properly sized. As an example, Figures 9-1 and 9-2 show a graphical asset before and after it is scaled in the most common model.

Figure 9-1. Original graphic

Figure 9-2. Traditional scaling of the graphic in Figure 9-1

Notice in Figure 9-2 that the graphic was scaled, including the rounded corners. Although this is sometimes the desired result, more often you will be interested in scaling both the width and the height of the graphic while keeping the corner radius consistent, as seen in Figure 9-3.

Figure 9-3. Graphic in Figure 9-2 scaled, with corners remaining consistent

This is particularly important in regard to skinning components, and here Scale-9 becomes indispensable. It allows you to divide a graphic into a 3-by-3 grid, with the four corner squares remaining consistent in size while the other squares scale to fill the needed area. Figure 9-4 shows the original graphic from Figure 9-1, but with the grid drawn on top of it.

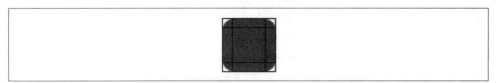

Figure 9-4. Graphic from Figure 9-1, but with Slice-9 guides drawn

Now when the graphic from Figure 9-4 is scaled, it will maintain the corner radius graphics, as seen in Figure 9-5, without scaling the corners.

Figure 9-5. Graphic from Figure 9-4, scaled with Slide-9 guides drawn

To use Scale-9, you have to define the coordinates of the scaling grid. You can define grid coordinates in several ways. The simplest and most common way is to specify them within the Embed( ) directive.

The Embed( ) directive, when used with a graphic, supports the special parameters scaleGridTop, scaleGridBottom, scaleGridLeft, and scaleGridRight for just this purpose. These parameters take an integer value and their registration point is the top left of the graphic. As an example, the following code of an embedded graphic has the Scale-9 grid defined:

```
<?xml version="1.0" encoding="utf-8"?>
<mx:Application xmlns:mx="http://www.adobe.com/2006/mxml">
    <mx:Image width="100" height="100" source="@Embed(source='assets/cube.
GIF',scaleGridTop='10',scaleGridLeft='10',
scaleGridBottom='90',scaleGridRight='90')"/>
</mx:Application>
```

This example uses the same graphic shown in Figure 9-4 and defines the properties within MXML, but you can achieve the same result in ActionScript and CSS. The box has an original width and height of 100 pixels. In this example, we are defining the guides 10 pixels away from each edge. Notice that scaleGridBottom and scaleGridRight are not set to 10, but are set to 100 minus 10 because the registration point of where Flash Player calculates things is the top left. Also, the distance from each edge does not need to be equal, but all values need to be defined. If you forget to define one of the scale grid properties, you will receive a compiler error.

 Scale-9 with embedded content can also be implemented outside of Flex within a SWF graphic from tools that produce the needed data within the resulting SWF. Adobe Flash Professional is one such tool, and when a graphic is compiled into a SWF with Scale-9 grid data embedded, Flex automatically uses the already defined data with the SWF. If you define values within both an Embed( ) directive and a SWF that already includes the grid data, the SWF file data will be used. Defining the grid in a SWF file is useful when a designer wants to configure the grid as part of the material a designer provides to a development team.

Working with SWF libraries

If you're working on a team that plans to produce graphical assets in Adobe Flash Professional, which supports creating SWF libraries, creating such libraries may be an ideal choice because it allows you to provide a single file that contains many, if not all, of the assets needed for an application. This also allows a designer to update a single file throughout the development process, in a single step.

In the following code, a SWF library item is used as a button icon:

```
<?xml version="1.0" encoding="utf-8"?>
<mx:Application xmlns:mx="http://www.adobe.com/2006/mxml">
    <mx:Button label="Click me" source="@Embed(source='assets/library.SWF',
symbol='circleAnimation')"/>
</mx:Application>
```

In this example, the circleAnimation symbol within the *library.swf* file is being embedded. The syntax for doing so is the same as that used to embed other content, except for the addition of the symbol parameter for the Embed( ) directive. The symbol parameter is a special parameter supported only with SWF libraries. If the referenced symbol is not valid, the Flex compiler returns an error.

If a SWF library contains many library items, but only some of the items are referenced in an application, only those library items are embedded within the final SWF. Finally, you may have noticed that you didn't have to specify the type of asset. If it was a bitmap, video, or animation, the Flex compiler automatically embeds it for you. If the type of symbol with the SWF library changes—for example, from a vector graphic to Flash video—you don't need to change anything within your code to handle the embedding process differently. However, if your code relies on a specific type for an asset, you may need to update it to reflect the new asset type.

Building an asset library using a static class in Flex

Another way to improve asset management is to define ActionScript classes that are dedicated to defining all the assets in an application. This allows you to centrally store the definition of all your assets and easily reference the assets throughout an application by referencing the asset class members.

To begin, you define the class that contains all the embedded assets. The asset will contain public static constant properties, which you can reference within your application. In the following example, the class is small, and you have a single class. In a large application, the class will likely be larger, with many assets and you may have several asset classes defined if you feel the need to split different types of assets.

```
package com.oreilly.programmingflex.assets
{
    public class Images
    {
        [Embed(source="/assets/btnOver.png")]
        public static const LOGO:Class;
        [Embed(source="/assets/sun.jpg")]
        public static const LOGOUT_ICON:Class;
    }
}
```

Now that you've defined the class that will contain the embedded assets, you can reference the embedded resources within MXML or ActionScript. Here is an example in MXML:

```
<?xml version="1.0" encoding="utf-8"?>
<mx:Application xmlns:mx="http://www.adobe.com/2006/mxml">
    <mx:Script>
        <![CDATA[
            import com.oreilly.programmingflex.assets.Images;
        ]]>
    </mx:Script>
    <mx:Image source="{Images.LOGO}"/>
    <mx:Button label="Logout" icon="{Images.LOGOUT_ICON}"/>
</mx:Application>
```

This method allows you to centralize all your assets and keep a manageable list of what assets are included within the application. When adding and redefining assets you need to edit only the class. This also allows you to reference the same asset throughout your application, be it from MXML or ActionScript, in one place.

Working with SWF animations

The Flash platform began its life as an animation tool for the Web, and as such, it only makes sense that Flex would be able to take advantage of that strength. Flex allows any Flash content to be embedded or loaded, including animated content. Usually such content is produced by a graphic designer or animator using animation software, and the result is a SWF file that doesn't contain any code but does contain a Flash animation.

For example, say you wanted to include an animated character to guide users through an application. You could reproduce the character in ActionScript, but that would take a lot of time, and chances are a developer would not be interested in producing such content. Tools such as Adobe Flash Professional (*http://www.adobe.com/go/flash*) are better suited for this purpose. For the purposes of our discussion, we won't be covering how to use such tools. Instead, we will focus on how such content is incorporated.

Here are some important items to keep in mind when working with SWF animations:

Frame rate
> The frame rate of an animation is not the frame rate that is ultimately used during playback. When content is added to a Flex application, the frame rate of the application is used (the main SWF) rather than the content's frame rate. The default frame rate used in Flex is 24 frames per second. It is a good idea to develop animated content to match that frame rate. Also, although it's not advisable (unless you are careful), you could change the frame rate of your application to match the SWF content by setting the -default-frame-rate compiler flag to match that of the SWF content you plan to embed.

Transparency
> SWF files support full transparency. Content loaded into a Flex application typically has no background; instead, the items below the animation on the Z index within Flash Player are used. Alpha transparency is also possible.

Animation size
> Sometimes referred to as *canvas* or *movie* size, animated content size is dictated by the bounding box of the animation. If you attempt to retrieve the width and height of the content, the currently used area is returned. This means that when an animation that is playing causes the size of the bounding box to change, the value returned by the width and height properties changes as well.

Embedding versus loading
> As with SWF graphics files, SWF animations can be loaded or embedded. If the animation exists within a SWF library, embedding is the only option. You will have to decide what approach to take based on the file size of the SWF animation and the need for immediately availability.

ActionScript communication

If the SWF animation is loaded and contains ActionScript code, you can communicate between your Flex application and the ActionScript code. If the SWF is compiled for Flash Player 9 with ActionScript 3.0 code, you will have more power to control the asset. If you are loading a SWF with an older version of ActionScript, you will have to implement the LocalConnection interface on both the loaded SWF and the main application to bridge the communication.

If a SWF is embedded and not loaded, the ActionScript code within the SWF is removed and the only interactivity you will be able to perform is to control the playback of the animation as you would any other MovieClip instance.

Working with Audio and Video

You can add audio and video to a Flex application through embedding, loading, and streaming. In practice, though, because audio and video content tends to produce large files, you will load or stream such media rather than embed it. Loading audio and video works the same with audio and video as graphics, except for having some additional capabilities specific to the media type, such as controlling playback. Streaming is similar to loading because it can occur anytime after an application is initialized. With streaming, you rely on a server to continuously return to the client the media data, broken up into smaller parts. This allows the user to begin playing the content more quickly and seek to the middle of the content without having to download the entire file.

Adding a sound effect

The Flex framework provides the SoundEffect component for handling sound effects in an application when an effect event occurs. The SoundEffect component makes it easy to play back a sound that is tied to a Flex effect. For more information on effects, see Chapter 11.

When an effect event occurs, the audio can be played back using SoundEffect. The SoundEffect component is not used for just any audio playback, only specifically when tied to a Flex effect event. The following code causes the sound effect to play when a user clicks on the button labeled "Click me":

```
<?xml version="1.0" encoding="utf-8"?>
<mx:Application xmlns:mx="http://www.adobe.com/2006/mxml">
    <mx:SoundEffect id="clickSound" source="assets/click.MP3"/>
    <mx:Button label="Click me" mouseDownEffect="{clickSound}"/>
</mx:Application>
```

In this example, when a user clicks the "Click me" button, the *click.mp3* file is loaded and played. By default, the SoundEffect class plays up to 500 milliseconds of an audio file. You can change the duration by setting the duration property, or if you want the entire audio file to play through no matter the duration, you can set useDuration to false.

Advanced sound control

The SoundEffect component is great when you want to add an audio effect that doesn't need to be controlled and when it ties in nicely to the Flex framework effects system. In other instances, when you may want to play an audio file and provide full audio controls, Flash Player exposes the low-level flash.media package that contains classes which provide granular control over media playback and handling. The most important classes to become familiar with are the Sound, SoundChannel, and SoundTransform classes. Together these classes enable you to load an MP3 file, control playback and volume, and retrieve metainformation from the file.

The Sound class is a factory object used to create an instance of an MP3 file and play it back. The play() instance method of the Sound class returns a SoundChannel instance lets you work directly with the playing instance. At first it may seem counterintuitive to have this extra step, but when you want to play multiple channels of the same audio, this separation is needed. SoundChannel also provides a reference to the SoundTransform instance that allows you to control the channel's audio level and panning.

The following code includes a reusable SoundPlayer class for loading an MP3 file, starting playback, and allowing the user to stop and pause playback:

```
package com.oreilly.programmingflex
{
    import flash.media.SoundChannel;
    import flash.media.Sound;
    import flash.net.URLStream;
    import flash.events.Event;
    import flash.media.ID3Info;
    import flash.net.URLRequest;
    import flash.events.EventDispatcher;

    public class SoundPlayer extends EventDispatcher
    {
        [Bindable]
        public var songName:String = "Loading";

        private var _sound:Sound;
        private var _soundChannel:SoundChannel;
        private var _currentPosition:Number;

        public function SoundPlayer(url:String)
        {
            _sound = new Sound(new URLRequest(url));
            //Subscribe to the ID3 event so we can retrieve the songName
            _sound.addEventListener(Event.ID3,id3Handler);
            play();
        }

        public function stop():void
        {
            _soundChannel.stop();
```

```
            //reset the position so play() start from the begining
            _currentPosition = 0;
        }

        public function pause():void
        {
            //store the position so we can resume playback
            _currentPosition = _soundChannel.position;
            _soundChannel.stop();
        }

        public function play():void
        {
            //If it is already playing, stop playback
            if(_soundChannel != null)
            {
                _soundChannel.stop();
            }
            //Store a reference to the playing channel
            _soundChannel = _sound.play(_currentPosition);
            //Set the volume, valid values are from 0 to 1
            _soundChannel.soundTransform.volume = .7;
        }

        private function id3Handler(id3Event:Event):void
        {
            songName = _sound.id3.songName;
            dispatchEvent(new Event("songNameChanged"));
        }
    }
}
```

And here is an example of using the SoundPlayer class:

```
<?xml version="1.0" encoding="utf-8"?>
<mx:Application xmlns:mx="http://www.adobe.com/2006/mxml">
    <mx:Script>
        <![CDATA[
            import com.oreilly.programmingflex.SoundPlayer;
            //Initialize the soundPlayer as soon as the application start
            public var soundPlayer:SoundPlayer = new SoundPlayer("assets/sound.MP3");
        ]]>
    </mx:Script>
    <mx:VBox>
        <mx:Text text="{soundPlayer.songName}" id="songName" width="100%"/>
        <mx:HBox width="100%">
            <mx:Button label="Play" click="soundPlayer.play()"/>
            <mx:Button label="Stop" click="soundPlayer.stop()"/>
            <mx:Button label="Pause" click="soundPlayer.pause()"/>
        </mx:HBox>
    </mx:VBox>
</mx:Application>
```

Although the preceding example is a simple MP3 player, it demonstrates much of what is needed in order to have deeper control over audio. This functionality is not exposed through any Flex component, but it is available within Flash Player.

Working with video

Flex also support the ability to display full-motion video. Flash Player supports the Flash video format, and currently three codecs are supported: On2 VP6, Sorenson Spark, and Screen. Generally, the On2 VP6 codec will be optimal because it currently has the best support for high-quality video playback; however, the Spark and Screen codecs have their own benefits as well. For instance, the Sorenson Spark codec is ideal for low-latency real-time video broadcast and for low CPU usage needs, such as for playback on handheld devices. It is the only codec currently available for client-to-server transmission and capturing, which allows you to capture an end user's web camera, for example. The Screen codec, meanwhile, is ideal for screen capturing, which typically is useful for video screen captures.

 Codecs are compression algorithms that are used when digitally encoding video. There tends to be some trade-offs among the different codecs available today. Some of the trade-offs include faster encoding speed for lower latency in real-time applications, higher quality and resolution, the ability to better handle specific use cases such as screen capturing, and wider adoption. When beginning work on an application that will use a lot of video, it is a good idea to compare the different codecs to find which best meets your needs.

As you can with audio, you can load, embed, and stream Flash video. You probably won't want to embed video within your application; typically you will be loading video or streaming it, because video files can be very large.

For working with video, the Flex framework provides the VideoDisplay component, which allows you to load and display video. Here is an example of the VideoDisplay component with playback and volume controls of a loaded video:

```
<?xml version="1.0" encoding="utf-8"?>
<mx:Application xmlns:mx="http://www.adobe.com/2006/mxml">
    <mx:Panel title="Video Viewer">
        <mx:VideoDisplay id="videoViewer" source="assets/video.flv"
volume="{volumeControl.value}"/>
        <mx:ControlBar>
            <mx:Label text="{videoViewer.playheadTime.toPrecision(2)}"/>
            <mx:Button label="Play" click="videoViewer.play()"/>
            <mx:Button label="Pause" click="videoViewer.pause()"/>
            <mx:Button label="Stop" click="videoViewer.stop()"/>
            <mx:HSlider id="volumeControl" maximum="1" width="80"/>
        </mx:ControlBar>
    </mx:Panel>
</mx:Application>
```

Even with such a short example, we have a fully functioning video player. The VideoDisplay component loads the video once it is initialized. The control bar contains a label displaying the time as the playback progresses; the buttons allow the user to pause, play, and stop playback; and the slider allows the user to control the volume. The playback is controlled through the VideoDisplay methods play( ), pause( ), and stop( ). The volume is controlled by data binding the volume property of the VideoDisplay component to the value property of the slider. The valid volume range is between zero and one, with one being the maximum.

Streaming media

Streaming is similar to loading, except that allows the user to seek to any point of a media file without needing to download the entire file, and it allows the user to download only a small portion of the file, rather than the entire file, before being able to play it. It does this by segmenting the media file into chunks that are sent to the player, which in turn buffers enough chunks to begin playback with the ability to keep adding to the buffer as playback continues. This can be beneficial when bandwidth consumption is a concern or when serving large files that users will often want to seek within rather than just starting from the beginning of the file.

The Flash Player supports streaming through the Real Time Messaging Protocol (RTMP). RTMP was developed by Macromedia (now Adobe) and is a part of Adobe's Flash Media Server product (*http://www.adobe.com/go/fms*).

Assuming you have an FLV file hosted on a local server with the URL *rtmp:// localhost/pf/video/video.flv*, here is code that uses the VideoDisplay component to display a streamed video:

```
<?xml version="1.0" encoding="utf-8"?>
<mx:Application xmlns:mx="http://www.adobe.com/2006/mxml">
    <mx:Panel title="Video Viewer">
        <mx:VideoDisplay bufferTime="3" id="videoViewer"
source="rtmp://localhost/pf2/video/video.flv" volume="{volumeControl.value}"/>
        <mx:ControlBar>
            <mx:Label text="{videoViewer.playheadTime.toPrecision(2)}"/>
            <mx:Button label="Play" click="videoViewer.play( )"/>
            <mx:Button label="Pause" click="videoViewer.pause( )"/>
            <mx:Button label="Stop" click="videoViewer.stop( )"/>
            <mx:HSlider id="volumeControl" maximum="1" width="80"/>
        </mx:ControlBar>
    </mx:Panel>
</mx:Application>
```

Notice how this example is almost identical to the previous one, except for the addition of the bufferTime property and a change to the value of the source property. The source property accepts a reference to an RTMP video stream and it takes care of communicating with the streaming server. bufferTime is a property of the VideoDisplay component that affects only streamed video. In the example, bufferTime is set to 3 seconds, which means the player will buffer for 3 seconds before playing back the stream to ensure that playback in not interrupted. You may not need to set this value very often, but if you find that your video is having difficulty playing continuously, typically because of network performance, you may want to compensate by setting the value of `bufferTime` to a higher value.

Summary

Throughout this chapter, you have seen how Flex can easily allow developers to harness the power of Flash Player in adding images, animations, video, and audio. The different types of media can be embedded, loaded, and in some cases, streamed.

Managing State

In Flex terminology, a *state* is a collection of changes (called *overrides*) to a view. The overrides can comprise additions or removals of components as well as changes to their properties and behaviors. Every Flex application has at least one state, referred to as its *base state*. Flex states enable you to more easily change the view for an application, whether at a macro or a micro level. For example, you can define two states that act as screens in an application (e.g., a login screen and a menu screen). Using states for screens is an example of a macro-level use. At the micro level, you can use states to manage cascading forms and even different views for components (e.g., roll-over changes).

The Flex framework provides an entire library for states and state management. You can create and manage states from MXML or ActionScript. Furthermore, you can use states in conjunction with other Flex features, such as transitions and history management, to create robust, responsive, and engaging applications and user interfaces with relative ease. In this chapter, you'll learn how to work with Flex states.

Creating States

You can create states at the application level and at the component level. The process for creating states at either level is identical. Although you can create states using ActionScript, it is far more common and practical to create all states using MXML. States are part of the view of an application, and as with any part of the view in a Flex application, you should use MXML unless there is a very good reason to use ActionScript. For that reason, much of this chapter focuses on creating states with MXML.

Every application and component has a states property that allows you to define an array of states. From MXML you can use the following syntax to populate the states array:

```
<mx:states>
    <!-- State elements -->
</mx:states>
```

States are instances of the mx.states.State class, and you can create a new state using the <mx:State> tag in MXML. When you create a new state you should—at a minimum—specify a name. The name for a state is the identifier by which you can reference it, and it must adhere to variable name rules (i.e., only alphanumeric characters and underscores). The following MXML creates a new state with a name of exampleState:

```
<mx:State name="exampleState"></mx:State>
```

Within the opening and closing <mx:State> tags, you can specify the state definition. A state definition consists of override elements that do the following:

- Add or remove components
- Set properties
- Set styles
- Set event handlers
- Perform custom overrides

The next several sections discuss each of these element types in more detail.

Applying States

By default, the base state is applied to an application or component. You can define many states for each application and component, but you can apply only one state at any one time. You can apply a state using the currentState property. Example 10-1 defines a state that adds a checkbox (see the upcoming section, "Adding and Removing Components" for details on adding components to states). The state is applied when the user clicks the button in the base state.

Example 10-1. Applying a state

```
<?xml version="1.0" encoding="utf-8"?>
<mx:Application xmlns:mx="http://www.adobe.com/2006/mxml" layout="absolute">

    <mx:states>
        <mx:State name="newCheckbox">
            <mx:AddChild relativeTo="{vbox}">
                <mx:CheckBox id="checkbox" label="New Checkbox" />
            </mx:AddChild>
        </mx:State>
    </mx:states>

    <mx:VBox id="vbox">
        <mx:Button label="Click" click="currentState='newCheckbox'" />
    </mx:VBox>

</mx:Application>
```

Note that the value of the currentState property is a string specifying the name of the state to apply. In the preceding example, when the user clicks the button, the value of newCheckbox is assigned to the currentState property of the application. The Flex framework then looks for a state with a name attribute of newCheckbox and applies that state. In the preceding example, the state with the name of newCheckbox uses an <mx:AddChild> tag to add a new checkbox to the VBox instance.

 If you want to return to the base state, you can assign a null value or an empty string to the currentState property.

The currentState property is a property inherited from the UIComponent class. That means each application and each component has its own currentState property, and you can set the states of each independently.

Defining States Based on Existing States

By default, all states are based on the base state. For example, the new checkbox in the example from the preceding section is added to the VBox. When the new state is applied, the VBox and nested button from the base state continue to exist. However, note that states are not applied cumulatively. For instance, Example 10-2 defines two states in addition to the base state. The base state has two buttons. Each button applies one of the states. When applying the newCheckbox state, a new checkbox is added. When applying the newTextArea state, a new text area is added, but if the checkbox had been previously added, it is removed.

Example 10-2. Defining a state based on an existing state

```
<?xml version="1.0" encoding="utf-8"?>
<mx:Application xmlns:mx="http://www.adobe.com/2006/mxml" layout="absolute">

    <mx:states>
        <mx:State name="newCheckbox">
            <mx:AddChild relativeTo="{vbox}">
                <mx:CheckBox id="checkbox" label="New Checkbox" />
            </mx:AddChild>
        </mx:State>
        <mx:State name="newTextArea">
            <mx:AddChild relativeTo="{vbox}">
                <mx:TextArea id="textarea" />
            </mx:AddChild>
        </mx:State>
    </mx:states>
```

Example 10-2. Defining a state based on an existing state (continued)

```
    <mx:VBox id="vbox">
        <mx:Button label="Click" click="currentState='newCheckbox'" />
        <mx:Button label="Click" click="currentState='newTextArea'" />
    </mx:VBox>

</mx:Application>
```

 Note that when components are removed by changing states, the components are still stored in memory.

If you want to define a state so that it's based on a state other than the base state, use the basedOn attribute of the <mx:State> tag. You can assign the name of a state to the basedOn attribute of a different state, and the state with the basedOn value automatically inherits the state's overrides, specified in the basedOn attribute. For example, rewrite the newTextArea state definition so that the <mx:State> tag appears as follows:

```
    <mx:State name="newTextArea" basedOn="newCheckbox">
```

When the newTextArea state is rewritten with the basedOn attribute (as in the preceding line of code), the newTextArea state adds both a checkbox and a text area.

Adding and Removing Components

One of the most common uses of states is adding and removing components. You can use the <mx:AddChild> tag to add a component or components. The following defines a state named newTextInput that adds a button component instance:

```
    <?xml version="1.0" encoding="utf-8"?>
    <mx:Application xmlns:mx="http://www.adobe.com/2006/mxml" layout="vertical">
        <mx:states>
            <mx:State name="newTextInput">
                <mx:AddChild>
                    <mx:TextInput id="textinput" />
                </mx:AddChild>
            </mx:State>
        </mx:states>
        <mx:Button id="button" label="Click" click="currentState='newTextInput'" />
    </mx:Application>
```

The default behavior of the <mx:AddChild> tag is to add the component or components to the application container or component for which the state is defined. However, if you want to define an explicit target to the component (or components) you added, use the relativeTo attribute. Example 10-3 adds the new button as a child of the VBox instance with an id of vbox.

Example 10-3. Adding a component

```xml
<?xml version="1.0" encoding="utf-8"?>
<mx:Application xmlns:mx="http://www.adobe.com/2006/mxml" layout="vertical">
    <mx:states>
        <mx:State name="newTextInput">
            <mx:AddChild relativeTo="{vbox}">
                <mx:TextInput id="textinput" />
            </mx:AddChild>
        </mx:State>
    </mx:states>
    <mx:VBox id="vbox">
        <mx:CheckBox id="checkbox1" label="One" />
        <mx:CheckBox id="checkbox2" label="Two" />
        <mx:Button id="button" label="Click" click="currentState='newTextInput'" />
    </mx:VBox>
</mx:Application>
```

When adding child components, the new instance is added as the last child of the target by default. For instance, in the preceding example, the new button is added below the two checkboxes in the base state. However, you can control where the new instances are added using the position attribute. The default value is lastChild, but you can optionally specify firstChild to add the new instance(s) to the beginning of the target container.

When you use lastChild or firstChild as the position value, the target value is interpreted as the container to which you want to add the child component(s). When you use a value of before or after for the position attribute, the target is interpreted as a sibling of the component(s) you are adding. If you want to add the child component(s) immediately before or after an existing component, you can specify the sibling component as the target and then use the value of before or after for the position attribute. Example 10-4 adds the new text input immediately after the first checkbox in the base state.

Example 10-4. Adding a component using the position property

```xml
<?xml version="1.0" encoding="utf-8"?>
<mx:Application xmlns:mx="http://www.adobe.com/2006/mxml" layout="absolute">
    <mx:states>
        <mx:State name="newTextInput">
            <mx:AddChild relativeTo="{checkbox1}" position="after">
                <mx:TextInput id="textinput" />
            </mx:AddChild>
        </mx:State>
    </mx:states>
    <mx:VBox id="vbox">
        <mx:CheckBox id="checkbox1" label="One" />
        <mx:CheckBox id="checkbox2" label="Two" />
        <mx:Button id="button" label="Click" click="currentState='newTextInput'" />
    </mx:VBox>
</mx:Application>
```

You remove components with the <mx:RemoveChild> tag, and the process generally is simpler than adding components. The <mx:RemoveChild> tag requires just one attribute, called target. The target attribute allows you to specify a reference to a component you want to remove. Example 10-5 has two checkboxes in the base state. The noCheckboxes state uses the <mx:RemoveChild> tag to remove both checkboxes.

Example 10-5. Removing a component

```
<?xml version="1.0" encoding="utf-8"?>
<mx:Application xmlns:mx="http://www.adobe.com/2006/mxml" layout="absolute">
    <mx:states>
        <mx:State name="noCheckboxes">
            <mx:RemoveChild target="{checkbox1}" />
            <mx:RemoveChild target="{checkbox2}" />
        </mx:State>
    </mx:states>
    <mx:VBox id="vbox">
        <mx:CheckBox id="checkbox1" label="One" />
        <mx:CheckBox id="checkbox2" label="Two" />
        <mx:Button id="button" label="Click" click="currentState='noCheckboxes'" />
    </mx:VBox>
</mx:Application>
```

Setting Properties

Using the <mx:SetProperty> tag you can set the property value for any component existing within the state. For example, you can set the text for a label, toggle the enabled property for a text input, change the x and y coordinates for a box, or even apply a filter, such as a blur effect. The <mx:SetProperty> tag requires target, name, and value attributes. The target attribute value needs to be a reference to the object to which you want to apply the new property value. The name attribute allows you to specify the name of the property you want to set. The value attribute allows you to specify the value you want to assign to the property. Example 10-6 uses two buttons to toggle between the base state and a state that enables a text input.

Example 10-6. Setting properties

```
<?xml version="1.0" encoding="utf-8"?>
<mx:Application xmlns:mx="http://www.adobe.com/2006/mxml" layout="absolute">
    <mx:states>
        <mx:State name="enabled">
            <mx:SetProperty target="{textinput}" name="enabled" value="{true}" />
        </mx:State>
    </mx:states>
    <mx:HBox id="hbox">
        <mx:Button id="enableButton" label="Enable" click="currentState='enabled'" />
        <mx:Button id="disableButton" label="Disable" click="currentState=null" />
        <mx:TextInput id="textinput" enabled="false" text="example text" />
    </mx:HBox>
</mx:Application>
```

Setting Styles

Use the `<mx:SetStyle>` tag to set styles for components when defining states. You set styles when you want to change the appearance (such as the color or font) of a component when its state changes. The `<mx:SetStyle>` tag has the same attributes as the `<mx:SetProperty>` tag. The target property allows you to reference the component to which you want to apply the style, the name attribute allows you to specify the style you want to set, and the value attribute allows you to set the value of the style.

Example 10-7 uses three buttons to toggle among three states. Each state sets the color styles of checkboxes to highlight groups of transportation types (land, air, and water). For example, when the user clicks the Land button, the car, train, and motorcycle checkbox labels are displayed using a red font.

Example 10-7. Setting styles

```
<?xml version="1.0" encoding="utf-8"?>
<mx:Application xmlns:mx="http://www.adobe.com/2006/mxml" layout="absolute">
    <mx:states>
        <mx:State name="landState">
            <mx:SetStyle target="{car}" name="color" value="0xFF0000" />
            <mx:SetStyle target="{train}" name="color" value="0xFF0000" />
            <mx:SetStyle target="{motorcycle}" name="color" value="0xFF0000" />
        </mx:State>
        <mx:State name="airState">
            <mx:SetStyle target="{helicopter}" name="color" value="0xFF0000" />
            <mx:SetStyle target="{airplane}" name="color" value="0xFF0000" />
        </mx:State>
        <mx:State name="waterState">
            <mx:SetStyle target="{boat}" name="color" value="0xFF0000" />
            <mx:SetStyle target="{submarine}" name="color" value="0xFF0000" />
        </mx:State>
    </mx:states>
    <mx:VBox id="vbox">
        <mx:HBox>
            <mx:Button id="land" label="Land" click="currentState='landState'" />
            <mx:Button id="air" label="Air" click="currentState='airState'" />
            <mx:Button id="water" label="Water" click="currentState='waterState'" />
        </mx:HBox>
        <mx:CheckBox id="helicopter" label="Helicopter" />
        <mx:CheckBox id="motorcycle" label="Motorcycle" />
        <mx:CheckBox id="car" label="Car" />
        <mx:CheckBox id="airplane" label="Airplane" />
        <mx:CheckBox id="train" label="Train" />
        <mx:CheckBox id="boat" label="Boat" />
        <mx:CheckBox id="submarine" label="Submarine" />
    </mx:VBox>
</mx:Application>
```

Setting Event Handlers

Use the `<mx:SetEventHandler>` tag to add or change an event handler for a component. The tag requires that you specify values for `target`, `name`, and `handler` attributes. The `target` attribute value needs to be a reference to the component for which you want to add or change an event handler. The `name` attribute value needs to be the name of the event handler. The `handler` attribute specifies the new event handler.

Example 10-8 modifies Example 10-6 so that it uses one button rather than two to toggle the enabled state of a text input. It does this by changing the event handler for the button (as well as the label) when it is clicked.

Example 10-8. Setting event handlers

```
<?xml version="1.0" encoding="utf-8"?>
<mx:Application xmlns:mx="http://www.adobe.com/2006/mxml" layout="absolute">
    <mx:states>
        <mx:State name="enabled">
            <mx:SetProperty target="{textinput}" name="enabled" value="{true}" />
            <mx:SetEventHandler target="{button}" name="click"
                handler="currentState=''" />
            <mx:SetProperty target="{button}" name="label" value="Disable" />
        </mx:State>
    </mx:states>
    <mx:HBox id="hbox">
        <mx:Button id="button" label="Enable" click="currentState='enabled'" />
        <mx:TextInput id="textinput" enabled="false" text="example text" />
    </mx:HBox>
</mx:Application>
```

Note that the `SetEventHandler` tag does not overwrite existing event handlers. Rather, it adds a new event handler to the queue of existing event handlers.

Using ActionScript to Define States

In most cases, it's more appropriate to use MXML than ActionScript to define states. However, sometimes you want to define states dynamically (in which case, you must use ActionScript). One such example is when you want to define a multipage form based on data loaded at runtime. Creating the form dynamically is advantageous because you can change the form without recompiling and republishing the SWF. However, because form elements aren't known at compile time, you cannot use MXML to define the states.

The ActionScript used to work with states corresponds to the MXML. In the following sections, you'll learn about the ActionScript equivalents to the MXML you learned about earlier.

Defining States

When defining states using ActionScript, you use the `mx.states.State` class. You can use the constructor as part of a new statement to define a new `State` instance:

```
var stateA:State = new State();
```

You can assign a name to a state using the `name` property, in much the same way as you'd use the `name` attribute of the `<mx:State>` tag:

```
stateA.name = "exampleStateA";
```

And just as you can use the `basedOn` attribute of the `<mx:State>` tag to define state inheritance, you can use the `basedOn` property of the `State` class. The following code defines a new state that is based on the state constructed in the previous two code snippets. Note that the `basedOn` property expects a string specifying the `name` of the state upon which you want to base the new state; you cannot assign it a reference to the `State` object.

```
var stateB:State = new State();
stateB.name = "exampleStateB";
stateB.basedOn = "exampleStateA";
```

Adding States

With MXML, you use the `<mx:states>` tag to define an array of states for an application or component. With ActionScript, you use the `states` property. The `states` property is defined in `UIComponent`, and it is inherited by all applications and components. The data type of `states` is `Array`, but by default, the property has a value of `null`. If you want to add states to an application or component using only Action-Script, you must first instantiate an array, as follows:

```
states = new Array();
```

Once defined, add states to the array:

```
states.push(stateA);
states.push(stateB);
```

Adding Overrides

As you'll read in the next few sections, you can define overrides (e.g., `AddChild` and `SetProperty`) using ActionScript. However, in addition to defining the overrides, you also must add the overrides to a state. Using MXML, you simply nest the override tags within the `<mx:State>` tag. With ActionScript, you must use the `overrides` property of the `State` class.

The overrides property is defined as an array data type. However, by default, the overrides property value of a `State` object is undefined. Therefore, you must first define the overrides property as an array before you can add overrides to a state using ActionScript:

```
stateA.overrides = new Array();
```

Once you've defined the overrides property as an array, you can add overrides to the array:

```
stateA.overrides.push(exampleAddChild);
```

Adding and Removing Child Elements

You can add and remove child elements in MXML using the <mx:AddChild> and <mx:RemoveChild> tags. The corresponding ActionScript classes are mx.states. AddChild and mx.states.RemoveChild.

When you want to add child elements using the AddChild class, you must first construct a new instance:

```
var addChild:AddChild = new AddChild();
```

When using MXML, nest the component tag within the <mx:AddChild> tag. When using ActionScript, you must assign a component reference to the target property of the AddChild object:

```
var button:Button = new Button();
button.label = "Example";
addChild.target = button;
```

If you want to specify a parent, you can use the relativeTo property. Simply assign a reference to the relativeTo component:

```
addChild.relativeTo = vbox;
```

Also, just as you can specify where you want to add the child element using the position attribute of the <mx:AddChild> tag, you can use the position property of the AddChild class. The property accepts the same values (firstChild, lastChild, before, and after) as the corresponding attribute. The values have the same effects as when working with MXML. When you specify a value of firstChild or lastChild, the child element is added as a child of the target. When you specify a value of before or after, the child element is added as a sibling of the target. If you don't specify any value or you assign a value of null, the default behavior is that the component is added as the last child of the target:

```
addChild.position = "firstChild";
```

When you want to remove a child element, use the RemoveChild object and specify the child using the target property:

```
var removeChild:RemoveChild = new RemoveChild();
removeChild.target = button;
```

Setting Properties and Styles

To set properties and styles with ActionScript you use the `mx.states.SetProperty` and `mx.states.SetStyle` classes. Each class has properties that correspond exactly to the attributes of the `<mx:SetProperty>` and `<mx:SetStyle>` tags. Both classes define `target`, `name`, and `value` properties. To simplify things you can also pass the `target`, `name`, and `value` to the constructors. The following examples illustrate how to use the `SetProperty` and `SetStyle` classes:

```
var setProperty:SetProperty = new SetProperty(button, "width", 200);
var setStyle:SetStyle = new SetStyle(button, "color", 0xFF00FF);
```

Setting Event Handlers

The `mx.states.SetEventHandler` class corresponds to the `<mx:SetEventHandler>` tag for setting event handlers. The class defines target and name properties that correspond to the target and name attributes of the `<mx:SetEventHandler>` tag. To make things even simpler, the `SetEventHandler` constructor allows you to pass the target and name parameters:

```
var setEventHandler:SetEventHandler = new SetEventHandler(button, "click");
```

When you use the `<mx:SetEventHandler>` tag, you use the `handler` attribute to specify the ActionScript to call when the event occurs. However, when working with a `SetEventHandler` object, you use the `handlerFunction` property. The `handlerFunction` property requires a reference to a function/method. Flash Player then calls that function/method when the event occurs. The following instructs Flash Player to call a function named `clickHandler` when the user clicks the button:

```
setEventHandler.handlerFunction = clickHandler;
```

Using Dynamic States

To better understand how to use ActionScript's dynamic states created at runtime, let's look at an example. Example 10-9 builds a multipage form from XML data and loads it at runtime. The form is composed of states for each page.

For the purposes of this example, the following XML data is used and saved in a file called *forms.xml*.

Example 10-9. forms.xml

```
<forms>
    <form id="1" label="Name">
        <item type="textinput" name="firstName" label="First Name" />
        <item type="textinput" name="lastName" label="Last Name" />
    </form>
    <form id="2" label="Address">
        <item type="textinput" name="address" label="Street Address" />
        <item type="textinput" name="city" label="City" />
```

Example 10-9. forms.xml (continued)

```
        <item type="textinput" name="state" label="State" />
        <item type="textinput" name="postalCode" label="Postal Code" />
    </form>
    <form id="3" label="Phone and Email">
        <item type="textinput" name="phone" label="Phone Number" />
        <item type="textinput" name="email" label="Email" />
    </form>
    <form id="4" label="Address">
        <item type="textarea" name="agreement" label="">
        Example Corporation reserves all rights.
        </item>
        <item type="checkbox" itemName="city" label="I agree" />
    </form>
</forms>
```

To work with the data, you can define several classes: CustomFormItem, CustomForm, and CustomFormManager.

The CustomFormItem class can be used to represent an item from the form. An item can consist of a label and a form control such as a text input, text area, or checkbox. Example 10-10 defines the CustomFormItem class.

Example 10-10. CustomFormItem.as

```
package com.oreilly.programmingflex.states {

    public class CustomFormItem {

        private var _type:String;
        private var _label:String;
        private var _name:String;
        private var _value:String;

        public function CustomFormItem(type:String, label:String,
                                       name:String, value:String) {
            _type = type;
            _label = label;
            _name = name;
            _value = value;
        }

        public function getType():String {
            return _type;
        }

        public function getLabel():String {
            return _label;
        }

        public function getName():String {
            return _name;
        }
```

Example 10-10. CustomFormItem.as (continued)

```
    public function getValue( ):String {
        return _value;
    }

    public static function parseFromXML(xml:XML):CustomFormItem {
        var type:String = xml.@type;
        var label:String = xml.@label;
        var name:String = xml.@itemName;
        var value:String = null;
        if(type == "textarea") {
            value = xml.children()[0].toString( );
        }
        return new CustomFormItem(type, label, name, value);
    }


    }
}
```

The CustomForm class (Example 10-11) is essentially a collection of form items with the addition of a method that constructs a new state based on the form.

Example 10-11. CustomForm.as

```
package com.oreilly.programmingflex.states {

    import mx.states.State;
    import mx.containers.GridRow;
    import mx.containers.GridItem;
    import mx.controls.Label;
    import mx.core.UIComponent;
    import mx.controls.TextInput;
    import mx.controls.CheckBox;
    import mx.controls.TextArea;
    import mx.states.AddChild;
    import com.oreilly.programmingflex.states.CustomFormItem;
    import mx.containers.Grid;

    public class CustomForm {

        private var _label:String;
        private var _items:Array;

        public function CustomForm(label:String, items:Array) {
            _label = label;
            _items = items;
        }

        public function getLabel( ):String {
            return _label;
        }
```

Example 10-11. CustomForm.as (continued)

```
public function getItems():Array {
    return _items.concat();
}

public function toState(parent:Grid):State {
    var state:State = new State();
    state.overrides = new Array();
    var gridRow:GridRow;
    var gridItem:GridItem;
    var count:uint = _items.length;
    var i:uint;
    var type:String;
    var label:Label;
    var component:UIComponent;
    var item:com.oreilly.programmingflex.states.CustomFormItem;
    var addChild:AddChild;
    for(i = 0; i < count; i++) {
        item = _items[i];
        gridRow = new GridRow();
        type = item.getType();
        if(type != "checkbox" && item.getLabel().length > 0) {
            label = new Label();
            label.text = item.getLabel();
            gridItem = new GridItem();
            gridItem.addChild(label);
            gridRow.addChild(gridItem);
        }
        if(type == "textinput") {
            component = new TextInput();
        }
        else if(type == "checkbox") {
            component = new CheckBox();
            CheckBox(component).label = item.getLabel();
        }
        else if(type == "textarea") {
            component = new TextArea();
            component.width = 200;
            TextArea(component).text = _items[i].getValue();
        }
        component.id = "component";
        gridItem = new GridItem();
        gridItem.addChild(component);
        gridRow.addChild(gridItem);
        addChild = new AddChild();
        addChild.relativeTo = parent;
        addChild.target = gridRow;
        state.overrides.push(addChild);
    }
    return state;
}
```

Example 10-11. CustomForm.as (continued)

```
    public static function parseFromXML(xml:XML):CustomForm {
        var label:String = xml.@label;
        var items:Array = new Array( );
        var i:uint;
        for(i = 0; i < xml.children().length( ); i++) {
            items.push(CustomFormItem.parseFromXML(xml.children( )[i]));
        }
        return new CustomForm(label, items);
    }


  }
}
```

The CustomFormManager class (Example 10-12) is a Singleton class that loads the XML data and provides an interface to a collection of forms.

Example 10-12. CustomFormManager.as

```
package com.oreilly.programmingflex.states {

    import flash.events.Event;
    import flash.events.ProgressEvent;
    import flash.events.IOErrorEvent;
    import flash.net.URLRequest;
    import flash.net.URLLoader;
    import flash.events.EventDispatcher;

    public class CustomFormManager extends EventDispatcher {

        private static var _instance:CustomFormManager;

        private var _forms:Array;
        private var _index:uint;

        public function CustomFormManager(enforcer:SingletonEnforcer) {
        }

        public static function getInstance( ):CustomFormManager {
            if(_instance == null) {
                _instance = new CustomFormManager(new SingletonEnforcer( ));
            }
            return _instance;
        }

        public function load(url:String):void {
            var request:URLRequest = new URLRequest(url);
            var loader:URLLoader = new URLLoader( );
            loader.load(request);
            loader.addEventListener(Event.COMPLETE, dataHandler);
        }
```

Example 10-12. CustomFormManager.as (continued)

```
        public function hasNextForm( ):Boolean {
            return _index < _forms.length;
        }

        public function getNextForm( ):CustomForm {
            if(_index >= _forms.length) {
                return null;
            }
            return _forms[_index++];
        }

        public function hasPreviousForm( ):Boolean {
            return _index > 0;
        }

        public function getPreviousForm( ):CustomForm {
            if(_index < 0) {
                return null;
            }
            return _forms[_index--];
        }

        private function dataHandler(event:Event):void {
            _index = 0;
            _forms = new Array( );
            var xml:XML = new XML(event.target.data);
            var forms:XMLList = xml.children( );
            var i:uint;
            var form:CustomForm;
            for(i = 0; i < forms.length( ); i++) {
                form = CustomForm.parseFromXML(forms[i]);
                _forms.push(form);
            }
            dispatchEvent(new Event(Event.COMPLETE));
        }

    }
}
class SingletonEnforcer {}
```

The MXML (with embedded ActionScript) in Example 10-13 illustrates how to use the preceding code to construct dynamic states based on XML data.

Example 10-13. Dynamic states

```
<?xml version="1.0" encoding="utf-8"?>
<mx:Application xmlns:mx="http://www.adobe.com/2006/mxml" layout="absolute"
initialize="initializeHandler(event)">
    <mx:Script>
        <![CDATA[
            import mx.states.SetProperty;
            import mx.states.SetEventHandler;
```

Example 10-13. Dynamic states (continued)

```
import mx.states.State;
import com.oreilly.programmingflex.states.CustomForm;

import com.oreilly.programmingflex.states.CustomFormManager;

private var _stateIndex:uint;
private var _stateCount:uint;

private function initializeHandler(event:Event):void {
    var formManager:CustomFormManager = CustomFormManager.getInstance( );
    formManager.load("forms.xml");
    formManager.addEventListener(Event.COMPLETE, dataHandler);
}

private function dataHandler(event:Event):void {
    _stateIndex = 1;
    _stateCount = 0;
    var formManager:CustomFormManager = CustomFormManager.getInstance( );
    var form:CustomForm;
    states = new Array( );
    var state:State;
    var index:uint = 1;
    var setProperty:SetProperty;
    var hasPreviousForm:Boolean;
    while(formManager.hasNextForm( )) {
        hasPreviousForm = formManager.hasPreviousForm( );
        _stateCount++;
        form = formManager.getNextForm( );
        state = form.toState(grid);
        setProperty = new SetProperty(next, "visible",
          formManager.hasNextForm( ));
        state.overrides.push(setProperty);
        setProperty = new SetProperty(previous, "visible",
          hasPreviousForm);
        state.overrides.push(setProperty);
        state.name = "form" + index++;
        states.push(state);
    }
    currentState = "form1";
}

private function nextForm( ):void {
    currentState = "form" + ++_stateIndex;
}

private function previousForm( ):void {
    currentState = "form" + --_stateIndex;
}

        ]]>
    </mx:Script>
    <mx:VBox id="vbox">
        <mx:Label id="formLabel" />
```

Example 10-13. Dynamic states (continued)

```
        <mx:HBox>
            <mx:Button id="previous" label="Previous" visible="false"
                click="previousForm( )" />
            <mx:Button id="next" label="Next" click="nextForm( )" />
        </mx:HBox>
        <mx:Grid id="grid">
        </mx:Grid>
    </mx:VBox>
</mx:Application>
```

Managing Object Creation Policies (Preloading Objects)

By default, components added by nonbase states aren't instantiated until the state is first requested. The MXML in Example 10-14 illustrates this. The trace( ) statement outputs null because button is not yet defined when the application first starts.

Example 10-14. Understanding object creation policies: default policy

```
<?xml version="1.0" encoding="utf-8"?>
<mx:Application xmlns:mx="http://www.adobe.com/2006/mxml" layout="absolute"
initialize="initializeHandler(event)">
    <mx:states>
        <mx:State name="example">
            <mx:AddChild>
                <mx:Button id="button" label="Example" />
            </mx:AddChild>
        </mx:State>
    </mx:states>
    <mx:Script>
        <![CDATA[

            private function initializeHandler(event:Event):void {
                trace(button);
            }

        ]]>
    </mx:Script>
</mx:Application>
```

However, you can manage when components added by states are instantiated using a creation policy. The default creation policy setting is auto, which means the component is instantiated when the state is first requested. You can set creation policies for each added component using the creationPolicy attribute of the <mx:AddChild> tag, or the creationPolicy property of the AddChild class. The possible values are auto (default), all, and none.

When you set the creation policy of an added component to all, the component is instantiated when the application first starts. The MXML in Example 10-15 illustrates how that works. Because the creation policy of the button is now set to all, the trace( ) statement outputs the reference to the component.

Example 10-15. Understanding object creation policies: policy all

```xml
<?xml version="1.0" encoding="utf-8"?>
<mx:Application xmlns:mx="http://www.adobe.com/2006/mxml" layout="absolute"
initialize="initializeHandler(event)">
    <mx:states>
        <mx:State name="example">
            <mx:AddChild creationPolicy="all">
                <mx:Button id="button" label="Example" />
            </mx:AddChild>
        </mx:State>
    </mx:states>
    <mx:Script>
        <![CDATA[

            private function initializeHandler(event:Event):void {
                trace(button);
            }

        ]]>
    </mx:Script>
</mx:Application>
```

When the creation policy is set to none, the component isn't instantiated until you explicitly call the createInstance( ) method of the AddChild object. If you're defining the AddChild object using the <mx:AddChild> tag, you must assign an id. Example 10-16 illustrates how the none creation policy works. The first trace( ) statement outputs null because the component hasn't been instantiated. The second trace( ) statement outputs the reference to the component because it is called immediately following the call to createInstance( ).

Example 10-16. Understanding object creation policy: policy none

```xml
<?xml version="1.0" encoding="utf-8"?>
<mx:Application xmlns:mx="http://www.adobe.com/2006/mxml" layout="absolute"
initialize="initializeHandler(event)">
    <mx:states>
        <mx:State name="example">
            <mx:AddChild creationPolicy="none" id="exampleAddChild">
                <mx:Button id="button" label="Example" />
            </mx:AddChild>
        </mx:State>
    </mx:states>
    <mx:Script>
        <![CDATA[

            private function initializeHandler(event:Event):void {
                trace(button);
                exampleAddChild.createInstance( );
                trace(button);
            }

        ]]>
    </mx:Script>
</mx:Application>
```

In most applications, the default (auto) creation policy is the correct setting. However, there are several reasons you might want to select a different creation policy. The all policy, for example, is useful in at least two scenarios:

The added component requires a long time to initialize
If the component isn't initialized until the state is requested, the user might experience a delay. By setting the policy to all, the component is initialized when the application first starts; that should mitigate any issues related to component initialization times and delays when changing states.

You want to reference the added component before first requesting the state
For example, when you create a component with several states, you might want to reference added components via an accessor method.

The none policy may not seem immediately useful; however, consider that the auto and all policies are very black and white:

- When you select auto, components aren't instantiated until the state is requested.

- When you select all, components are instantiated when the application initializes.

There are reasons you might want to ensure that a component initializes before a state is requested, but you don't want to force the component to instantiate when the application initializes. For example, a complex application might contain many states, each of which has components that take a long time to initialize. If you set the creation policy of all the AddChild objects to all, the user might have to wait a long time before the application initializes. However, it might be a better user experience if the application starts right away while the components for the rest of the states initialize in the background. Using the none creation policy allows you to do just that. Simply call the createInstance() method of the AddChild object to instantiate the child component.

Handling State Events

Four events are associated with state changes:

- When a state change is requested, the application or component containing the state dispatches a currentStateChanging event. The event occurs before the state actually changes.

- Once the state has changed, the application or component dispatches a currentStateChanged event. Both events are of type mx.events.StateChangeEvent (use the constants CURRENT_STATE_CHANGING and CURRENT_STATE_CHANGED to add listeners). Neither event is cancelable, which means you cannot prevent a state change from occurring by canceling a currentStateChanging event, for example. Rather, both events are used primarily by the transitions framework to detect when a transition should occur.

- The `enterState` and `exitState` events occur when the state starts and stops:
  - The `enterState` event occurs as soon as the state has started but before it is applied to the view.
  - The `exitState` event occurs as soon as the state is about to stop.

  Both events are of type `mx.events.FlexEvent` (use the constants `ENTER_STATE` and `EXIT_STATE` to add listeners).
- The `enterState` event is dispatched by a `State` object when the state starts, and by an application or component when returning to the base state. The `exitState` event is dispatched by a `State` object when the state stops, and by an application or component when exiting the base state.

When to Use States

States are a powerful and extremely useful feature of the Flex framework. You can accomplish many things using states. In fact, you can use states for so many things that it's possible to use them in ways for which they are not really designed. States are very closely associated with the view, so they should be used for things that affect the view or changes in behavior associated with the view (in the case of setting event handlers). Although you could easily use states to change data models, for example, it's not an appropriate use. To better understand the most appropriate use of states, consider the following guidelines for when to use them:

For applying a transition effect
  If you want to use a transition, you ought to use states.

For changing or replacing all or part of a screen
  If you're adding or removing components, states are usually the most appropriate choice.

There are some gray areas that make states an unlikely choice. For example, you might have a form with a text input control that is disabled until the user selects a checkbox. You *could* use states for that, but unless you want to apply a transition, it is probably much more appropriate to simply use ActionScript triggered by the `click` event of the checkbox.

Summary

In this chapter, you learned about Flex view states. You learned what they are and how to create them. States consist of overrides, which are the parts of a state that specify how the state differs from another state. Overrides frequently consist of things such as adding and removing components as well as setting styles, properties, and event listeners.

CHAPTER 11

Using Effects and Transitions

Flex applications always consist of one or more user interface and/or container components. At a minimum, a Flex application has an application container, but usually it has many additional components. Although the default behavior for components is fairly static, you can liven up an application with the use of effects. An *effect* is an action that takes place, such as moving, fading, or zooming into or out of a component. An effect can even be a nonvisual behavior, such as playing a sound. Using effects, you can create applications that are more visually (and audibly) interesting. Perhaps more importantly, you can use effects to direct focus and help users better understand how to use applications.

Another way in which you can use effects is to create transitions between states. In Chapter 10, you learned about creating state views. However, so far in the book you've learned how to create only sudden state changes. Using effects as transitions, you can create more interesting and seamless changes between states. For example, rather than an added component suddenly appearing, it can fade in. Not only does this generally create a more visually engaging user experience, but also effects can be used to show emphasis and to highlight change.

In this chapter, we'll look at how to work with effects and transitions. We'll discuss how to trigger effects, how to programmatically control effects, and even how to create custom effects. We'll also discuss how to use an effect as a transition between states, as well as how to create custom transition types.

Using Effects

Effects are actions that you can apply to components. Common examples of effects are fades, moves, and zooms. The Flex framework includes many standard effects, as you'll see later in Table 11-1. However, you are not limited to using those effects exclusively. You can also create composite effects both in sequence (e.g., fade, then move) and in parallel (e.g., fade and move). You can also write custom effects using ActionScript. These custom effects can then be used in exactly the same ways as standard effects.

Working with Effects

In order to use an effect you, must first create an instance of the effect. There are two basic ways to create an effect instance: using MXML or using ActionScript. We'll look at each technique.

MXML is arguably the most common way to create an effect instance. You need merely to add a tag of the appropriate type and give it an ID. You should place the tag as a child of the root document element. For example, you can place the tag as a child of an Application tag. The tag should never be nested within other tags (i.e., within other child components). The following example creates a new move effect instance:

```
<mx:Move id="moveEffect" />
```

Table 11-1 lists all the standard effects.

Table 11-1. Standard effects

Effect	Description
Blur	Animate a blur.
Move	Animate the motion of a component in the x and/or y direction.
Fade	Animate the alpha value of a component.
Dissolve	Animate the alpha value of a rectangular overlay.
Glow	Apply a glow to a component, and animate the appearance/disappearance of the glow.
Resize	Animate the width and height of a component.
Rotate	Rotate a component.
Zoom	Animate the x and y scales of a component.
WipeLeft WipeRight WipeUp WipeDown	Apply a mask that moves to reveal or hide a component.
Iris	Apply a mask that scales to hide or reveal a component.
AnimateProperty	You can use this effect to animate any numeric property of a component.

Each of the effects in Table 11-1 has a different set of properties that you can set to customize the effect. For example, by default a move effect moves both to and from the component's current location. The result is that the effect doesn't seem to do anything. However, you can specify the xFrom, xTo, yFrom, and/or yTo property to affect how the component will move. The following example creates an effect that moves the component along the x-axis from −100 to the current x coordinate value:

```
<mx:Move id="moveEffect" xFrom="-100" />
```

You can also construct effects using the appropriate constructor as part of a new statement. For example, the following code creates a new Move instance:

```
private var moveEffect:Move = new Move();
```

Regardless of how you construct the effect instance, you can set the properties using ActionScript:

```
moveEffect.xFrom = -100;
```

Playing Effects

There are two ways in which you can play effects: using the play( ) method or using a trigger. We'll look at the play( ) method first because it is the most straightforward way to use an effect. Then we'll look at using triggers.

Manually playing effects

You can use the play( ) method of an effect to manually play the effect. In order for an effect to play, it must have a target to which it applies the settings. For example, if you have created a move effect instance that is supposed to move a component from −100 to its current location, you must tell it what component to use as the target. You can accomplish that using the target property:

```
moveEffect.target = textInput;
```

You can then use the play( ) method to start the playback of the effect:

```
moveEffect.play( );
```

Example 11-1 uses a move effect and applies it to four text input controls when they are created.

Example 11-1. Applying a simple effect

```
<?xml version="1.0" encoding="utf-8"?>
<mx:Application xmlns:mx="http://www.adobe.com/2006/mxml" layout="absolute">

    <mx:Script>
        <![CDATA[

            private function applyEffect(event:Event):void {
                moveEffect.target = event.currentTarget;
                moveEffect.play( );
            }

        ]]>
    </mx:Script>

    <mx:Move id="moveEffect" xFrom="-100" />

    <mx:VBox>
        <mx:TextInput id="textInput1" creationComplete="applyEffect(event)" />
        <mx:TextInput id="textInput2" creationComplete="applyEffect(event)" />
        <mx:TextInput id="textInput3" creationComplete="applyEffect(event)" />
        <mx:TextInput id="textInput4" creationComplete="applyEffect(event)" />
    </mx:VBox>

</mx:Application>
```

In this example, the text inputs each appear to slide from the left.

You can also specify more than one target at one time for an effect, using the `targets` property. With the `targets` property, you can specify an array of targets to which the effect should be applied. In Example 11-2, the result is visually identical to the preceding code, but this time the effect is played just once rather than four times.

Example 11-2. Applying an effect to many targets

```
<?xml version="1.0" encoding="utf-8"?>
<mx:Application xmlns:mx="http://www.adobe.com/2006/mxml" layout="absolute">

    <mx:Script>
        <![CDATA[

            private function applyEffect(event:Event):void {
                moveEffect.targets = [textInput1, textInput2, textInput3, textInput4];
                moveEffect.play();
            }

        ]]>
    </mx:Script>

    <mx:Move id="moveEffect" xFrom="-100" />

    <mx:VBox creationComplete="applyEffect(event)">
        <mx:TextInput id="textInput1" />
        <mx:TextInput id="textInput2" />
        <mx:TextInput id="textInput3" />
        <mx:TextInput id="textInput4" />
    </mx:VBox>

</mx:Application>
```

It's also worth noting that you can apply an effect to a container. In the case of the move effect applied in the preceding examples, it would be much simpler to apply the effect to the VBox instance, as shown in Example 11-3.

Example 11-3. Applying an effect to a container

```
<?xml version="1.0" encoding="utf-8"?>
<mx:Application xmlns:mx="http://www.adobe.com/2006/mxml" layout="absolute">

    <mx:Script>
        <![CDATA[

            private function applyEffect(event:Event):void {
                moveEffect.target = vbox;
                moveEffect.play();
            }

        ]]>
    </mx:Script>
```

Example 11-3. Applying an effect to a container (continued)

```
    <mx:Move id="moveEffect" xFrom="-100" />

    <mx:VBox id="vbox" creationComplete="applyEffect(event)">
        <mx:TextInput id="textInput1" />
        <mx:TextInput id="textInput2" />
        <mx:TextInput id="textInput3" />
        <mx:TextInput id="textInput4" />
    </mx:VBox>

</mx:Application>
```

However, note that this works only when the result of the effect is the same when applied to the container as when applied to the child components. The preceding examples have the same visual result because the effect (move) works identically if applied to the container or the child components. This is not true for all effects; for example, a rotate effect will have a different result if applied to a container or if applied to the child components. The code in Example 11-4 applies a rotate effect first to the individual child components.

Example 11-4. Applying a rotate effect to individual components

```
<?xml version="1.0" encoding="utf-8"?>
<mx:Application xmlns:mx="http://www.adobe.com/2006/mxml" layout="absolute">

    <mx:Script>
        <![CDATA[

            private function applyEffect(event:Event):void {
                rotateEffect.target = event.currentTarget;
                rotateEffect.originX = event.currentTarget.width / 2;
                rotateEffect.originY = event.currentTarget.height / 2;
                rotateEffect.play();
            }

        ]]>
    </mx:Script>

    <mx:Rotate id="rotateEffect" />

    <!-- Set clipContent to false so that the components aren't masked
        while rotating -->
    <mx:VBox id="vbox" x="400" y="400" clipContent="false">
        <mx:TextInput id="textInput1" creationComplete="applyEffect(event)" />
        <mx:TextInput id="textInput2" creationComplete="applyEffect(event)" />
        <mx:TextInput id="textInput3" creationComplete="applyEffect(event)" />
        <mx:TextInput id="textInput4" creationComplete="applyEffect(event)" />
    </mx:VBox>

</mx:Application>
```

When applied this way, the individual text inputs rotate independently, each around their own center point. In Example 11-5, we'll use the same effect, but we'll apply it to the VBox instance instead.

Example 11-5. Applying a rotate effect to a container

```
<?xml version="1.0" encoding="utf-8"?>
<mx:Application xmlns:mx="http://www.adobe.com/2006/mxml" layout="absolute">

    <mx:Script>
        <![CDATA[

            private function applyEffect(event:Event):void {
                rotateEffect.target = event.currentTarget;
                rotateEffect.originX = event.currentTarget.width / 2;
                rotateEffect.originY = event.currentTarget.height / 2;
                rotateEffect.play();
            }

        ]]>
    </mx:Script>

    <mx:Rotate id="rotateEffect" />

    <mx:VBox id="vbox" x="400" y="400" clipContent="false"
creationComplete="applyEffect(event)">
        <mx:TextInput id="textInput1" />
        <mx:TextInput id="textInput2" />
        <mx:TextInput id="textInput3" />
        <mx:TextInput id="textInput4" />
    </mx:VBox>

</mx:Application>
```

This change causes the entire container to rotate, rather than each child component rotating independently.

Using triggers

Triggers occur within a Flex application to start an effect. Using triggers allows you to create and apply effects entirely with MXML. This is not necessarily better or worse than using the play( ) method. It is just a different way of applying effects.

 In Flex terminology, a trigger combined with an effect is called a *behavior*.

There are standard triggers available to all components. Table 11-2 lists these common triggers.

Table 11-2. Standard triggers

Trigger	Description
addedEffect	The component was added to the display list.
removedEffect	The component was removed from the display list.
creationCompleteEffect	The component has been created and initialized.
focusInEffect	The component has received focus.
focusOutEffect	The focus has moved from the component.
hideEffect	The component has been hidden (made not visible).
showEffect	The component has been shown (made visible).
rollOverEffect	The user has moved the mouse over the component.
rollOutEffect	The user has moved the mouse out of the component.
mouseDownEffect	The user has pressed the mouse button over the component.
mouseUpEffect	The user has released the mouse button over the component.
moveEffect	The x and/or y property of the component has changed.
resizeEffect	The width and/or height of the component has changed.

You can assign an effect instance to the trigger for a component, and the effect will be applied automatically when that trigger occurs. When you use triggers, you do not have to set a target for the effect. Instead, the target is automatically set when the effect is triggered. The following example uses triggers to apply a move effect to each of four text input controls as they are created:

```
<?xml version="1.0" encoding="utf-8"?>
<mx:Application xmlns:mx="http://www.adobe.com/2006/mxml" layout="absolute">

    <mx:Move id="moveEffect" xFrom="-100" />

    <mx:VBox>
        <mx:TextInput id="textInput1" creationCompleteEffect="{moveEffect}" />
        <mx:TextInput id="textInput2" creationCompleteEffect="{moveEffect}" />
        <mx:TextInput id="textInput3" creationCompleteEffect="{moveEffect}" />
        <mx:TextInput id="textInput4" creationCompleteEffect="{moveEffect}" />
    </mx:VBox>

</mx:Application>
```

Of course, you can apply effects to containers using triggers as well. The following example applies the move effect to the container rather than the child components:

```
<?xml version="1.0" encoding="utf-8"?>
<mx:Application xmlns:mx="http://www.adobe.com/2006/mxml" layout="absolute">

    <mx:Move id="moveEffect" xFrom="-100" />

    <mx:VBox creationCompleteEffect="{moveEffect}">
        <mx:TextInput id="textInput1" />
```

```
        <mx:TextInput id="textInput2" />
        <mx:TextInput id="textInput3" />
        <mx:TextInput id="textInput4" />
    </mx:VBox>

</mx:Application>
```

Oftentimes, triggers are the simplest way to apply an effect. As you can see, you typically need fewer lines of code to apply an effect using a trigger than you would need if you were using ActionScript. However, triggers typically work best for simple uses of effects. When you need to customize how the effect is applied, it can get more difficult to use triggers, and in those cases, it is typically better to use ActionScript.

Effect Events

All effects dispatch events that notify listeners when the effects start and when they end. Those events are called effectStart and effectEnd. The effect events are of type mx.events.EffectEvent. Example 11-6 illustrates how to use the effectEnd event to set the alpha of a container after it has moved from the left.

Example 11-6. Listening for an effectEnd event

```
<?xml version="1.0" encoding="utf-8"?>
<mx:Application xmlns:mx="http://www.adobe.com/2006/mxml" layout="absolute">

    <mx:Script>
        <![CDATA[
            import mx.events.EffectEvent;

            private function effectEndHandler(event:EffectEvent):void {
                // The initial alpha is .5. Once the effect is complete set the alpha to
1.
                vbox.alpha = 1;
            }

        ]]>
    </mx:Script>

    <mx:Move id="moveEffect" xFrom="-100" effectEnd="effectEndHandler(event)" />

    <mx:VBox id="vbox" alpha=".5" creationCompleteEffect="{moveEffect}">
        <mx:TextInput id="textInput1" />
        <mx:TextInput id="textInput2" />
        <mx:TextInput id="textInput3" />
        <mx:TextInput id="textInput4" />
    </mx:VBox>

</mx:Application>
```

The `EffectEvent` type inherits the standard event properties such as `target` and `currentTarget`. However, effects use factories to create the effect instances, and the `target` property of an `EffectEvent` object references the factory used to create the effect, not the effect instance. A factory is a programming construct that is responsible for creating objects. In this case, a `Move` object (or any other effect type) is a factory that creates the actual instances of the effect that get applied to components. If you need to retrieve a reference to the actual effect instance (rather than the factory), you can use the `effectInstance` property. Example 11-7 illustrates this by reversing a move effect once it has played.

Example 11-7. Reversing an effect

```
<?xml version="1.0" encoding="utf-8"?>
<mx:Application xmlns:mx="http://www.adobe.com/2006/mxml" layout="absolute">

    <mx:Script>
        <![CDATA[
            import mx.events.EffectEvent;

            private function effectEndHandler(event:EffectEvent):void {
                event.effectInstance.reverse();
                event.effectInstance.play();
            }

        ]]>
    </mx:Script>

    <mx:Move id="moveEffect" xFrom="-100" effectEnd="effectEndHandler(event)" />

    <mx:VBox creationCompleteEffect="{moveEffect}">
        <mx:TextInput id="textInput1" />
        <mx:TextInput id="textInput2" />
        <mx:TextInput id="textInput3" />
        <mx:TextInput id="textInput4" />
    </mx:VBox>

</mx:Application>
```

The preceding examples illustrate how to add a handler for an event using an attribute. Of course, you can also add a handler using ActionScript. With ActionScript you use `addEventListener` as you would normally when registering any listener for any event. In that case, you can use the `EffectEvent.EFFECT_START` and `EffectEvent.EFFECT_END` constants, as shown here:

```
moveEffect.addEventListener(EffectEvent.EFFECT_START, effectStartHandler);
moveEffect.addEventListener(EffectEvent.EFFECT_END, effectEndHandler);
```

All effects dispatch `effectStart` and `effectEnd` events. Most, though not all, also dispatch `tweenStart`, `tweenUpdate`, and `tweenEnd` events. The tween events are inherited by all subclasses of `TweenEffect` and `MaskEffect`, which include all the effects listed in Table 11-1. The only effects that don't dispatch tween events are composite effects (which are discussed in the next section).

Tween is a word carried over from Flash. Tween is short for *in between*, which refers to an animation technique in which starting and ending values are given, and the intermediate values are automatically calculated. The result is that an animation (such as a translation, scale, or rotation) can be achieved quite simply by providing just the starting and ending values along with a duration.

Tween events are of type `mx.events.TweenEvent`. The `tweenStart` event occurs as a tween begins, which is immediately after the `effectStart` event in most cases. The `tweenUpdate` event occurs for each change to the tweened property or properties. That means that there might be many `tweenUpdate` events. Then, once a tween effect has completed, it dispatches a `tweenEnd` event. The `tweenEnd` event always follows the last `tweenUpdate` event and precedes the `effectEnd` event.

The `TweenEvent` class defines a value property in addition to the inherited event properties. The value property contains the current value of the property or properties being changed over time. For example, for a rotate effect, the `TweenEvent` object's value property is a number corresponding to the current `rotation` property of the component being rotated. Yet if the effect affects more than one property, the value property of the `TweenEvent` object is an array of the values of the affected properties. For example, a move effect animates the x and y properties of a component. The `TweenEvent` dispatched by a move effect has a value property that is an array with two elements corresponding to the x and y values.

Composite Effects

Not only can you create simple effects using the standard effect types, but you also can create composite effects by combining them. There are two ways you can combine effects: in sequence or in parallel.

The Sequence component allows you to group together effects that you want to occur one after the other. For example, you can use a Sequence component to first apply a fade effect and then apply a move effect. From MXML, you can simply nest the effects you want to sequence within a Sequence tag, as follows:

```
<mx:Sequence id="sequenceEffect">
  <mx:Fade />
  <mx:Move xTo="100" />
</mx:Sequence>
```

Note that in the preceding example, the Sequence instance has the id attribute, indicating that you will only need to refer to the Sequence instance rather than the nested, sequenced effects:

```
<mx:TextInput creationCompleteEffect="{sequenceEffect}" />
```

You can add a pause between sequenced effects using a pause effect. You can affect the length of the pause by specifying a value (in milliseconds) for the duration property. The following example fades a target, pauses 1,000 milliseconds, and then moves the target:

```
<mx:Sequence id="sequenceEffect">
  <mx:Fade />
  <mx:Pause duration="1000" />
  <mx:Move xTo="100" />
</mx:Sequence>
```

The Parallel component allows you to group together effects that you want to play at the same time. For example, if you want to fade and move a component at the same time, you can use the following parallel effect:

```
<mx:Parallel id="parallelEffect">
  <mx:Fade />
  <mx:Move xFrom="-100" />
</mx:Parallel>
```

You can also nest composite effects within other composite effects. For example, the following will fade and move a target at the same time, pause for 1,000 milliseconds, and then rotate 360 degrees:

```
<mx:Sequence id="sequenceEffect">
  <mx:Parallel>
    <mx:Fade />
    <mx:Move xFrom="-100" />
  </mx:Parallel>
  <mx:Pause duration="1000" />
  <mx:Rotate />
</mx:Sequence>
```

You can also create composite effects using ActionScript. All the same rules apply to creating composite effects via ActionScript as when creating standard effects using ActionScript. The only difference is that you need a way to programmatically group effects within the composite effect. To accomplish that, use the addChild( ) method for the Parallel or Sequence object:

```
var sequenceEffect:Sequence = new Sequence( );
sequenceEffect.addChild(rotateEffect);
```

Note that although effects and display objects both have addChild( ) methods, you cannot add an effect to the display list, nor can you add a display object to an effect.

Pausing, Resuming, and Reversing Effects

By default, an effect plays straight through. However, you can pause, resume, and even reverse an effect. All effects have pause( ) and resume( ) methods that pause and resume the playback of an effect, respectively.

You can reverse the playback of an effect using the reverse( ) method. If you call the reverse( ) method while an effect is currently playing, it will reverse from that point and play back to the start. If the effect is not playing, calling the reverse( ) method will not play the effect, but it will configure the effect so that the next time it is triggered or played, it will play in reverse.

Delaying and Repeating Effects

When you want to delay an effect, you have several options depending on what you are trying to accomplish. If you want to wait to start an effect until a user or system event occurs, you should associate the effect with the correct trigger or you should call the effect's play( ) method in response to an event. If you want to add a timed delay before an effect starts after it's been triggered or played, you can specify a value for the startDelay property of the effect. The startDelay property allows you to specify how many milliseconds the effect will pause before playback starts. The default value is 0, which means there is no delay. The following example creates a fade effect that adds a 1,000-millisecond delay:

```
<mx:Fade id="fadeEffect" startDelay="1000" />
```

The repeatCount property allows you to repeat the effect. The default value is 1, which means the effect plays exactly once. If you specify a value greater than 1, the effect will repeat the specified number of times. For example, the following plays the fade effect twice:

```
<mx:Fade id="fadeEffect" repeatCount="2" />
```

If you specify a value of 0, the effect repeat untils you explicitly call the end( ) method.

You can add a delay between repeats using the repeatDelay property. The default value is 0. The value is interpreted as milliseconds.

Customizing Animation Easing

For all tween effects (blur, move, fade, glow, etc.), you can control the *easing* that gets applied to the effect. Easing refers to the rate at which the effect is applied. The default easing type is linear, meaning the effect is applied at a fixed rate from start to end. However, you may want to apply effects in a nonlinear fashion. You can apply custom easing to effects using the easingFunction property.

The easingFunction property allows you to assign a reference to a function that accepts four numeric parameters (playback time, initial value, total change in value, and duration of effect) and returns the new value to use. The effect then calls that function automatically every time it needs to update the value of a property for the target component. While you can certainly create custom easing functions, you may find it more convenient to try one of the many easing functions that are included in the Flex framework's mx.effects.easing package.

The `mx.effects.easing` package includes an assortment of classes such as `Cubic`, `Elastic`, `Exponential`, `Quadratic`, and so on. Each class has static methods called `easeIn`, `easeOut`, and `easeInOut`. You can reference these functions for use with effects. Here's an example that applies an elastic `easeOut` to a fade effect:

```
<mx:Fade id="fadeEffect" easingFunction="{mx.effects.easing.Elastic.easeOut}" />
```

Using Effects and Fonts

You can use effects with any UI component. However, if the component contains text (e.g., labels, text inputs, etc.), the fade and rotate effects will not work as intended unless you embed the font. By default, all text in UI controls uses system fonts rather than embedded fonts. Flash Player does not properly render text for system fonts if the font in the `alpha` property is set to anything other than 1 or if the `rotation` property is not 0. Because the fade effect changes the `alpha` property, and the rotate effect changes the `rotation` property, these effects will not work properly unless you embed the font. In the case of a fade effect, the text portion of the control will always be opaque. In the case of a rotate effect, the text will not be visible, except when the rotation is set to 0.

See Chapter 9 for more information about embedding fonts.

Creating Custom Effects

Although you can use standard effects and composite effects to solve most of the effects needs of an application, sometimes these off-the-shelf solutions won't achieve the intended result. For those cases, the Flex framework allows you to create your own custom effects that you can use exactly as you would use other standard effects.

Creating custom effects requires a more thorough understanding of the effect framework structure. Because working with effects is so simple, it's not necessary to look at the inner workings of the effect framework until you want to write a custom effect.

The effect framework consists of two basic types of classes: *effect factories* and *effect instances*. When you create a new effect object using MXML or ActionScript, you are working with an effect factory class. However, when the effect is applied to a component, the actual object utilized is an effect instance. The effect objects that you create using MXML and/or ActionScript using classes such as `Move` or `Resize` utilize a design pattern called the *Factory Method*. The Factory Method pattern means that the factory class is responsible for creating the effect instances, which are what are applied to the components.

Next we'll look at how to define factory and instance classes.

Defining an Effect Instance Class

The effect instance class is the one used as the blueprint for the actual objects that apply the effect to the components. You don't directly create instances of this class normally. That is handled by the factory class. For example, when you use a move effect, the actual effect object that is applied to a component is of type MoveInstance. You don't typically create a MoveInstance object directly. Rather, that instance is automatically created by the Move factory object. We'll look at how to create factories in the next section. First, let's look at how to create an effect instance class.

All effect instance classes must inherit from mx.effects.EffectInstance, and at a minimum, all EffectInstance subclasses must override the play( ) method, and the overridden play( ) method must also call the super.play( ) method. Additionally, all effect instance classes should have constructors that accept one parameter typed as Object. The parameter is the target for the effect instance that is automatically passed to the constructor when it is called by the factory. The constructor should call super( ) and pass it the parameter. Example 11-8 is a simple example that merely places a red dot in the upper-right corner of a component.

Example 11-8. FlagInstance class as an example of a custom effect instance

```
package com.oreilly.programmingflex.effects {
    import mx.effects.EffectInstance;
    import flash.display.Shape;

    // The class must extend EffectInstance.
    public class FlagInstance extends EffectInstance {

        // Allow for configuration of the color.
        private var _color:Number;

        public function set color(value:Number):void {
            _color = value;
        }

        public function get color( ):Number {
            return _color;
        }

        // The constructor must accept a parameter and pass that
        // along to the super constructor.
        public function FlagInstance(newTarget:Object) {
            super(newTarget);
        }

        // All effect instances must override play( ).
        override public function play( ):void {

            // Call the super.play( ) method.
            super.play( );
```

Example 11-8. FlagInstance class as an example of a custom effect instance (continued)

```
            // Create a shape with a red dot.
            var shape:Shape = new Shape();
            shape.graphics.lineStyle(0, 0, 0);
            shape.graphics.beginFill(_color, 1);
            shape.graphics.drawCircle(0, 0, 5);
            shape.graphics.endFill();

            // Move the shape to the upper right corner of the component.
            shape.x = target.x + target.width;
            shape.y = target.y;

            // Add the shape to the display list.
            target.parent.rawChildren.addChild(shape);
        }

    }
}
```

Defining an Effect Factory Class

All effect factory classes must extend the `mx.effects.Effect` class. When you subclass `Effect`, you must override the `getAffectedProperties()` and `initInstance()` methods, and you must assign a reference to the `instanceClass` property.

The `getAffectedProperties()` method should return an array of all the names of the properties affected. If the effect doesn't affect any properties, the method should return an empty array.

The `initInstance()` method should accept one parameter of type `EffectInstance`. It should always call `super.initInstance()`, and then it should set any properties of the instance necessary. For example, if you want to pass through any settings from the factory to the instance, you should do so in the `initInstance()` method.

The `instanceClass` property is a property inherited from `Effect` that determines what class is used by the factory to create instances. You must set the `instanceClass` property. Typically, you should do this in the constructor.

Example 11-9 is a simple factory class corresponding to the `FlagInstance` class from the preceding section.

Example 11-9. Flag class as an example of an effect

```
package com.oreilly.programmingflex.effects {
    import mx.effects.Effect;
    import mx.effects.EffectInstance;

    // All factory classes must inherit from Effect.
    public class Flag extends Effect {

        // Allow for the configuration of the color. Use a default of red.
        private var _color:Number = 0xFF0000;
```

Example 11-9. Flag class as an example of an effect (continued)

```
    public function set color(value:Number):void {
        _color = value;
    }

    public function get color( ):Number {
        return _color;
    }

    // The constructor must call the super constructor, and it should also
    // assign the instance class reference to instanceClass.
    public function Flag(newTarget:Object = null) {
        super(newTarget);
        instanceClass = FlagInstance;
    }

    // In this example there are no affected properties for the target.
    override public function getAffectedProperties( ):Array {
        return [];
    }

    override protected function initInstance(instance:EffectInstance):void {
        super.initInstance(instance);

        // Since instance is typed as EffectInstance you must cast as FlagInstance
        // to set the color property.
        FlagInstance(instance).color = _color;
    }

    }
}
```

Using Custom Effects

Once you've created a custom effect, you can use it just as you would use a standard effect. The following example illustrates this by applying the flag effect to text input controls as the user moves focus:

```
<?xml version="1.0" encoding="utf-8"?>
<mx:Application xmlns:mx="http://www.adobe.com/2006/mxml" layout="absolute" xmlns:
pf="com.oreilly.programmingflex.effects.*">

    <pf:Flag id="flagEffect" color="0xFFFFFF" />

    <mx:VBox x="164" y="187">
        <mx:TextInput focusOutEffect="{flagEffect}" />
        <mx:TextInput focusOutEffect="{flagEffect}" />
        <mx:TextInput focusOutEffect="{flagEffect}" />
        <mx:TextInput focusOutEffect="{flagEffect}" />
    </mx:VBox>

</mx:Application>
```

Creating Tween Effects

When you want to create effects that cause changes over time, you should create a tween effect. Tween effect classes extend `TweenEffect` and `TweenEffectInstance` rather than `Effect` and `EffectInstance`. We'll talk more about that in just a moment. First, we'll look at how to use the `mx.effects.Tween` class to create animated changes.

The `Tween` class constructor requires that you pass it four parameters: a callback object, a starting value, an ending value, and a duration in milliseconds. For example, the following creates a `Tween` object that automatically sends notifications at intervals for 5,000 milliseconds. Each notification includes a value from 0 to 100. The progression of values is a linear change from 0 to 100. The notifications are sent to the this object.

```
new Tween(this, 0, 100, 5000);
```

Unlike most of the Flex framework, the `Tween` class does not use the normal event model. Instead, it uses a callback model in which the callback object must define methods with specific names. Those methods are then called in response to specific events. In the case of the `Tween` class, the callback object can define the `onTweenUpdate()` and `onTweenEnd()` methods. The `onTweenUpdate()` method receives notifications as the value changes over time. The `onTweenEnd()` method receives notifications when the tween has completed.

Once you construct a `Tween` object, it automatically starts running. It calls the methods on the callback method at the appropriate intervals, sending the current value of the range over which it is changing over time. For example, on the first `onTweenUpdate()` method call, the `Tween` object passes it a value of 0 based on the preceding example, but the second call to `onTweenUpdate()` will be a value slightly larger than 0, with each successive call passing the method a larger value. Once the value reaches the maximum value in the range (100 in our example), the `Tween` object calls `onTweenEnd()`.

Most of the standard effects such as move, rotate, and blur are tween effects. Because `TweenEffect` and `TweenEffectInstance` extend `Effect` and `EffectInstance`, respectively, implementing a concrete subclass of each of these types is very similar to implementing classes that directly extend `Effect` and `EffectInstance`. In fact, all the rules discussed in the preceding sections are applicable to tween effects as well. Apart from extending `TweenEffect`, all tween effect factory classes have the same rules as nontween effects. Tween effect instance classes, however, must follow several rules.

`TweenEffectInstance` subclasses should construct a `Tween` object in the `play()` method, and the `Tween` object should use the this object as the callback object. Furthermore, the subclass must override the `onTweenUpdate()` method at a minimum. The `onTweenUpdate()` method should accept one parameter typed as `Object`. And the `onTweenUpdate()` method should be responsible for updating the property or properties of the target.

Example 11-10, WobbleInstance, is a TweenEffectInstance subclass that uses Tween objects to cause the target to appear to wobble a specified number of times.

Example 11-10. WobbleInstance class as an example of a tween effect instance

```
package com.oreilly.programmingflex.effects {
    import mx.effects.effectClasses.TweenEffectInstance;
    import mx.effects.Tween;

    // The class must extend TweenEffectInstance.
    public class WobbleInstance extends TweenEffectInstance {

        // The _wobbleRepeat property determines how many times the target should
        // wobble. The _wobbleCount property counts how many wobbles have occurred.
        private var _wobbleRepeat:uint;
        private var _wobbleCount:uint;

        public function set wobbleRepeat(value:uint):void {
            _wobbleRepeat = value;
        }

        public function get wobbleRepeat():uint {
            return _wobbleRepeat;
        }

        // The constructor looks very much like a regular Effect subclass.
        public function WobbleInstance(newTarget:Object) {
            super(newTarget);
        }

        // The play() method calls super.play(). Then it creates a new Tween object.
        // In this case the Tween object changes from 0 to 2 over the course of 100
        // milliseconds.
        override public function play():void {
            super.play();
            _wobbleCount = 0;
            new Tween(this, 0, 2, 100);
        }

        // The onTweenUpdate() method is required. In this case onTweenUpdate() simply
        // sets the rotation property of the target.
        override public function onTweenUpdate(value:Object):void {
            super.onTweenUpdate(value);
            target.rotation = value;
        }

        // The onTweenEnd() method is not strictly required. However, in this case we
        // need to override it so that it can create new Tween objects for as long as
        // the target is supposed to wobble.
        override public function onTweenEnd(value:Object):void {
            super.onTweenEnd(value);
            if(_wobbleCount < _wobbleRepeat) {
                new Tween(this, value, value == 2 ? -2 : 2, 200);
```

Example 11-10. WobbleInstance class as an example of a tween effect instance (continued)

```
        }
        else if(_wobbleCount == _wobbleRepeat) {
            new Tween(this, value, 0, 100);
        }
        _wobbleCount++;
    }

    }
}
```

Example 11-11 shows the Wobble factory class. Notice that it looks very similar to a regular effect factory class.

Example 11-11. Wobble class as an example tween effect factory

```
package com.oreilly.programmingflex.effects {
    import mx.effects.TweenEffect;
    import mx.effects.EffectInstance;

    public class Wobble extends TweenEffect {

        private var _wobbleRepeat:uint = 2;

        public function set wobbleRepeat(value:uint):void {
            _wobbleRepeat = value;
        }

        public function get wobbleRepeat( ):uint {
            return _wobbleRepeat;
        }

        public function Wobble(newTarget:Object = null) {
            super(newTarget);
            instanceClass = WobbleInstance;
        }

        override public function getAffectedProperties( ):Array {
            return ["rotation"];
        }

        override protected function initInstance(instance:EffectInstance):void {
            super.initInstance(instance);
            WobbleInstance(instance).wobbleRepeat = _wobbleRepeat;
        }

    }
}
```

Here is the effect applied to components:

```
<?xml version="1.0" encoding="utf-8"?>
<mx:Application xmlns:mx="http://www.adobe.com/2006/mxml" layout="absolute" xmlns:
pf="com.oreilly.programmingflex.effects.*">

    <pf:Wobble id="wobbleEffect" wobbleRepeat="10" />

    <mx:VBox x="164" y="187">
        <mx:TextInput focusOutEffect="{wobbleEffect}" />
        <mx:TextInput focusOutEffect="{wobbleEffect}" />
        <mx:TextInput focusOutEffect="{wobbleEffect}" />
        <mx:TextInput focusOutEffect="{wobbleEffect}" />
    </mx:VBox>

</mx:Application>
```

Using Transitions

Transitions allow you to apply effects to state view changes. Utilizing transitions is very simple. The prerequisite for transitions is that you have two or more states between which you want to apply the transition. Once you have the states defined, you next create the transitions you want to use.

You can create transitions using MXML or ActionScript. First we'll look at how to create transitions using MXML. Then we'll look at how to accomplish the same thing using ActionScript.

Creating Transitions with MXML

As shown in Chapter 10, all applications and components have a states property that you can use to define all the states they use. Likewise, all applications and components have a transitions property that is an array of all the transitions you want to use. In MXML, you can define the transitions property value using the following code within an application or component root tag:

```
<mx:transitions>
  <!-- All transitions appear here. -->
</mx:transitions>
```

All the elements of the transitions array must be Transition objects. In MXML, you create Transition instances using the Transition tag. All Transition objects must define fromState and toState properties, and these properties should be the names of the states from and to which the transition should apply. For example, the following code creates a transition from a state called A to a state called B:

```
<mx:Transition fromState="A" toState="B" />
```

If you want to use a transition for all changes to or from a particular state, you can use the asterisk (*) as a wildcard that means "all states." The following example creates a transition from all states to a state named B:

```
<mx:Transition fromState="*" toState="B" />
```

Transition objects have an effect property that determines what effect is applied during the state change. The effect property is the default property when you create the Transition object using MXML, which means you can simply nest an effect tag within a Transition tag, as in the following example:

```
<mx:Transition fromState="*" toState="B">
  <mx:Move target="{vbox}" />
</mx:Transition>
```

Notice that in this example, the effect specifies a target. In most cases, the effect must specify a target or targets when used as a transition. If you want to specify more than one target, you can use the targets property of an effect and specify an array of targets, as in the following example:

```
<mx:Transition fromState="*" toState="B">
  <mx:Move targets="{[textInput1, textInput2, textInput3, textInput4]}" />
</mx:Transition>
```

In many cases, you don't need to set the effect properties specifying things such as alphas or x and y coordinates. When effects are applied as transitions, the to and from properties are automatically set to the values of the targets' properties in the from and to states. For example, when you apply a move effect as a transition, the xFrom and yFrom properties are automatically set to the x and y property values of the target in the from state, and the xTo and yTo properties are automatically set to the x and y property values of the target in the to state. However, if you want to set the effect properties explicitly, you can do that as you would for any normal effect, and those settings will override any automatic settings. For instance, the following example creates a transition that uses a rotate effect with explicit settings for angleFrom and angleTo:

```
<mx:Transition fromState="*" toState="B">
  <mx:Rotate target="{vbox}" angleFrom="0" angleTo="360" />
</mx:Transition>
```

Now that we've had the opportunity to discuss all the fundamentals of working with transitions, let's look at a working example. Example 11-12 creates four title windows and four states—each state featuring one of the windows larger than the others. This example uses a transition that animates all the state changes so that the windows move and resize.

Example 11-12. Applying transitions between states

```xml
<?xml version="1.0" encoding="utf-8"?>
<mx:Application xmlns:mx="http://www.adobe.com/2006/mxml" layout="absolute">

    <mx:states>
        <mx:State name="A">
            <mx:SetProperty target="{windowA}" name="width" value="500"/>
            <mx:SetProperty target="{windowA}" name="height" value="300"/>
            <mx:SetProperty target="{windowC}" name="width" value="150"/>
            <mx:SetProperty target="{windowC}" name="height" value="150"/>
            <mx:SetProperty target="{windowC}" name="y" value="333"/>
            <mx:SetProperty target="{windowD}" name="x" value="373"/>
            <mx:SetProperty target="{windowD}" name="width" value="150"/>
            <mx:SetProperty target="{windowD}" name="height" value="150"/>
            <mx:SetProperty target="{windowD}" name="y" value="333"/>
            <mx:SetProperty target="{windowB}" name="x" value="23"/>
            <mx:SetProperty target="{windowB}" name="y" value="333"/>
            <mx:SetProperty target="{windowB}" name="width" value="150"/>
            <mx:SetProperty target="{windowB}" name="height" value="150"/>
            <mx:SetProperty target="{windowC}" name="x" value="200"/>
        </mx:State>
        <mx:State name="B">
            <mx:SetProperty target="{windowD}" name="width" value="150"/>
            <mx:SetProperty target="{windowD}" name="height" value="150"/>
            <mx:SetProperty target="{windowC}" name="width" value="150"/>
            <mx:SetProperty target="{windowC}" name="height" value="150"/>
            <mx:SetProperty target="{windowA}" name="width" value="150"/>
            <mx:SetProperty target="{windowA}" name="height" value="150"/>
            <mx:SetProperty target="{windowB}" name="width" value="500"/>
            <mx:SetProperty target="{windowB}" name="height" value="300"/>
            <mx:SetProperty target="{windowA}" name="y" value="333"/>
            <mx:SetProperty target="{windowC}" name="x" value="200"/>
            <mx:SetProperty target="{windowC}" name="y" value="333"/>
            <mx:SetProperty target="{windowB}" name="x" value="23"/>
            <mx:SetProperty target="{windowD}" name="x" value="373"/>
            <mx:SetProperty target="{windowD}" name="y" value="333"/>
        </mx:State>
        <mx:State name="C">
            <mx:SetProperty target="{windowD}" name="width" value="150"/>
            <mx:SetProperty target="{windowD}" name="height" value="150"/>
            <mx:SetProperty target="{windowB}" name="width" value="150"/>
            <mx:SetProperty target="{windowB}" name="height" value="150"/>
            <mx:SetProperty target="{windowA}" name="width" value="150"/>
            <mx:SetProperty target="{windowA}" name="height" value="150"/>
            <mx:SetProperty target="{windowC}" name="width" value="500"/>
            <mx:SetProperty target="{windowC}" name="height" value="300"/>
            <mx:SetProperty target="{windowA}" name="y" value="333"/>
            <mx:SetProperty target="{windowB}" name="x" value="200"/>
            <mx:SetProperty target="{windowB}" name="y" value="333"/>
            <mx:SetProperty target="{windowC}" name="x" value="23"/>
            <mx:SetProperty target="{windowC}" name="y" value="19"/>
            <mx:SetProperty target="{windowD}" name="x" value="373"/>
            <mx:SetProperty target="{windowD}" name="y" value="333"/>
        </mx:State>
```

Example 11-12. Applying transitions between states (continued)

```
        <mx:State name="D">
            <mx:SetProperty target="{windowC}" name="width" value="150"/>
            <mx:SetProperty target="{windowC}" name="height" value="150"/>
            <mx:SetProperty target="{windowB}" name="width" value="150"/>
            <mx:SetProperty target="{windowB}" name="height" value="150"/>
            <mx:SetProperty target="{windowA}" name="width" value="150"/>
            <mx:SetProperty target="{windowA}" name="height" value="150"/>
            <mx:SetProperty target="{windowD}" name="width" value="500"/>
            <mx:SetProperty target="{windowD}" name="height" value="300"/>
            <mx:SetProperty target="{windowA}" name="y" value="333"/>
            <mx:SetProperty target="{windowB}" name="x" value="200"/>
            <mx:SetProperty target="{windowB}" name="y" value="333"/>
            <mx:SetProperty target="{windowD}" name="x" value="23"/>
            <mx:SetProperty target="{windowD}" name="y" value="19"/>
            <mx:SetProperty target="{windowC}" name="x" value="373"/>
            <mx:SetProperty target="{windowC}" name="y" value="333"/>
        </mx:State>
    </mx:states>

    <mx:transitions>
        <mx:Transition fromState="*" toState="*">
            <mx:Parallel targets="{[windowA, windowB, windowC, windowD]}">
                <mx:Move />
                <mx:Resize />
            </mx:Parallel>
        </mx:Transition>
    </mx:transitions>

    <mx:TitleWindow x="23" y="19" width="250" height="200" layout="absolute" title="A"
id="windowA" click="currentState='A'" />
    <mx:TitleWindow x="309" y="19" width="250" height="200" layout="absolute" title="B"
id="windowB" click="currentState='B'" />
    <mx:TitleWindow x="23" y="260" width="250" height="200" layout="absolute" title="C"
id="windowC" click="currentState='C'" />
    <mx:TitleWindow x="309" y="260" width="250" height="200" layout="absolute" title="D"
id="windowD" click="currentState='D'" />

</mx:Application>
```

Creating Transitions with ActionScript

Transitions work much the same way in both MXML and ActionScript inasmuch as
you must set the same properties and all the properties work in the same way regardless of whether you're using MXML or ActionScript.

You can construct a new `mx.states.Transition` instance using the constructor:

```
    var transition:Transition = new Transition( );
```

You can then set the `fromState` and `toState` properties:

```
    transition.fromState = "*";
    transition.toState = "*";
```

Now you can assign an effect to the effect property:

```
var move:Move = new Move( );
move.targets = [textInput1, textInput2];
transition.effect = move;
```

Finally you simply need to add the transition to the transitions property of the application or component:

```
transitions = [transition];
```

There's no real advantage to using transitions from ActionScript or MXML. How you determine which you should use should be based on the type of document for which you are trying to define the states. If you are adding transitions to an MXML document, you should use MXML to define the transitions, and if you are adding transitions to an ActionScript class, you should use ActionScript for the transitions.

Using Transition Filters

When you apply transitions the effects are applied to all targets all the time. Often that is the correct behavior. However, sometimes you want to make the application of some effects conditional for some targets based on what changes are taking place for the targets. For instance, consider the following rewrite of the transition in Example 11-12:

```
<mx:transitions>
    <mx:Transition fromState="*" toState="*">
        <mx:Sequence targets="{[windowA, windowB, windowC, windowD]}">
            <mx:Blur blurYFrom="0" blurYTo="10" duration="100" />
            <mx:Parallel>
                <mx:Move />
                <mx:Resize />
            </mx:Parallel>
            <mx:Blur blurYFrom="10" blurYTo="0" duration="100" />
        </mx:Sequence>
    </mx:Transition>
</mx:transitions>
```

In this example, a blur is first applied to all the targets, the move and resize effects are then applied, and then the blur is applied again in reverse (essentially removing the blur). This creates a nice effect that depicts a motion blur when the windows are moving. However, there is one problem with this transition: the blur is always applied to all targets even when the target isn't actually going to move at all. This is a good case for using *transition effect filters*.

A filter on a transition effect allows you to make the application of the effect conditional. Table 11-3 shows all the filter values.

Table 11-3. Transition effect filter values

Filter value	Description
add	The target was added using AddChild.
remove	The target was removed using RemoveChild.
show	The target was made visible using SetProperty to set the visible property to true.
hide	The target was made nonvisible using SetProperty to set the visible property to false.
move	The target's x and y properties change during the transition.
resize	The target's width and height properties change during the transition.

The following rewrite of the transition from the preceding example corrects the blur problem by applying the blur only to the targets that are moving during the transition:

```
<mx:transitions>
    <mx:Transition fromState="*" toState="*">
        <mx:Sequence targets="{[windowA, windowB, windowC, windowD]}">
            <mx:Blur blurYFrom="0" blurYTo="10" duration="100" filter="move" />
            <mx:Parallel>
                <mx:Move />
                <mx:Resize />
            </mx:Parallel>
            <mx:Blur blurYFrom="10" blurYTo="0" duration="100" filter="move" />
        </mx:Sequence>
    </mx:Transition>
</mx:transitions>
```

Creating Custom Transitions

As you've already seen, transitions use effects. That means you can create custom transitions the same way you create custom effects. The only difference when creating custom transitions is that the effect instance class needs to handle the fallback rules for automatically determining the starting and ending property values. For example, we've seen that if you don't explicitly set the xFrom, yFrom, xTo, and yTo properties for an effect used as a transition, the values are automatically retrieved from the target in the from and to states. When you create an effect instance class that you intend to use as a transition, you should include the ability to automatically detect these default property values.

EffectInstance subclasses automatically inherit a property called propertyChanges, which is of type mx.effects.effectClasses.PropertyChanges. The propertyChanges property has two properties: start and end. These properties are associative arrays containing the affected property values of the target in the from and to states.

Summary

In this chapter, you learned about working with effects and transitions in Flex 2. You learned that effects are frequently paired with a trigger to create what is known as a behavior. You also learned that effects can be applied declaratively using MXML tags or through ActionScript, and that transitions allow you to apply animated changes between Flex component states.

CHAPTER 12

Working with Data

Although some Flex applications use data more extensively than others, nearly all use data to some extent. The Flex SDK is a robust set of tools for working with data. This chapter examines how to work with data on the client side without an extensive discussion of client-server data communication, which is covered in Chapter 16. Rather, this chapter focuses primarily on the following topics: modeling data and data binding.

When working with data, you generally want to store it in some sort of data repository within memory. These repositories are known as *data models*. In the first section of this chapter, we'll look at each of the three basic ways to store data in data models.

You can use ActionScript for all your data management needs, but then you're not really using the power of the Flex framework. To simplify linking data from a data model to a control or from one control to another control or component, you can use a powerful feature called *data binding*.

Once you know the basics of working with data in a Flex application, you'll have a foundation for sending and receiving data. That topic is discussed further in Chapter 16.

Using Data Models

You can work with data in many ways in Flex applications, including as low-level ActionScript solutions and high-level MXML solutions; this section looks at both techniques. You can use these data models as a repository for data retrieved from a remote procedure call (RPC) such as a web service method call. You can also use a data model to store user input data before sending it to the server. You can even use a data model simply as a mechanism for populating form input, such as a combo box.

Using the Model Tag

The <mx:Model> tag allows you to create an object that represents a data structure using MXML. To use the tag practically, you must always specify an id attribute:

```
<mx:Model id="example" />
```

Once you've created a model this way, you can do one of two things:

- Create a data structure using tags.
- Specify a source attribute to populate the model from a file.

Creating tag-based model structures

If you want to populate a model object within your MXML document, you can specify the structure using *tags*. Tags are useful when you want to use the data model for storing user input or data you retrieve from an RPC. The tags are arbitrary XML tags that you select to represent the data structure. The data model must contain only one root node. The following example uses a data model to represent a user:

```
<mx:Model id="userData">
    <user>
        <email></email>
        <phone></phone>
        <address>
            <city></city>
            <state></state>
        </address>
    </user>
</mx:Model>
```

Of course, you can populate the data model with real data, as in the next example:

```
<mx:Model id="userData">
    <user>
        <email>example@example.com</email>
        <phone>123 555-1212</phone>
        <address>
            <city>Exampleville</city>
            <state>CA</state>
        </address>
    </user>
</mx:Model>
```

However, in most cases when you want to initialize a data model with data, you should use an external file, as described in the next section. When you create the structure of a data model in the MXML document in this fashion, you won't initialize the object with data. Instead, you'll use it with data binding (discussed in the "Data Binding" section, later in this chapter) to store data from user input or data retrieved with RPCs.

Populating a model from a file

If you want to use a data model to store static data, often the best approach is to load that data from a file rather than define the structure and initialize the object data, all from the MXML document. For example, consider a data model in which you want to store all the U.S. state names. If you define the structure and initialize it within the MXML document, your MXML document becomes cluttered with lots of lines that are not used to define the user interface or the business logic, but rather are used just to populate a data model. It is better to place that data in a separate file and simply reference it in the MXML document. The <mx:Model> tag makes that an easy task.

If you specify a source attribute for an <mx:Model> tag, the object looks to the file you specify, and it loads the data from that file at compile time, not at runtime. Specifying the source attribute achieves exactly the same effect as placing the contents of the source file within the <mx:Model> tag, but it allows you to place the data in a separate file to clean up the MXML. Once the *.swf* is compiled, you won't need to distribute the data source file with the *.swf* file because all the data is compiled into the *.swf*.

Consider the following XML document called *states.xml*, an XML file that contains the names of all 50 U.S. states (to save space, this example has been shortened, but you can assume the actual file contains all 50 states):

```
<states>
    <state>Alabama</state>
    <state>Alaska</state>
    <state>Arizona</state>
    <state>Arkansas</state>
    <state>California</state>
    <state>Colorado</state>
    <state>Connecticut</state>
    <state>Delaware</state>
    <state>Florida</state>
    <state>Georgia</state>
    <state>Hawaii</state>
    <state>Idaho</state>
    <state>Illinois</state>
    <!-- additional states... -->
</states>
```

You can populate a model with that data by adding the source attribute to the <mx:Model> tag, as shown in the following example:

```
<mx:Model id="statesModel" source="states.xml" />
```

 The preceding example assumes that *states.xml* is in the same directory as the main MXML file for the application.

Referencing model data

Having a data model doesn't do you much good unless you can reference the data stored within it—either to update it or to retrieve it. In many, if not most cases, you will use data binding to reference model data. (The details of data binding are discussed later in this chapter, in the "Data Binding" section.) You can also reference a model using ActionScript. You'll see how the same concepts apply when using data binding later in this chapter.

To understand how to reference data in a data model, it's important to understand how an <mx:Model> tag translates into ActionScript. Unlike many MXML tags, the <mx:Model> tag does not correspond to an ActionScript class by the same name. There is no Model class; rather, an object created using the <mx:Model> tag is an instance of the ObjectProxy class. An ObjectProxy object is essentially a wrapper for an Object instance. In practical terms, you can treat an ObjectProxy object exactly as you would an Object instance. The primary purpose of ObjectProxy is to enable data binding, which would not be available for a simple Object instance.

The fact that an object created with <mx:Model> is an ObjectProxy object in Action-Script immediately tells you that you can access the data using standard Action-Script dot syntax. The only thing you need to now know about these objects is how the tag-based data structure translates to ActionScript. As we've discussed, a model created with <mx:Model> can have only one root node. That root node is always synonymous with the model object itself. The child nodes of the root node become properties of the ObjectProxy object, and the child nodes of the child nodes become properties of the properties of the object.

The following example defines a simple data model and a button. When the user clicks the button, it calls trace( ) and displays the value of the email property of the data model. Because the root node of the data model (user) is synonymous with the data model object (userData), you do not need to (nor can you) treat the root node as a child of the data model; to retrieve the email value, userData.email is used, not userData.user.email:

```
<mx:Model id="userData">
    <user>
        <email>example@example.com</email>
        <phone>123 555-1212</phone>
        <address>
            <city>Exampleville</city>
            <state>CA</state>
        </address>
    </user>
</mx:Model>
<mx:Button click="trace(userData.email)" />
```

You can also assign values to the data model properties using standard ActionScript expressions. The following example uses the same data model as the preceding example, but with two buttons—one that updates the city value by appending a random number and one that traces the value:

```
<mx:VBox>
    <mx:Button click="userData.address.city = 'Exampleville' +
                    Math.round(Math.random( ) * 10)" />
    <mx:Button click="trace(userData.address.city)" />
</mx:VBox>
```

There is one conversion that takes place that might not be intuitive. When a data model structure consists of two or more sibling nodes with the same name, they are converted into an array. Consider the states example again:

```
<states>
    <state>Alabama</state>
    <state>Alaska</state>
    <state>Arizona</state>
    <state>Arkansas</state>
    <state>California</state>
    <state>Colorado</state>
    <state>Connecticut</state>
    <state>Delaware</state>
    <state>Florida</state>
    <state>Georgia</state>
    <state>Hawaii</state>
    <state>Idaho</state>
    <state>Illinois</state>
    <!-- additional states... -->
</states>
```

The states data is loaded into a data model using the source attribute, as follows:

```
<mx:Model id="statesModel" source="states.xml" />
```

Here, statesModel.state is an array that contains the name of each state as an element. The following traces true when the user clicks the button because statesModel.state is an array:

```
<mx:Button click="trace(statesModel.state is Array)" />
```

The following example uses an ActionScript function to loop through all the elements of the array and display them in a text area:

```
<mx:Script>
    <![CDATA[

        private function displayStates( ):void {
            for(var i:uint = 0; i < statesModel.state.length; i++) {
                statesTextArea.text += statesModel.state[i] + "\n";
            }
        }

    ]]>
</mx:Script>
```

```
<mx:Model id="statesModel" source="states.xml" />
<mx:VBox>
    <mx:Button click="displayStates( )" />
    <mx:TextArea id="statesTextArea" height="500" />
</mx:VBox>
```

Using XML

The <mx:Model> tag is useful when you want to work with data stored in traditional types such as objects, strings, and arrays. If you want to work with XML-formatted data, you can use the <mx:XML> tag to create an XML-based data model.

The <mx:Model> and <mx:XML> tags are structurally very similar. As with <mx:Model>, you should always specify an id attribute when creating an <mx:XML> tag:

```
<mx:XML id="example" />
```

Also, as with <mx:Model>, there are two ways to create the structure and/or initialize an <mx:XML> data model:

- Create a data structure using tags.
- Specify a source attribute to populate the model from a file.

Specifying XML structure with tags

You can specify an XML structure using tags in the MXML document much as you would for an ObjectProxy-based model created with <mx:Model>. The following defines the structure for an <mx:XML> tag:

```
<mx:XML id="chaptersXml" xmlns="">
    <chapters label="Chapters">
        <chapter label="Chapter 1">
            <file label="File 1.1" />
        </chapter>
        <chapter label="Chapter 2">
            <file label="File 2.1" />
        </chapter>
    </chapters>
</mx:XML>
```

 As with <mx:Model>, the structure for <mx:XML> must have only one root node.

The MXML parser uses namespaces extensively, and it is important that the XML tag has a unique namespace from the default namespace of the containing MXML document. For this reason, Flex Builder adds xmlns="", as in the preceding example.

Loading XML from a file

You can load the XML data for an <mx:XML> tag using the source attribute just as you would with <mx:Model>. When you use the source attribute, that data is loaded at compile time, and it is compiled into the *.swf*. That means that you do not need to distribute the source file with the *.swf* and that the data is static. The following loads the data from *chapters.xml*:

```
<mx:XML id=chaptersXml" source="chapters.xml" />
```

Referencing XML data

When you use an <mx:XML> tag, it creates an XML object in ActionScript. By default, the XML object is a top-level E4X XML object. However, you can use the format attribute to specify whether to use an E4X XML object or a legacy flash.xml.XMLNode object. The default value for the format attribute is e4x. Setting the value to xml creates an XMLNode object instead. For all the examples in this book, E4X XML data models are used unless otherwise noted.

When you want to reference the data from a model created using <mx:XML>, the root node of the data is synonymous with the data model object. The following uses E4X syntax to trace the label attribute of the first <chapter> child node:

```
<mx:XML id="chaptersXml">
    <chapters label="Chapters">
        <chapter label="Chapter 1">
            <file label="File 1.1" />
        </chapter>
        <chapter label="Chapter 2">
            <file label="File 2.1" />
        </chapter>
    </chapters>
</mx:XML>
<mx:Button click="trace(chaptersXml.chapter[0].@label)" />
```

This example assigns the data model as the data provider for a tree component:

```
<mx:XML id="chaptersXml">
    <chapters label="Chapters">
        <chapter label="Chapter 1">
            <file label="File 1.1" />
        </chapter>
        <chapter label="Chapter 2">
            <file label="File 2.1" />
        </chapter>
    </chapters>
</mx:XML>
<mx:VBox>
    <mx:Button click="chapters.dataProvider = chaptersXml" />
    <mx:Tree id="chapters" width="200" labelField="@label" />
</mx:VBox>
```

Using ActionScript Classes

Although the <mx:Model> and <mx:XML> data models provide a simple and convenient way to work with data, they are not the ideal solution in most cases. Even though they work well for simple, static data (such as a list of U.S. state names), they are not well suited for complex data, dynamic data, or data that has rules applied to it. In those cases, it is better to use a custom ActionScript class as the data model. Here are some advantages of using a custom ActionScript class:

Strong typing
> With <mx:Model> and <mx:XML> you cannot enforce data types, but with Action-Script classes you can (i.e., a string must be a string, and an int must be an int).

Data testing/consistency
> You cannot verify that a value assigned to an object created using <mx:Model> or <mx:XML> is a valid value. For example, if a particular property can have values onlt in the range from 1 to 10, you cannot verify that when assigning values to <mx:Model> or <mx:XML>. However, an ActionScript class setter method can test for valid values. If a value is invalid, the class can discard the new assignment, convert the value to a value in the valid range, or throw an error.

Business logic
> When you assign a value to a property of an instance created from <mx:Model> or <mx:XML>, you are simply assigning a value without the ability to run any business logic. However, with an ActionScript class, you can run any ActionScript operations you want when getting or setting values.

Design patterns
> You cannot employ sophisticated design patterns with <mx:Model> and <mx:XML>, yet you can with an ActionScript class. For example, you may need to have a single, managed instance of a data model such as a user account data model. That way, it is accessible throughout the application. With an ActionScript class, you can employ the Singleton design pattern to accomplish this goal.

> It's worth noting that the main application class is a type of Singleton class in that there is only one instance per application, and that one instance is globally accessible (via mx.core.Application.application). You could, theoretically, add a data model instance to the main class and access it globally through the main class. Although that would accomplish the goal, the architectural soundness of that decision is questionable. It is generally advisable to use an ActionScript class as the data model.

Writing an ActionScript class as a data model is quite simple. You merely need to define a new class with public accessor methods for all the properties. The class in Example 12-1 defines a data model for a user. Note that all the getters and setters are strongly typed, and several of the setters use data testing.

Example 12-1. User class

```
package com.oreilly.programmingflex.data {

    public class User {

        private var _nameFirst:String;
        private var _nameLast:String;
        private var _email:String;
        private var _lastLogin:Date;
        private var _userType:uint;

        public function get nameFirst():String {
            return _nameFirst;
        }

        public function set nameFirst(value:String):void {
            _nameFirst = nameFirst;
        }

        public function get nameLast():String {
            return _nameLast;
        }

        public function set nameLast(value:String):void {
            _nameLast = nameLast;
        }

        public function get email():String {
            return _email;
        }

        public function set email(value:String):void {
            var expression:RegExp = /\b[A-Z0-9._%-]+@[A-Z0-9.-]+\.[A-Z]{2,4}\b/i;
            if(expression.test(value)) {
                _email = value;
            }
            else {
                _email = "invalid email";
            }
        }

        public function get lastLogin():Date {
            return _lastLogin;
        }

        public function set lastLogin(value:Date):void {
            _lastLogin = lastLogin;
        }

        public function get userType():uint {
            return _userType;
        }
```

Example 12-1. User class (continued)

```
    public function set userType(value:uint):void {
        if(userType <= 2) {
            _userType = userType;
        }
    }

    public function User( ) {}


    }
}
```

You can then create an instance of the model class using MXML or ActionScript. With MXML, you have to define the namespace, then use `<namespace:Class>` to create the instance:

```
<?xml version="1.0" encoding="utf-8"?>
<mx:Application xmlns:mx="http://www.adobe.com/2006/mxml" xmlns:data="com.oreilly.
programmingflex.data.*" layout="absolute">

    <data:User id="user" email="example@example.com" lastLogin="{new Date( )}"
               nameFirst="Abigail" nameLast="Smith" userType="1" />

</mx:Application>
```

With ActionScript, you need to import the class, and then use the constructor as part of a new statement:

```
import com.oreilly.programmingflex.data.User;
private var user:User;

private function initializeHandler(event:Event):void {
    user = new User( );
    user.email = "example@example.com";
    // etc.
}
```

In the next section, we'll look at data binding. If you want to enable the data binding feature for a custom ActionScript-based data model, you must use the `[Bindable]` metatag when declaring the class:

```
[Bindable]
public class User {
```

If you create the instance using MXML, the instance is automatically enabled for data binding, assuming the class uses the `[Bindable]` metatag. However, if you create the instance using ActionScript, you must also use the `[Bindable]` tag when declaring the variable you use to store the reference:

```
[Bindable]
private var user:User;
```

We'll talk more about data binding and the `[Bindable]` metatag in the next section.

Data Binding

Flex applications typically utilize lots of data retrieved from both RPCs (server-side method calls) and user input collected in forms. One way you can work with data is to use extensive ActionScript. ActionScript provides low-level access to all the data in your Flex application. Yet the ActionScript code can be redundant, and it can be time-consuming to write. Although extensive ActionScript may be necessary in some cases, the Flex framework provides a feature called *data binding* that simplifies working with data in most cases.

Data binding lets you associate data from one object with another. There are lots of ways to use data binding. The following examples list a few of the most common uses for data binding:

- Link form input controls (text inputs, checkboxes, etc.) with data models.
- Link two or more controls (e.g., display a slider value in a text component).

In the following sections, we'll look at the rules of data binding as well as examples of different ways to use data binding.

Understanding Data Binding Syntax

There are three ways to apply data binding:

- Curly brace ({}) syntax
- `<mx:Binding>`
- `BindingUtils`

Each technique for applying data binding has advantages and disadvantages, which we'll discuss in the next few sections.

Curly braces

Using curly braces to apply data binding is the simplest and fastest technique. Throughout the early part of this book, you've seen quite a few examples of curly-brace syntax. Placing curly braces around any expression causes it to be evaluated. Consider the following example with a combo box and a text input control:

```
<mx:HBox>
    <mx:ComboBox id="level">
        <mx:Array>
            <mx:Object label="A" data="1" />
            <mx:Object label="B" data="2" />
            <mx:Object label="C" data="3" />
            <mx:Object label="D" data="4" />
        </mx:Array>
    </mx:ComboBox>

    <mx:TextInput id="selectedLevel" text="level.value" />
</mx:HBox>
```

In this example, the text attribute of the text input is set to level.value. In that format, the value is interpreted literally, so the string level.value displays in the text input. Changing the text input tag to the following makes a big difference:

```
<mx:TextInput id="selectedLevel" text="{level.value}" />
```

With this change, the text input now selects the data corresponding to the selected combo box item. As the user selects a different combo box item, the value in the text input also updates. This is because the text level.value is now placed within curly braces, so it is treated as an expression rather than as literal text.

More than just evaluating the expression, the curly braces attempt to make a data binding association. If the association is successful, as the value of the target (in the example, the target is level.value) changes, the listening property (the text property of the text input in this example) also updates. The preceding example illustrates this because as the combo box value changes, so does the value displayed in the text input. For a more dramatic example, consider the following:

```
<mx:Panel id="panel" width="{panelWidth.value}" height="{panelHeight.value}">
    <mx:NumericStepper id="panelWidth"  value="200" minimum="200"
                        maximum="400" stepSize="10" height="22"/>
    <mx:NumericStepper id="panelHeight"  value="200" minimum="200"
                        maximum="400" stepSize="10" height="22"/>
</mx:Panel>
```

In this example, the panel contains two nested numeric steppers. The panel uses data binding to link the width property to the value of the first numeric stepper and the height property to the value of the second stepper. The result is that as the user changes the values of the numeric steppers, the width and height of the panel change accordingly.

There are many scenarios in which you can use curly brace syntax for data binding. As you've seen in the preceding example, you can use the syntax to directly associate a target property with a property of a form control such as a text input. You can also link a value from a control to a data model, as the following example illustrates:

```
<mx:Model id="dataModel">
    <userData>
        <email>{email.text}</email>
        <phone>{phone.text}</phone>
        <city>{city.text}</city>
        <state>{state.value}</state>
    </userData>
</mx:Model>

<mx:VBox>
    <mx:Label text="Email" />
    <mx:TextInput id="email" />
    <mx:Label text="Phone" />
    <mx:TextInput id="phone" />
    <mx:Label text="City" />
    <mx:TextInput id="city" />
```

```
    <mx:Label text="State" />
    <mx:ComboBox id="state">
        <mx:Array>
            <mx:Object label="CA" />
            <mx:Object label="MA" />
        </mx:Array>
    </mx:ComboBox>
</mx:VBox>
```

The preceding code uses data binding to link the values from form controls to a data model. You can use data binding both to assign values to a data model, as in the preceding example, and to retrieve data from a data model and display it. And you can even use data binding in both directions at the same time. The following code, used in conjunction with the preceding example, formats and displays the text from the data model in a text area, updating as the user changes the values in the controls bound to the model:

```
<mx:TextArea width="200" height="200" text="{'Contact Information\nEmail: ' +
            dataModel.email + '\nPhone: ' + dataModel.phone + '\nLocation: ' +
            dataModel.city + ', ' + dataModel.state}" />
```

Perhaps an even more useful example is one in which you use data binding to link data either directly from controls or from a data model to an RPC component such as a RemoteObject component. Using data binding in this way allows you to make RPCs without having to write much, if any, ActionScript. The following example uses data binding to link the data from the data model in the preceding example to a RemoteObject instance as the parameters for a method call:

```
<mx:RemoteObject id="example" destination="exampleService">
    <mx:method name="saveContactInformation">
        <mx:arguments>
            <email>{dataModel.email}</email>
            <phone>{dataModel.phone}</phone>
            <city>{dataModel.city}</city>
            <state>{dataModel.state}</state>
        </mx:arguments>
    </mx:method>
</mx:RemoteObject>
```

As the values in the data model update via data binding, so too will the values in the RemoteObject method arguments update. This allows you to call the method by simply calling a send( ) method with no parameters, as in the following example:

```
<mx:Button label="Save" click="example.saveContactInformation.send( )" />
```

This is a very simple example of working with RemoteObject. The same principles are true when working with HTTPService and WebService as well. All of these RPC techniques are discussed in more detail in Chapter 14.

Because curly brace syntax allows you to evaluate any ActionScript expression, you can also use data binding with E4X expressions. That means you can use data binding not only to link XML data with control values, but also to link controls and RPC components to XML values using E4X expressions. For instance, instead of using a Model object, as in the earlier example, you can use an XML object as follows:

```
<mx:XML id="xmlData">
    <userData email="{email.text}" phone="{phone.text}"
              city="{city.text}" state="{state.value}" />
</mx:XML>
```

You can then use E4X expressions to link the text area value to values from the XML object:

```
<mx:TextArea width="200" height="200" text="{'Contact Information\nEmail: ' +
             xmlData.@email + '\nPhone: ' + xmlData.@phone + '\nLocation: ' +
             xmlData.@city + ', ' + xmlData.@state}" />
```

<mx:Binding>

The <mx:Binding> tag allows you to do exactly the same things as curly brace syntax, but with MXML tags rather than inline expressions. The <mx:Binding> tag requires the following attributes:

source
> The origin of the data you want to link

destination
> The point which you want notified when the value changes from the source

For the following example, the same basic premise is used as in the first example of the curly brace discussion: we'll link the value from a combo box to a text input so that when the user changes the value in the combo box, the value in the text input also changes. First, we'll add the controls:

```
<mx:HBox>
    <mx:ComboBox id="level">
        <mx:Array>
            <mx:Object label="A" data="1" />
            <mx:Object label="B" data="2" />
            <mx:Object label="C" data="3" />
            <mx:Object label="D" data="4" />
        </mx:Array>
    </mx:ComboBox>

    <mx:TextInput id="selectedLevel" />
</mx:HBox>
```

Notice that we're not setting the text property of the text input. With curly brace syntax, we'd set the text property inline. With the <mx:Binding> tag we'll use a separate tag to achieve the goal of data binding. To link the source (level.value) and the destination (selectedLevel.text), you can add the following tag to your code (note that the tag must appear outside of any layout container tags):

```
<mx:Binding source="level.selectedItem.data" destination="selectedLevel.text" />
```

This code works identically to how the curly brace example worked, yet it uses a different mechanism to achieve that goal.

You can use `<mx:Binding>` with data models and RPC components as well. We can rewrite the earlier data model example to illustrate this point. First, add the data model, the `RemoteObject`, and the controls. Note that in this example, the data model and the remote method arguments do not define any values inline:

```
<mx:Model id="dataModel">
    <userData>
        <email></email>
        <phone></phone>
        <city></city>
        <state></state>
    </userData>
</mx:Model>

<mx:RemoteObject id="example" destination="exampleService">
    <mx:method name="saveContactInformation">
        <mx:arguments>
            <email></email>
            <phone></phone>
            <city></city>
            <state></state>
        </mx:arguments>
    </mx:method>
</mx:RemoteObject>

<mx:VBox>
    <mx:Label text="Email" />
    <mx:TextInput id="email" />
    <mx:Label text="Phone" />
    <mx:TextInput id="phone" />
    <mx:Label text="City" />
    <mx:TextInput id="city" />
    <mx:Label text="State" />
    <mx:ComboBox id="state">
        <mx:Array>
            <mx:Object label="CA" />
            <mx:Object label="MA" />
        </mx:Array>
    </mx:ComboBox>
    <mx:TextArea id="summary" width="200" height="200" />
</mx:VBox>
```

Next, we need to define the data bindings using the `<mx:Binding>` tag:

```
<mx:Binding source="email.text" destination="dataModel.email" />
<mx:Binding source="phone.text" destination="dataModel.phone" />
<mx:Binding source="city.text" destination="dataModel.city" />
<mx:Binding source="state.value" destination="dataModel.state" />
<mx:Binding source="'Contact Information\nEmail: ' + dataModel.email +
    '\nPhone: ' + dataModel.phone + '\nLocation: ' + dataModel.city + ', ' +
    dataModel.state" destination="summary.text" />
```

```
<mx:Binding source="dataModel.email"
             destination="example.saveContactInformation.arguments.email" />
<mx:Binding source="dataModel.phone"
             destination="example.saveContactInformation.arguments.phone" />
<mx:Binding source="dataModel.city"
             destination="example.saveContactInformation.arguments.city" />
<mx:Binding source="dataModel.state"
             destination="example.saveContactInformation.arguments.state" />
```

You can also use E4X expressions with the <mx:Binding> tag. Assume you change the data model from a Model object to an XML object as follows:

```
<mx:XML id="xmlData">
    <userData email="{email.text}" phone="{phone.text}"
              city="{city.text}" state="{state.value}" />
</mx:XML>
```

You can then change the <mx:Binding> tags as follows:

```
<mx:Binding source="email.text" destination="xmlData.@email" />
<mx:Binding source="phone.text" destination="xmlData.@phone" />
<mx:Binding source="city.text" destination="xmlData.@city" />
<mx:Binding source="state.value" destination="xmlData.@state" />
<mx:Binding source="'Contact Information\nEmail: ' + xmlData.@email + '\nPhone: ' +
            xmlData.@phone + '\nLocation: ' + xmlData.@city + ', ' +
            xmlData.@state" destination="summary.text" />
<mx:Binding source="xmlData.@email"
            destination="example.saveContactInformation.arguments.email" />
<mx:Binding source="xmlData.@phone"
            destination="example.saveContactInformation.arguments.phone" />
<mx:Binding source="xmlData.@city"
            destination="example.saveContactInformation.arguments.city" />
<mx:Binding source="xmlData.@state"
            destination="example.saveContactInformation.arguments.state" />
```

The <mx:Binding> tag requires more code than the curly brace syntax. Curly brace syntax can appear inline within existing tags, whereas <mx:Binding> syntax requires that you add additional tags to your code. This may seem like a disadvantage at first; however, in the long run it is advantageous to use <mx:Binding> in most cases because it allows you to create a cleaner separation between UI layout and the data used. Using the <mx:Binding> tag is a cleaner implementation of data binding, yet it does not allow any greater functionality than curly brace syntax. If you need more functionality (such as dynamically changing data binding end points at runtime) you can use BindingUtils, discussed in the next section.

BindingUtils

In most cases, you should use curly brace or <mx:Binding> syntax for data binding. However, neither technique allows you to dynamically configure data binding at runtime. The mx.binding.utils.BindingUtils class has a static method called bindProperty() that allows you to configure data binding from ActionScript. This ActionScript solution provides the most flexibility and the lowest-level access to data binding of all the techniques. As such, the `BindingUtils.bindProperty()` method can be a useful resource in those special cases in which you require more flexibility than the other techniques afford you.

The syntax for the `bindProperty()` method is as follows:

```
BindingUtils.bindProperty(destinationObject, destinationProperty,
                          sourceObject, sourceProperty);
```

The destination and source object parameters are object references, and the property parameters are strings. The following example links the value from a combo box so that it displays in a text input:

```
BindingUtils.bindProperty(textInput, "text", comboBox, "value");
```

Because `BindingUtils` is ActionScript, you can place the code anywhere that you can place ActionScript code. The following example uses a button to enable data binding between a combo box and a text input when the user clicks the button:

```
<mx:Script>
    <![CDATA[
        import mx.binding.utils.BindingUtils;
    ]]>
</mx:Script>

<mx:VBox>
  <mx:ComboBox id="comboBox">
    <mx:Array>
      <mx:Object label="1" />
      <mx:Object label="2" />
      <mx:Object label="3" />
      <mx:Object label="4" />
    </mx:Array>
  </mx:ComboBox>
  <mx:TextInput id="textInput" />
  <mx:Button label="enable data binding"
            click="BindingUtils.bindProperty(textInput, 'text', comboBox, 'value')"
  />
</mx:VBox>
```

In the preceding example, the combo box and the text input are not initially linked. However, when the user clicks on the button, it calls the `bindProperty()` method, which links the controls such that the combo box value is displayed in the text input, and the display changes as the value changes. To use `BindingUtils`, you must add an `import` statement, as in the example.

The `bindProperty()` method returns a reference to a new `mx.binding.utils.ChangeWatcher` object. The `ChangeWatcher` class defines a class of objects that represents the actual data binding link between a source and a destination. Using `bindProperty()` by itself allows you to enable data binding at runtime, but if you want to further modify that data binding, you'll have to work with a `ChangeWatcher` object. Using a `ChangeWatcher` object, you can disable data binding or change the source point.

The ChangeWatcher object returned by a bindProperty( ) method call represents that data binding association, and if you want to change that association or stop it, you must use the ChangeWatcher object. You can stop a data binding association between two points by calling the unwatch( ) method of the ChangeWatcher object:

```
changeWatcher.unwatch( );
```

You can retrieve the current source value using the getValue( ) method:

```
changeWatcher.getValue( );
```

You can change the source object using the reset( ) method. The reset( ) method accepts one parameter specifying the new source object:

```
changeWatcher.reset(newSourceObject);
```

The reset( ) method does not allow you to change the property of the source object. If you want to change the property, you must call unwatch( ) to stop the current data binding association. You can then start a new association using BindingUtils. bindProperty( ):

```
changeWatcher.unwatch( );
changeWatcher = BindingUtils.bindProperty(newSource, newProperty, destination,
destinationProperty);
```

Example 12-2 uses BindingUtils and ChangeWatcher to toggle the source object between two combo boxes. The example uses two combo boxes, a text input, and a button. When the application initializes, it calls the initializeHandler( ) method because that is assigned to the Application initialize handler. The initializeHandler( ) method sets data binding between the level combo box and the selectedLevel text input. When the user clicks the button it calls the toggleDataBinding( ) method, which uses the reset( ) method of the ChangeWatcher object to change the source object.

Example 12-2. Working withBindingUtils

```
<?xml version="1.0" encoding="utf-8"?>
<mx:Application xmlns:mx="http://www.adobe.com/2006/mxml" layout="absolute" in
itialize="initializeHandler(event)">

  <mx:Script>
   <![CDATA[

      import mx.binding.utils.BindingUtils;
      import mx.binding.utils.ChangeWatcher;

      private var _changeWatcher:ChangeWatcher;
      private var _currentHost:ComboBox;

      private function initializeHandler(event:Event):void {
          // Set the initial data binding, and assign the ChangeWatcher
          // object to the _changeWatcher property.
          _changeWatcher = BindingUtils.bindProperty(selectedLevel, "text",
                                          level, "value");
```

Example 12-2. Working withBindingUtils (continued)

```
        // Save a reference to the current source object.
        _currentHost = level;
    }

    private function toggleDataBinding(event:Event):void {

        // Determine the new source object. If the current source
        // object is level, set the new source to subLevel. If the
        // current source object is subLevel then set the new
        // source to level.
        _currentHost = _currentHost == level ? subLevel : level;

        // Use the reset() method to change the source object.
        _changeWatcher.reset(_currentHost);

        // Calling reset() changes the source for the data binding, but it does
        // not immediately update the destination. For that, you need to
        // manually update the destination value by retrieving the source value
        // using the getValue() method of the ChangeWatcher object.
        selectedLevel.text = _changeWatcher.getValue().toString();
    }

  ]]>
</mx:Script>

<mx:VBox>
  <mx:ComboBox id="level">
      <mx:Array>
          <mx:Object label="A" data="1" />
          <mx:Object label="B" data="2" />
          <mx:Object label="C" data="3" />
          <mx:Object label="D" data="4" />
      </mx:Array>
  </mx:ComboBox>

  <mx:ComboBox id="subLevel">
      <mx:Array>
          <mx:Object label="A" data="1.1" />
          <mx:Object label="B" data="1.2" />
          <mx:Object label="C" data="1.3" />
          <mx:Object label="D" data="1.4" />
      </mx:Array>
  </mx:ComboBox>

  <mx:TextInput id="selectedLevel" />

  <mx:Button label="enable data binding" click="toggleDataBinding(event)" />

</mx:VBox>
</mx:Application>
```

Enabling Data Binding for Custom Classes

Data binding is enabled for some types of objects by default, but it won't work for instances of custom classes by default. You must enable data binding with the [Bindable] metatag. The [Bindable] metatag tells the Flex compiler to configure whatever it precedes so that it works with data binding. You can use [Bindable] with the following:

- A class
- A property
- An implicit getter method
- An implicit setter method

 Note that for data binding to work properly when using implicit getters and setters, you should have both a getter and a setter for every property for which you want to use data binding.

When you use the [Bindable] metatag before a class declaration, it marks all the public properties and all the getter and setter pairs as data binding-enabled:

```
[Bindable]
public class Example {
```

When you use [Bindable] before a property declaration, it sets just that property as data binding-enabled:

```
[Bindable]
private var _exampleProperty;
```

When you use [Bindable] before a getter and/or setter method, it marks that getter/setter method as data binding-enabled. If you have both a getter and a setter with the same name, you need to place the [Bindable] metatag before only one of them. If you have only a getter method, the method works only as the source for data binding, and if you have only a setter method, the method works only as the destination for data binding:

```
[Bindable]
public function get exampleGetter():String {
    return "example";
}
```

In practical terms, you must always enable both the contents of a custom class and an instance of the class to use the instance for data binding. For instance, consider the simple class in Example 12-3.

Example 12-3. Basic data binding class example

```
package com.oreilly.programmingflex.binding {

    [Bindable]
    public class DataBindableExample {

        private var _example:String;

        public function get example( ):String {
            return _example;
        }

        public function set example(value:String):void {
            _example = value;
        }

        public function DataBindableExample( ) {
            _example = "example";
        }


    }
}
```

The class in Example 12-4 uses [Bindable] to enable the entire class. However, if you want to use an instance of the class in an MXML document as either the source or the destination for data binding, you must declare the instance using the [Bindable] tag as well.

Example 12-4. Implementation of basic data binding

```
<?xml version="1.0" encoding="utf-8"?>
<mx:Application xmlns:mx="http://www.adobe.com/2006/mxml" layout="absolute"
initialize="initializeHandler(event)">

    <mx:Script>
        <![CDATA[

            import com.oreilly.programmingflex.binding.DataBindableExample;

            [Bindable]
            private var _dataBindableExample:DataBindableExample;

            private function initializeHandler(event:Event):void {
                _dataBindableExample = new DataBindableExample( );
            }

        ]]>
    </mx:Script>
    <mx:VBox>
        <mx:TextInput id="input" />
        <mx:TextInput id="output" />
    </mx:VBox>
```

Example 12-4. Implementation of basic data binding (continued)

```
    <mx:Binding source="input.text" destination="_dataBindableExample.example" />
    <mx:Binding source="_dataBindableExample.example" destination="output.text" />
</mx:Application>
```

The preceding example uses the DataBindableExample instance as an intermediary between the two text inputs. This particular example does not demonstrate a useful use case, but it does illustrate a simple working example that shows which elements are necessary to build a custom class that works with data binding. We'll look at more practical, more complex examples later in this chapter, when we talk about building proxies for end points that wouldn't otherwise be data binding-enabled.

Customizing Data Binding

Data binding works by dispatching events using the standard Flash Player event model. If you were to look at the generated ActionScript for an application that uses data binding, you would see that classes with bindable properties dispatch events, and where MXML uses data binding syntax, the generated ActionScript class registers event listeners. When you use the [Bindable] tag, the default event type that gets dispatched is propertyChange. In many cases, this is perfectly workable. However, it can introduce inefficiencies when one class has several properties using data binding, because anytime any of the properties changes, all listeners for all changes in all bindable properties for the object instance will receive a notification. It is far more efficient if each property dispatches a unique event name. You can achieve this by adding an event setting for the [Bindable] tag as follows:

```
    [Bindable(event="customEvent")]
```

In the cases where you customize the event name, you must also manually dispatch the event, as in the following:

```
    dispatchEvent(new Event("customEvent"));
```

Obviously, when you customize the event name, you must add a [Bindable] tag before each property (or getter/setter), rather than using one tag just prior to the class declaration. Example 12-5 uses custom event names.

Example 12-5. Customized data binding

```
package com.oreilly.programmingflex.binding {

    import flash.events.Event;
    import flash.events.EventDispatcher;

    public class CustomizedDataBindableExample extends EventDisaptcher {

        private var _a:String;
        private var _b:String;
```

Example 12-5. Customized data binding (continued)

```
    [Bindable(event="aChange")]
    public function get a( ):String {
        return _a;
    }

    public function set a(value:String):void {
        _a = value;
        dispatchEvent(new Event(A_CHANGE));
    }

    [Bindable(event="bChange")]
    public function get b( ):String {
        return _b;
    }

    public function set b(value:String):void {
        _b = value;
        dispatchEvent(new Event(B_CHANGE));
    }

    public function CustomizedDataBindableExample( ) {
        _a = "a";
        _b = "b";
    }

    }
}
```

Data Binding Examples

In the next few sections, we'll look at examples that use data binding to achieve a variety of goals.

Controlling Images

Example 12-6 uses data binding to work with images. Using a combo box, the user can select an image to view. Using data binding, the value of the combo box is linked to the source property of an image component. Additionally, the example uses three slider controls to control the alpha, width, and height of the image, all of which are linked using data binding.

Example 12-6. Data binding example

```
<?xml version="1.0" encoding="utf-8"?>
<mx:Application xmlns:mx="http://www.adobe.com/2006/mxml" layout="absolute">

    <mx:VBox x="0" y="0" height="100%" horizontalAlign="center">
```

Example 12-6. Data binding example (continued)

```
        <!-- Add a combo box with several options. Each option has a label
             and then a data property that contains a URL to an image. -->
        <mx:ComboBox id="imageUrl">
            <mx:Array>
                <mx:Object label="Water Lilies" data="file:///C|/
Documents and Settings/All Users/Documents/My Pictures/
Sample Pictures/Water lilies.jpg" />
                <mx:Object label="Sunset" data="file:///C|/
Documents and Settings/All Users/Documents/My Pictures/
Sample Pictures/Sunset.jpg" />
            </mx:Array>
        </mx:ComboBox>

        <!-- Place the image within a canvas with a fixed size so that when the
             image resizes it won't cause the rest of the layout to change -->
        <mx:Canvas width="160" height="120">
            <!-- Make sure maintainAspectRatio is set to false so you can change
                 the width and height independently. -->
            <mx:Image id="image" width="160" height="120" alpha="0"
                maintainAspectRatio="false" />
        </mx:Canvas>

        <!-- Add three labels and sliders. -->
        <mx:Label text="Alpha"/>
        <mx:HSlider id="imageAlpha" minimum="0" maximum="1" value="1"
            liveDragging="true" />
        <mx:Label text="Width"/>
        <mx:HSlider id="imageWidth" minimum="0" maximum="160" value="160"
            liveDragging="true" />
        <mx:Label text="Height"/>
        <mx:HSlider id="imageHeight" minimum="0" maximum="120" value="120"
            liveDragging="true" />
    </mx:VBox>

    <!-- Define the data binding between the components. The image alpha,
         width, and height properties are linked to the slider values.
         The image source is linked to the combo box value. -->
    <mx:Binding source="imageAlpha.value" destination="image.alpha" />
    <mx:Binding source="imageWidth.value" destination="image.width" />
    <mx:Binding source="imageHeight.value" destination="image.height" />
    <mx:Binding source="imageUrl.value" destination="image.source" />
</mx:Application>
```

Working with Web Services

In this example, we build a simple application that calls web service methods. In the first part, we'll use data binding to link the result of a web service method call to text input controls. In the second part, we'll link the values from numeric steppers to the parameters for a web service method.

In this first part, we'll initially add the WebService object and define the first operation. The WSDL is *http://www.rightactionscript.com/webservices/FlashSurvey. php?wsdl*, and the operation is called getAverages. The operation does not require any parameters.

```
<?xml version="1.0" encoding="utf-8"?>
<mx:Application xmlns:mx="http://www.adobe.com/2006/mxml" layout="absolute">

    <mx:WebService id="survey" wsdl="http://www.rightactionscript.com/webservices/
FlashSurvey.php?wsdl">
        <mx:operation name="getAverages" resultFormat="object" />
    </mx:WebService>

</mx:Application>
```

Next, we'll add the controls to call the method and display the results. Note that the click event handler for the button calls the send( ) method of the web service operation:

```
<?xml version="1.0" encoding="utf-8"?>
<mx:Application xmlns:mx="http://www.adobe.com/2006/mxml" layout="absolute">

    <mx:WebService id="survey" wsdl="http://www.rightactionscript.com/webservices/
FlashSurvey.php?wsdl">
        <mx:operation name="getAverages" resultFormat="object" />
    </mx:WebService>

    <mx:HBox>
        <mx:VBox>
            <mx:Button id="getAveragesButton" label="Get Averages" click="survey.
getAverages.send( )" />
            <mx:TextInput id="resultFlash" enabled="false" />
            <mx:TextInput id="resultActionScript" enabled="false" />
        </mx:VBox>
    </mx:HBox>

</mx:Application>
```

Now we can use data binding to link the results to the text input controls. The getAverages web service method for this web service returns an object with two properties: flash and actionscript. The return value is stored in the lastResult property of the operation object. That means we can use survey.getAverages. lastResult.flash and survey.getAverages.lastResult.actionscript as the sources for the bindings:

```
<?xml version="1.0" encoding="utf-8"?>
<mx:Application xmlns:mx="http://www.adobe.com/2006/mxml" layout="absolute">

    <!-- Existing application code -->

    <mx:Binding source="survey.getAverages.lastResult.flash"
                destination="resultFlash.text" />
```

```
    <mx:Binding source="survey.getAverages.lastResult.actionscript"
destination="resultActionScript.text" />

</mx:Application>
```

When you test this application and click on the button, you'll see the averages returned and displayed (assuming you have a working Internet connection).

Now we'll add one more operation, called takeSurvey. The takeSurvey method requires two parameters, called years_flash and years_actionscript:

```
<?xml version="1.0" encoding="utf-8"?>
<mx:Application xmlns:mx="http://www.adobe.com/2006/mxml" layout="absolute">

    <mx:WebService id="survey" wsdl="http://www.rightactionscript.com/webservices/
FlashSurvey.php?wsdl">
        <mx:operation name="getAverages" resultFormat="object" />
        <mx:operation name="takeSurvey">
            <mx:request>
                <years_flash></years_flash>
                <years_actionscript></years_actionscript>
            </mx:request>
        </mx:operation>
    </mx:WebService>

    <!-- Existing application code -->

</mx:Application>
```

Now that the operation is defined, you can add the controls to allow the user to select the values for the parameters and call the method. For that purpose, add two numeric steppers and a button with a click handler:

```
<?xml version="1.0" encoding="utf-8"?>
<mx:Application xmlns:mx="http://www.adobe.com/2006/mxml" layout="absolute">

    <!-- Existing application code -->

    <mx:HBox>
        <!-- Existing application code -->
        <mx:VBox>
            <mx:Button id="sendValuesButton" label="Take Survey"
                click="survey.takeSurvey.send( )" />
            <mx:NumericStepper id="flashValue" />
            <mx:NumericStepper id="actionScriptValue" />
        </mx:VBox>
    </mx:HBox>

    <!-- Existing application code -->

</mx:Application>
```

The remaining step is to define the data binding for the numeric steppers and the operation request parameters:

```
<?xml version="1.0" encoding="utf-8"?>
<mx:Application xmlns:mx="http://www.adobe.com/2006/mxml" layout="absolute">

    <!-- Existing application code -->

    <mx:Binding source="flashValue.value"
        destination="survey.takeSurvey.request.years_flash" />
    <mx:Binding source="actionScriptValue.value" destination="survey.takeSurvey.
request.years_actionscript" />

</mx:Application>
```

Now you can run the application, select values from the numeric steppers, and click the button to take the survey. If you click on the button to get the averages, you'll notice that the numbers have changed from the previous time you viewed the values.

Building Data Binding Proxies

Some types of objects and some elements in Flex applications cannot use data binding directly. For example, you cannot use data binding directly with component styles. Yet you can build an elegant solution that uses something called *delegation*. Delegation is what occurs when a class called a *proxy* wraps an object, and it passes along requests to the object it wraps. The goal of delegation may be different in different scenarios, but in this case, the goal is to provide a layer of indirection so that the data binding-enabled proxy can accept requests in place of the object that cannot accept those requests.

A proxy class generally uses the following structure:

```
package {

    public class ProxyClass {

        private var _object:Object;

        public function ProxyClass(object:Object) {
            _object = object;
        }

        public function method():void {
            _object.method();
        }

    }

}
```

Obviously, the preceding format is overly simplified, and each proxy class may vary the format slightly. We'll look at two specific implementations of proxy classes designed to facilitate data binding in the next two subsections. Hopefully you'll then be able to generalize this solution so that you can apply it to similar scenarios when you need to enable data binding for an object that doesn't natively support data binding.

Using Data Binding with a Shared Object

You cannot use data binding with shared objects. Yet you can use a proxy to enable data binding. For this example, we'll use a very simple case that stores one user preference in a local shared object. That one preference is a Boolean value indicating whether to show a form in the application. Of course, you could accomplish this task through ActionScript, yet you could also enable data binding with a proxy class that wraps the shared object. For this example, here's our proxy class definition:

```
package com.oreilly.programmingflex.binding.proxies {
    import flash.net.SharedObject;

    [Bindable]
    public class UserPreferences {

        private var _sharedObject:SharedObject;

        // Retrieve the value from the shared object.
        public function get showForm( ):Boolean {
            return _sharedObject.data.showForm;
        }

        // Assign the value to the shared object, and call flush( )
        // to ensure it writes to disk immediately.
        public function set showForm(value:Boolean):void {
            _sharedObject.data.showForm = value;
            _sharedObject.flush( );
        }

        // The class wraps a shared object. Pass the reference to the constructor,
        // and the assign that reference to a private property.
        public function UserPreferences(sharedObject:SharedObject):void {
            _sharedObject = sharedObject;
        }

    }
}
```

You can then use the following MXML to demonstrate how the proxy works:

```
<?xml version="1.0" encoding="utf-8"?>
<mx:Application xmlns:mx="http://www.adobe.com/2006/mxml" layout="absolute"
initialize="initializeHandler(event)">
```

```
<mx:Script>
    <![CDATA[
        import com.oreilly.programmingflex.binding.proxies.UserPreferences;
        import flash.net.SharedObject;

        // Declare a variable for the instance of the UserPreferences
        // class. Make the variable data binding enabled with the
        // [Bindable] metatag.
        [Bindable]
        private var _userPreferences:UserPreferences;

        // When the application starts construct the UserPreferences object,
        // passing it a reference to a local shared object.
        private function initializeHandler(event:Event):void {
            _userPreferences =
            new UserPreferences(SharedObject.getLocal("userPreferences"));
        }

        // This is the function we call via data binding when the
        // shared object showForm property changes. Toggle the
        // current state.
        private function set toggleForm(value:Boolean):void {
            currentState = value ? null : "hideForm";
        }

    ]]>
</mx:Script>

<!-- Define a state that removes the form -->
<mx:states>
    <mx:State name="hideForm">
        <mx:RemoveChild target="{form}" />
    </mx:State>
</mx:states>

<!-- Define a form and a checkbox -->
<mx:VBox id="vbox">
    <mx:Form id="form">
        <mx:FormHeading label="Form"/>
        <mx:FormItem label="First Name">
            <mx:TextInput id="firstName"/>
        </mx:FormItem>
        <mx:FormItem label="Last Name">
            <mx:TextInput id="lastName"/>
        </mx:FormItem>
    </mx:Form>
    <mx:CheckBox id="showForm" label="Show Form" />
</mx:VBox>

<!-- Define data bindings between the checkbox and proxy object as well
     as between the proxy object and the toggleForm( ) function. -->
<mx:Binding source="_userPreferences.showForm"
    destination="showForm.selected" />
<mx:Binding source="showForm.selected"
```

```
        destination="_userPreferences.showForm" />
    <mx:Binding source="_userPreferences.showForm" destination="toggleForm" />

</mx:Application>
```

This example toggles the state, and it remembers the state every time you return to the application because it's storing the data in the shared object.

Summary

In this chapter, you learned about the basics of working with data. You read about using data models, both the Flex framework tag-based data models and the preferred ActionScript class-based data models. You also learned about using data binding to link data to components and ensure that the data is always in sync.

CHAPTER 13
Validating and Formatting Data

When working with data, you'll frequently need to ensure that the data adheres to certain rules. When the data is from user input, this is called *validation*. When the data is being displayed or needs to be in a particular form before storing it or sending it to a service method, this is called *formatting*. The Flex framework provides mechanisms for both of these types of operations. In this chapter, we will look at both validating and formatting data.

Validating User Input

When you work with user input, you frequently may want to validate that input before submitting it for some sort of course of action, either client-side or server-side. For example, if you want to submit form data to a server script that inserts the data to a database, you may need to verify that the values are in the correct format so that you can insert them (e.g., a numeric value needs to be a number, and a date needs to be formatted so that your script can parse it into the format you require for the database).

You can write your own validation procedures for this purpose. Yet most validations require rewriting the same basic code time after time. All that redundancy leads to a lot of time spent rewriting the same basic code rather than focusing on new tasks. For this reason, the Flex framework ships with a type of component called a *validator*, which you can use to assist with validating user input. There are a handful of standard validator types, including `StringValidator`, `NumberValidator`, `DateValidator`, `PhoneValidator`, and `ZipCodeValidator`. The next few sections discuss how to work with each of the standard validators and show you how to build custom validator types.

Using Validators

There are two ways you can work with validators: with MXML or with ActionScript. For many use cases, MXML is sufficient for your validation needs. Although it is common to work with validators in MXML, there are many cases in which you'll work with validators both in MXML *and* in ActionScript for the same project—creating the validators using MXML, and adding extra functionality with ActionScript. In a few cases, you'll work with validators entirely in ActionScript. Those are special cases in which you need to be able to build the validators dynamically at runtime because the exact user input controls and validation needs are not known at compile time.

Validator basics

All validator types inherit from a base type called `Validator`. Although you'll work with subtypes more frequently (e.g., `StringValidator`), you can work with `Validator` for very basic validation requirements, and all the validator types inherit the basic functionality and properties of the `Validator` type.

When you create a validator, you must specify at least two properties, called `source` and `property`. The `source` is a reference to the object containing the data you want to validate, and the `property` is the property of that object that contains the data. You can create a validator that uses MXML with the following structure:

```
<mx:Validator source="{sourceObject}" property="sourceProperty" />
```

By default, the behavior of a validator is simply to validate that the user has specified a value. All validators have a property called `required` that defaults to `true`. The following achieves exactly the same result as the preceding code example:

```
<mx:Validator source="{sourceObject}" property="sourceProperty" required="true" />
```

The default trigger for a validator is a `valueCommit` event. All input controls dispatch `valueCommit` events when the value is changed programmatically, or when the focus shifts away from the control. Example 13-1 illustrates a very basic validator use. The application consists of a form with a text input and a button. The validator uses the text input as the source, and it validates that the user has input at least one character. The validator runs when the user moves focus away from the text input. That means you must first move focus to the text input (by clicking in it) and then shift focus away either by clicking on the button or by pressing the Tab key.

Example 13-1. Basic form validation

```
<?xml version="1.0" encoding="utf-8"?>
<mx:Application xmlns:mx="http://www.adobe.com/2006/mxml" layout="absolute">

    <mx:Form>
        <mx:FormHeading label="Sample Form"/>
        <mx:FormItem label="Name">
```

Example 13-1. Basic form validation (continued)

```
            <mx:TextInput id="username"/>
        </mx:FormItem>
        <mx:FormItem>
            <mx:Button id="button" label="Submit"/>
        </mx:FormItem>
    </mx:Form>

    <mx:Validator source="{username}" property="text" />

</mx:Application>
```

When a validator runs, there are two possible outcomes: either it will validate the data successfully or it won't. If it validates the data, the default behavior is to do nothing. If it does not successfully validate the data, the default behavior for a validator is to apply a red outline to the input control and display a message when the user moves the mouse over the control.

As mentioned earlier, it is far more common to create validators using MXML than ActionScript. Yet there are valid use cases that require you to create the validators using ActionScript. For example, if you create a form at runtime based on XML data, you must also create the validators at runtime, and that requires ActionScript. To create a validator at runtime, use a standard new statement with the constructor for the validator type. For example, the following creates a Validator object:

```
    _validator = new Validator( );
```

You must always set both the source and the property properties as well:

```
    _validator.source = sourceObject;
    _validator.property = "sourceProperty";
```

Example 13-2 achieves exactly the same thing as Example 13-1, but in this case, the validator is created using ActionScript.

Example 13-2. ActionScript-based validator

```
<?xml version="1.0" encoding="utf-8"?>
<mx:Application xmlns:mx="http://www.adobe.com/2006/mxml" layout="absolute"
initialize="initializeHandler(event)">
    <mx:Script>
        <![CDATA[
            import mx.validators.Validator;

            private var _validator:Validator;

            private function initializeHandler(event:Event):void {
                _validator = new Validator( );
                _validator.source = username;
                _validator.property = "text";
            }

        ]]>
    </mx:Script>
```

Example 13-2. ActionScript-based validator (continued)

```
<mx:Form>
    <mx:FormHeading label="Sample Form"/>
    <mx:FormItem label="Name">
        <mx:TextInput id="username"/>
    </mx:FormItem>
    <mx:FormItem>
        <mx:Button id="button" label="Submit"/>
    </mx:FormItem>
</mx:Form>

</mx:Application>
```

Unless stated otherwise, all properties of all validators can be set using MXML or ActionScript.

Customizing validator messages

When a validator runs and fails to successfully validate the data, it displays a message by default. The message type depends on the type of validator as well as the way in which the validator failed. The `Validator` class defines just one type of message that appears when a required field contains no data. The default message is "This field is required." That message may be appropriate in most cases, but if your application requires a custom message, you can change the value using the `requiredFieldError` property:

```
<mx:Validator source="{sourceObject}" property="sourceProperty"
requiredFieldError="Hey, fill out this item" />
```

All validator types inherit the `required` and `requiredFieldError` properties, and so you can set a custom `requiredFieldError` message for any validator type. However, many validator types may fail for reasons other than the field simply being required. For example, a `PhoneNumberValidator` can fail if the data contains an invalid character. Each validator type also defines properties allowing you to customize the error messages for each type of possible error. For example, the following customizes the error message when the user specifies an invalid character for a phone number:

```
<mx:PhoneNumberValidator source="{sourceObject}" property="sourceProperty"
    invalidCharError="You really ought to use the proper characters" />
```

We'll look at all the possible errors for each validator type later in this chapter.

Handling validator events

Validators dispatch two basic types of events: valid and invalid. When a validator runs successfully, it dispatches a valid event; when it doesn't, it dispatches an invalid event. By default, the source control receives and handles the events. All input controls are configured to respond to valid and invalid events, typically by applying a red outline and displaying a message. For this reason, it's not necessary to explicitly handle the validator events. However, if you want to modify the default behavior, you need to listen for and handle the validator events. You can handle the events in one of the following ways:

- Specify values for the valid and invalid attributes of the MXML tag used to create the validator:

```
<mx:Validator source="{sourceObject}" property="sourceProperty"
    valid="validHandler(event)" invalid="invalidHandler(event)" />
```

- Use addEventListener( ) to register listeners for the events via ActionScript. To do so, use the mx.events.ValidationResultEvent.VALID and mx.events.ValidationResultEvent.INVALID constants:

```
validator.addEventListener(ValidationResultEvent.VALID, validHandler);
validator.addEventListener(ValidationResultEvent.INVALID, invalidHandler);
```

Example 13-3 handles the valid and invalid events such that in addition to the default behavior, the form item label also changes.

Example 13-3. Handling validator events

```
<?xml version="1.0" encoding="utf-8"?>
<mx:Application xmlns:mx="http://www.adobe.com/2006/mxml" layout="absolute">
    <mx:Script>
        <![CDATA[

            import mx.events.ValidationResultEvent;

            private function invalidHandler(event:ValidationResultEvent):void {
                usernameItem.setStyle("color", 0xFF0000);
                usernameItem.label = "*Name";
            }

            private function validHandler(event:ValidationResultEvent):void {
                usernameItem.setStyle("color", 0x000000);
                usernameItem.label = "Name";
            }

        ]]>
    </mx:Script>

    <mx:Form>
        <mx:FormHeading label="Sample Form"/>
        <mx:FormItem id="usernameItem" label="Name">
            <mx:TextInput id="username"/>
        </mx:FormItem>
        <mx:FormItem>
            <mx:Button id="button" label="Submit" />
        </mx:FormItem>
    </mx:Form>

    <mx:Validator id="validator" source="{username}" property="text"
invalid="invalidHandler(event)" valid="validHandler(event)" />

</mx:Application>
```

Every validator can have a listener that is automatically configured to listen to validator events. By default, the listener is the source object. As mentioned, all user input controls can listen for the validator events and respond to them in a default manner. If you want to specify a different, nondefault listener for a validator, you can use the listener property to assign a reference to a new object. The listener object must be an object that implements the IValidatorListener interface. The UIComponent class implements IValidatorListener, so you can assign any UIComponent instance (including any user input control) as the listener. Although slightly convoluted, the following example illustrates how the listener property can work. In this example, the validator is applied to a data model rather than a control. The data model value is assigned via data binding from a text input:

```
<?xml version="1.0" encoding="utf-8"?>
<mx:Application xmlns:mx="http://www.adobe.com/2006/mxml" layout="absolute">

    <mx:Model id="userData">
        <userData>
            <username></username>
        </userData>
    </mx:Model>

    <mx:Form>
        <mx:FormHeading label="Sample Form"/>
        <mx:FormItem id="usernameItem" label="Name">
            <mx:TextInput id="username"/>
        </mx:FormItem>
        <mx:FormItem>
            <mx:Button id="button" label="Submit" />
        </mx:FormItem>
    </mx:Form>

    <mx:Binding source="username.text" destination="userData.username" />

    <mx:Validator id="validator" source="{userData}" property="username" />

</mx:Application>
```

Although the validator is applied to the data model field, it does not actually do anything useful. This is for two reasons, the first of which is that the normal trigger for the validator won't work because data models don't dispatch valueCommit events. We'll talk more about alternative ways of triggering validators in the next section, but for now you can simply define the validator's trigger property so that it's a reference to the input control. That tells the validator to listen for valueCommit events from the input control rather than the data model:

```
<mx:Validator id="validator" source="{userData}" property="username"
    trigger="{username}" />
```

However, even with the preceding change, the application won't display any sort of notification when the validation fails. That's due to the second reason, which is that a validator's default listener is the source object—a data model in this case.

However, a data model does not know how to handle those events. Instead, if you want a listener object to handle the events, you must override the default listener value by setting the listener property for the validator. With the following change to the validator, it uses the input control as the listener:

```
<mx:Validator id="validator" source="{userData}" property="username"
    trigger="{username}" listener="{username}" />
```

This example isn't very practical, though. There is no reason in this case for you to validate data in a data model rather than in the text input. However, it does illustrate the basics of how a listener works. Now let's look at two more useful examples, the first of which is extremely simple.

As you saw earlier in this section, you can explicitly handle valid and invalid events. However, when doing so, you might have noticed that the default listener behavior (the red outline and message applied to the source control) is still applied. If you want to use explicit event handlers for the valid and invalid events without the default listener behavior, you must override the default listener setting by using a value of null. Example 13-4 uses a null value for the listener along with explicit event handlers. In this example, the label changes when validator events occur, but the default listener behavior does not.

Example 13-4. Overriding default validator behavior

```
<?xml version="1.0" encoding="utf-8"?>
<mx:Application xmlns:mx="http://www.adobe.com/2006/mxml" layout="absolute">
    <mx:Script>
        <![CDATA[

            import mx.events.ValidationResultEvent;

            private function invalidHandler(event:ValidationResultEvent):void {
                usernameItem.setStyle("color", 0xFF0000);
                usernameItem.label = "*Name";
            }

            private function validHandler(event:ValidationResultEvent):void {
                usernameItem.setStyle("color", 0x000000);
                usernameItem.label = "Name";
            }

        ]]>
    </mx:Script>

    <mx:Form>
        <mx:FormHeading label="Sample Form"/>
        <mx:FormItem id="usernameItem" label="Name">
            <mx:TextInput id="username"/>
        </mx:FormItem>
        <mx:FormItem>
            <mx:Button id="button" label="Submit" />
```

Example 13-4. Overriding default validator behavior (continued)

```
        </mx:FormItem>
    </mx:Form>

    <mx:Validator id="validator" source="{username}" property="text"
invalid="invalidHandler(event)" valid="validHandler(event)" listener="{null}" />

</mx:Application>
```

You can also assign a nondefault listener when you want to use a customized listener. The customized listener might do any number of things, such as auto-correcting a value. To register a custom listener, the class must implement the mx.validators. IValidatorListener interface, which requires public properties (or getter/setters) called errorString and validationSubField as well as a public method called validationResultHandler(), which accepts a parameter of type mx.events. ValidationResultEvent. Example 13-5 shows a simple class that implements the interface. This class allows you to pass it any control with a text property, and it attempts to auto-correct the field. In this example, the auto-correction is very limited in scope: it auto-corrects only the string abc, and makes it abcd.

Example 13-5. Customized validator listener

```
package com.oreilly.programmingflex.validation.listeners {

    import mx.events.ValidationResultEvent;
    import mx.validators.IValidatorListener;
    import mx.core.UIComponent;

    public class AutoCorrectTextListener implements IValidatorListener {

        private var _errorString:String;
        private var _validationSubField:String;
        private var _control:Object;
        private var _passThroughEvent:Boolean;

        // Implement the errorString and validationSubField getters and setters.
        // They simply act as accessor methods for corresponding private properties.
        public function get errorString():String {
            return _errorString;
        }

        public function set errorString(value:String):void {
            _errorString = value;
        }

        public function get validationSubField():String {
            return _validationSubField;
        }

        public function set validationSubField(value:String):void {
            _validationSubField = value;
        }
```

Example 13-5. Customized validator listener (continued)

```
        // The constructor accepts two parameters: the control with a text
        // property you want to target, and an optional parameter specifying
        // whether or not to pass through the event to the control if it
        // cannot auto-correct.
        public function AutoCorrectTextListener(control:Object,
                                                passThroughEvent:Boolean = true) {
            _control = control;
            _passThroughEvent = passThroughEvent;
        }

        // This method gets called when the validator dispatches an event. The code
        // auto-corrects the text if possible (in this case it only auto-corrects
        // one case). If it cannot auto-correct, it passes the event (if
        // applicable) to the control.
        public function validationResultHandler(event:ValidationResultEvent):void {
            if(_control.text == "abc" || _control.text == "abcd") {
                _control.text = "abcd";
            }
            else {
                if(_passThroughEvent) {
                    _control.validationResultHandler(event);
                }
            }
        }

    }
}
```

The MXML in Example 13-6 uses this custom listener.

Example 13-6. Using a customized validator listener

```
<?xml version="1.0" encoding="utf-8"?>
<mx:Application xmlns:mx="http://www.adobe.com/2006/mxml" layout="absolute"
initialize="initializeHandler(event)">
    <mx:Script>
        <![CDATA[

            import com.oreilly.programmingflex.validation.listeners.
AutoCorrectTextListener;

            private var _listener:AutoCorrectTextListener;

            private function initializeHandler(event:Event):void {

                // Create a new listener that targets the text input control.
                _listener = new AutoCorrectTextListener(username);

                // Register the listener with the validator. The validator is
                // created via MXML later in the document. The MXML id attribute
                // is set to validator, which is the reason you can reference the
                // object by that name here.
```

Example 13-6. Using a customized validator listener (continued)

```
                validator.listener = _listener;
            }

        ]]>
    </mx:Script>

    <mx:Form>
        <mx:FormHeading label="Sample Form"/>
        <mx:FormItem id="usernameItem" label="Name">
            <mx:TextInput id="username"/>
        </mx:FormItem>
        <mx:FormItem>
            <mx:Button id="button" label="Submit" />
        </mx:FormItem>
    </mx:Form>

    <mx:Validator id="validator" source="{username}" property="text" />

</mx:Application>
```

When you test this application you can try using any text other than abc or abcd, and the event will be passed to the control with the standard behavior following. If you use the text abc, it auto-corrects to abcd.

Triggering validators

To run, a validator must first be *triggered*. As you've already seen, the default `trigger` for a validator is the `valueCommit` event, which is dispatched by the `source` object. In many cases, that is appropriate because the `valueCommit` event occurs for all input controls when the value is set programmatically or when the focus shifts from the control. However, there are reasons you may want to change the default trigger for a validator. For example, although the most common use case for validators is to employ a user input control as the source, you could theoretically use any object and any property. If the object type you use as the source does not dispatch a `valueCommit` event, the default trigger will never occur. Another, more common scenario for changing the default trigger is one in which you want a different object to trigger the validator. For example, rather than triggering a validator when the user moves focus from a text input, you might want to trigger the validator when the user clicks on a button.

The two properties you can use with a validator to change the trigger are `trigger` and `triggerEvent`. The `trigger` property requires a reference to an object that you want to use as the trigger. The `triggerEvent` property requires the name of the event you want to use to trigger the validator. The following example uses the `click` event for the button to trigger the validator:

```
    <?xml version="1.0" encoding="utf-8"?>
    <mx:Application xmlns:mx="http://www.adobe.com/2006/mxml" layout="absolute">
```

```
<mx:Form>
    <mx:FormHeading label="Sample Form"/>
    <mx:FormItem label="Name">
        <mx:TextInput id="username"/>
    </mx:FormItem>
    <mx:FormItem>
        <mx:Button id="button" label="Submit" />
    </mx:FormItem>
</mx:Form>

<mx:Validator source="{username}" property="text" trigger="{button}"
    triggerEvent="click" />

</mx:Application>
```

You can have still further control over how and when validators run by using Action-Script to run the validators. All validators have a validate( ) method that you can call to run the validator. If you want to call the validate( ) method for a validator, you must ensure that the object has an id; whether you set the id property when creating the validator via MXML or you assign the validator to a variable when creating it with ActionScript. The following example sets the trigger property of a validator to null so that the default trigger does not work:

```
<?xml version="1.0" encoding="utf-8"?>
<mx:Application xmlns:mx="http://www.adobe.com/2006/mxml" layout="absolute">

    <mx:Form>
        <mx:FormHeading label="Sample Form"/>
        <mx:FormItem label="Name">
            <mx:TextInput id="username"/>
        </mx:FormItem>
        <mx:FormItem>
            <mx:Button id="button" label="Submit" />
        </mx:FormItem>
    </mx:Form>

    <mx:Validator id="validator" source="{username}" property="text"
        trigger="{null}" />

</mx:Application>
```

If you test the preceding code, you'll find that the validator does not run automatically because the trigger is null. Now you can add an event listener to the button so that it calls a function when clicked by the user. The validate( ) method of the validator can be called with the function, as shown here:

```
<?xml version="1.0" encoding="utf-8"?>
<mx:Application xmlns:mx="http://www.adobe.com/2006/mxml" layout="absolute">

    <mx:Script>
        <![CDATA[
```

```
        private function runValidator(event:MouseEvent):void {
            validator.validate( );
        }

    ]]>
</mx:Script>

<mx:Form>
    <mx:FormHeading label="Sample Form"/>
    <mx:FormItem label="Name">
        <mx:TextInput id="username"/>
    </mx:FormItem>
    <mx:FormItem>
        <mx:Button id="button" label="Submit" click="runValidator(event)" />
    </mx:FormItem>
</mx:Form>

<mx:Validator id="validator" source="{username}" property="text"
    trigger="{null}" />

</mx:Application>
```

If you want to achieve the same result as with the standard trigger, it is far simpler to use the default behavior rather than writing all the extra code (as in the preceding example). However, the validate( ) method allows you greater control over how the application behaves.

The validate( ) method not only runs the validator, but it also returns a ValidationResultEvent object, which tells you whether the validation succeeded. The type property of the object is either valid or invalid (for which you can use the ValidationResultEvent.VALID and ValidationResultEvent.INVALID constants, respectively). Example 13-7 uses validate( ) to display an alert when the user clicks on the button but doesn't properly fill in a required field.

Example 13-7. Running validation with ActionScript

```
<?xml version="1.0" encoding="utf-8"?>
<mx:Application xmlns:mx="http://www.adobe.com/2006/mxml" layout="absolute">
    <mx:Script>
        <![CDATA[
            import mx.events.ValidationResultEvent;
            import mx.controls.Alert;

            private function runValidators(event:Event):void {
                // Run the validate( ) method and assign the result to a variable.
                var validationResultEvent:ValidationResultEvent =
validator.validate(null, true);

                // If the result of the validate( ) method call is invalid then
                // display an alert.
                if(validationResultEvent.type == ValidationResultEvent.INVALID) {
                    Alert.show("You must specify a value");
```

Example 13-7. Running validation with ActionScript (continued)

```
                }
            }

        ]]>
    </mx:Script>

    <mx:Form>
        <mx:FormHeading label="Sample Form"/>
        <mx:FormItem id="usernameItem" label="Name">
            <mx:TextInput id="username"/>
        </mx:FormItem>
        <mx:FormItem>
            <mx:Button id="button" label="Submit" click="runValidators(event)" />
        </mx:FormItem>
    </mx:Form>

    <mx:Validator id="validator" source="{username}" property="text"


</mx:Application>
```

When you're working with more than one validator, and you want to call the validate( ) method of each, you can explicitly call the method of each, or you can use a static Validator class method called validateAll( ). The validateAll( ) method requires an array parameter for which every element is a validator object. The validateAll( ) method then returns an array with all the ValidationResultEvent objects for every validator that returned an invalid response. If all the validations passed, the return array is empty. Example 13-8 uses four validators. When the user clicks the button, the button dispatches an event that calls a function that runs validateAll( ), and it displays an alert notifying the user if any of the fields did not validate properly.

Example 13-8. Using validateAll( )

```
<?xml version="1.0" encoding="utf-8"?>
<mx:Application xmlns:mx="http://www.adobe.com/2006/mxml" layout="absolute"
initialize="initializeHandler(event)">
    <mx:Script>
        <![CDATA[
            import mx.events.ValidationResultEvent;
            import mx.controls.Alert;
            import mx.validators.Validator;

            private var _validators:Array;

            private function initializeHandler(event:Event):void {
                // Create an array with the validators.
                _validators = [usernameValidator, phoneValidator, emailValidator,
zipCodeValidator];
            }
```

Example 13-8. Using validateAll() (continued)

```
        private function runValidators(event:Event):void {
            // Run all the validators.
            var results:Array = Validator.validateAll(_validators);

            // If the results array is empty then everything passed. If it's not
            // empty then at least one validator didn't pass.
            if(results.length > 0) {
                var message:String = "The following fields are incorrect:\n";

                // Loop through all the results, and retrieve the id of the
                // source for the corresponding validator.
                for(var i:uint = 0; i < results.length; i++) {
                    message += results[i].target.source.id + "\n";
                }
                Alert.show(message);
            }
        }

    ]]>
</mx:Script>

<mx:Form>
    <mx:FormHeading label="Sample Form"/>
    <mx:FormItem id="usernameItem" label="Name">
        <mx:TextInput id="username"/>
    </mx:FormItem>
    <mx:FormItem label="Phone">
        <mx:TextInput id="phone"/>
    </mx:FormItem>
    <mx:FormItem label="Email">
        <mx:TextInput id="email"/>
    </mx:FormItem>
    <mx:FormItem label="Zip Code">
        <mx:TextInput id="zipcode"/>
    </mx:FormItem>
    <mx:FormItem>
        <mx:Button id="button" label="Submit" click="runValidators(event)" />
    </mx:FormItem>
</mx:Form>

<mx:Validator id="usernameValidator" source="{username}" property="text" />
<mx:PhoneNumberValidator id="phoneValidator" source="{phone}" property="text" />
<mx:EmailValidator id="emailValidator" source="{email}" property="text" />
<mx:ZipCodeValidator id="zipCodeValidator" source="{zipcode}" property="text" />

</mx:Application>
```

Using Standard Framework Validators

The Flex framework includes not only the base validator, `Validator`, but also many validators for common sorts of data formats. The framework ships with the following validators:

- `StringValidator`
- `NumberValidator`
- `DateValidator`
- `EmailValidator`
- `PhoneNumberValidator`
- `ZipCodeValidator`
- `CreditCardValidator`
- `CurrencyValidator`
- `SocialSecurityValidator`
- `RegExpValidator`

All the validator types are subtypes of `Validator`, and they inherit all the same properties and methods. However, each subtype implements specialized validation behaviors. Each validator type is discussed in greater detail in the next few sections.

StringValidator

The `StringValidator` allows you to verify that a string value length is within a specific range. You can define `minLength` and `maxLength` property values for `StringValidators`, as in the following example:

```
<mx:StringValidator source="{sourceObject}" property="sourceProperty"
    minLength="5" maxLength="10" />
```

You can also specify custom error messages, just in case the validation fails, using the `tooShortError` and `tooLongError` properties:

```
<mx:StringValidator source="{sourceObject}" property="sourceProperty"
    minLength="5" maxLength="10" tooShortError="You gotta use a
longer number, buddy" tooLongError="Whoa! Shorter numbers, please" />
```

NumberValidator

The `NumberValidator` allows you to validate all sorts of number values. You can specify a range of allowable values using the `minValue` and `maxValue` properties:

```
<mx:NumberValidator source="{sourceObject}" property="sourceProperty"
    minValue="-5" maxValue="5" />
```

The default value for `minValue` and `maxValue` is NaN (not a number), which means that no limit is placed on the range. If you set a value for either property and you later want to remove the limit, just assign a value of NaN to the validator, as shown here:

```
numberValidator.minValue = NaN;
```

If you want to allow or disallow negative numbers, you can use the `allowNegative` property. The default value is `true`, but setting it to `false` disallows negative numbers:

```
<mx:NumberValidator source="{sourceObject}" property="sourceProperty"
    allowNegative="false" />
```

By default, a `NumberValidator` allows any number type, but you can explicitly specify whether you want to accept all number types (`real`) or just integers (`int`) using the domain property. The default value is `real`, but the following example allows only integers:

```
<mx:NumberValidator source="{sourceObject}" property="sourceProperty"
    domain="int" />
```

When allowing real numbers you can also control the allowable precision. The precision is the measure of the number of decimal places. The `precision` property controls this setting, and it has a default value of –1, which allows all precisions. A value of 0 effectively accomplishes the same thing as setting domain to int (meaning all values must be integers). Positive integer values for precision limit the number of allowable decimal places. The following allows only up to four decimal places:

```
<mx:NumberValidator source="{sourceObject}" property="sourceProperty"
    precision="4" />
```

By default, a `NumberValidator` validates using the thousands place marker and decimal marker characters used in the United States: the comma for thousands and the dot for a decimal place. However, if you need to validate using different marker characters, you can specify those values using the `thousandsSeparator` and `decimalSeparator` properties, respectively. The only rules for these properties are that they must not be digits, and they cannot each have the same value. The following example uses the characters used by many European countries:

```
<mx:NumberValidator source="{sourceObject}" property="sourceProperty"
    thousandsSeparator="." decimalSeparator="," />
```

You can also specify many custom errors using the properties of a `NumberValidator`, including the following: `decimalPointCountError`, `exceedsMaxError`, `integerError`, `invalidCharError`, `invalidFormatCharsError`, `lowerThanMinError`, `negativeError`, `precisionError`, and `separationError`. Each property is documented at *http://livedocs. macromedia.com/flex/2/langref/mx/validators/NumberValidator.html*.

DateValidator

`DateValidator` allows you to validate values as dates. There are several basic properties you can configure to customize this type of validator, and there are advanced properties that allow you to use the validator with several inputs at once.

The basic properties you can use with a `DateValidator` are `allowedFormatChars` and `inputFormat`. The `allowedFormatChars` property allows you to specify which characters are allowable as delimiters between year, month, and date. The default value is /\-., which means any of the following is valid:

```
1/20/2010
1 20 2010
1.20.2010
1-20-2010
1\20\2010
```

The following allows only the asterisk character as a delimiter:

```
<mx:DateValidator source="{sourceObject}" property="sourceProperty"
    allowedFormatChars="*" />
```

The `inputFormat` property determines the order of the year, month, and date parts. You can use the strings YYYY, MM, and DD to represent each of those parts. You can use any of the default delimiter characters as delimiters in the `inputFormat` string. The default value is MM/DD/YYYY. The following example requires that the date appear with the year followed by the month followed by the date:

```
<mx:DateValidator source="{sourceObject}" property="sourceProperty"
    inputFormat="YYYY/MM/DD" />
```

Unlike most of the validators, the `DateValidator` allows you to use one validator to validate more than one input. This is because date inputs frequently may span three inputs: one for the year, one for the month, and one for the date. When you specify a source property value for a `DateValidator`, it assumes you want to validate just one input. However, you have the option to specify three different sources and properties using the `yearSource`, `monthSource`, `daySource`, `yearProperty`, `monthProperty`, and `dayProperty` properties:

```
<?xml version="1.0" encoding="utf-8"?>
<mx:Application xmlns:mx="http://www.adobe.com/2006/mxml" layout="absolute">

    <mx:VBox>
        <mx:TextInput id="year" />
        <mx:TextInput id="month" />
        <mx:TextInput id="day" />
        <mx:Button click="trace(validator.validate())" />
    </mx:VBox>
    <mx:DateValidator id="validator" yearSource="{year}" yearProperty="text"
        monthSource="{month}" monthProperty="text" daySource="{day}"
        dayProperty="text" inputFormat="YYYY/MM/DD" />

</mx:Application>
```

EmailValidator

The `EmailValidator` is easy to implement, as it doesn't require any additional properties aside from the standard source and property. It simply validates the source value as a valid email address:

```
<mx:EmailValidator source="{sourceObject}" property="sourceProperty" />
```

PhoneNumberValidator

The PhoneNumberValidator allows you to verify that a value is in a valid format for a phone number. According to the PhoneNumberValidator rules, a valid phone number consists of at least 10 numeric characters as well as possible additional formatting characters. There is just one property you can use to customize the rules a PhoneNumberValidator uses. The allowedFormatChars property allows you to specify the valid nonnumeric characters that are allowable in a phone number value. The default set of allowable characters consist of (,), -, ., +, and a space. The following allows for phone number values in which the only valid formatting characters are dots:

```
<mx:PhoneNumberValidator source="{sourceObject}" property="sourceProperty"
    allowedFormatChars="." />
```

ZipCodeValidator

The ZipCodeValidator validates that the value is in the format of a valid U.S. zip code or a Canadian postal code. You can specify what type of code it validates using the domain property. The default value is set to the ZipCodeValidatorDomainType.US_ONLY value, which means the validator won't validate Canadian-style postal codes. Optionally, you can use the ZipCodeValidatorDomainType.US_OR_CANADA constant to recognize Canadian postal codes, as shown here:

```
<mx:ZipCodeValidator source="{sourceObject}" property="sourceProperty"
domain="{ZipCodeValidatorDomainType.US_OR_CANADA}" />
```

You can also use the allowedFormatChars property to specify a set of allowable formatting characters consisting of nonalphanumeric characters; the default set consists of a space or a hyphen (-).

CreditCardValidator

The CreditCardValidator allows you to validate that a number is in the proper format and follows the basic rules for credit card numbers. Although it cannot verify that the number is a valid credit card number, it can provide a simple test to ensure that there was no user error causing an incorrect number of digits or the wrong prefix for a card type. The CreditCardValidator can test for American Express, Diners Club, Discover, MasterCard, and Visa number formats. This validator type requires two input sources: one for the card type (usually a radio button group or a combo box) and one for the card number (usually a text input). Here's an example:

```
<?xml version="1.0" encoding="utf-8"?>
<mx:Application xmlns:mx="http://www.adobe.com/2006/mxml" layout="absolute">

    <mx:VBox>
        <mx:ComboBox id="cardType">
            <mx:dataProvider>
                <mx:ArrayCollection>
                    <mx:Array>
```

```
                    <mx:String>American Express</mx:String>
                    <mx:String>Diners Club</mx:String>
                    <mx:String>Discover</mx:String>
                    <mx:String>MasterCard</mx:String>
                    <mx:String>Visa</mx:String>
                </mx:Array>
            </mx:ArrayCollection>
        </mx:dataProvider>
    </mx:ComboBox>
    <mx:TextInput id="cardNumber" />
    <mx:Button click="trace(validator.validate( ))" />
    </mx:VBox>
    <mx:CreditCardValidator id="validator" cardNumberSource="{cardNumber}"
cardNumberProperty="text" cardTypeSource="{cardType}" cardTypeProperty="value" />

</mx:Application>
```

CurrencyValidator

The CurrencyValidator validates currency values, such as dollar amounts. Obviously, currency formatting and numeric formatting have much in common, and for that reason there are many similarities between CurrencyValidator and NumberValidator. For example, CurrencyValidator's minValue, maxValue, precision, allowNegative, decimalSeparator, and thousandsSeparator properties work exactly as they do for a NumberValidator. In addition, a CurrencyValidator allows you to specify currencySymbol and alignSymbol properties. The default value for currencySymbol is the U.S. dollar sign ($). You can use the alignSymbol property to specify where the currency symbol must appear relative to the numeric value.

Valid values are CurrencyValidatorAlignSymbol.LEFT, CurrencyValidatorAlignSymbol. RIGHT, and CurrencyValidatorAlignSymbol.ANY. The default value is CurrencyValidatorAlignSymbol.LEFT.

SocialSecurityValidator

The SocialSecurityValidator validates a value that adheres to the rules for a U.S. Social Security number (###-##-####). This validator allows you to customize the validation rules by specifying the allowable formatting characters via the allowedFormatChars property; the default values are a space or a hyphen (-).

RegExpValidator

The RegExpValidator allows you to use regular expressions to validate values. You can use the RegExpValidator for any type of validation that isn't covered by the other standard validators. The RegExpValidator requires that you set at least one property, expression, which is the regular expression you want to use to validate the data. In addition, you can optionally specify a value for the flags property, which can use any combination of the valid regular expression flags: i, g, m, s, and x.

The following example validates a text area to ensure that it contains at least 50 words:

```
<mx:RegExpValidator expression="(\b\w+\b\W*)\{50,\}" flags="ig"
    source="{comments}" property="text" />
```

Writing Custom Validators

If one of the standard validators doesn't run the sort of validation you require, you can write a custom validator. To write a custom validator, you must write an Action-Script class that extends mx.validators.Validator, and the class must override the doValidation() method. The doValidation() method is protected; it requires an Object parameter and returns an array. If the validation does not succeed, the method returns an array of ValidationResult objects. If the validation does succeed, the method returns an empty array. The WordCountValidator in Example 13-9 is a simple example that validates a value based on minimum word count.

Example 13-9. Custom validator

```
package com.oreilly.programmingflex.validators {

    import mx.validators.Validator;
    import mx.validators.ValidationResult;

    public class WordCountValidator extends Validator {

        private var _count:int;

        public function get count():int {
            return _count;
        }

        public function set count(value:int):void {
            _count = value;
        }

        public function WordCountValidator() {
            super();
            _count = -1;
        }

        override protected function doValidation(value:Object):Array {
            var results:Array = new Array();
            results = super.doValidation(value);
            if(results.length > 0) {
                return results;
            }
            if(_count > -1) {
                var expression:RegExp = /\b\w+\b\W*/ig;
                var matches:Array = String(value).match(expression);
                if(matches.length < _count) {
```

Example 13-9. Custom validator (continued)

```
                    results.push(new ValidationResult(true, null, "tooFewWords",
"You must enter at least " + _count + " words."));
            }
        }
        return results;
    }

  }
}
```

The MXML in Example 13-10 illustrates how you might use `WordCountValidator`.

Example 13-10. Using a custom validator

```
<?xml version="1.0" encoding="utf-8"?>
<mx:Application xmlns:mx="http://www.adobe.com/2006/mxml" xmlns:validators="com.oreilly.
programmingflex.validators.*" layout="absolute">

    <mx:Form>
        <mx:FormHeading label="Sample Form"/>
        <mx:FormItem label="Comments">
            <mx:TextArea id="comments" />
        </mx:FormItem>
        <mx:FormItem>
            <mx:Button id="button" label="Submit"/>
        </mx:FormItem>
    </mx:Form>

    <validators:WordCountValidator source="{comments}" property="text" count="5" />

</mx:Application>
```

Formatting Data

The Flex framework provides a group of components that allow you to format values. You can use these formatters to format data for any reason, though they're most useful for displaying data.

Flex ships with a handful of formatters, such as `NumberFormatter` and `PhoneFormatter`, and you can even build custom formatters based on the same framework. Each formatter uses different properties, but all the formatters work in the same basic manner. First you must create the formatter either with MXML or with ActionScript, assigning property values as necessary. You can then call the `format( )` method of the formatter, passing it the value you want to format. The `format( )` method returns a string. If the formatter cannot format a string, it dispatches an error event.

You can create a formatter using MXML with the corresponding MXML tag. For example, the following creates a `NumberFormatter` instance. This example uses all the default property values, though you could also set the property values in the MXML.

Note that you should always assign an `id` value to formatters because you'll need to reference them with ActionScript.

```
<mx:NumberFormatter id="numberFormatter" />
```

You can optionally create a formatter with ActionScript using the constructor, as shown here:

```
var numberFormatter:NumberFormatter = new NumberFormatter();
```

Once you've created a formatter object, you must call the `format()` method to apply the formatting. The `format()` method requires that you pass it the value you want to format. The method does not change the original value, but it returns a new string formatted according to the rules set by the formatter and its properties:

```
var formattedValue:String = numberFormatter.format(userInput.text);
```

NumberFormatter

The `NumberFormatter` allows you to format (as a string) any number or value that can be converted to a number. You can see the default formatting using the following code:

```
<mx:TextInput text="{numberFormatter.format('1234.56789')}" />
<mx:NumberFormatter id="numberFormatter" />
```

The preceding example displays 1,234.56789. The default formatting doesn't affect the precision of the number, it merely adds a thousands place marker.

With a `NumberFormatter`, you can control whether and how a number is rounded with the rounding property. The default value is none, although you can optionally specify a value of up, down, or nearest. The following example displays 1,235, as it rounds up to the nearest whole number:

```
<mx:TextInput text="{numberFormatter.format('1234.56789')}" />
<mx:NumberFormatter id="numberFormatter" rounding="nearest" />
```

You can also control the precision of the formatted output using the `precision` property. The default value is -1, which doesn't enforce any precision constraints. A nonnegative integer value for the `precision` property rounds the decimal places to that many, if necessary. The `rounding` property value is used to determine how to round for precision, if necessary. The following displays 1,234.56:

```
<mx:TextInput text="{numberFormatter.format('1234.56789')}" />
<mx:NumberFormatter id="numberFormatter" precision="2" />
```

If the input value uses decimal and/or thousands place markers, the formatter needs to know how to interpret them. `NumberFormatter` uses the `decimalSeparatorFrom` and `thousandsSeparatorFrom` properties for this purpose. The default values are the dot (.) and the comma (,); however, you can specify different values. The following example uses the delimiting characters as they are used in many European countries (the formatted text is 1,234.56789):

```
<mx:TextInput text="{numberFormatter.format('1.234,56789')}" />
<mx:NumberFormatter id="numberFormatter" decimalSeparatorFrom=","
    thousandsSeparatorFrom="." />
```

You can also specify the delimiting characters to use in the formatted output by way of the decimalSeparatorTo and thousandsSeparatorTo properties. The following example displays 1.234,56789:

```
<mx:TextInput text="{numberFormatter.format('1,234.56789')}" />
<mx:NumberFormatter id="numberFormatter" decimalSeparatorTo=","
    thousandsSeparatorTo="." />
```

You can also specify whether to use the thousands delimiter at all with the useThousandsSeparator property; the default value is true. A value of false won't display the thousands place delimiter.

The useNegativeSign property allows you to specify how negative numbers are formatted. The default value is true, and it results in a number preceded by a negative sign (e.g., -1). If the property is set to false, the number is surrounded by parentheses (e.g., (1)).

DateFormatter

The DateFormatter allows you to format the data from a Date object as a string. There is one configurable property that you can use with a DateFormatter. That property, called formatString, allows you to specify the way in which the elements of a Date object (year, month, day, hours, etc.) should be formatted in the output string. The default value is MM/DD/YYYY, which is the month followed by the day of the month followed by the four-digit year. The following characters have special meaning in the formatString value:

- Y: year
- M: month
- D: day of month
- E: day of week
- A: AM/PM
- J: hour (0–23)
- H: hour (1–24)
- K: hour (0–11 for use with AM/PM)
- L: hour (1–12 for use with AM/PM)
- N: minute
- S: second

Y, M, D, and E yield different results when used in different groupings. For example, YY results in a two-digit year, whereas YYYY results in a four-digit year. This same pattern is generally true for each of these characters. For example, M/D/YYYY displays 1/2/2010 for January 2, 2010, but MM/DD/YYYY displays 01/02/2010. M and E also result in abbreviations and full names of the months and days of the week when used in groups of three and four. For example, MMM can display Jan., and MMMM displays January.

You can use any other characters in a formatString value, and they are interpreted literally. The following example displays January 2, 2010 at 4:25:10 PM:

```
<mx:TextInput text="{dateFormatter.format(new Date(2010, 0, 2, 16, 25, 10))}" />
<mx:DateFormatter id="dateFormatter" formatString="MMMM D, YYYY at L:N:S A" />
```

CurrencyFormatter

The CurrencyFormatter works very much like the NumberFormatter except that it adds a currency symbol in addition to formatting a number value. CurrencyFormatter uses all the same properties as NumberFormatter, but it adds two additional properties: currencySymbol and alignSymbol. The default value for currencySymbol is the U.S. dollar sign ($). The default value for alignSymbol is left; the other possible value is right.

PhoneFormatter

The PhoneFormatter takes any number or string that can be converted to a number, and it formats that as a phone number. The PhoneFormatter allows you to configure the format of the output using the formatString property. The default value of the formatString property is (###) ###-####, in which the # is a placeholder for a digit. The following example outputs 123.456.7890:

```
<mx:TextInput text="{phoneFormatter.format(1234567890)}" />
<mx:PhoneFormatter id="phoneFormatter" formatString="###.###.####" />
```

By default, the formatString property allows only a specific set of characters. That set of characters is dictated by the validPatternChars property, which has a default value set consisting of +, (,), #, -, ., and a space. You can customize the allowable characters in the pattern if you want. The following example outputs 123*456*7890:

```
<mx:TextInput text="{phoneFormatter.format(1234567890)}" />
<mx:PhoneFormatter id="phoneFormatter" formatString="###*###*####"
    validPatternChars="#*" />
```

You can also specify the area code using an areaCode property. The areaCode property defaults to −1, which means that no area code is prepended to the formatted string. However, if you specify a non-negative integer value for the areaCode property, it gets prepended to the phone number. For example, the following displays (123) 456-7890:

```
<mx:TextInput text="{phoneFormatter.format(4567890)}" />
<mx:PhoneFormatter id="phoneFormatter" formatString="###-####" areaCode="123" />
```

If you want to specify the pattern for the area code, you can use the areaCodeFormat property. The default value is (###). The following example displays 123 456-7890:

```
<mx:TextInput text="{phoneFormatter.format(4567890)}" />
<mx:PhoneFormatter id="phoneFormatter" formatString="###-####"
    areaCode="123" areaCodeFormat="### " />
```

Note that when you use a specific value for the areaCode property, the formatter will not place a space between the area code and the formatted number. Therefore, in the preceding example, we added a space as the last character of the areaCodeFormat property.

ZipCodeFormatter

The ZipCodeFormatter allows you to format a number or string as a zip or postal code in U.S. or Canadian format. You can configure the formatter via the formatString property. The default value is #####, which formats a value as a U.S. zip code. The only other possible formatString property values are #####-#### (U.S. zip+4 format), ##### #### (U.S. zip+4 format with a space), ###-### (Canadian format), and ### ### (Canadian format with a space). The following formats the number in U.S. zip+4 format:

```
<mx:TextInput text="{zipCodeFormatter.format(123456789)}" />
<mx:ZipCodeFormatter id="zipCodeFormatter" formatString="#####-####" />
```

Writing Custom Formatters

If one of the standard formatters does not assist you in a particular formatting requirement, you can write a custom formatter. To write a custom formatter, you must write an ActionScript class that extends mx.formatters.Formatter. The class must override the format( ) method. Example 13-11 applies zero-fill to numbers.

Example 13-11. Creating a custom formatter

```
package com.oreilly.programmingflex.formatters {
    import mx.formatters.Formatter;

    public class ZeroFillFormatter extends Formatter {

        private var _count:int;

        // The count getter/setter allows the user of the formatter
        // to set the number of total characters up to which the value
        // may require zero-fill.
```

Example 13-11. Creating a custom formatter (continued)

```
    public function set count(value:int):void {
        _count = value;
    }

    public function get count():int {
        return _count;
    }

    // Call the superclass constructor, and set _count to -1, which is
    // used as the value to indicate no zero-fill should be applied.
    public function ZeroFillFormatter() {
        super();
        _count = -1;
    }

    // The format() method signature must match that of Formatter.
    override public function format(value:Object):String {

        // If necessary, convert the parameter to a string. Otherwise,
        // cast to a string.
        var stringValue:String;
        if(!(value is String)) {
            stringValue = value.toString();
        }
        else {
            stringValue = String(value);
        }

        // If the length of the string value is less than _count,
        // prepend zeros.
        while(_count > stringValue.length) {
            stringValue = "0" + stringValue;
        }
        return stringValue;
    }

    }
}
```

Example 13-12 illustrates how to use this custom formatter.

Example 13-12. Using a custom formatter

```
<?xml version="1.0" encoding="utf-8"?>
<mx:Application xmlns:mx="http://www.adobe.com/2006/mxml" xmlns:formatters="com.oreilly.
programmingflex.formatters.*" layout="absolute">

    <mx:TextInput text="{zeroFillFormatter.format(123456789)}" />
    <formatters:ZeroFillFormatter id="zeroFillFormatter" count="15" />

</mx:Application>
```

The preceding example displays 000000123456789 in the text input control.

Summary

In this chapter, you learned about additional ways to work with data. This chapter covered two main topics: validating and formatting. Validating data means ensuring that the data meets certain rules prior to submitting it for some course of action. This is useful when you want to verify that user input data is in the correct form. Formatting data typically means displaying data to the user in a particular way, such as adding hyphens, parentheses, decimal place separators, and so on.

Customizing Application Appearance

The Flex framework has a great deal of functionality built into it, making it relatively easy to start building applications. All the user interface components and layout containers greatly simplify the process of creating a new application because you can utilize all the functionality of the components without having to write all the code to make them work. However, as great as that is, it would be nearly useless in most cases if you could not customize the appearance of the components. Yet, as we'll see in this chapter, customizing the appearance of Flex components is another built-in feature.

There are essentially two ways to customize the appearance of components:

- Apply styles.
- Change skins.

Styles are settings such as color, font face, border settings, row height, and so on. These are settings that you can customize entirely programmatically both at compile time and at runtime. Styles allow you to customize a great deal of the appearance of components, yet they can go only so far. For example, if you want to change the background color of a button, you can do that using styles, but if you want to completely change the shape of a button (from a rounded rectangle to a trapezoid, for instance), you need to use a different technique in which you change the skins of the component. *Skins* can be graphical elements (PNG files, for example) or programmatic elements (classes), and they allow you to not only customize the existing elements of a component, but also completely change which elements are used. Therefore, using custom skins allows you to alter the appearance of a component so completely that it is unrecognizable from its original default appearance. You can use both styles and skins at the same time (although oftentimes applying a skin will cancel out certain style settings).

In this chapter, we'll look more closely at all the techniques you can use to customize application appearance through the use of styles and skins. We'll also look at working with fonts, using Cascading Style Sheets (CSS), customizing an application preloader, and creating custom themes for styling.

Using Styles

Styles allow you to control a great many aspects of an application's appearance, including colors, fonts, spacing, animation settings, and more. You can define and apply styles in many ways, each with its own advantages and disadvantages. These can be categorized as follows:

- Instance styles
- Class selectors (stylesheets)
- Type selectors (stylesheets)
- Global styles

Because there are so many ways to apply styles, it is actually possible to apply different values for the same style to a component using different ways to apply that style. For example, you can set the color of a button component using an instance style as well as using a type selector. Because this is possible, it's necessary for Flex to have an order of precedence for the application of styles. That order (from greatest precedence to least) is the same as the list preceding this paragraph. That means that if Flex has to decide between an instance style and a type selector, it will use the value from the instance style.

Style Value Formats

There are lots of different styles, and each style has a required data type for its value. For example, the style used to set the font face (fontFamily) requires a string value specifying the name of the font to use, yet the style used to set the font size (fontSize) requires a numeric value. Behind the scenes, all styles accept values of one of these two data types: string and number. However, for convenience, some styles accept more than one type of value. For example, color styles should be specified using numeric values, but you can also specify one of the color strings, such as red or green. Those values are translated to number values behind the scenes. Also, some styles actually require number values of 0 or 1, but you can optionally specify a Boolean value of true or false. This next example sets the dropShadowEnabled property to 1, but it could also use the value true to achieve the same effect:

```
<mx:Style>
    VBox {
        backgroundColor: green;
        borderStyle: solid;
        dropShadowEnabled: 1;
    }
</mx:Style>
<mx:VBox width="200" height="200">
```

Some styles allow you to specify a unit of measurement. However, Flex ignores all units of measurement, using only the numeric portion of the value. For example, when you specify a font size, you can also specify a unit of measurement such as pixels or points, though the result will always be the same regardless of what unit of measurement is specified (or if none is specified). This allows you to use the same stylesheets for your Flex applications that you might use with HTML applications. The following example sets the font-size property of a class selector to 15px, which is interpreted simply as 15 by Flex:

```
.example {
    font-size: 15px
}
```

 The Flex Style Explorer allows you to see what styles are available for Flex components, and you can adjust those settings in real time and see the generated CSS to create the style settings. You can view the Flex Style Explorer at *http://www.adobe.com/go/flex_styles_explorer_app*.

Instance Styles

Instance styles are the styles set for a specific component instance. You can set instance styles using MXML or ActionScript. Setting instance styles using MXML is often referred to as setting an inline style because you simply set the value for an attribute in the component tag. Here's an example of a button component for which we're setting the color style:

```
<mx:Button label="Example" color="red" />
```

You can set many inline styles at the same time. Here's the same button with additional styles set inline:

```
<mx:Button label="Example" color="red" borderColor="yellow"
    cornerRadius="10" fontStyle="italic" />
```

You can also set styles on an instance using ActionScript via the setStyle( ) method. The setStyle( ) method is defined by UIComponent, which means that you can call the method for all (visual) Flex components. The setStyle( ) method requires two parameters: the name of the style property as a string (e.g., color) and the value for the property. Here's an example that sets a button component's color style:

```
button.setStyle("color", "red");
```

If you want to set many styles for a component, you need to call setStyle( ) for each style. Here's an example that sets many styles for one component:

```
button.setStyle("color", "red");
button.setStyle("borderColor", "yellow");
button.setStyle("cornerRadius", 10);
button.setStyle("fontStyle", "italic");
```

If you apply styles using setStyle( ), you can change styles at runtime. That means you can use setStyle( ) to change a style even if it was set inline. Example 14-1 sets the color style both inline and with ActionScript. Because setStyle( ) is called after the inline style was applied, the button label appears in red rather than green.

Example 14-1. Setting a style with setStyle( )

```
<?xml version="1.0" encoding="utf-8"?>
<mx:Application xmlns:mx="http://www.adobe.com/2006/mxml"
    initialize="initializeHandler(event)">
    <mx:Script>
        <![CDATA[
            private function initializeHandler(event:Event):void {
                button.setStyle("color", "red");
            }
        ]]>
    </mx:Script>
    <mx:Button id="button" label="Example" color="green" />
</mx:Application>
```

If you want to retrieve the style value for a specific instance, you can use the getStyle( ) method. The getStyle( ) method requires a parameter specifying the name of the style. The method then returns the current value of the style. The following example retrieves the color style value for the button and displays it:

```
<mx:Button id="button" label="Example" color="red" />
<mx:TextInput text="{button.getStyle('color').toString(16)}" />
```

Using CSS

You can use CSS to define styles for components. Although you can use CSS that gets loaded at runtime, this section deals only with CSS that is compiled into the Flex application. (We'll look at runtime CSS in the "Runtime CSS section, later in this chapter.)

CSS is a standard way to apply styles across platforms, languages, and frameworks. The syntax of CSS in Flex is identical to the syntax of CSS as it is used by HTML. For example, here's a sample class selector for a Flex application written in CSS:

```
.example {
    color: red;
}
```

Note that even though the syntax of CSS in Flex is identical to that used by HTML, not all the style properties available in HTML are also available in Flex.

When you define CSS for Flex applications, you have two basic options: external stylesheets and local style definitions. In both cases, the CSS is compiled into the Flex application, so they are functionally identical. However, there are advantages to each. External stylesheets enable you to more cleanly distinguish between layout (MXML) and style definitions (external CSS document). Additionally, when you use external stylesheets you can define the styles in one location but use them in many MXML documents without having to redefine them. On the other hand, local style definitions are more convenient when you intend to use the style or styles in just one MXML file.

An external stylesheet is a text file that you compile into a Flex application by using the source attribute of a Style MXML tag. The following code is an example of a Style tag that compiles in an external stylesheet defined in *styles.css*. The styles defined in the external document are then available within the MXML document within which the Style tag appears.

```
<mx:Style source="styles.css" />
```

If you want to define local style selector definitions, you can simply place the CSS between opening and closing Style tags, as in the following example:

```
<mx:Style>
    .example {
        color: red;
    }
</mx:Style>
```

Whether you're using external stylesheets or local style definitions, you can define the same sorts of style selectors: class selectors and type selectors. Class selector names always start with a dot (.), as in the preceding example. A selector can define one or more styles. The preceding example defines just one style for the selector. The following example defines two styles for the selector:

```
.example {
    color: red;
    font-style: italic;
}
```

When you want to apply a class selector to a component, you must set the styleName property of the component. The styleName value should be the name of the class selector without the initial dot. The following example sets the styleName property of a button to the example style selector:

```
<mx:Button label="Example" styleName="example" />
```

If you want to set the styleName property of a component using ActionScript, use the standard dot syntax, as follows:

```
button.styleName="example";
```

The other type of selector is called a type selector, and it automatically applies to all components of the type that match the name of the selector. For example, you can define a type selector called Button, and it automatically gets applied to all buttons:

```
Button {
    color: red;
}
```

Type selectors always take precedence over class selectors. Example 14-2 defines a type selector and a class selector. In this case, the font style is italic because the type selector sets it. However, because the class selector defines the color as green, the button label is green rather than red.

Example 14-2. Selector precedence

```
<?xml version="1.0" encoding="utf-8"?>
<mx:Application xmlns:mx="http://www.adobe.com/2006/mxml">
    <mx:Style>
        Button {
            color: red;
            font-style: italic;
        }
        .example {
            color: green;
        }
    </mx:Style>
    <mx:Button label="Example" styleName="example" />
</mx:Application>
```

Neither local style definitions nor external stylesheets take precedence inherently. If you use both in one document, you will see that the order in which they appear in the document is what determines which takes precedence. Let's look at a complete example that illustrates this. Here's *styles.css*, an external stylesheet document. It contains just one style definition, a class selector called example:

```
.example {
    color: red;
    font-style: italic;
}
```

Example 14-3 is the MXML document that both uses this external stylesheet and has a local style definition for the same class selector. In this case, the button has a green and italicized label because the local style definition takes precedence over the external stylesheet, only because it appears after the external stylesheet include in the code.

Example 14-3. Order of style tags affects styles (part 1)

```
<?xml version="1.0" encoding="utf-8"?>
<mx:Application xmlns:mx="http://www.adobe.com/2006/mxml">
    <mx:Style source="styles.css" />
    <mx:Style>
        .example {
            color: green;
        }
    </mx:Style>
    <mx:Button label="Example" styleName="example" />
</mx:Application>
```

Yet, if you reverse the order of the two Style tags, as in Example 14-4, you'll see that the button label is now red.

Example 14-4. Order of style tags affects styles (part 2)

```
<?xml version="1.0" encoding="utf-8"?>
<mx:Application xmlns:mx="http://www.adobe.com/2006/mxml">
    <mx:Style>
        .example {
            color: green;
        }
    </mx:Style>
    <mx:Style source="styles.css" />
    <mx:Button label="Example" styleName="example" />
</mx:Application>
```

Style Properties

In Flex, all style property names must be capable of being treated as variables. For this reason, it's necessary that all style property names follow the naming rules for variables, meaning they must consist of alphabetical and numeric characters. Notably, variable names cannot contain hyphens. However, traditional CSS style property names use hyphens (e.g., font-family), and for this reason, Flex supports both hyphenated and camel-case style property names in CSS. (Flex converts hyphenated style property names to the camel-case equivalent behind the scenes.) For example, if you want to set the font name, you can use the style property font-family or fontFamily when using CSS. However, you cannot use hyphenated style properties in ActionScript using setStyle( ) or with inline styles.

Using StyleManager

Behind the scenes, Flex converts all CSS to ActionScript instructions that are managed by a class called mx.managers.StyleManager. In most cases, it is not necessary to work directly with the StyleManager class. However, in the event that you want to have greater runtime control over styles applied as either class selectors or type selectors, you'll need to work with StyleManager.

The StyleManager class allows you to access and configure existing selectors that were created via CSS, and it allows you to add new selectors programmatically. To access an existing selector, use the static method called getStyleDeclaration( ). The method requires a string parameter specifying the name of the selector. The name of the selector should include the initial dot for class selectors. The method returns an mx.styles.CSSStyleDeclaration object representing the selector:

```
var selector:CSSStyleDeclaration =
StyleManager.getStyleDeclaration(".exampleSelector");
```

If you try to access a selector that does not exist, the Flex application throws a runtime error.

You can use the setStyle( ) method for a CSSStyleDeclaration object to edit the styles for that object. The setStyle( ) method for CSSStyleDeclaration is identical to the method of the same name for UIComponent. You pass it the name of the style and the new value, as in the following example:

```
selector.setStyle("color", "red");
```

If you want to add a new selector at runtime that wasn't defined at compile time, you can do so by constructing a new CSSStyleDeclaration object and then adding it to the StyleManager using the setStyleDeclaration( ) method. The setStyleDeclaration( ) method allows you to specify the name of the selector (specifying null causes the StyleManager to use the name of the selector from the CSSStyleDeclaration object), the CSSStyleDeclaration object, and a Boolean value indicating whether to immediately update the styles for affected components:

```
var selector:CSSStyleDeclaration = new CSSStyleDeclaration(".newSelector");
StyleManager.setStyleDeclaration(null, selector, true);
```

Setting a style declaration is a computationally expensive operation. If you are going to set more than one style declaration at a time, it is best to set the third parameter of the setStyleDeclaration( ) method to false for all but the last method call:

```
StyleManager.setStyleDeclaration(".newSelector1", selector1, false);
StyleManager.setStyleDeclaration(".newSelector2", selector2, false);
StyleManager.setStyleDeclaration(".newSelector3", selector3, false);
StyleManager.setStyleDeclaration(".newSelector4", selector4, true);
```

You should be careful when using setStyleDeclaration( ) that you don't mistakenly overwrite an existing selector. Most component types already have type selectors defined in the *defaults.css* document (found in the default theme used by Flex, as discussed in the discussion of themes, later in this chapter) that is compiled into Flex applications by default. That means that even if you didn't define a Button type selector, your Flex application is probably using one that it compiled in from *defaults.css*. Thus, if you replace the Button type selector with a call to setStyleDeclaration( ), you will lose all the style settings that buttons have by default if you haven't explicitly given values to those styles in your new selector. The better option in most cases is to get a reference to the existing CSSStyleDefinition object and edit the style values for that object using setStyle( ).

Global Styles

You can apply global styles using the `global` selector. You can set the `global` selector in external stylesheets, local style definitions, or using `StyleManager`. Global styles always have the lowest precedence, which means that a global style is applied only if it's not overridden by a higher-priority setting such as a type selector, a class selector, or an instance style. Example 14-5 uses a `global` selector along with a class selector. In this example, the first button is green and italic, and the second button uses just the global style settings.

Example 14-5. Using a global selector with a class selector

```
<?xml version="1.0" encoding="utf-8"?>
<mx:Application xmlns:mx="http://www.adobe.com/2006/mxml" layout="vertical">
    <mx:Style>
        global {
            color: red;
            font-style: italic;
        }
        .example {
            color: green
        }
    </mx:Style>
    <mx:Button label="Example 1" styleName="example" />
    <mx:Button label="Example 2" />
</mx:Application>
```

Reviewing Style Precedence

Style precedence can be a little confusing at first because there are simply so many ways to set styles. For that reason, we'll now summarize the precedence. From highest precedence to lowest, here's the list:

1. Instance style set with `setStyle( )`
2. Inline style
3. Class selector set with `StyleManager`
4. Class selector set in stylesheet
5. Type selector set with `StyleManager`
6. Type selector set stylesheet
7. Global styles

Working with Fonts

When you want to customize the font used by components within your Flex application, you'll need to know the specifics of how to work with font outlines. The first important thing to understand in regard to this topic is how Flex differentiates between types of fonts. In terms of how Flex deals with fonts, there are three types of fonts:

System fonts

These are the fonts that are installed on the user's system. Just as an HTML page can display text using a font installed on the user's system, so too can Flex applications.

Device fonts

There are three device fonts: _sans, _serif, and _typewriter, which resolve to the most similar system font on the user's computer.

Embedded fonts

Flex applications allow you to embed font outlines within the *.swf* file, so you can guarantee that all users will see the same font even if they don't have it installed on their system.

System fonts

When you use system fonts, you add no additional file size to the Flex application by embedding fonts. You can specify system fonts simply by specifying the name of the system font to use for the fontFamily (or font-family) style, as in this example:

```
font-family: Verdana;
```

The problem with system fonts is that the user must have the font. Otherwise, the text will render using the default system font. For this reason, it's usually a good idea to specify system fonts as a fallback list. You can specify the value for font-family as a comma-delimited list of font names. The Flex application tries to use the first font on the list, and if it cannot find that system font, it uses the next font on the list:

```
font-family: Verdana, Arial, Helvetica;
```

Device fonts

Device fonts are not specific fonts, but rather names of font categories. Flex recognizes three device fonts: _sans, _serif, and _typewriter. These device fonts resolve to a system font that is in a general font category. For example, _sans usually resolves to Arial or Helvetica, _serif usually resolves to Times New Roman, and _typewriter usually resolves to Courier or Courier New. Using device fonts is a way to virtually guarantee that the text will appear in a general style (i.e., sans-serif, serif, or monotype). When you use a device font name in CSS, you must enclose the value in quotation marks:

```
font-family: "_sans";
```

 Often when you use system fonts, it is advisable to add a device font as the last font in the fallback list, as in the following example:

```
font-family: Verdana, Arial, Helvetica, "_sans";
```

Embedded fonts

Although there are use cases for system fonts and device fonts, the fonts most frequently used in Flex applications are embedded fonts. Embedded fonts compile the font outlines into the *.swf*, guaranteeing that all users will see the text in the same font. The potential downside of embedded fonts is that they increase the size of the *.swf* file. However, considering that Flex applications are rich Internet applications, the actual file size increase for an embedded font is usually unsubstantial. The exception to that would be the use of extended characters and multibyte fonts, for use with languages such as Japanese and Chinese. Yet even in some of those cases, the file size increase can sometimes be mitigated by embedding only the outlines for the fonts required by the application.

There are other reasons to embed fonts aside from just wanting to guarantee consistent fonts for all users. Embedded fonts solve a few problems with system fonts. System fonts in Flex applications cannot be rotated, nor can you adjust the alpha of system fonts. If you attempt to rotate system fonts, the text disappears. If you attempt to adjust the alpha of a system font, you will not see an effect. However, if you embed the font, you can both rotate the text and adjust the alpha. Furthermore, system fonts are not antialiased; when you increase the size of system fonts, the aliasing is more apparent, and it will look like the text has jagged edges. Embedded fonts are anti-aliased, meaning they look better at larger sizes. (Note that this is a double-edged sword because antialiased text is less legible at smaller font sizes. We'll look at the solution to this in the "Using FlashType" section, later in this chapter.)

There are a handful of ways to embed fonts. First we'll look at how to embed fonts when you have the font file (a *.ttf* file). You can embed these fonts using the `Embed` metadata tag within ActionScript. To embed the font this way, use the `source` attribute to specify the path to the *.ttf* file and the `fontName` attribute to specify the name of the font because you will want to reference it throughout your application. In order for the metadata tag to work, you must place it just before a variable declaration of type `Class`. You will not need to use the variable at all, but the compiler requires this. Here's an example that embeds a font called Century Gothic from the *.ttf* file using the `fontName` of gothicCentury:

```
[Embed(source="C:\\WINDOWS\\Fonts\\GOTHIC.ttf", fontName="gothicCentury")]
private var _centuryGothic:Class;
```

Once you've embedded the font, you can use the `fontName` value to reference it just as you would any other font, as shown in Example 14-6.

Example 14-6. Embedding a font using the Embed metadata tag

```
<?xml version="1.0" encoding="utf-8"?>
<mx:Application xmlns:mx="http://www.adobe.com/2006/mxml">
    <mx:Style>
        global {
            fontFamily: gothicCentury;
        }
```

Example 14-6. Embedding a font using the Embed metadata tag (continued)

```
    </mx:Style>
    <mx:Script>
        <![CDATA[

            [Embed(source="C:\\WINDOWS\\Fonts\\GOTHIC.ttf", fontName="gothicCentury")]
            private var _centuryGothic:Class;

        ]]>
    </mx:Script>
    <mx:TextArea text="Example Text" />
</mx:Application>
```

When you embed a font, only one set of the font outlines is embedded. In Example 14-6, only the standard font outlines are embedded, not the bold or italic outlines. In Example 14-7, you can clearly see the effects of this when you try to add a button instance to the preceding example.

Example 14-7. Missing font outlines cause default fonts to appear

```
<?xml version="1.0" encoding="utf-8"?>
<mx:Application xmlns:mx="http://www.adobe.com/2006/mxml">
    <mx:Style>
        global {
            fontFamily: gothicCentury;
        }
    </mx:Style>
    <mx:Script>
        <![CDATA[

            [Embed(source="C:\\WINDOWS\\Fonts\\GOTHIC.ttf", fontName="gothicCentury")]
            private var _centuryGothic:Class;

        ]]>
    </mx:Script>
    <mx:TextArea text="Example Text" />
    <mx:Button label="Example" />
</mx:Application>
```

Because buttons default to using the bold version of a font, Example 14-7 uses the Century Gothic font for the text area, but it uses the default system font for the button label. In order to fix this, we must also embed the bold font outlines for the same font using the same fontName value. However, this time we need to set the fontWeight attribute to bold; see Example 14-8. (If you want to embed the italicized font outlines, you should set fontStyle to italic.)

Example 14-8. Embedding standard and bold font outlines

```
<?xml version="1.0" encoding="utf-8"?>
<mx:Application xmlns:mx="http://www.adobe.com/2006/mxml">
    <mx:Style>
```

Example 14-8. Embedding standard and bold font outlines (continued)

```
            global {
                fontFamily: gothicCentury;
            }
        </mx:Style>
        <mx:Script>
            <![CDATA[

                [Embed(source="C:\\WINDOWS\\Fonts\\GOTHIC.ttf", fontName="gothicCentury")]
                private var _centuryGothic:Class;

                [Embed(source="C:\\WINDOWS\\Fonts\\GOTHICB.ttf", fontName="gothicCentury",
    fontWeight="bold")]
                private var _centuryGothicBold:Class;

            ]]>
        </mx:Script>
        <mx:TextArea text="Example Text" />
        <mx:Button label="Example" />
    </mx:Application>
```

You can also embed fonts from CSS using the @font-face directive. This is particularly useful when you use external stylesheets because you can compile them to use as themes or as runtime CSS. However, it's also equally okay to use this technique for local style definitions simply because you prefer the syntax to the Embed metadata tag. In the following examples, we'll use local style definitions for the sake of simplicity and clarity.

The @font-face directive allows for all the same attributes/properties as the Embed metadata tag when embedding fonts. The exceptions are that the source attribute of the metadata tag is called src in the @font-face directive and fontName from the metadata tag is called fontFamily in the directive. Furthermore, the value of the src attribute should be wrapped in url( ), as shown in the following example:

```
    @font-face {
        src: url("C:\\WINDOWS\\Fonts\\GOTHIC.ttf");
        fontFamily: gothicCentury;
    }
```

Example 14-9 is the earlier MXML example rewritten with @font-face directives.

Example 14-9. Using the @font-face directive

```
<?xml version="1.0" encoding="utf-8"?>
<mx:Application xmlns:mx="http://www.adobe.com/2006/mxml">
    <mx:Style>
        @font-face {
            src: url("C:\\WINDOWS\\Fonts\\GOTHIC.ttf");
            fontFamily: gothicCentury;
        }
        @font-face {
            src: url("C:\\WINDOWS\\Fonts\\GOTHICB.ttf");
```

Example 14-9. Using the @font-face directive (continued)

```
        fontFamily: gothicCentury;
        fontWeight: bold;
    }
    global {
        fontFamily: gothicCentury;
    }
</mx:Style>
<mx:TextArea text="Example Text" />
<mx:Button label="Example" />
</mx:Application>
```

Flex allows you to embed a font in a different manner as well. Rather than embedding the font by way of the *.ttf* file, you can use the font name as it's recognized by the computer system. When you want to do this, you can use the Embed metadata tag. Rather than using the source attribute, you should use the systemFont and specify the name of the font as it's known by the system. Additionally, when you specify a system font name, you must also specify the MIME type by using the mimeType attribute. The value should be either application/x-font or application/x-font-truetype. Example 14-10 uses system font names to embed fonts.

Example 14-10. Embedding fonts by system name

```
<?xml version="1.0" encoding="utf-8"?>
<mx:Application xmlns:mx="http://www.adobe.com/2006/mxml">
    <mx:Style>
        global {
            fontFamily: gothicCentury;
        }
    </mx:Style>
    <mx:Script>
        <![CDATA[

            [Embed(systemFont="Century Gothic", fontName="gothicCentury",
mimeType="application/x-font")]
            private var _centuryGothic:Class;

            [Embed(systemFont="Century Gothic", fontName="gothicCentury",
fontWeight="bold", mimeType="application/x-font")]
            private var _centuryGothicBold:Class;

        ]]>
    </mx:Script>
    <mx:TextArea text="Example Text" />
    <mx:Button label="Example" />
</mx:Application>
```

You can also embed fonts by name using CSS. To do so, you should wrap the src value using local( ) rather than url( ). The following example illustrates how this works:

```
<?xml version="1.0" encoding="utf-8"?>
<mx:Application xmlns:mx="http://www.adobe.com/2006/mxml">
    <mx:Style>
        @font-face {
            src: local("Century Gothic");
            fontFamily: gothicCentury;
        }
        @font-face {
            src: local("Century Gothic");
            fontFamily: gothicCentury;
            fontWeight: bold;
        }
        global {
            fontFamily: gothicCentury;
        }
    </mx:Style>
    <mx:TextArea text="Example Text" />
    <mx:Button label="Example" />
</mx:Application>
```

Embedding font subsets

When you embed a font, by default all the outlines are embedded, regardless of what characters are used in the application. In some cases, your application may not use all the font outlines, and in those cases, it is unnecessary and wasteful to embed all the font outlines. For that reason, Flex allows you to specify ranges of characters to embed using the unicodeRange attribute for @font-face or the Embed metadata tag. The unicodeRange attribute allows you to specify one or more Unicode values or ranges of Unicode values. The Unicode values must be in the form U+*code*, such as U+00A1. You can specify ranges by placing a hyphen between two values, as in U+00A1-U+00FF. You can specify more than one value or range by delimiting them with commas, as in Example 14-11.

Example 14-11. Embedding font subset ranges

```
<?xml version="1.0" encoding="utf-8"?>
<mx:Application xmlns:mx="http://www.adobe.com/2006/mxml">
    <mx:Style>
        @font-face {
            src: url("C:\\WINDOWS\\Fonts\\GOTHIC.ttf");
            fontFamily: gothicCentury;
            unicodeRange: U+0041-U+007F;
        }
        @font-face {
            src: url("C:\\WINDOWS\\Fonts\\GOTHICB.ttf");
            fontFamily: gothicCentury;
            fontWeight: bold;
            unicodeRange: U+0041-U+007F;
```

Example 14-11. Embedding font subset ranges (continued)

```
        }
        global {
            fontFamily: gothicCentury;
        }
    </mx:Style>
    <mx:TextArea text="++ Example Text ++" />
    <mx:Button label="Example" />
</mx:Application>
```

Example 14-11 embeds the range of standard Latin alphabet characters, but not the + character. That means the alphabetic characters in the components show up, but the + characters do not. Example 14-12 embeds the + character as well.

Example 14-12. Embedding lists of font subsets

```
<?xml version="1.0" encoding="utf-8"?>
<mx:Application xmlns:mx="http://www.adobe.com/2006/mxml">
    <mx:Style>
        @font-face {
            src: url("C:\\WINDOWS\\Fonts\\GOTHIC.ttf");
            fontFamily: gothicCentury;
            unicodeRange: U+0041-U+007F,U+002B;
        }
        @font-face {
            src: url("C:\\WINDOWS\\Fonts\\GOTHICB.ttf");
            fontFamily: gothicCentury;
            fontWeight: bold;
            unicodeRange: U+0041-U+007F,U+002B;
        }
        global {
            fontFamily: gothicCentury;
        }
    </mx:Style>
    <mx:TextArea text="++ Example Text ++" />
    <mx:Button label="Example" />
</mx:Application>
```

You can also use named ranges that you define in the compiler configuration file you specify using the -load-config attribute. If you want to add named ranges to the compiler configuration file, you must add the values in the following format:

```
<flex-config>
    <compiler>
        <fonts>
            <languages>
                <language-range>
                    <lang>Alpha And Plus</lang>
                    <range>U+0041-U+007F,U+002B</range>
                </language-range>
            </languages>
        </fonts>
    </compiler>
</flex-config>
```

If you want to add more than one named range, you can simply add more language-range tags nested within the languages tag.

You can then specify the named range as the value for the unicodeRange attribute. The name must appear in quotes, as in Example 14-13.

Example 14-13. Embedding fonts by named ranges

```
<?xml version="1.0" encoding="utf-8"?>
<mx:Application xmlns:mx="http://www.adobe.com/2006/mxml">
    <mx:Style>
        @font-face {
            src: url("C:\\WINDOWS\\Fonts\\GOTHIC.ttf");
            fontFamily: gothicCentury;
            unicodeRange: "Alpha And Plus";
        }
        @font-face {
            src: url("C:\\WINDOWS\\Fonts\\GOTHICB.ttf");
            fontFamily: gothicCentury;
            fontWeight: bold;
            unicodeRange: "Alpha And Plus";
        }
        global {
            fontFamily: gothicCentury;
        }
    </mx:Style>
    <mx:TextArea text="++ Example Text ++" />
    <mx:Button label="Example" />
</mx:Application>
```

To simplify things, you can use predefined ranges. The predefined ranges are in the *flash-unicode-table.xml* document in the *frameworks* subdirectory of the *SDK* directory. If you want to use these predefined ranges, you can copy and paste the language-range tags from the *flash-unicode-table.xml* document to your configuration file.

Using FlashType

In Flex 2.0.1 and higher, it is possible to leverage greater control over embedded fonts using something called FlashType. In the initial version of Flex 2, it was necessary to use Flash authoring to export *.swf* files with embedded fonts that you could then embed into your Flex 2 applications to have greater control over the text. However, the Flex compilers in 2.0.1 and higher are capable of compiling with FlashType enabled, without the additional step of first exporting from Flash authoring.

FlashType allows you to control text appearance with additional styles:

fontSharpness

A value from −400 to 400 (the default value is 0) specifying how crisp the edges of the font appear. The higher the value is, the crisper the edges. Lowering the value for smaller fonts usually makes the fonts more legible.

fontThickness

A value from −200 to 200 (the default value is 0) specifying how thick the edges of the font should be.

 FlashType also allows you to use the fontAntiAliasType and fontGridFitType styles, which are beyond the scope of this book. You can consult the Flex documentation for more details on these styles.

Example 14-14 uses two sliders that allow you to adjust the sharpness and thickness of the font in order to see the effects.

Example 14-14. Adjusting FlashType properties

```
<?xml version="1.0" encoding="utf-8"?>
<mx:Application xmlns:mx="http://www.adobe.com/2006/mxml">
    <mx:Style>
        global {
            fontFamily: gothicCentury;
            fontSize: 50;
        }
    </mx:Style>
    <mx:Script>
        <![CDATA[

            [Embed(systemFont="Century Gothic", fontName="gothicCentury",
mimeType="application/x-font")]
            private var _centuryGothic:Class;

            [Embed(systemFont="Century Gothic", fontName="gothicCentury",
fontWeight="bold", mimeType="application/x-font")]
            private var _centuryGothicBold:Class;

            private function sharpnessChangeHandler(event:Event):void {
                StyleManager.getStyleDeclaration("global").setStyle("fontSharpness",
sharpnessSlider.value);
            }

            private function thicknessChangeHandler(event:Event):void {
                StyleManager.getStyleDeclaration("global").setStyle("fontThickness",
thicknessSlider.value);
            }


        ]]>
```

Example 14-14. Adjusting FlashType properties (continued)

```
    </mx:Script>
    <mx:Button label="Example" />
    <mx:HSlider id="sharpnessSlider" value="0" minimum="-400" maximum="400"
liveDragging="true" change="sharpnessChangeHandler(event)" />
    <mx:HSlider id="thicknessSlider" value="0" minimum="-200" maximum="200"
liveDragging="true" change="thicknessChangeHandler(event)" />
</mx:Application>
```

FlashType is enabled for embedded fonts by default. Although there is no difference in runtime performance between FlashType and non-FlashType fonts, there are compile-time performance hits when using FlashType. If you don't intend to use any of the styles enabled by FlashType and you are embedding a lot of fonts and notice compiler slowness, you can disable FlashType for the fonts using the `flashType` attribute in the `@font-face` directive or `Embed` metadata tag:

```
@font-face {
    src: url("C:\\WINDOWS\\Fonts\\GOTHIC.ttf");
    fontFamily: gothicCentury;
    flashType: false;
}
```

Skinning Components

Although styles are an excellent way to customize components, they can do only so much. If you want to change the color, font, or spacing settings for components, styles are perfect solutions. However, if you want to completely change the appearance of a component so that it uses a different shape, you'll need to use skins instead of (or in addition to) styles.

Component skins are graphics or classes that you can specify for states and/or parts of a component that will completely replace the standard appearance of the component. Every component type will have different skins that you can set. For example, buttons have skins such as `upSkin`, `overSkin`, and `downSkin` that determine the appearance of the button in the up, over, and down states. You can use embedded graphics such as *.jpg* files or *.png* files, or you can use programmatic skins. We'll discuss both options in the following sections.

Applying Skins

You can apply skins in the same way you apply styles: using inline skin settings, `setStyle()`, CSS, or `StyleManager`. Each component type has skin settings that are treated like styles. The skin styles for each component type vary. For example, buttons have skin styles such as `upSkin`, `overSkin`, and `downSkin` and text input components have skin styles such as `borderSkin`.

The values for skin styles must always reference a class. For graphical skins, the value should be a class created by an embedded image (see Chapter 9 for more information about embedding images). For programmatic skins, the value should be a reference to the skin class. We'll look at the details of both types in the following sections.

Graphical Skinning

Graphical skinning is often the fastest and simplest way to create highly customized component appearances. Graphical skins consist of embedded images or *.swf* content that is substituted for the default artwork for component states or parts of components. Typically the workflow is to create the artwork for each skin (determined by the available skin styles for the component you want to customize), output that artwork in an embeddable format (*.png*, *.jpg*, *.swf*, etc.), embed the artwork, and set the skin styles to point to the embedded artwork. The format of the artwork you want to embed often depends on what you are trying to achieve as well as the skill set of the designer creating the artwork. As a general rule, bitmap formats will contribute the most to file size and will pixelate when scaled; vector artwork from *.svg* or *.swf* files will contribute the least to file size (assuming the vector artwork is relatively simple) and will scale without pixelating. Furthermore, within the bitmap category, *.gif* and *.png* (PNG24) support transparency, and vector formats also support transparency. This is an important consideration if the artwork you want to use for skins requires transparency (e.g., nonrectangular edges/corners).

You can set graphical skins in one of three ways: inline, using setStyle( ), or using CSS.

Inline graphical skins

Inline graphical skins work just like inline styles, except that the value must be a reference to a class for an embedded graphical element. The most common way to achieve this is to add an @Embed directive within the inline value. The @Embed directive has the following syntax:

```
@Embed(source='path to asset')
```

Here's an example that sets the upSkin, overSkin, and downSkin of a button using this inline technique to embed the assets:

```
<mx:Button upSkin="@Embed('/assets/buttonUp.png')"
           overSkin="@Embed('/assets/buttonOver.png')"
           downSkin="@Embed('/assets/buttonDown.png')" />
```

Setting graphical skins with setStyle

When you use setStyle( ) to set a skin style, you must reference a class that points to the embedded asset. The way to achieve that is to embed the asset, point it to a variable of type Class, and then use that variable as the value for the setStyle( ) method. Here's an example:

```
[Embed(source="/assets/buttonUp.png")]
private var upSkin:Class;
[Embed(source="/assets/buttonOver.png")]
private var overSkin:Class;
[Embed(source="/assets/buttonDown.png")]
private var downSkin:Class;

private function initialize(event:Event):void {
    button.setStyle("upSkin", upSkin);
    button.setStyle("overSkin", overSkin);
    button.setStyle("downSkin", downSkin);
}
```

Using CSS to set graphical skins

You can use external stylesheets or local style definitions to assign skin styles for graphical skins. When using CSS for this purpose, you can add an Embed directive directly to the CSS, and Flex will automatically embed the asset and use that asset for the specified skin style. Here's an example:

```
.example {
    upSkin: Embed("/assets/buttonUp.png");
    overSkin: Embed("/assets/buttonOver.png");
    downSkin: Embed("/assets/buttonDown.png");
}
```

Using Scale-9

When you use graphical skins, it's important to consider whether the component will need to scale. If so, you'll frequently want to use Scale-9 (see Chapter 9 for more details). This is particularly important when the graphical skin has corners or edges that will distort when they scale. Figure 14-1 shows an example of such an image. In the following examples, we'll use this image as the background skin for a VBox to see the difference when Scale-9 is applied.

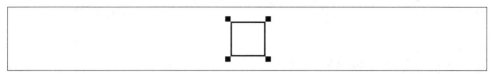

Figure 14-1. An image to be used as a skin for a VBox

First, Example 14-15 uses the image as the background image for a VBox without Scale-9.

Example 14-15. Embedding a skin without Scale-9

```
<?xml version="1.0" encoding="utf-8"?>
<mx:Application xmlns:mx="http://www.adobe.com/2006/mxml">
    <mx:Style>
        VBox {
            backgroundImage: Embed("vbox_background.png");
            backgroundSize: "100%";
        }
    </mx:Style>
    <mx:VBox height="200" width="200" />
</mx:Application>
```

Figure 14-2 shows the distortion caused by the preceding code.

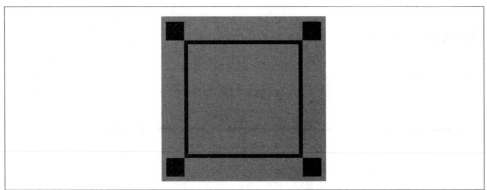

Figure 14-2. Distorted version of image

Example 14-16 is the same code using Scale-9.

Example 14-16. Embedding a skin with Scale-9

```
<?xml version="1.0" encoding="utf-8"?>
<mx:Application xmlns:mx="http://www.adobe.com/2006/mxml">
    <mx:Style>
        VBox {
            backgroundImage: Embed("vbox_background.png",
scaleGridTop="5", scaleGridLeft="5", scaleGridBottom="29", scaleGridRight="29");
            backgroundSize: "100%";
        }
    </mx:Style>
    <mx:VBox height="200" width="200" />
</mx:Application>
```

With the preceding code, the image no longer distorts. Figure 14-3 shows the improvement.

Figure 14-3. Image that scales without distortion

Using Flash Library symbols

You can embed entire *.swf* files for use as graphical skins. For example, the following embeds three *.swf* files to use as button states:

```
<mx:Button upSkin="@Embed('/assets/buttonUp.swf')"
           overSkin="@Embed('/assets/buttonOver.swf')"
           downSkin="@Embed('/assets/buttonDown.swf')" />
```

However, you can embed individual symbols from the library of the *.swf* file by adding the symbol parameter to the directive. In order for this to work, you must have exported the *.swf* file from Flash authoring with the symbols set to export for Action-Script using linkage identifiers. The values of the symbol parameters should be equal to the linkage identifiers for the symbols you want to embed. The following code embeds the individual symbols from one *.swf* file:

```
<mx:Button upSkin="@Embed('buttonSkins.swf', symbol='buttonUp')"
           overSkin="@Embed('buttonSkins.swf', symbol='buttonOver')"
           downSkin="@Embed('buttonSkins.swf', symbol='buttonDown')" />
```

Programmatic Skinning

Programmatic skinning is far more complex than graphical skinning. However, programmatic skinning does provide advantages. Programmatic skinning allows greater control because you can respond to everything that occurs to the skin during runtime, such as state changes and scaling. Because programmatic skinning uses code rather than graphical assets, it may require a smaller file size than the graphical equivalent. Furthermore, programmatic skinning allows you to use low-level features such as display object filters (drop shadows, bevels, glows, etc.).

When you want to create a programmatic skin, you should create a subclass of one of the following classes:

mx.skins.ProgrammaticSkin
> Most programmatic skins subclass ProgrammaticSkin, and this is an appropriate superclass for almost all skins.

mx.skins.Border
> The Border class is a subclass of ProgrammaticSkin, and it adds support for borderMetrics for skins that are borders.

mx.skins.RectangularBorder
> This class is a subclass of Border, and it adds support for backgroundImage.

All programmatic skins must implement the updateDisplayList( ) method. The updateDisplayList( ) method is a protected method that you must override. It expects two numeric parameters specifying the width and height of the skin, and the method return type should be void. The updateDisplayList( ) method gets called automatically every time the component needs to draw or redraw the skin; this is where you should place the code that does the drawing. Example 14-17 is a simple skin class. This version merely draws a white rectangle.

Example 14-17. A programmatic skin class

```
package com.oreilly.programmingflex.styles {
    import mx.skins.ProgrammaticSkin;

    public class ButtonSkin extends ProgrammaticSkin {

        public function ButtonSkin( ) {}

        override protected function updateDisplayList(unscaledWidth:Number,
unscaledHeight:Number):void {
            var backgroundColor:Number = 0xFFFFFF;
            graphics.clear( );
            graphics.lineStyle(0, 0, 0);
            graphics.beginFill(backgroundColor, 1);
            graphics.drawRect(0, 0, unscaledWidth, unscaledHeight);
            graphics.endFill( );
        }

    }
}
```

Once you've defined the programmatic skin class, you can assign that class as the skin using any of the techniques you can use for graphical skins: inline, setStyle( ), or CSS. The difference, however, is that in each case you must specify a reference to the programmatic skin class (see Example 14-18).

Example 14-18. Using a programmatic skin class

```
<?xml version="1.0" encoding="utf-8"?>
<mx:Application xmlns:mx="http://www.adobe.com/2006/mxml">
    <mx:Script>
        <![CDATA[
            import com.oreilly.programmingflex.styles.ButtonSkin;
        ]]>
    </mx:Script>
    <mx:Button upSkin="{ButtonSkin}" overSkin="{ButtonSkin}" downSkin="{ButtonSkin}"
label="Example" />
</mx:Application>
```

Note that in Example 14-18, we use curly braces to evaluate the skin classes in the
inline values. This is required if you want to import the class and reference the class
by its shortened name (e.g., ButtonSkin rather than com.oreilly.programmingflex.
styles.ButtonSkin). However, you can optionally specify the values as strings if you
reference the fully qualified class name each time, as in Example 14-19.

Example 14-19. Using a programmatic skin class by fully qualified name

```
<?xml version="1.0" encoding="utf-8"?>
<mx:Application xmlns:mx="http://www.adobe.com/2006/mxml">
    <mx:Button upSkin="com.oreilly.programmingflex.styles.ButtonSkin"
               overSkin="com.oreilly.programmingflex.styles.ButtonSkin"
               downSkin="com.oreilly.programmingflex.styles.ButtonSkin"
               label="Example" />
</mx:Application>
```

Using setStyle( ), you should simply pass a reference to the class as the second
parameter, as in Example 14-20.

Example 14-20. Using a programmatic skin class using setStyle()

```
<?xml version="1.0" encoding="utf-8"?>
<mx:Application xmlns:mx="http://www.adobe.com/2006/mxml"
initialize="initializeHandler(event)">
    <mx:Script>
        <![CDATA[
            import com.oreilly.programmingflex.styles.ButtonSkin;

            private function initializeHandler(event:Event):void {
                button.setStyle("upSkin", ButtonSkin);
                button.setStyle("overSkin", ButtonSkin);
                button.setStyle("downSkin", ButtonSkin);
            }
        ]]>
    </mx:Script>
    <mx:Button id="button" label="Example" />
</mx:Application>
```

Using CSS, you must specify the fully qualified class name as a string wrapped by a ClassReference directive, as in Example 14-21.

Example 14-21. Using a programmatic skin class using CSS

```
<?xml version="1.0" encoding="utf-8"?>
<mx:Application xmlns:mx="http://www.adobe.com/2006/mxml">
    <mx:Style>
        Button {
            upSkin:
ClassReference("com.oreilly.programmingflex.styles.ButtonSkin");
            overSkin:
ClassReference("com.oreilly.programmingflex.styles.ButtonSkin");
            downSkin:
ClassReference("com.oreilly.programmingflex.styles.ButtonSkin");
        }
    </mx:Style>
    <mx:Button id="button" label="Example" />
</mx:Application>
```

You'll note that in the preceding examples, we set the skins for all the button states to the same class. Although this is not necessary, it is possible. Furthermore, it's possible to code the programmatic skin class so that it is able to detect the name of the skin to which it is applied. The ProgrammaticSkin class defines a name property that you can access from a subclass. The name property returns a string specifying the name of the skin. For instance, in the preceding examples, the possible values for the name property are upSkin, overSkin, and downSkin. Example 14-22 is a modification to the ButtonSkin class that uses different settings based on the skin name. This example also adds a drop-shadow filter to illustrate something you can achieve with programmatic skins.

Example 14-22. Detecting a programmatic skin name

```
package com.oreilly.programmingflex.styles {
    import mx.skins.ProgrammaticSkin;
    import flash.filters.DropShadowFilter;

    public class ButtonSkin extends ProgrammaticSkin {

        public function ButtonSkin( ) {}

        override protected function updateDisplayList(unscaledWidth:Number,
unscaledHeight:Number):void {
            var backgroundColor:Number = 0xFFFFFF;
            var distance:Number = 4;
            switch (name) {
                case "overSkin":
                    backgroundColor = 0xCCCCCC;
                    break;
                case "downSkin":
                    distance = 0;
                    backgroundColor = 0x7F7F7F;
            }
```

Example 14-22. Detecting a programmatic skin name (continued)

```
            graphics.clear( );
            graphics.lineStyle(0, 0, 0);
            graphics.beginFill(backgroundColor, 1);
            graphics.drawRect(0, 0, unscaledWidth, unscaledHeight);
            graphics.endFill( );
            var shadow:DropShadowFilter = new DropShadowFilter(distance);
            filters = [shadow];
        }


    }
}
```

Another thing that programmatic skins can do is respond to styles. Up to this point, the programmatic skin has used a hardcoded background color value. However, using styles we can enable greater flexibility with this button skin. Rather than an always white background, we can specify a background color to be made for each button instance using styles. In order to accomplish this, we need only to retrieve the style value within the programmatic skin class using the getStyle( ) method. The getStyle( ) method requires the name of the style as a string parameter, and it returns the value. Example 14-23 is the new ButtonSkin class that accepts a backgroundColor style. Note that we also have to add a method that adjusts luminosity for the background color in the over and down states.

Example 14-23. Detecting style property values in a programmatic skin class

```
package com.oreilly.programmingflex.styles {
    import mx.skins.ProgrammaticSkin;
    import flash.filters.DropShadowFilter;

    public class ButtonSkin extends ProgrammaticSkin {

        public function ButtonSkin( ) {}

        override protected function updateDisplayList(unscaledWidth:Number,
          unscaledHeight:Number):void {

            // If the backgroundColor style is defined then use that value.
            // Otherwise, default to 0xFFFFFF.
            var backgroundColor:Number = getStyle("backgroundColor")
             ? getStyle("backgroundColor") : 0xFFFFFF;
            var distance:Number = 4;
            switch (name) {
                case "overSkin":
                    backgroundColor = setLuminosity(backgroundColor, .8);
                    break;
                case "downSkin":
                    distance = 0;
                    backgroundColor = setLuminosity(backgroundColor, .5);
            }
            graphics.clear( );
```

Example 14-23. Detecting style property values in a programmatic skin class (continued)

```
            graphics.lineStyle(0, 0, 0);
            graphics.beginFill(backgroundColor, 1);
            graphics.drawRect(0, 0, unscaledWidth, unscaledHeight);
            graphics.endFill( );
            var shadow:DropShadowFilter = new DropShadowFilter(distance);
            filters = [shadow];
        }

        // The setLuminosity method takes a color value, splits it apart into
        // the red, green, and blue parts, multiplies each part by a value
        // (multiplier should be from 0 to 1), and recombines the parts to
        // make one RGB value. The result is an RGB value that is a luminosity
        // variant of the original color.
        private function setLuminosity(color:Number, percent:Number):Number {
            var red:Number = (color >> 16) * percent;
            var green:Number = (color >> 8 & 0xFF) * percent;
            var blue: Number = (color & 0xFF) * percent;
            return red << 16 | green << 8 | blue;
        }

    }
}
```

The MXML code in Example 14-24 illustrates how you can apply this style setting.

Example 14-24. Applying a style to a programmatic skin instance

```
<?xml version="1.0" encoding="utf-8"?>
<mx:Application xmlns:mx="http://www.adobe.com/2006/mxml">
    <mx:Style>
        Button {
            upSkin:
              ClassReference("com.oreilly.programmingflex.styles.ButtonSkin");
            overSkin:
              ClassReference("com.oreilly.programmingflex.styles.ButtonSkin");
            downSkin:
              ClassReference("com.oreilly.programmingflex.styles.ButtonSkin");
            backgroundColor: red;
        }
    </mx:Style>
    <mx:Button id="button" label="Example" />
</mx:Application>
```

Skinning Application Backgrounds

Almost universally, you'll want to customize the background of your Flex application. You can skin the application background using the backgroundImage skin style setting. You can use graphical skins or programmatic skins for application backgrounds. Here's an example that embeds a *.png* file to use as the application background:

```
<?xml version="1.0" encoding="utf-8"?>
<mx:Application xmlns:mx="http://www.adobe.com/2006/mxml"
    backgroundImage="@Embed('/assets/application_background.png')">
</mx:Application>
```

Skinning Tool Tips

You can skin tool tips as you would any other component—either graphically or programmatically. Simply set the value for the ToolTip type selector's borderSkin style. Example 14-25 is a programmatic skin for tool tips.

Example 14-25. An example tool tip skin class

```
package com.oreilly.programmingflex.styles {
    import mx.skins.ProgrammaticSkin;
    import flash.filters.DropShadowFilter;

    public class ToolTipSkin extends ProgrammaticSkin {

        public function ToolTipSkin( ) {}

        override protected function updateDisplayList(unscaledWidth:Number,
          unscaledHeight:Number):void {
            graphics.clear( );
            graphics.lineStyle(0, 0, 0);
            graphics.beginFill(0xFFFFFF, .8);
            graphics.drawRoundRectComplex(0, 0, unscaledWidth,
              unscaledHeight, 0, 10, 10, 10);
            graphics.endFill( );
            filters = [new DropShadowFilter( )];
        }

    }
}
```

You can then apply the customized skin as shown in Example 14-26.

Example 14-26. Using a programmatic tool tip skin class

```
<?xml version="1.0" encoding="utf-8"?>
<mx:Application xmlns:mx="http://www.adobe.com/2006/mxml">
    <mx:Style>
        ToolTip {
            borderSkin:
                ClassReference("com.oreilly.programmingflex.styles.ToolTipSkin");
        }
    </mx:Style>
    <mx:Button label="Example" toolTip="Example Tool Tip" />
</mx:Application>
```

Figure 14-4 shows what this customized tool tip looks like.

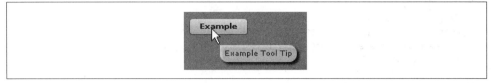

Figure 14-4. Customized tool tip

Customizing the Preloader

By default, all Flex applications use a standard preloader progress bar screen while the application itself is downloading. If you choose, you can create a custom preloader screen. This is possible and relatively simple to accomplish. There are two steps:

1. Create a class that subclasses `mx.preloaders.DownloadProgressBar` or subclasses `Sprite` and implements the `mx.preloaders.IPreloaderDisplay` interface.

2. Set the `preloader` property of the `Application` object to the path to the class from the preceding step.

The first of these two steps is the more complicated of the two, but it is still reasonably trivial. You have two options: either subclass `mx.preloaders.DownloadProgressBar` or create a `Sprite` subclass that also implements `mx.preloaders.IPreloader`. Let's look at the `DownloadProgressBar` subclass first.

Technically you can subclass `DownloadProgressBar` as an all-purpose solution. However, from an academic standpoint, it's better to subclass `DownloadProgressBar` only when you intend to customize the default preloader screen. When subclassing `DownloadProgressBar`, you'll want to ensure that you always called the super constructor from the constructor of the subclass:

```
package com.oreilly.programmingflex.preloader {

    import mx.preloaders.DownloadProgressBar;

    public class CustomPreloaderSubclass extends DownloadProgressBar {

        public function CustomPreloaderSubclass( ) {
            super( );
        }

    }
}
```

The super constructor ensures that the proper event handlers are configured for the class. Then you need only to override the event handler methods necessary for the particular subclass. If you consult the documentation for `DownloadProgressBar`, you'll see that it has the following protected event handler methods that you can override: initProgressHandler, progressHandler, completeHandler, rslProgressHandler, rslCompleteHandler, and rslErrorHandler. Example 14-27 is a simple example that overrides just progressHandler. This example displays the bytes loaded and total bytes in the label field rather than the default value of Loading.

Example 14-27. Example custom preloader class

```
package com.oreilly.programmingflex.preloader {

    import mx.preloaders.DownloadProgressBar;
    import flash.events.ProgressEvent;

    public class CustomPreloaderSubclass extends DownloadProgressBar {

        public function CustomPreloaderSubclass() {
            super();
        }

        override protected function progressHandler(event:ProgressEvent):void {
            super.progressHandler(event);
            label = event.bytesLoaded + " of " + event.bytesTotal + " bytes";
        }

    }
}
```

Once you've created a custom preloader class, you can assign the class name to the preloader property of the Application tag for the project, as in Example 14-28.

Example 14-28. Setting thepreloader for an application

```
<?xml version="1.0"?>
<mx:Application xmlns:mx="http://www.adobe.com/2006/mxml" layout="absolute"
preloader=" com.oreilly.programmingflex.preloader.CustomPreloaderSubclass">
<mx:Script>
    <![CDATA[

        // This example embeds a file so that there is a significant amount of data
        // to load and you will be able to see the preloader screen.
        [Embed(source="file.mp3")]
        private var _file:Class;

    ]]>
</mx:Script>
</mx:Application>
```

 You may need to upload the application to a web server to see the preloader screen for more than just a second.

When you want to completely customize the preloader screen, you can still subclass DownloadProgressBar and simply not call the super constructor and/or override the createChildren( ) method. However, doing so misses the intent of subclassing. A subclass should use at least part of the implementation of the superclass. Therefore, it is better in such cases to write a class that instead subclasses Sprite and implements IPreloaderDisplay. If you view the documentation for IPreloaderDisplay, you'll see that an implementing class must define the public properties backgroundAlpha, backgroundColor, backgroundImage, backgroundSize, preloader, stageWidth, and stageHeight, as well as a method called initialize.

Example 14-29 is a simple customized preloader. This example uses a circle and animates a radial line moving around the axis as the application downloads.

Example 14-29. A preloader class subclassing Sprite

```
package com.oreilly.programmingflex.preloader {
    import mx.preloaders.IPreloaderDisplay;
    import flash.display.Sprite;
    import flash.display.Shape;
    import flash.events.Event;
    import flash.events.ProgressEvent;
    import mx.events.FlexEvent;
    import mx.preloaders.Preloader;

    public class CustomPreloaderScreen extends Sprite implements
IPreloaderDisplay {

        private var _progress:Shape;
        private var _preloader:Preloader;
        private var _backgroundAlpha:Number;
        private var _backgroundColor:uint;
        private var _backgroundImage:Object;
        private var _backgroundSize:String;
        private var _stageHeight:Number;
        private var _stageWidth:Number;

        public function set preloader(value:Sprite):void {
            _preloader = value as Preloader;
            value.addEventListener(ProgressEvent.PROGRESS, progressEventHandler);
            value.addEventListener(FlexEvent.INIT_COMPLETE,
initCompleteEventHandler);
        }

        public function set backgroundAlpha(value:Number):void {
            _backgroundAlpha = value;
        }

        public function get backgroundAlpha( ):Number {
            return _backgroundAlpha;
        }
```

Example 14-29. A preloader class subclassing Sprite (continued)

```
    public function set backgroundColor(value:uint):void {
        _backgroundColor = value;
    }

    public function get backgroundColor():uint {
        return _backgroundColor;
    }

    public function set backgroundImage(value:Object):void {
        _backgroundImage = value;
    }

    public function get backgroundImage():Object {
        return _backgroundImage;
    }

    public function set backgroundSize(value:String):void {
        _backgroundSize = value;
    }

    public function get backgroundSize():String {
        return _backgroundSize;
    }

    public function set stageWidth(value:Number):void {
        _progress.x = value / 2;
        _stageWidth = value;
    }

    public function get stageWidth():Number {
        return _stageWidth;
    }

    public function set stageHeight(value:Number):void {
        _progress.y = value / 2;
        _stageHeight = value;
    }

    public function get stageHeight():Number {
        return _stageHeight;
    }

    public function CustomPreloaderScreen() {
        _progress = new Shape();
        addChild(_progress);
    }

    private function progressEventHandler(event:ProgressEvent):void {
        _progress.graphics.clear();
        _progress.graphics.lineStyle(0, 0, 1);
        _progress.graphics.drawCircle(0, 0, 20);
        _progress.graphics.moveTo(0, 0);
        _progress.graphics.lineTo(0, 20);
```

Example 14-29. A preloader class subclassing Sprite (continued)

```
            _progress.graphics.moveTo(0, 0);
            var angle:Number = event.bytesLoaded / event.bytesTotal * Math.PI * 2;
            var newX:Number = Math.sin(angle) * 20;
            var newY:Number = Math.cos(angle) * 20;
            _progress.graphics.lineTo(newX, newY);
        }

        public function initialize( ):void {
            _progress.x = stage.stageWidth / 2;
            _progress.y = stage.stageHeight / 2;
        }

        private function initCompleteEventHandler(event:FlexEvent):void {
            dispatchEvent(new Event(Event.COMPLETE));
        }


    }
}
```

You can test this preloader in the same way as the earlier example. This time use the name CustomPreloaderScreen for the application's preloader property (see Example 14-30).

Example 14-30. Setting the preloader class for the application

```
<?xml version="1.0"?>
<mx:Application xmlns:mx="http://www.adobe.com/2006/mxml" layout="absolute"
preloader=" com.oreilly.programmingflex.preloader.CustomPreloaderScreen">
<mx:Script>
    <![CDATA[

        // This example embeds a file so there is a significant amount of data
         // to load and you will be able to see the preloader screen.
        [Embed(source="file.mp3")]
        private var _file:Class;

    ]]>
</mx:Script>
</mx:Application>
```

Themes

Themes provide a way to compile all *.css* files, graphical skin asset files, and programmatic skin classes in an *.swc* file that you can then tell the Flex compiler to use for your Flex application. This has two primary advantages:

- It allows you to precompile style and skin assets so that application compilation is faster.
- It allows you to more easily distribute and drop in preconfigured styles and skins for Flex applications.

Themes are fantastic when, say, you have a corporate style guide that you need to implement across many applications. Rather than having to distribute all the *.css* files, graphical elements, and programmatic skin classes, you can distribute just one *.swc* file.

Setting a Theme

Setting a theme for a Flex application is very simple. All that is necessary is to add a -theme compiler option to mxmlc. If you are compiling from the command line (or using Ant or another automatic build program), simply add -theme *themeFile*.swc to the compiler options, as in this example:

```
mxmlc -theme corporate.swc Main.mxml
```

If you are using Flex Builder to build your application, you should open the project properties, select the Flex Compiler option, and add -theme *themeFile*.swc to the additional compiler arguments field.

Creating a Theme

In order to use a theme, you clearly must have a theme first. A theme must contain at least one *.css* file, and likely contains additional assets such as image assets and/or a programmatic skin class. A theme file must be precompiled as an *.swc* file. You can compile an *.swc* file using compc, the command-line components compiler. When you compile a theme file, you should specify -include-file options for each *.css* and/or graphical skin asset file you want to add to the *.swc*. The -include-file option requires two parameters: the name by which you refer to the file in the *.css* and the path to the file. Here's an example:

```
compc -include-file corporate_styles.css ../assets/themes/corporate.css
-include-file background.jpg ../assets/themes/background.jpg -o corporate.swc
```

If you want to add programmatic skin classes to the theme *.swc* file, you can use the -include-classes option. The -include-classes option allows you to specify one or more fully qualified class names in a space-delimited list:

```
compc -include-file corporate_styles.css ../assets/themes/corporate.css
-include-classes com.company.styles.ButtonSkin com.company.styles.ToolTipSkin
```

As you can see, even with just two included files or classes, the command-line statement starts to get unwieldy, and adding more files just exacerbates the problem. A more elegant solution is to use the configuration file. The following is a sample configuration file called *example_theme.xml*:

```
<?xml version="1.0"?>
<flex-config xmlns="http://www.adobe.com/2006/flex-config">
    <output>corporate.swc</output>
    <include-file>
        <name>corporate.css</name>
        <path>../assets/themes/corporate.css</path>
    </include-file>
```

```
    <include-file>
        <name>background.jpg</name>
        <path>../assets/themes/background.jpg</path>
    </include-file>
    <include-classes>
        <class>com.company.styles.ButtonSkin</class>
        <class>com.company.styles.ToolTipSkin</class>
    </include-classes>
</flex-config>
```

You can then compile using the -load-config option of compc as follows:

```
compc -load-config example_theme.xml
```

Flex ships with sample themes in an uncompiled format. You can find the theme files in the *frameworks/themes* directory of the Flex SDK. (If you're using Flex Builder, the SDK is located in the *FlexSDK* directory of the Flex Builder installation.) To compile and use a theme, do the following:

1. Create a new Flex project with the main *.mxml* file code in Example 14-31.

   Example 14-31. Main MXML document

   ```
   <?xml version="1.0" encoding="utf-8"?>
   <mx:Application xmlns:mx="http://www.adobe.com/2006/mxml">
       <mx:ComboBox>
           <mx:dataProvider>
               <mx:ArrayCollection>
                   <mx:String>a</mx:String>
                   <mx:String>b</mx:String>
                   <mx:String>c</mx:String>
                   <mx:String>d</mx:String>
               </mx:ArrayCollection>
           </mx:dataProvider>
       </mx:ComboBox>
       <mx:Button label="Example" />
   </mx:Application>
   ```

2. Navigate to the *themes* directory, and copy *Smoke.css* and *smoke_bg.jpg*.

3. Paste the copies of the Smoke theme files in the new Flex project.

4. In the new Flex project, create a new file called *smoke_config.xml*, and add the code in Example 14-32 to the file.

   Example 14-32. smoke_config.xml

   ```
   <?xml version="1.0"?>
   <flex-config xmlns="http://www.adobe.com/2006/flex-config">
       <output>smoke_theme.swc</output>
       <include-file>
           <name>Smoke.css</name>
           <path>Smoke.css</path>
       </include-file>
       <include-file>
   ```

Example 14-32. smoke_config.xml (continued)

```
        <name>smoke_bg.jpg</name>
        <path>smoke_bg.jpg</path>
    </include-file>
</flex-config>
```

5. From a command prompt, change to the directory with the *.xml* file, and run the following command, which will compile the assets into an *.swc* file:

```
compc -load-config smoke_config.xml
```

6. You can delete the copies of *Smoke.css* and *smoke_bg.jpg* as well as *smoke_config.xml*; they are no longer necessary in order to use the theme now that the .*swc* file has been created.

7. Compile your Flex application with the -theme option set to *smoke_config.swc*.

When you run the Flex application you'll see the Smoke theme applied, as shown in Figure 14-5.

Figure 14-5. The Smoke theme

Runtime CSS

In Flex 2.0.1 and higher, you can use runtime CSS. Thus far in the chapter, when we've talked about CSS, we've talked exclusively about CSS that gets compiled into the Flex application. Now we'll look at how you can load and apply CSS at runtime, effectively restyling an application at runtime.

Because Flex styles often require embedded resources such as skin assets, classes, and fonts, Flex runtime CSS must be precompiled into *.swf* files. When using Flex 2.0.1 you can use the `mxmlc` compiler to compile a *.css* file into an *.swf* that includes all assets embedded by the *.css* file. In order to compile the *.css* file, simply pass the path to the file as the one compiler argument, as in the following example:

```
mxmlc styles.css
```

The preceding example compiles *styles.css* into a file called *styles.swf*. You can then load *styles.swf* into your Flex applications at runtime without having to include the .*css* or any of the embedded assets in the main Flex application. That means you can update the styles for an application without having to recompile and redeploy the application itself. All you have to do is update the styles file. Furthermore, you can have many styles files that the user can choose from at runtime.

In order to load CSS at runtime, you use the `StyleManager.loadStyleDeclarations()` method. The `loadStyleDeclarations()` method requires at least one parameter—the path to the *.swf* file containing the CSS:

```
StyleManager.loadStyleDeclarations("styles.swf");
```

If you're loading only one stylesheet, as soon as you've loaded the styles, you'll want to apply them. By default, `loadStyleDeclarations()` behaves in this way. However, if you are loading several stylesheets (runtime stylesheets have the same cumulative potential as compile-time stylesheets), you likely don't want to apply the styles until after you've loaded the last stylesheet. This is because applying styles is a relatively expensive operation, and it is best to defer applying the styles until they have all loaded. You can achieve this by specifying `false` for the second parameter of all but the last `loadStyleDeclarations()` method call. Then specify a value of `true` (or do not specify a value because the default is true) for the last `loadStyleDeclarations()` method call. Here's an example:

```
StyleManager.loadStyleDeclarations("stylesA.swf", false);
StyleManager.loadStyleDeclarations("stylesB.swf", false);
StyleManager.loadStyleDeclarations("stylesC.swf", false);
StyleManager.loadStyleDeclarations("stylesD.swf", true);
```

The `loadStyleDeclarations()` method allows you to load stylesheets from the same domain as the Flex application or from different domains. However, if you load the stylesheet *.swf* file from a different domain, you'll need to specify `true` for the third (optional) parameter for `loadStyleDeclarations()`:

```
StyleManager.loadStyleDeclarations("http://www.differentdomain.com/styles.swf",
    true, true);
```

Because styles are applied cumulatively, you need a mechanism for clearing loaded CSS. You can achieve that using the `StyleManager.unloadStyleDeclarations()` method. The `unloadStyleDeclarations()` method requires that you specify the path to the *.swf* file that was originally loaded, and you can optionally specify whether to immediately unload the styles or wait until you've unloaded other styles:

```
StyleManager.unloadStyleDeclarations("styles.swf");
```

In order to best understand runtime CSS, here's a simple exercise:

1. Create a file called *a.css* with the CSS in Example 14-33.

Example 14-33. a.css

```
@font-face {
    src: url("C:\\WINDOWS\\Fonts\\ARIAL.ttf");
    fontFamily: arial;
}
@font-face {
    src: url("C:\\WINDOWS\\Fonts\\ARIALBD.ttf");
    fontFamily: arial;
    fontWeight: bold;
}
global {
    fontFamily: arial;
}
Button {
    cornerRadius: 10;
}
```

2. From a command prompt, compile *a.css* to *a.swf* using the following command (make sure you've added `mxmlc` to your path):

```
mxmlc a.css
```

3. Create a file called *b.css* with the CSS in Example 14-34.

Example 14-34. b.css

```
@font-face {
    src: url("C:\\WINDOWS\\Fonts\\GOTHIC.ttf");
    fontFamily: gothicCentury;
}
@font-face {
    src: url("C:\\WINDOWS\\Fonts\\GOTHICB.ttf");
    fontFamily: gothicCentury;
    fontWeight: bold;
}
global {
    fontFamily: gothicCentury;
}
Application {
    themeColor: green;
}
Button {
    cornerRadius: 25;
}
ToolTip {
    borderSkin: ClassReference("com.oreilly.programmingflex.styles.ToolTipSkin");
}
```

4. From a command prompt, compile *b.css* to *b.swf* using the following command:

```
mxmlc b.css
```

5. Create a new document called *RuntimeCSS.mxml* with the code in Example 14-35.

Example 14-35. RuntimeCSS.mxml

```
<?xml version="1.0" encoding="utf-8"?>
<mx:Application xmlns:mx="http://www.adobe.com/2006/mxml"
initialize="initializeHandler(event)">
    <mx:Script>
        <![CDATA[

            private var _currentStyle:String;

            private function initializeHandler(event:Event):void {
                StyleManager.loadStyleDeclarations("a.swf");
                _currentStyle = "a.swf";
            }

            private function clickHandler(event:Event):void {
                StyleManager.unloadStyleDeclarations(_currentStyle);
                StyleManager.loadStyleDeclarations(stylesOptions.value.toString());
                _currentStyle = stylesOptions.value as String;
            }
        ]]>
    </mx:Script>
    <mx:ComboBox id="stylesOptions" toolTip="Select a Style Sheet">
        <mx:dataProvider>
            <mx:ArrayCollection>
                <mx:String>a.swf</mx:String>
                <mx:String>b.swf</mx:String>
            </mx:ArrayCollection>
        </mx:dataProvider>
    </mx:ComboBox>
    <mx:Button label="Change Style" click="clickHandler(event)" />
</mx:Application>
```

6. Compile and run *RuntimeCSS.mxml*.

When you run this test, you'll be able to switch between two runtime stylesheets and see the effects. Notice the difference if you comment the unloadStyleDeclarations( ) line.

Summary

In this chapter, you learned how to customize the appearance of a Flex application. We discussed using styles and skins to change the appearance of components within the application. You also learned how to apply these settings using MXML, Action-Script, and CSS.

Client Data Communication

Flex applications are capable of many types of data communication, from the simple to the complex. Often when we think of data communication in Flex applications, we think of client-server communications such as RPCs. However, some types of data communication occur entirely on the client side, and these types are the subject of this chapter.

At a minimum, all Flex applications require a client-side element in the form of a *.swf* file running in Flash Player. Some Flex applications even use several *.swf* files running in one or more instances of Flash Player on the client machine. The client-side portion of a Flex application is capable of several types of client data communication intended for a variety of purposes.

There are three ways a Flex application can run data communications on the client:

Local connections

A local connection allows two *.swf* files to communicate as long as they are running on the same client machine at the same time. The *.swf* files can be running in two different instances of Flash Player. They can even be running in different host environments. For example, one *.swf* can be running in a web browser while one is running embedded within an executable.

Shared objects

Local shared objects allow the application to store and retrieve persistent data on the client machine. For example, a user can save preferences that the application can retrieve automatically the next time the application runs.

External interface

The external interface is a mechanism by which a Flex application can communicate with the host environment. This allows the Flex application to run as an integrated part of a larger application.

The Flex framework does not provide special behaviors for working with client data communications. Rather, all the topics in this book use low-level Flash Player API ActionScript.

Local Connections

Local connections are a way in which two *.swf* files can communicate even if they are running in two different Flash Player instances. Local connections allow you to create integrated applications composed of two or more *.swf* files running in separate Flash Player instances, such as several pods or modules that are part of a complex rich Internet application (RIA) that uses both Flex elements and HTML elements. Furthermore, local connections allow you to communicate between Flash 9 content (Flex applications) and older, legacy Flash content (Flash 8 or earlier).

Local connections use AMF, a binary messaging format, as the protocol for local connection data packets. A local connection request uses one AMF packet, and the maximum size for a local connection AMF packet is 40 KB. Local connections also use AMF0 exclusively. This is in contrast with other ActionScript classes that can use AMF0 as well as AMF3. AMF0 is compatible with older Flash content, making local connections a good way to communicate from Flex applications to older Flash content.

Basic Local Connection Communication

Typically when implementing local connection, at least two *.swf* files are needed: one that sends the requests and one that receives the requests. You cannot establish a local connection with a *.swf* without its explicit consent because the receiving *.swf* must have the necessary code to listen for the specific requests.

Technically it is possible to use a local connection to send and receive requests all within one *.swf*. However, in all practical cases, you will use two *.swf* files.

Both the sending and receiving *.swf* files use the flash.net.LocalConnection object. The LocalConnection object communicates over a named connection channel. The name of the channel is arbitrary and is a string value, but for the communication to work, the sending and receiving *.swf* files must send and receive over a channel with the same name.

The sending *.swf* uses the send( ) method of a LocalConnection object to send the request. The send( ) method requires at least two parameters specifying the name of the channel and the name of the method to call on the receiving *.swf*. The following example creates a new LocalConnection instance and calls the send( ) method:

```
var localConnection:LocalConnection = new LocalConnection( );
localConnection.send("channel", "exampleMethod");
```

If the method in the receiving *.swf* expects parameters, you can pass them to the send( ) method following the name of the method to call. For example, this calls exampleMethod on the receiving *.swf* and passes it integer parameters:

```
localConnection.send("channel", "exampleMethod", 10, 25);
```

The receiving *.swf* must listen for requests on the same channel as the sending *.swf* sends them. You can instruct a LocalConnection object to listen for requests by calling the connect( ) method, passing it the name of the channel to which to listen:

```
var receivingLocalConnection:LocalConnection = new LocalConnection( );
receivingLocalConnection.connect("channel");
```

 If you do not call the connect( ) method, the *.swf* will have no way of knowing that it should be listening for requests.

You must also tell the LocalConnection object where to direct the requests. For example, when the sending *.swf* makes a request for exampleMethod, the receiving LocalConnection object needs to know where it can find exampleMethod. You can tell it where to find the method by assigning a reference to the appropriate object to the client property of the LocalConnection object. For example, the following tells the LocalConnection object on the receiver application where it can find the requested methods as methods of this class:

```
receivingLocalConnection.client = this;
```

 The methods that you expose via a local connection must be declared as public. Otherwise, the application will throw an error.

This step of setting the client is essential. Without setting the client property, the LocalConnection object will throw errors when it receives requests.

Example 15-1 requires two MXML files compiled into two *.swf* files. The first MXML file creates the sending *.swf*. It contains a text area and a button. When the user clicks the button, the event handler sends a local connection request to call a method named displayMessage with a parameter equal to the value of the text area text.

Example 15-1. Local connection send example

```
<?xml version="1.0" encoding="utf-8"?>
<mx:Application xmlns:mx="http://www.adobe.com/2006/mxml">

    <mx:Script>
        <![CDATA[

            import flash.net.LocalConnection;
```

Example 15-1. Local connection send example (continued)

```
        private var _localConnection:LocalConnection = new LocalConnection( );

        private function sendMessage(event:MouseEvent):void {
            _localConnection.send("dataChannel", "displayMessage", message.text);
        }

    ]]>
    </mx:Script>

    <mx:VBox id="vbox">
        <mx:TextArea id="message" />
        <mx:Button click="sendMessage(event)" />
    </mx:VBox>

</mx:Application>
```

The second MXML document defines the receiving *.swf*. This file (Example 15-2) contains a text area.

Example 15-2. Local connection receive example

```
<?xml version="1.0" encoding="utf-8"?>
<mx:Application xmlns:mx="http://www.adobe.com/2006/mxml" layout="absolute"
initialize="initializeHander(event)">

    <mx:Script>
        <![CDATA[

        import flash.net.LocalConnection;

        private var _localConnection:LocalConnection;

        private function initializeHandler(event:Event):void {
            _localConnection = new LocalConnection( );
            _localConnection.connect("dataChannel");
            _localConnection.client = this;
        }

            // Note that this method is declared as public because it is
            // exposed as a method to a local connection.
        public function displayMessage(message:String):void {
            output.text += message + "\n";
        }

    ]]>
    </mx:Script>

    <mx:TextArea id="output"  width="539" height="589"/>

</mx:Application>
```

The initializeHandler( ) method runs when the application initializes because it is set to handle the application initialize event. It creates the LocalConnection object, connects to the channel to listen for requests, and designates this as the client for the requests, meaning that the requests get routed to methods of the same name defined for the MXML document. Notice that displayMessage( ) is declared as public. Methods called via a local connection must be declared as public.

Legacy Communication

One nonobvious use for local connections is to allow inter-.*swf* communication between Flash 9 (Flex) applications and content published to Flash 8 or earlier. Flex applications can load any sort of .*swf*, whether it was published from Flex or any version of Flash authoring. However, because Flash 9 applications use a fundamentally different virtual machine than older Flash content, it's not possible for a Flash 9 application to communicate directly with a .*swf* published from Flash 8 or earlier. If a Flash 9 application loads a Flash 9 .*swf*, they can communicate directly. However, that's not possible when a Flash 9 application loads a Flash 8 or earlier .*swf*.

Local connection communication is a solution for interoperability, because it is supported by both older Flash content as well as Flash 9 applications. You can create a local connection API in the legacy content that the Flex application can call once it loads the .*swf*.

Cross-Domain Communication

In our discussion of local connection communication, we have thus far assumed that all communicating .*swf* files are in the same domain. By default, Flash Player disallows local connection communication when the .*swf* files are being loaded from different domains. However, you can explicitly allow cross-domain communication for a specific receiving .*swf*.

There are two basic types of cross-domain local connection communication: *known domains* and *unknown domains*. Known domains communication occurs when both the sending and receiving applications know about one another and the domains from which they are hosted. However, there are many cases in which the domains are not necessarily known at compile time. For example, you may use a local connection to create a plugin-style application that can interact with many different applications. In such a case, you don't necessarily know what all the possible domains are ahead of time.

The technique for unknown domains works for both unknown and known domains, but it is also more lax. Therefore, it is recommended that you use the known-domains technique whenever possible. If you must enable cross-domain communication but you do not know the domains from which the .*swf* files will be hosted, you can use the unknown-domains technique.

To allow cross-domain local connection communication for known domains you must do two things: explicitly tell the receiving LocalConnection object to allow requests from the sending domain, and prefix the sending request channel name with the domain of the receiving *.swf*. Use the allowDomain( ) method to specify a list of all the domains to allow.

For the next example, assume that the sending *.swf* is hosted at *www.a.com* and the receiving *.swf* is hosted at *www.b.com*. The following illustrates the code to send a request:

```
var localConnection:LocalConnection = new LocalConnection( );
localConnection.send("www.b.com:channel", "exampleMethod");
```

The following illustrates the code necessary to receive the request with an application hosted at *www.a.com*:

```
var receivingLocalConnection:LocalConnection = new LocalConnection( );
receivingLocalConnection.allowDomain("www.a.com");
receivingLocalConnection.connect("channel");
receivingLocalConnection.client = this;
```

When the domains are unknown, you can use the wildcard character (*) when calling allowDomain( ), and rather than prefixing the channel with the receiving domain, you can name the channel with an initial underscore:

```
// Sending .swf
var localConnection:LocalConnection = new LocalConnection( );
localConnection.send("_channel", "exampleMethod");

// Receiving .swf
var receivingLocalConnection:LocalConnection = new LocalConnection( );
receivingLocalConnection.allowDomain("*");
receivingLocalConnection.connect("channel");
receivingLocalConnection.client = this;
```

 When testing cross-domain communication, it is useful to run the application using the debugger, which notifies you if there is a problem.

Persistent Data

Many applications need to store persistent data on the client computer, and Flex applications are no exception. For example, a Flex application may display a start page for new users, yet the application may give the user the option to hide the start page on subsequent visits. Though you could store that preference remotely, a more common method is to store the preference on the client side.

Flash Player security is a top priority at Adobe, and for this reason Flash Player can't write to arbitrary files on the client computer. However, Flash Player does have a designated area on the client computer where it can write to very specific files that are controlled and managed entirely by Flash Player. These files are called *local shared objects*, and you can use ActionScript to write to and read from these files.

Flash Player uses the `flash.net.SharedObject` class to manage access to local shared object data. Although the data is stored in files on the client machine, the access to those files is controlled exclusively through the `SharedObject` interface. This both simplifies working with shared objects and improves security to protect Flex application users from malicious programmers.

 Note that the `SharedObject` class also allows you to work with *remote* shared objects. For this reason, you may notice that the `SharedObject` class API includes many properties and methods not discussed in this chapter. Remote shared objects allow real-time data synchronization across many clients, but they also require server software such as Flash Media Server. In this book, we discuss local shared objects, not remote shared objects.

Creating Shared Objects

Unlike many ActionScript classes, the `SharedObject` constructor is never used directly, and you cannot meaningfully create a new instance using the constructor. Rather, the `SharedObject` class defines a static, lazy instantiation factory method called `getLocal( )`. The `getLocal( )` method returns a `SharedObject` instance that acts as a proxy to a local shared object file on the client computer. There can obviously be many local shared objects on a client computer, so you must specify the specific shared object you want to reference by passing a string parameter to `getLocal( )`. If the file does not yet exist, Flash Player first creates the file and then opens it for reading and writing. If the file already exists, Flash Player simply opens it for reading and writing. The following code retrieves a reference to a shared object called `example`:

```
var sharedObject:SharedObject = SharedObject.getLocal("example");
```

Reading and Writing to Shared Objects

Once you've retrieved the reference to the shared object, you can read and write to it using the data property of the object, which is essentially an associative array. You must write all data that you want to persist to disk to the data property. You can use dot syntax or array-access notation to read and write arbitrary keys and values. In general, dot syntax is marginally optimal because it yields slightly faster performance. The following writes a value of `true` to the shared object for a key called `hideStartScreen`:

```
sharedObject.data.hideStartScreen = true;
```

You should use array-access notation when you want to read or write using a key that uses characters that are not valid for use in variable/property names. For example, if you want to use a key that contains spaces, you can use array-access notation:

```
sharedObject.data["First Name"] = "Bob";
```

Data is not written to disk as you write it to the SharedObject instance. By default, Flash Player attempts to write the data to disk when the *.swf* closes. However, this can fail silently for several reasons. For example, the user might not have allocated enough space or the user might have disallowed writing to shared objects entirely. In these cases, the shared object data will not write to disk, and the Flex application will have no notification. For this reason, it is far better to explicitly write the data to disk.

You can explicitly write data to disk using the flush( ) method. The flush( ) method serializes all the data and writes it to disk. If the user has disallowed local data storage for Flash Player for the domain, flush( ) throws an error:

```
try {
  sharedObject.flush( );
}
catch {
  Alert.show("You must allow local data storage.");
}
```

The flush( ) method also returns a string value corresponding to either the PENDING or the FLUSHED constants of flash.net.SharedObjectFlushStatus. If the return value is FLUSHED, the data was successfully saved to disk. If the return value is PENDING, it means that the user has not allocated enough disk space for the amount of data the shared object is trying to write to disk, and Flash Player is displaying a settings dialog to the user, prompting her to allow the necessary allocation. When the user selects either to allow or disallow the allocation, the shared object dispatches a netStatus event. You can listen for the event using the flash.events.NetStatusEvent. NET_STATUS constant:

```
sharedObject.addEventListener(NetStatusEvent.NET_STATUS, flushStatusHandler);
```

The NetStatusEvent type defines a property called info that contains a property called code. The code property will have a string value of either SharedObject.Flush. Success or SharedObject.Flush.Failed. Example 15-3 tries to write to disk. If the user has disallowed local data storage or does not allocate the space when prompted, the application displays an alert.

Example 15-3. Shared object example

```
<?xml version="1.0" encoding="utf-8"?>
<mx:Application xmlns:mx="http://www.adobe.com/2006/mxml" layout="absolute"
initialize="initializeHandler(event)">

    <mx:Script>
        <![CDATA[

            import flash.net.SharedObject;
            import mx.controls.Alert;

            private var _sharedObject:SharedObject;
```

Example 15-3. Shared object example (continued)

```
        private function initializeHandler(event:Event):void {
            _sharedObject = SharedObject.getLocal("example");
            if(_sharedObject.data.count == null) {
                _sharedObject.data.count = 20;
                try {
                    var status:String = _sharedObject.flush();
                    if(status == SharedObjectFlushStatus.PENDING) {
                        _sharedObject.addEventListener(NetStatusEvent.NET_STATUS,
flushStatusHandler);
                    }
                }
                catch (error:Error) {
                    Alert.show("You must allow local data storage.");
                }
            }
            else {
                Alert.show("Shared object data: " + _sharedObject.data.count);
            }
        }

        private function flushStatusHandler(event:NetStatusEvent):void {
            event.target.removeEventListener(NetStatusEvent.NET_STATUS,
flushStatusHandler);
            if(event.info.code == "SharedObject.Flush.Failed") {
                Alert.show("You must allow local data storage.");
            }
        }

    ]]>
    </mx:Script>

</mx:Application>
```

By default, Flash Player attempts to allocate enough space for the shared object data. If the shared object is likely to grow over time, Flash Player might prompt the user to allocate more space with each incremental increase. If you know that a shared object will require more disk space in the future, you can preallocate space by calling `flush()` with the number of bytes you want to allocate. For example, the following attempts to allocate 512,000 bytes:

```
sharedObject.flush(512000);
```

The default allocation is 100 KB. Unless the user has changed his Flash Player settings, you can generally assume that you can store up to 100 KB of data in a local shared object without prompting the user.

Controlling Scope

By default, every shared object is specific to the *.swf* from which it originates. However, you can allow several *.swf* files to access the same shared object(s) by specifying a path when calling getLocal( ). The default path is the path to the *.swf*. For example, if the *.swf* is at *http://www.example.com/flex/client/a.swf*, the path is */flex/client/a.swf*, which means only *a.swf* can access the shared object. For this example, we'll assume that *a.swf* retrieves a reference to a shared object called example as follows:

```
var sharedObject:SharedObject = SharedObject.getLocal("example");
```

If *b.swf* is in the same directory as *a.swf*, and *b.swf* also tries to retrieve a reference to a shared object called example using the exact same code as appears in *a.swf*, *b.swf* will retrieve a reference to a different shared object—one that is scoped specifically to the path */flex/client/b.swf*. If you want *a.swf* and *b.swf* to be able to access the same shared object, you must specify a path parameter using a common path that they both share, such as */flex/client*:

```
var sharedObject:SharedObject = SharedObject.getLocal("example", "/flex/client");
```

In order for *.swf* files to have access to the same shared objects, they must specify a path that they have in common. For example, both *a.swf* and *b.swf* have */flex/client* in common. They also share the paths */flex* and */*. If *http://www.example.com/main.swf* wants to use the same shared object as *a.swf* and *b.swf*, all three *.swf* files must specify a path of */* for the shared object because that is the only path they have in common.

 Shared objects can be shared by all *.swf* files within a domain. However, *.swf* files in two different domains cannot access the same local shared object.

Using Local Shared Objects

Thus far we've talked about local shared objects in theory. In this section, we'll build a simple application that uses a shared object in a practical way. This example displays a log-in form in a pop up. However, the user has the option to set a preference so that the application will remember her.

This example application uses an MXML component that displays the login window. It also uses a User Singleton class that allows the user to authenticate. Note that in this example, the application uses hardcoded values against which it authenticates. In a real application, the authentication would be against data from a database, LDAP, or some similar data store.

The User class looks like Example 15-4.

Example 15-4. User class for shared object example

```
package com.oreilly.programmingflex.lso.data {

    import flash.events.EventDispatcher;
    import flash.events.Event;

    public class User extends EventDispatcher {

        // The managed instance.
        private static var _instance:User;

        // Declare two constants to use for event names.
        public static const AUTHENTICATE_SUCCESS:String = "success";
        public static const AUTHENTICATE_FAIL:String = "fail";

        public function User() {}

        // The Singleton accessor method.
        public static function getInstance():User {
            if(_instance == null) {
                _instance = new User();
            }
            return _instance;
        }

        // The authenticate() method tests if the username and password are valid.
        // If so it dispatches an AUTHENTICATE_SUCCESS event. If not it dispatches
        // an AUTHENTICATE_FAIL event.
        public function authenticate(username:String, password:String):void {
            if(username == "user" && password == "pass") {
                dispatchEvent(new Event(AUTHENTICATE_SUCCESS));
            }
            else {
                dispatchEvent(new Event(AUTHENTICATE_FAIL));
            }
        }

    }
}
```

The login form component looks like Example 15-5 (name the file *LogInForm.mxml* and save it in the root directory for the project).

Example 15-5. LogInForm.mxml

```
<?xml version="1.0" encoding="utf-8"?>
<mx:TitleWindow xmlns:mx="http://www.adobe.com/2006/mxml">
    <mx:Script>
        <![CDATA[

            import mx.managers.PopUpManager;
            import com.oreilly.programmingflex.lso.data.User;
```

Example 15-5. LogInForm.mxml (continued)

```
            // This method handles click events from the button.
            private function onClick(event:MouseEvent):void {
                // If the user selected the remember me check box then save the username
                // and password to the local shared object.
                if(rememberMe.selected) {
                    var sharedObject:SharedObject = SharedObject.getLocal("userData");
                    sharedObject.data.user = {username: username.text,
                     password: password.text};
                    sharedObject.flush( );
                }
                // Authenticate the user.
                User.getInstance( ).authenticate(username.text, password.text);
            }

        ]]>
    </mx:Script>
    <mx:Form>
        <mx:FormHeading label="Log In" />
        <mx:FormItem label="Username">
            <mx:TextInput id="username" />
        </mx:FormItem>
        <mx:FormItem label="Password">
            <mx:TextInput id="password" displayAsPassword="true" />
        </mx:FormItem>
        <mx:FormItem>
            <mx:Button id="submit" label="Log In" click="onClick(event)" />
        </mx:FormItem>
        <mx:FormItem>
            <mx:CheckBox id="rememberMe" label="Remember Me" />
        </mx:FormItem>
    </mx:Form>
</mx:TitleWindow>
```

The application MXML file itself is shown in Example 15-6.

Example 15-6. Main MXML file for shared object example

```
<?xml version="1.0" encoding="utf-8"?>
<mx:Application xmlns:mx="http://www.adobe.com/2006/mxml" layout="absolute"
initialize="initializeHandler(event)">

    <mx:Script>
        <![CDATA[
            import mx.containers.Form;
            import mx.managers.PopUpManager;
            import com.oreilly.programmingflex.lso.data.User;
            import com.oreilly.programmingflex.lso.ui.LogInForm;

            private var _logInForm:LogInForm;

            private function initializeHandler(event:Event):void {
```

Example 15-6. Main MXML file for shared object example (continued)

```
            // Retrieve the same shared object used to store the data from the
            // log in form component.
            var sharedObject:SharedObject = SharedObject.getLocal("userData");

            // Listen for events from the User instance.
            User.getInstance( ).addEventListener(User.AUTHENTICATE_SUCCESS,
             removeLogInForm);
            User.getInstance( ).addEventListener(User.AUTHENTICATE_FAIL,
             displayLogInForm);

            // If the shared object doesn't contain any user data then display the log
in
            // form. Otherwise, authenticate the user with the data retrieved from the
            // local shared object.
            if(sharedObject.data.user == null) {
                displayLogInForm( );
            }
            else {
                User.getInstance( ).authenticate(sharedObject.data.user.username,
                 sharedObject.data.user.password);
            }
        }

        private function displayLogInForm(event:Event = null):void {
            if(_logInForm == null) {
                _logInForm = new LogInForm( );
                PopUpManager.addPopUp(_logInForm, this, true);
            }
        }

        private function removeLogInForm(event:Event = null):void {
            if(_logInForm != null) {
                PopUpManager.removePopUp(_logInForm);
                _logInForm = null;
            }
        }

    ]]>
    </mx:Script>
    <mx:TextArea x="10" y="10" text="Application"/>

</mx:Application>
```

This simple application illustrates a practical use of local shared objects. When you test this example, use the username user and the password pass.

Customizing Serialization

Many built-in types are automatically serialized and deserialized. For example, strings, numbers, Boolean values, Date objects, and arrays are all automatically serialized and deserialized. That means that even though shared object data is ultimately saved to a flat file, when you read a Date object or an array from a shared object, it is automatically recognized as the correct type. Flash Player automatically serializes all public properties (including public getters/setters) for custom types as well. However, Flash Player does not automatically store the class type. That means that when you retrieve data of a custom type from a shared object, it does not deserialize to the custom type by default. For instance, consider the class shown in Example 15-7.

Example 15-7. Account class

```
package com.oreilly.programmingflex.serialization {
    public class Account {

        private var _firstName:String;
        private var _lastName:String;

        public function get firstName():String {
            return _firstName;
        }

        public function set firstName(value:String):void {
            _firstName = value;
        }

        public function get lastName():String {
            return _lastName;
        }

        public function set lastName(value:String):void {
            _lastName = value;
        }

        public function Account() {}

        public function getFullName():String {
            return _firstName + " " + _lastName;
        }

    }
}
```

If you try to write an object of this type to a shared object, it correctly serializes the firstName and lastName properties (getters/setters). That means that when you read the data back from the shared object, it displays those values properly. However, it will throw an error if you attempt to call getFullName() because the deserialized object will not be of type User. To test this, we'll use two MXML applications called A and B. A is defined as shown in Example 15-8, and it sets the shared object data.

Example 15-8. Application A

```
<?xml version="1.0" encoding="utf-8"?>
<mx:Application xmlns:mx="http://www.adobe.com/2006/mxml" layout="absolute"
initialize="initializeHandler(event)">

    <mx:Script>
        <![CDATA[

            import flash.net.SharedObject;
            import mx.controls.Alert;
            import com.oreilly.programmingflex.serialization.Account;

            private var _sharedObject:SharedObject;

            private function initializeHandler(event:Event):void {
                _sharedObject = SharedObject.getLocal("test", "/");
                var account:Account = new Account();
                account.firstName = "Joey";
                account.lastName = "Lott";
                _sharedObject.data.account= account;
                try {
                    var status:String = _sharedObject.flush();
                    if(status == SharedObjectFlushStatus.PENDING) {
                        _sharedObject.addEventListener(NetStatusEvent.NET_STATUS,
                         flushStatusHandler);
                    }
                }
                catch (error:Error) {
                    Alert.show("You must allow local data storage.");
                }
            }

            private function flushStatusHandler(event:NetStatusEvent):void {
                event.target.removeEventListener(NetStatusEvent.NET_STATUS,
                 flushStatusHandler);
                if(event.info.code == "SharedObject.Flush.Failed") {
                    Alert.show("You must allow local data storage.");
                }
            }

        ]]>
    </mx:Script>

</mx:Application>
```

B, shown in Example 15-9 reads the shared object data, and attempts to display the data in alert pop ups. Note that it will correctly display firstName and lastName, but it will throw an error on getFullName().

Example 15-9. Application B

```
<?xml version="1.0" encoding="utf-8"?>
<mx:Application xmlns:mx="http://www.adobe.com/2006/mxml" layout="absolute"
initialize="initializeHandler(event)">

    <mx:Script>
        <![CDATA[

            import flash.net.SharedObject;
            import flash.utils.describeType;
            import com.oreilly.programmingflex.serialization.Account;
            import mx.controls.Alert;

            private var _sharedObject:SharedObject;

            private function initializeHandler(event:Event):void {
                _sharedObject = SharedObject.getLocal("test", "/");
                try {
                    Alert.show(_sharedObject.data.account.firstName + "
                      " + _sharedObject.data.account.lastName);
                    Alert.show(_sharedObject.data.account.getFullName());
                }
                catch (error:Error) {
                    Alert.show(error.toString());
                }
            }

        ]]>
    </mx:Script>

</mx:Application>
```

If you want to store the type in the serialized data, you can use flash.net. registerClassAlias(). The registerClassAlias() function allows you to map the class to an alias. The alias is written to the serialized data. When the data is deserialized, Flash Player automatically instantiates the object as the specified type. The following revisions to A and B cause the User data to deserialize as a User object.

Example 15-10 shows the new A, which creates the User object and saves it to the shared object. Since the code now registers the class to the alias, User, it will store the alias in the serialized data as well.

Example 15-10. Application A registering a class alias

```
<?xml version="1.0" encoding="utf-8"?>
<mx:Application xmlns:mx="http://www.adobe.com/2006/mxml" layout="absolute"
initialize="initializeHandler(event)">

    <mx:Script>
        <![CDATA[

            import flash.net.SharedObject;
```

Example 15-10. Application A registering a class alias (continued)

```
        import mx.controls.Alert;
        import com.oreilly.programmingflex.serialization.Account;
        import flash.net.registerClassAlias;

        private var _sharedObject:SharedObject;

        private function initializeHandler(event:Event):void {
            registerClassAlias("Account", Account);
            _sharedObject = SharedObject.getLocal("test", "/");
            var account:Account = new Account( );
            account.firstName = "Joey";
            account.lastName = "Lott";
            _sharedObject.data.account = account;
            try {
                var status:String = _sharedObject.flush( );
                if(status == SharedObjectFlushStatus.PENDING) {
                    _sharedObject.addEventListener(NetStatusEvent.NET_STATUS,
                        flushStatusHandler);
                }
            }
            catch (error:Error) {
                Alert.show("You must allow local data storage.");
            }
        }

        private function flushStatusHandler(event:NetStatusEvent):void {
            event.target.removeEventListener(NetStatusEvent.NET_STATUS,
                flushStatusHandler);
            if(event.info.code == "SharedObject.Flush.Failed") {
                Alert.show("You must allow local data storage.");
            }
        }

    ]]>
    </mx:Script>

</mx:Application>
```

Example 15-11 shows the updated B. Since this code also registers the class using the alias, User, it automatically deserializes the data from the local shared object as a User object because it matches the alias.

Example 15-11. Application B registering a class alias

```
<?xml version="1.0" encoding="utf-8"?>
<mx:Application xmlns:mx="http://www.adobe.com/2006/mxml" layout="absolute"
initialize="initializeHandler(event)">

    <mx:Script>
        <![CDATA[

        import flash.net.SharedObject;
```

Example 15-11. Application B registering a class alias (continued)

```
            import flash.utils.describeType;
            import mx.controls.Alert;
            import com.oreilly.programmingflex.serialization.Account;
            import flash.net.registerClassAlias;

            private var _sharedObject:SharedObject;

            private function initializeHandler(event:Event):void {
                registerClassAlias("Account", Account);
                _sharedObject = SharedObject.getLocal("test", "/");
                try {
                    Alert.show(_sharedObject.data.account.firstName + "
                       " + _sharedObject.data.account.lastName);
                    Alert.show(_sharedObject.data.account.getFullName( ));
                }
                catch (error:Error) {
                    Alert.show(error.toString( ));
                }
            }

        ]]>
    </mx:Script>

</mx:Application>
```

When you register a class using `registerClassAlias( )`, the class for which you are registering the alias must not have any required parameters in the constructor. If it does, Flash Player will throw an error when trying to deserialize the data.

The default serialization and deserialization for custom classes works well for standard value object-style data model types. However, if you want to serialize and deserialize any nonpublic state settings, you must implement `flash.utils.IExternalizable`. When a class implements `IExternalizable`, Flash Player automatically uses the custom serialization and deserialization you define rather than the standard. That allows you much more control over what and how the objects will store.

The `IExternalizable` interface requires two methods, called `writeExternal( )` and `readExternal( )`. The `writeExternal( )` method requires a `flash.utils.IDataOutput` parameter, and the `readExternal( )` method requires a `flash.utils.IDataInput` parameter. Both `IDataInput` and `IDataOutput` provide interfaces for working with binary data. `IDataInput` allows you to read data using methods such as `readByte( )`, `readUTF( )`, and `readObject( )`, and `IDataOutput` allows you to write data using methods such as `writeByte( )`, `writeUTF( )`, and `writeObject( )`. The `writeExternal( )` method gets called when the object needs to be serialized. You must write all data to the `IDataOutput` parameter that you want to store. The `readExternal( )` method gets called when the object is deserialized. You must read all the data from the `IDataInput` parameter. The data you read from the `IDataInput` parameter is in the same order as the data you write to the IDataOutput parameter. Example 15-12 rewrites Account using IExternalizable. Note that there is no setter method for either firstName or lastName, which proves that the data is set via the customized deserialization.

Example 15-12. Account rewritten to implement IExternalizable

```
package com.oreilly.programmingflex.serialization {
    import flash.utils.IExternalizable;
    import flash.utils.IDataInput;
    import flash.utils.IDataOutput;

    public class Account implements IExternalizable {

        private var _firstName:String;
        private var _lastName:String;

        public function get firstName():String {
            return _firstName;
        }

        public function get lastName():String {
            return _lastName;
        }

        public function Account(first:String = "", last:String = "") {
            _firstName = first;
            _lastName = last;
        }

        public function getFullName():String {
            return _firstName + " " + _lastName;
        }

        public function readExternal(input:IDataInput):void {
            _firstName = input.readUTF();
            _lastName = input.readUTF();
        }

        public function writeExternal(output:IDataOutput):void {
            // Verify that _firstName is not null because this method may get called
            // when the data is null. Only serialize when the object is non-null.
            if(_firstName != null) {
                output.writeUTF(_firstName);
                output.writeUTF(_lastName);
            }
        }

    }
}
```

Communicating with the Host Application

Flex applications require the Flash Player runtime environment to work. For this reason, it is common to think of Flex applications as being confined to Flash Player. However, it is entirely possible for a Flex application to communicate with the host application. For example, if a Flex application is running within a web browser, the application can interact with the browser. If a Flex application is running within a desktop executable, it can interact with that executable. This allows you to create integrated applications that span beyond the Flash Player context.

Flex application/host application communication takes place via a Flash Player class called `flash.external.ExternalInterface`. `ExternalInterface` allows you to make synchronous calls to host application methods from the Flex application, and from the host application to Flex application methods. `ExternalInterface` is quite simple to work with, and in most cases, it is quite appropriate.

Working with ExternalInterface

The `flash.external.ExternalInterface` class defines two static methods, named `call()` and `addCallback()`, enabling Flex-to-host-application communication and host-application-to-Flex communication, respectively.

The `call()` method allows you to call a method of the host application by passing it the name of the method. If the host application method expects parameters, you can pass those parameters to the `call()` method following the name of the host application method. For example, the following calls the `alert()` JavaScript method when the Flex application is run in a web browser:

```
ExternalInterface.call("alert", "Test message from Flex");
```

The `call()` method works synchronously. For example, the JavaScript `confirm()` function creates a new dialog with OK and Cancel buttons. The confirm dialog pauses the application until the user clicks on a button, at which time it returns either `true` (OK) or `false` (Cancel).

```
var option:Boolean = ExternalInterface.call("confirm",
                "Do you really want to close the application?");
```

Of course, the host application functions can be custom functions as well.

If you want to call a Flex method from the host application, you must register the method within the Flex application using `ExternalInterface.addCallback()`. The `addCallback()` method allows you to register a particular function or method with an alias by which the method or function may be called from the host application. For example, the following registers `Alert.show` as `showAlert`:

```
ExternalInterface.addCallback("showAlert", Alert.show);
```

You can then call the `Alert.show` method by way of the `showAlert` alias from the host application.

Within the host application, you must retrieve a reference to the Flash Player instance that is running the *.swf*. You can then call the method by its alias directly from the reference. For example, if `getFlexApplicationReference( )` is a function within the host application that returns a reference to the Flash Player instance, the following launches an alert:

```
getFlexApplicationReference( ).showAlert("Alert message from host application");
```

In JavaScript, the Flash Player reference is different depending on the type of browser (IE or non-IE). In IE you can retrieve a reference to the Flash Player instance by `window.id`, where *id* is the value of the `id` parameter of the `<object>` tag, and in non-IE browsers, the reference is `document.name`, where *name* is the value of the `name` attribute of the `<embed>` tag. The following JavaScript function determines the browser type and returns the correct reference in which both the `id` parameter and the `name` attribute are Example:

```
function getFlexApplicationReference( ) {
  if (navigator.appName.indexOf("Microsoft") != -1) {
    return window.Example;
  } else {
    return document.Example;
  }
}
```

Setting the Web Browser Status

`ExternalInterface` might seem a little confusing until you see an example or two. In this section and the next, we'll look at a few simple examples that should clarify how `ExternalInterface` works. This first application simply allows a Flex application to call to JavaScript in a hosting web browser so that it sets the status bar message as the user moves the mouse over Flex buttons.

 Firefox disables JavaScript access to `window.status` by default, and therefore this example might not work with the default Firefox configuration.

This application uses one simple MXML document and one HTML page. The MXML document should contain the code shown in Example 15-13.

Example 15-13. ExternalInterfaceExample.mxml

```
<?xml version="1.0" encoding="utf-8"?>
<mx:Application xmlns:mx="http://www.adobe.com/2006/mxml" layout="absolute">

  <mx:Script>
    <![CDATA[
```

Example 15-13. ExternalInterfaceExample.mxml (continued)

```
            private function rollOverHandler(event:MouseEvent):void {
                ExternalInterface.call("setStatus", event.currentTarget.label);
            }

        ]]>
    </mx:Script>
    <mx:VBox>
        <mx:Button label="A" rollOver="rollOverHandler(event)" />
        <mx:Button label="B" rollOver="rollOverHandler(event)" />
        <mx:Button label="C" rollOver="rollOverHandler(event)" />
        <mx:Button label="D" rollOver="rollOverHandler(event)" />
    </mx:VBox>

</mx:Application>
```

This MXML document creates four buttons. Each button has a different label. Using event handlers for the rollOver event, each button notifies the rollOverHandler( ) method when the user has moved the mouse over the button. The rollOverHandler( ) method uses ExternalInterface.call( ) to call the setStatus method that is defined using JavaScript in the HTML page within which the application is to be embedded. The label for the corresponding button gets passed to the setStatus function.

The HTML page should contain the standard HTML template for embedding Flex content. In addition, it must define the setStatus( ) JavaScript function as follows:

```
<script language="JavaScript" type="text/javascript">
<!--

  function setStatus(value) {
    window.status = value;
  }

// -->
</script>
```

When you test this application, the browser status bar message changes as you move the mouse over the Flex buttons.

Integrating HTML and Flex Forms

There are cases in which you may want to display the majority of a form in HTML, but you may want to use Flex components for one or more of the form elements. For example, you may want to use sliders, color pickers, or, as in this example, date choosers.

In this simple example, we'll create a basic HTML form with a checkbox and a small embedded Flex application. The Flex application consists of one date chooser component. The checkbox simply enables and disables the date chooser. Additionally, to highlight the synchronous nature of ExternalInterface, the Flex application makes a

---

request to the HTML page for an array of disabled dates, which it uses to disable those dates in the date chooser.

For this application, we'll first create the HTML page as shown in Example 15-14.

Example 15-14. ExternalInterface example HTML page

```html
<html>
    <script language="JavaScript" type="text/javascript">
    <!--

      function getFlexApplicationReference() {
        if (navigator.appName.indexOf("Microsoft") != -1) {
          return window.Flex2;
        } else {
          return document.Flex2;
        }
      }

      function getDisallowedDates() {
        return [new Date()]
      }


    -->
    </script>
    <input name="checkbox" type="checkbox" onChange="getFlexApplicationReference().
setEnabled(this.checked)" />
        <object classid="clsid:D27CDB6E-AE6D-11cf-96B8-444553540000"
            id="Flex2" width="175" height="180"
            codebase="http://fpdownload.macromedia.com/get/flashplayer/current/swflash.
cab">
            <param name="movie" value="Flex2.swf" />
            <param name="quality" value="high" />
            <param name="bgcolor" value="#FFFFFF" />
            <param name="allowScriptAccess" value="sameDomain" />
            <embed src="Flex2.swf" quality="high" bgcolor="#FFFFFF"
                width="175" height="180" name="Flex2" align="middle"
                play="true"
                loop="false"
                quality="high"
                allowScriptAccess="sameDomain"
                type="application/x-shockwave-flash"
                pluginspage="http://www.adobe.com/go/getflashplayer">
            </embed>
        </object>
</body>
</html>
```

In the preceding HTML code we've highlighted a few of the key things to notice. You'll see that the checkbox uses an onChange handler to call the setEnabled() method of the Flex application, passing it the checked value of the checkbox. This means that the Flex application must map a method to the setEnabled() name as a valid

ExternalInterface callback. You'll also see that the code defines several JavaScript methods called getFlexApplicationReference( ) and getDisallowedDates( ). The former simply returns the reference to the Flex application and the latter is callable from the Flex application to retrieve an array of Date objects.

The Flex application consists of just one MXML document, as shown in Example 15-15.

Example 15-15. ExternalInterface example MXML Flex2.mxml

```
<?xml version="1.0" encoding="utf-8"?>
<mx:Application xmlns:mx="http://www.adobe.com/2006/mxml" layout="absolute"
initialize="initializeHandler(event)" width="175" height="180">

    <mx:Script>
        <![CDATA[

            private function initializeHandler(event:Event):void {
                var disallowedDates:Array = ExternalInterface.call("getDisallowedDates");
                calendar.disabledRanges = disallowedDates;
                ExternalInterface.addCallback("setEnabled", setEnabled);
            }

            public function setEnabled(value:Boolean):void {
                calendar.enabled = value;
            }

        ]]>
    </mx:Script>
    <mx:DateChooser id="calendar" enabled="false" />

</mx:Application>
```

In this code, you'll notice that when the application initializes, it calls the getDisallowedDates( ) JavaScript function in a synchronous fashion, retrieving the returned value immediately. It then uses that value—an array of Date objects—to specify the disabled ranges for the date chooser instance. Since ExternalInterface automatically serializes and deserializes arrays and Date objects, this code works without having to further convert the returned values.

When the application initializes it also registers setEnabled( ) as an ExternalInterface callback. That is what allows the JavaScript-to-Flex communication.

The setEnabled( ) method takes the parameter and assigns it to the enabled property of the date chooser. Again, since Boolean values are automatically serialized and deserialized, the code works as is.

Summary

In this chapter, we looked at the three basic ways in which you can enable data communication that occurs entirely on the client. These mechanisms enable different types of behavior:

- Local connections allow communication between two or more *.swf* files running on the same computer.
- Local shared objects allow persistent data storage and retrieval on the client computer.
- ExternalInterface allows Flash and Flex applications to communicate with the application that hosts Flash Player.

CHAPTER 16

Remote Data Communication

Remote data communication occurs at runtime. It does not reside strictly in the client, but requires network connections to send and receive data between the client and the server. Flex applications support a variety of remote data communication techniques built on standards. There are three basic categories of Flex application remote data communication:

HTTP request/response-style communication
> This category consists of several overlapping techniques. Utilizing the Flex framework HTTPService component or the Flash Player API URLLoader class, you can send and load uncompressed data such as text blocks, URL encoded data, and XML packets. You can also send and receive SOAP packets using the Flex framework WebService component. And you can use a technology called Flash Remoting to send and receive AMF packets, which use a binary protocol that is similar to SOAP (but considerably smaller). Each technique achieves the similar goal of sending requests and receiving responses using HTTP or HTTPS.

Real-time communication
> This category consists of persistent socket connections. Flash Player supports two types of socket connections: those that require a specific format for packets (XMLSocket) and those that allow raw socket connections (Socket). In both cases, the socket connection is persistent between the client and the server, allowing the server to push data to the client—something not possible using standard HTTP request/response-style techniques.

File upload/download communication
> This category consists of the FileReference API which is native to Flash Player and allows file upload and download directly within Flex applications.

Of these three generalized categories, it is fairly easy to distinguish between file upload/download communication and the other two types. Clearly file upload/download communication applies only to cases in which the application requires file uploading and downloading. However, the distinction between HTTP request/response and real-time communication is not always as obvious.

HTTP request/response is far more common than real-time data communication. Although real-time data communication is necessary for some low-latency applications, it adds network overhead to the application because it requires a persistent socket connection for each user. In contrast, HTTP request/response communication is always initiated by the client in the form of a request. The server returns a response to the client, and then the connection is closed again until the client makes another request. In most cases, the request/response model is more efficient.

In this chapter, we'll focus primarily on two forms of remote data communication: request/response and file upload/download. We'll focus primarily on asynchronous (request/response) communication techniques because they make up the majority of remote data communication you'll use for Flex applications. We'll also discuss the basics of file upload and download.

Understanding Strategies for Data Communication

When you build Flex applications that utilize data communication, it's important to understand the strategies available for managing those communications and how to select the right strategy for an application. If you're new to working with Flash platform applications, it's important that you take the time to learn how data communication works within Flash Player and how that compares and contrasts with what you already know about developing for other platforms. For example, some of what you might know from working with HTML-based applications or Ajax applications may be useful, but you should never assume that Flex applications behave in the same way as applications built on other platforms.

As you already know by this time, all Flex applications run in Flash Player. With the exception of some Flex applications created using Flex Data Services, almost all Flex applications are composed of precompiled .swf files that are loaded in Flash Player on the client. The .swf files are initially requested from the server, but they run on the client. This means dynamic data (any data not statically compiled into the .swf) must be requested at runtime from the client to a server.

Because Flex applications are stateful and self-contained, they don't require new page requests and wholesale screen refreshes to make data requests and handle responses. This behavior is something Flex applications have in common with Ajax Rather than being page-driven, Flex applications are event-driven. Even as the view within a Flex application might not change, it can be making requests and receiving responses. Therefore, Flex data communication clearly requires different strategies from those employed by page-driven applications.

The Flex framework provides components for working with data communication using standard HTTP requests as well as SOAP requests. These components are beneficial when using the first of the common strategies for data communication: placing the code (the component) that makes a request within the class or MXML document that utilizes the data. This is often the most obvious strategy, and it is often the strategy that scales the least. This strategy decentralizes data communication, which causes several problems:

- Managing data communication is difficult when the code is decentralized, simply because it makes it difficult to locate the code at times.

- When data communication is tightly coupled with a particular view that uses the data, that data is not readily accessible to other parts of the application. This may not seem like a problem until you consider that many applications use the same data in many places, and if you place the data communication code within the views that use the data, you make it difficult to synchronize the data and you may require many requests for the same data.

- Decentralizing data communication code makes the application fragile because changing anything about the data communication process (protocols, APIs, etc.) can break the application in many places. In contrast, when data communication code is centralized, it is relatively easier to adapt the application when something in the data communication process changes.

Although the first strategy has these significant pitfalls associated with it, we still include discussions of the components within this chapter because the strategy is not completely without merit. The components often provide a much faster way to assemble data communication-ready applications. This is useful in cases of rapid prototypes, test applications, and small-scale (nonenterprise) applications with less demanding technical requirements.

The second strategy requires centralizing data communication using *remote proxy objects*. Remote proxies are objects that reside within the client tier where they can stand in for remote services. The remote proxy objects may even have the same APIs as the remote services. Remote proxies provide a centralized location for data communication code, and they hide the details of how data communication takes places from the rest of the application. Even if the implementation changes, the rest of the application can still continue to make calls on the remote proxy objects.

The second strategy is much more scalable than the first. Furthermore, because data communication code is centralized, this strategy is not susceptible to the same problems as the first strategy, such as duplication of data requests, synchronization problems, and adaptability issues. For these reasons, we strongly prefer the use of remote proxies for enterprise applications.

Working with Request/Response Data Communication

You can work with request/response data communication in three basic ways: via simple HTTP services, web services, and Flash Remoting. Each achieves the same basic goal of sending a request and receiving a response, and as such, you can use them for the same purposes within Flex applications. Which method you choose depends primarily on what type of service you have available. For example, if you want to load XML data from an XML document, you should use simple HTTP service communication. However, if you want to call a web service method, you should use web services communication.

Simple HTTP Services

The most basic type of HTTP request/response communication uses what we call *simple HTTP services*. These services include things such as text and XML resources, either in static documents or dynamically generated by something such as a ColdFusion page, a servlet, or an ASP.NET page. Simple HTTP services might also include pages that run scripts when called in order to do things such as insert data into or update databases, or send email. You can use simple HTTP services to execute these sorts of server behaviors, to load data, or to do both.

Flex provides two basic ways in which you can call simple HTTP services: using HTTPService, a Flex framework component; and using the Flash Player class flash. net.URLLoader.

HTTPService

HTTPService is a component that allows you to make requests to simple HTTP services such as text files, XML files, or scripts and pages that return dynamic data. You must always define a value for the url property of an HTTPService object. The url property tells the object where it can find the resource to which it should make the request. The value can be either a relative URL or an absolute URL. The following example uses MXML to create an HTTPService object that loads text from a file called *data.txt* saved in the same directory as the compiled *.swf* file:

    <mx:HTTPService id="textService" url="data.txt" />

Now that you know how to create a new HTTPService instance, let's discuss how to send requests, handle results, and pass parameters.

Sending requests

Creating an HTTPService object does not automatically make the request to load the data. In order to make the request, you must call the send( ) method. You can call the send( ) method in response to any framework or user event. For example, if you want to make the request as soon as the application initializes, you can call send( ) in response to the initialize event. If you want to load the data when the use clicks a button, you can call the send( ) method in response to a click event:

    textService.send( );

Handling results

The send( ) method makes the request, but a response is not likely to be returned instantaneously. Instead, the application must wait for a result event. The result event occurs when the entire response has been returned. The following example displays an alert when the data loads:

```
<mx:HTTPService id="textService" url="data.txt"
    result="mx.controls.Alert.show('Data loaded')" />
```

Of course, normally you would want to do something more useful than display an alert when the data loads. More commonly, you will want to use the data in some way. You can retrieve the response data (i.e., the data that has loaded) using the lastResult property. Plain text is always loaded as string data. However, the HTTPService component is capable of automatically converting serialized data into associative arrays. For this reason, the lastResult property is typed as Object. If you want to treat it as a string, you must cast it. Example 16-1 loads text from a file and then displays it in a text area.

Example 16-1. Loading text with HTTPService

```
<?xml version="1.0" encoding="utf-8"?>
<mx:Application xmlns:mx="http://www.adobe.com/2006/mxml" xmlns:remoting="com.oreilly.
programmingflex.rpc.*" layout="absolute" initialize="initializeHandler(event)">

    <mx:Script>
        <![CDATA[

            private function initializeHandler(event:Event):void {
                textService.send( );
            }

            private function resultHandler(event:Event):void {
                textArea.text = String(textService.lastResult);
            }

        ]]>
    </mx:Script>

    <mx:HTTPService id="textService" url="data.txt" result="resultHandler(event)" />

    <mx:TextArea id="textArea" />

</mx:Application>
```

Although you can explicitly handle the result event, it is far more common to use data binding. Example 16-2 accomplishes the same thing as Example 16-1, but it uses data binding.

Example 16-2. Using data binding with HTTPService

```
<?xml version="1.0" encoding="utf-8"?>
<mx:Application xmlns:mx="http://www.adobe.com/2006/mxml" xmlns:remoting="com.oreilly.
programmingflex.rpc.*" layout="absolute" initialize="initializeHandler(event)">

    <mx:Script>
        <![CDATA[

            private function initializeHandler(event:Event):void {
                textService.send( );
            }

        ]]>
    </mx:Script>

    <mx:HTTPService id="textService" url="data.txt" />

    <mx:TextArea id="textArea" text="{textService.lastResult}" />

</mx:Application>
```

When possible, HTTPService deserializes data it loads in much the same way as it would interpret data placed in a Model tag. For example, consider the following data:

```
<countries>
    <country>Select One</country>
    <country>Canada</country>
    <country>U.S.</country>
</countries>
```

If you attempt to load this data using HTTPService it will be parsed into an object named countries that contains an array named country, each element of which corresponds to the <country> elements. Example 16-3 illustrates this using a live XML file that contains the XML data shown in the preceding code block. It uses data binding to populate the combo box with the data.

Example 16-3. Loading XML with HTTPService

```
<?xml version="1.0" encoding="utf-8"?>
<mx:Application xmlns:mx="http://www.adobe.com/2006/mxml" layout="absolute"
initialize="initializeHandler(event)">

    <mx:Script>
        <![CDATA[

            private function initializeHandler(event:Event):void {
                countriesService.send( );
            }

        ]]>
    </mx:Script>
```

Example 16-3. Loading XML with HTTPService (continued)

```
<mx:HTTPService id="countriesService"
  url="http://www.rightactionscript.com/states/xml/countries.xml" />

<mx:VBox>
    <mx:ComboBox id="country"
        dataProvider="{countriesService.lastResult.countries.country}"  />
</mx:VBox>
```

```
</mx:Application>
```

As we've already seen, by default HTTPService results are interpreted as text if they are blocks of text, and if the results are XML data, they are parsed into an object. However, that is merely the default behavior. You can explicitly dictate the way in which the results are handled using the resultFormat property of the HTTPService object. The default value is object, which yields the default behavior you've already seen. You can optionally specify any of the following values:

text

The data is not parsed at all, but is treated as raw text.

flashvars

The data is assumed to be in URL-encoded format, and it will be parsed into an object with properties corresponding to the name/value pairs.

array

The data is assumed to be in XML format, and it is parsed into objects much the same as with the object settings. However, in this case, the result is always an array. If the returned data does not automatically parse into an array, the parsed data is placed into an array.

xml

The data is assumed to be in XML format, and it is interpreted as XML using the legacy XMLNode ActionScript class.

e4x

The data is assumed to be in XML format, and it is interpreted as XML using the ActionScript 3.0 XML class (E4X).

Sending parameters

When you want to pass parameters to the service, you can use the request property of the HTTPService instance. The request property requires an Object value. By default, the name/value pairs of the object are converted to URL-encoded format and are sent to the service using HTTP GET. You can assign an object using ActionScript, as in the following:

```
var parameters:Object = new Object();
parameters.a = "one";
parameters.b = "two";
service.request = parameters;
```

However, when creating an `HTTPService` object using MXML, it is often convenient to declare the parameters using MXML as well:

```
<mx:HTTPService id="service" url="script.php">
  <mx:request>
    <a>one</a>
    <b>two</b>
  </mx:request>
</mx:HTTPService>
```

Declaring the request in this way also allows you to use data binding with the parameters. To illustrate this with a working example, consider the code in Example 16-4, which builds on Example 16-3 by using a second `HTTPService` object to retrieve state names based on the selected country.

Example 16-4. Using HTTPService with input parameters

```
<?xml version="1.0" encoding="utf-8"?>
<mx:Application xmlns:mx="http://www.adobe.com/2006/mxml" layout="absolute"
initialize="initializeHandler(event)">

    <mx:Script>
        <![CDATA[

            private function initializeHandler(event:Event):void {
                countriesService.send( );
            }

            private function changeHandler(event:Event):void {
                statesService.send( );
            }

        ]]>
    </mx:Script>

    <mx:HTTPService id="countriesService"
      url="http://www.rightactionscript.com/states/xml/countries.xml" />

    <mx:HTTPService id="statesService"
      url="http://www.rightactionscript.com/states/xml/states.php">
        <mx:request>
            <country>
                {country.value}
            </country>
        </mx:request>
    </mx:HTTPService>

    <mx:VBox>
        <mx:ComboBox id="country"
            dataProvider="{countriesService.lastResult.countries.country}"
            change="changeHandler(event)" />
        <mx:ComboBox dataProvider="{statesService.lastResult.states.state}" />
    </mx:VBox>

</mx:Application>
```

In the preceding example, the first combo box is populated with a list of countries. When the user selects a country from the combo box, it sends a request to the second service, a PHP script, sending the selected country as a parameter. The return value is in the following format:

```
<states>
  <state>Alabama</state>
  <state>Alaska</state>
  <!-- etc. -->
</states>
```

As noted, by default, parameters are sent in URL-encoded format using HTTP GET. However, you can adjust those settings. The contentType property of the HTTPService object determines the format in which the content is sent. The default value is application/x-www-form-urlencoded, which sends the values in URL-encoded format. You can specify application/xml to send the data as XML if the service expects raw XML data:

```
<mx:HTTPService id="service" url="script.php" contentType="application/xml">
  <mx:request>
    <parameters>
      <a>one</a>
      <b>two</b>
    </parameters>
  </mx:request>
</mx:HTTPService>
```

The method property determines what transport method is used. The default is GET, but you can also specify a value of POST, HEAD, OPTIONS, PUT, TRACE, or DELETE.

Using HTTPService with ActionScript

Although the simplest and quickest way to use an HTTPService object is to primarily use MXML, this technique is best-suited to nonenterprise applications in which the data communication scenarios are quite simple. However, for more complex data communication requirements, it is advisable to use remote proxies, as discussed earlier in this chapter. Because HTTPService components provide significant data conversion advantages (such as automatic serialization of data), it is still frequently a good idea to use an HTTPService object within a remote proxy. However, it is generally necessary to then work with the HTTPService component entirely with ActionScript, including constructing the object and handling the responses.

When working with HTTPService objects entirely with ActionScript you'll want to import the mx.rpc.http.HTTPService class. You can then construct an instance with a standard new statement:

```
var httpRequest:HTTPRequest = new HTTPRequest();
```

You should then set the url property:

```
httpRequest.url = "data.txt";
```

Just as you would listen for any event from any object, you need to add listeners to HTTPService objects using addEventListener( ). HTTPService objects dispatch events of type ResultEvent when a response is returned, and they dispatch events of type FaultEvent when an error is returned from the server. The ResultEvent and FaultEvent classes are in the mx.rpc.events package:

```
httpRequest.addEventListener(ResultEvent.RESULT, resultHandler);
```

Example 16-5 is a simple working example that uses the recommended remote proxy approach in conjunction with HTTPService. This example accomplishes the same basic thing as previous MXML-based examples—displaying countries and states in combo boxes. However, this example uses several classes to accomplish this. The first class we'll look at is a simple data model class called ApplicationDataModel. Here's the code.

Example 16-5. ApplicationDataModel.as

```
package com.oreilly.programmingflex.remotedata {
    import mx.collections.ListCollectionView;

    public class ApplicationDataModel {

        private static var _instance:ApplicationDataModel;

        private var _countryNames:ListCollectionView;
        private var _statesNames:ListCollectionView;

        [Bindable]
        public function set countryNames(value:ListCollectionView):void {
            _countryNames = value;
        }

        public function get countryNames():ListCollectionView {
            return _countryNames;
        }

        [Bindable]
        public function set statesNames(value:ListCollectionView):void {
            _statesNames = value;
        }

        public function get statesNames():ListCollectionView {
            return _statesNames;
        }

        public function ApplicationDataModel() {}

        public static function getInstance():ApplicationDataModel {
            if(_instance == null) {
                _instance = new ApplicationDataModel();
            }
```

Example 16-5. ApplicationDataModel.as (continued)

```
        return _instance;
    }


}
}
```

In Example 16-6, we'll define StatesService, which is the remote proxy that loads XML data using HTTPService. The class defines two service methods: getCountries( ) and getStates( ). When the results are returned for the service method calls, they are assigned to the data model.

Example 16-6. StatesService.as

```
package com.oreilly.programmingflex.remotedata {
    import mx.rpc.http.HTTPService;
    import mx.rpc.events.ResultEvent;
    import mx.collections.XMLListCollection;
    import com.oreilly.programmingflex.remotedata.ApplicationDataModel;

    public class StatesService {

        private var _service:HTTPService;

        public function StatesService( ) {
            _service = new HTTPService( );
            _service.resultFormat = "e4x";
        }

        public function getCountries( ):void {
            _service.addEventListener(ResultEvent.RESULT, countriesResultHandler);
            _service.url = "http://rightactionscript.com/states/xml/countries.xml";
            _service.send( );
        }

        public function getStates(country:String):void {
            _service.addEventListener(ResultEvent.RESULT, statesResultHandler);
            _service.url = "http://rightactionscript.com/states/xml/states.php?country="
            + country;
            _service.send( );
        }

        private function countriesResultHandler(event:ResultEvent):void {
            _service.removeEventListener(ResultEvent.RESULT, countriesResultHandler);
            ApplicationDataModel.getInstance( ).countryNames = new XMLListCollection(_
service.lastResult.children( ) as XMLList);
        }

        private function statesResultHandler(event:ResultEvent):void {
            _service.removeEventListener(ResultEvent.RESULT, statesResultHandler);
            ApplicationDataModel.getInstance( ).statesNames = new XMLListCollection(_
service.lastResult.children( ) as XMLList);
```

Example 16-6. StatesService.as (continued)

```
        }


    }
}
```

Example 16-7 is the MXML application that utilizes both classes.

Example 16-7. Using the states service proxy and application data model

```
<?xml version="1.0" encoding="utf-8"?>
<mx:Application xmlns:mx="http://www.adobe.com/2006/mxml" layout="absolute"
creationComplete="creationCompleteHandler(event)">
    <mx:Script>
        <![CDATA[
            import mx.rpc.http.HTTPService;
            import mx.rpc.events.ResultEvent;
            import com.oreilly.programmingflex.remotedata.StatesService;
            import com.oreilly.programmingflex.remotedata.ApplicationDataModel;

            private var _statesService:StatesService;
            private function creationCompleteHandler(event:Event):void {
                _statesService = new StatesService();
                _statesService.getCountries();
            }
        ]]>
    </mx:Script>
    <mx:VBox>
        <mx:ComboBox id="countryMenu" dataProvider="{ApplicationDataModel.getInstance().
countryNames}" change="_statesService.getStates(countryMenu.selectedLabel)" />
        <mx:ComboBox dataProvider="{ApplicationDataModel.getInstance().statesNames}" />
    </mx:VBox>
</mx:Application>
```

In this example, the StatesService instance is created, and getCountries() is called immediately. The first combo box is data-bound to the countryNames property of the data model. As the user selects a value from the first combo box, it calls getStates(), passing it the selected country. The second combo box is data-bound to the statesNames property of the data model.

URLLoader

HTTPService allows you to use requests and handle responses to and from simple HTTP services. You can optionally use the Flash Player class called flash.net. URLLoader to accomplish the same tasks entirely with ActionScript, but at a slightly lower level.

The first step when working with a URLLoader object is always to construct the object using the constructor method, as follows:

```
    var loader:URLLoader = new URLLoader();
```

Once you've constructed the object, you can do the following:

- Send requests.
- Handle responses.
- Send parameters.

Sending requests

You can send requests using the load( ) method of a URLLoader object. The load( ) method requires that you pass it a flash.net.URLRequest object specifying at a minimum what URL to use when making the request. The following makes a request to a text file called *data.txt*:

```
loader.load(new URLRequest("data.txt"));
```

Handling responses

URLLoader objects dispatch complete events when a response has been returned. Any return value is stored in the data property of the URLLoader object. Example 16-8 loads XML data from a URL and handles the response.

Example 16-8. Loading XML usingURL Loader

```
<?xml version="1.0" encoding="utf-8"?>
<mx:Application xmlns:mx="http://www.adobe.com/2006/mxml" layout="absolute"
initialize="initializeHandler(event)">

    <mx:Script>
        <![CDATA[

            private var _countriesService:URLLoader;

            private function initializeHandler(event:Event):void {
              _countriesService = new URLLoader( );
              _countriesService.addEventListener(Event.COMPLETE,
                  countriesCompleteHandler);
            _countriesService.load(new URLRequest("http://localhost/states/xml/countries.xml"));
                XML.ignoreWhitespace = true;
            }

            private function countriesCompleteHandler(event:Event):void {
                var xml:XML = new XML(_countriesService.data);
                country.dataProvider = xml.children( );
            }

        ]]>
    </mx:Script>

    <mx:VBox>
        <mx:ComboBox id="country" />
    </mx:VBox>

</mx:Application>
```

When data is returned to a URLLoader object, it is interpreted as a string by default. In the preceding example, you can see that this is so because the data must be converted to an XML object.

It is possible to receive binary data and URL-encoded data in response to a URLLoader request. If you want to handle a binary response, you must set the dataFormat property of the URLLoader object to flash.net.URLLoaderDataFormat.BINARY. Binary data will then be interpreted as a ByteArray. If the returned data is in URL-encoded format, you can set the dataFormat property to flash.net.URLLoaderDataFormat. VARIABLES, and the returned data is interpreted as a flash.net.URLVariables object. URLVariables objects contain properties corresponding to the name/value pairs in the returned value. For example, if a URLLoader object is set to handle URL-encoded return data, a return value of a=one&b=two creates a URLVariables object with a and b properties accessible, as in the following:

```
trace(loader.data.a + " " + loader.data.b);
```

Sending parameters

You can send parameters using URLLoader as well. In order to send parameters, you assign a value to the data property of the URLRequest object used to make the request. The URLRequest object can send binary data or string data. If you assign a ByteArray to the data property, it's sent as binary. If you assign a URLVariables object to the data property the data is sent in URL-encoded format. Otherwise, the data is converted to a string. Example 16-9 builds on Example 16-8 to send a parameter when requesting state data.

Example 16-9. Sending parameters with URLLoader

```
<?xml version="1.0" encoding="utf-8"?>
<mx:Application xmlns:mx="http://www.adobe.com/2006/mxml" layout="absolute"
initialize="initializeHandler(event)">

    <mx:Script>
        <![CDATA[

            private var _countriesService:URLLoader;
            private var _statesService:URLLoader;

            private function initializeHandler(event:Event):void {
                _countriesService = new URLLoader( );
                _countriesService.addEventListener(Event.COMPLETE,
countriesCompleteHandler);
                _countriesService.load(new URLRequest("http://localhost/states/xml/
countries.xml"));
                _statesService = new URLLoader( );
                _statesService.addEventListener(Event.COMPLETE, statesCompleteHandler);
                XML.ignoreWhitespace = true;
            }
```

Example 16-9. Sending parameters with URLLoader (continued)

```
            private function countriesCompleteHandler(event:Event):void {
                var xml:XML = new XML(_countriesService.data);
                country.dataProvider = xml.children( );
            }

            private function statesCompleteHandler(event:Event):void {
                var xml:XML = new XML(_statesService.data);
                state.dataProvider = xml.children( );
            }

            private function changeHandler(event:Event):void {
                var request:URLRequest =
                  new URLRequest("http://localhost/states/xml/states.php");
                var parameters:URLVariables = new URLVariables( );
                parameters.country = country.value;
                request.data = parameters;
                _statesService.load(request);
            }

        ]]>
    </mx:Script>

    <mx:VBox>
        <mx:ComboBox id="country" change="changeHandler(event)" />
        <mx:ComboBox id="state" />
    </mx:VBox>

</mx:Application>
```

You can use the method property to specify how the data should be sent. Possible values are flash.net.URLRequestMethod.POST and flash.net.URLRequestMethod.GET.

Using URLLoader in a remote proxy

Now that you've had a chance to see the basics of working with URLLoader, here's an example that uses URLLoader in context. In the section titled "Using HTTPService with ActionScript," you saw a complete working example. You can use the same MXML document and data model class and make a few minor edits to the remote proxy class in order to use URLLoader instead of HTTPService. Example 16-10 is the new remote proxy class.

Example 16-10. StatesService.as

```
package com.oreilly.programmingflex.remotedata {
    import flash.net.URLLoader;
    import flash.net.URLRequest;
    import flash.events.Event;
    import flash.net.URLVariables;
    import mx.collections.XMLListCollection;
    import com.oreilly.programmingflex.remotedata.ApplicationDataModel
```

Example 16-10. StatesService.as (continued)

```
public class StatesService {

    private var _service:URLLoader;

    public function StatesService() {
        _service = new URLLoader();
    }

    public function getCountries():void {
        _service.addEventListener(Event.COMPLETE, countriesResultHandler);
        var request:URLRequest =
          new URLRequest("http://rightactionscript.com/states/xml/countries.xml");
        _service.load(request);
    }

    public function getStates(country:String):void {
        _service.addEventListener(Event.COMPLETE, statesResultHandler);
        var request:URLRequest =
          new URLRequest("http://rightactionscript.com/states/xml/states.php");
        var parameters:URLVariables = new URLVariables();
        parameters.country = country;
        request.data = parameters;
        _service.load(request);
    }

    private function countriesResultHandler(event:Event):void {
        _service.removeEventListener(Event.COMPLETE, countriesResultHandler);
        ApplicationDataModel.getInstance().countryNames =
          new XMLListCollection(new XML(_service.data).children() as XMLList);
    }

    private function statesResultHandler(event:Event):void {
        _service.removeEventListener(Event.COMPLETE, statesResultHandler);
        ApplicationDataModel.getInstance().statesNames =
          new XMLListCollection(new XML(_service.data).children() as XMLList);
    }


    }
}
```

You can test this new StatesService class using the same MXML document and ApplicationDataModel class from earlier in the chapter.

Web Services

Flash Player has no built-in support for SOAP web services. However, Flex provides a WebService component that uses built-in HTTP request/response support as well as XML support to enable you to work with SOAP-based web services. There are two ways you can work with the WebService components: using MXML and using ActionScript.

Using WebService Components with MXML

You can create a WebService component instance using MXML. When you do, you should specify an id and a value for the wsdl property, as in the following example:

```
<mx:WebService id="statesService" wsdl="http://www.rightactionscript.com/states/
webservice/StatesService.php?wsdl" />
```

Web services define one or more methods or operations. You must define the WebService instance so that it knows about the operations using nested operation tags. The operation tag requires that you specify the name at a minimum. The following example defines an operation called getCountries. This means that the WSDL document must also define a getCountries operation.

```
<mx:WebService id="statesService" wsdl="http://www.rightactionscript.com/states/
webservice/StatesService.php?wsdl">
  <mx:operation name="getCountries" />
</mx:WebService>
```

Once you've defined the WebService instance and an operation, you need to be able to call the method and handle the response, which we'll look at in the next few sections.

Calling web service methods

All operations that you define for a WebService component instance are accessible as properties of the instance. For example, in the preceding section, we created a WebService instance called statesService with an operation called getCountries. That means you can use ActionScript to reference the operation as statesService. getCountries.

You can then call getCountries just as though it were a method of statesService:

```
statesService.getCountries();
```

Optionally, you can call the send( ) method of getCountries:

```
statesService.getCountries.send();
```

Each of these ways of calling the operation is equivalent in many cases. The only time you must use one instead of the other is when you want to declaratively define operation parameters using MXML. In such cases, you must use the send( ) method.

Handling results

When a web service operation returns a result, you can handle it in one of two ways: explicitly handle the result event or use data binding. Then, once a result is returned, you can retrieve the result value from the lastResult property of the operation.

All web service operations dispatch a result event when the result is returned. The following code tells the application to call trace( ) when the result is returned:

```
<mx:WebService id="statesService" wsdl="http://www.rightactionscript.com/states/
webservice/StatesService.php?wsdl">
  <mx:operation name="getCountries" result="trace('result returned')" />
</mx:WebService>
```

Here we're using the same code, except we're tracing the result of the operation using statesService.getCountries.lastResult:

```
<mx:WebService id="statesService" wsdl="http://www.rightactionscript.com/states/
webservice/StatesService.php?wsdl">
  <mx:operation name="getCountries"
      result="trace(statesService.getCountries.lastResult)" />
</mx:WebService>
```

Example 16-11 is a simple example that loads an array of countries and uses data binding to populate a combo box.

Example 16-11. Using a WebService to load data

```
<?xml version="1.0" encoding="utf-8"?>
<mx:Application xmlns:mx="http://www.adobe.com/2006/mxml" layout="absolute"
initialize="initializeHandler(event)">

    <mx:Script>
        <![CDATA[

            private function initializeHandler(event:Event):void {
                statesService.getCountries.send( );
            }

        ]]>
    </mx:Script>

    <mx:WebService id="statesService"
    wsdl="http://www.rightactionscript.com/states/webservice/StatesService.php?wsdl">
        <mx:operation name="getCountries" />
    </mx:WebService>

    <mx:VBox>
        <mx:ComboBox id="country" dataProvider="{statesService.getCountries.lastResult}" /
>
    </mx:VBox>

</mx:Application>
```

In each of the preceding examples, the result returned by the operation is an array.

Sending parameters

You can send parameters to a web service method using the WebService component. When you want to send parameters, you have two basic options: you can pass the parameters when calling the method or you can declare the parameters when declaring the operation.

First we'll look at passing parameters to a web service method when calling it. When you want to pass parameters in this way, you must call the operation as a method of the WebService instance. You can then pass parameters to the method in the function call operator just as you would any standard method:

```
service.exampleOperation("a", "b");
```

If you want to pass parameters with dynamic values obtained from user input, you can use expressions, just as you would for any method. For example, the following assumes that textInput1 and textInput2 are text input controls:

```
service.exampleOperation(textInput1.text, textInput2.text);
```

Example 16-12 adds another operation, getStates, and calls the method passing it the selected country value.

Example 16-12. Calling a WebService method with parameters

```
<?xml version="1.0" encoding="utf-8"?>
<mx:Application xmlns:mx="http://www.adobe.com/2006/mxml" layout="absolute"
initialize="initializeHandler(event)">

    <mx:Script>
        <![CDATA[

            private function initializeHandler(event:Event):void {
                statesService.getCountries();
            }

            private function changeHandler(event:Event):void {
                statesService.getStates(country.value);
            }

        ]]>
    </mx:Script>

    <mx:WebService id="statesService" wsdl="http://www.rightactionscript.com/states/
webservice/StatesService.php?wsdl">
        <mx:operation name="getCountries" />
        <mx:operation name="getStates" />
    </mx:WebService>

    <mx:VBox>
        <mx:ComboBox id="country" dataProvider="{statesService.getCountries.lastResult}"
change="changeHandler(event)" />
        <mx:ComboBox dataProvider="{statesService.getStates.lastResult}" />
    </mx:VBox>

</mx:Application>
```

You can optionally use the send( ) method to call the operation. When you want to send parameters using the send( ) method, simply pass the parameters to the send( ) method:

```
statesService.getStates.send(country.value);
```

Another option when passing parameters to a web service method is to declare them when declaring the operation. You can do that by nesting a request tag in the operation tag. Then, within the request tag, you can create a structure of the parameters. You should use the names of the parameters as they are expected by the web service method (as defined in the WSDL). For example, the following code declares an operation that expects two parameters, called a and b:

```
<mx:WebService id="exampleService" wsdl="http://www.example.com/service.wsdl ">
  <mx:operation name="exampleOperation">
    <mx:request>
      <a>1</a>
      <b>2</b>
    </mx:request>
  </mx:operation>
</mx:WebService>
```

When you use this form of declarative parameter, you must call the operation using the send( ) method. You don't need to pass any parameters to the send( ) method.

```
exampleService.exampleOperation.send( );
```

Note that you can use data binding to bind to parameters as well, as in Example 16-13.

Example 16-13. Using the send() method

```
<?xml version="1.0" encoding="utf-8"?>
<mx:Application xmlns:mx="http://www.adobe.com/2006/mxml" layout="absolute"
initialize="initializeHandler(event)">

    <mx:Script>
        <![CDATA[

            private function initializeHandler(event:Event):void {
                statesService.getCountries.send( );
            }

            private function changeHandler(event:Event):void {
                statesService.getStates.send( );
            }

        ]]>
    </mx:Script>

    <mx:WebService id="statesService" wsdl="http://www.rightactionscript.com/states/
webservice/StatesService.php?wsdl">
        <mx:operation name="getCountries" />
        <mx:operation name="getStates">
```

Example 16-13. Using the send() method (continued)

```
            <mx:request>
                <country>
                    {country.value}
                </country>
            </mx:request>
        </mx:operation>
    </mx:WebService>

    <mx:VBox>
        <mx:ComboBox id="country" dataProvider="{statesService.getCountries.lastResult}"
change="changeHandler(event)" />
        <mx:ComboBox dataProvider="{statesService.getStates.lastResult}" />
    </mx:VBox>

</mx:Application>
```

This example first populates the list of states. It then uses parameter binding to link the selection from the country combo box to the parameter sent to the getStates operation.

Using WebService Components with ActionScript

You can use a WebService component using ActionScript instead of MXML. This is useful in cases where you want to fully separate the view from the controller and the model, such as in the recommended remote proxy approach. The MXML version of the WebService component is an instance of mx.rpc.soap.mxml.WebService, which is a subclass of mx.rpc.soap.WebService. When you use the component directly from ActionScript you should instantiate mx.rpc.soap.WebService directly:

```
// Assume the code already has an import statement for mx.rpc.soap.WebService.
var exampleService:WebService = new WebService( );
```

Once you have created a WebService instance, you need to specify the WSDL URL using the wsdl property:

```
exampleService.wsdl = "http://www.example.com/Service.wsdl";
```

Next, you must call a method called loadWSDL( ). You must call the method prior to calling any of the web service operations. Assuming you set the wsdl property, you don't need to pass any parameters to loadWSDL( ):

```
exampleService.loadWSDL( );
```

Sending requests

Once you've called the loadWSDL( ) method, you can call any operations defined by the web service. You can call the operations either as methods of the WebService object or by using the send( ) method:

```
// The following lines of code accomplish the same thing.
exampleService.testOperation( );
exampleService.testOperation.send( );
```

Sending parameters

If you want to pass parameters to an operation, you can pass them when calling the operation as a method, or you can pass them to the send( ) method:

```
// The following lines of code accomplish the same thing.
exampleService.testOperation(parameter);
exampleService.textOperation.send(parameter);
```

Handling results

You can handle the results of a web service operation either by listening for events or use data binding. If you want to use events, you can register listeners for result and error events dispatched by the operation(s). The result events are of type $mx.rpc.events.ResultEvent$, and the error events are of type $mx.rpc.events.FaultEvent$. The following example registers listeners for result and error events:

```
exampleService.testOperation.addEventListener(ResultEvent.RESULT, onResult);
exampleService.testOperation.addEventListener(FaultEvent.FAULT, onError);
```

If you want to use data binding, you must declare the WebService instance as bindable, as in Example 16-14.

Example 16-14. Using data binding with WebService

```
<?xml version="1.0" encoding="utf-8"?>
<mx:Application xmlns:mx="http://www.adobe.com/2006/mxml" layout="absolute"
initialize="initializeHandler(event)">

    <mx:Script>
        <![CDATA[
            import mx.rpc.soap.WebService;

            [Bindable]
            private var _statesService:WebService;

            private function initializeHandler(event:Event):void {
                _statesService = new WebService( );
                _statesService.wsdl = "http://www.rightactionscript.com/states/webservice/
StatesService.php?wsdl";
                _statesService.loadWSDL( );
                _statesService.getCountries.send( );
            }

            private function changeHandler(event:Event):void {
                _statesService.getStates.send(country.value);
            }

        ]]>
    </mx:Script>

    <mx:VBox>
```

Example 16-14. Using data binding with WebService (continued)

```
        <mx:ComboBox id="country" dataProvider="{_statesService.getCountries.lastResult}"
          change="changeHandler(event)" />
        <mx:ComboBox dataProvider="{_statesService.getStates.lastResult}" />
    </mx:VBox>

</mx:Application>
```

Using WebService with a remote proxy

In keeping with the previous sections, let's now look at how to use a WebService instance as part of a remote proxy class. Example 16-15 uses the same MXML document and data model class as Example 16-6 did. The only changes are to the remote proxy class shown here.

Example 16-15. StatesService.as

```
package com.oreilly.programmingflex.remotedata {
    import mx.rpc.soap.WebService;
    import mx.rpc.events.ResultEvent;
    import mx.collections.ArrayCollection;
    import com.oreilly.programmingflex.remotedata.ApplicationDataModel;

    public class StatesService {

        private var _service:WebService;

        public function StatesService( ) {
            _service = new WebService( );
            _service.wsdl = "http://www.rightactionscript.com/states/webservice/
StatesService.php?wsdl";
            _service.loadWSDL( );
        }

        public function getCountries( ):void {
            _service.getCountries.addEventListener(ResultEvent.RESULT,
                                            countriesResultHandler);
            _service.getCountries( );
        }

        public function getStates(country:String):void {
            _service.getStates.addEventListener(ResultEvent.RESULT,
                                        statesResultHandler);
            _service.getStates(country);
        }

        private function countriesResultHandler(event:ResultEvent):void {
            _service.getCountries.removeEventListener(ResultEvent.RESULT,
                                            countriesResultHandler);
            ApplicationDataModel.getInstance( ).countryNames =
              _service.getCountries.lastResult;
        }
```

Example 16-15. StatesService.as (continued)

```
        private function statesResultHandler(event:ResultEvent):void {
            _service.getStates.removeEventListener(ResultEvent.RESULT,
                                            statesResultHandler);
            ApplicationDataModel.getInstance().statesNames =
_service.getStates.lastResult;
        }


    }
}
```

Data Type Conversion

One of the advantages of using web services is that the result packets specify not only
the return value, but also the type. For example, the result packets for the
getCountries() and getStates() operations of the web service used in the preceding sections specify that the return value is an array. The result packet can specify
that the return data is an integer, a floating-point number, an array, a string, a date, a
Boolean value, or any number of custom data types. The Flex framework WebService
class automatically converts the result to the appropriate ActionScript type.
Table 16-1 describes common types and how they are converted to ActionScript.

Table 16-1. Common types and how they are converted to ActionScript

Data-type name	SOAP type	ActionScript type
String	xsd:string	String
Integer	xsd:int	Int
Floating-point number	xsd:float	Number
Boolean	xsd:boolean	Boolean
Date	xsd:date	Date
Array	xsd:string[], etc.	mx.collections.ArrayCollection

Flash Remoting

Flash Remoting is a technology for HTTP-based request/response data communication. Flash Remoting has many advantages, including the following:

- Data serialization and deserialization are handled automatically. That means
  when you send a Date object from a Flex application it is automatically converted to the correct corresponding type on the server (and vice versa). This is
  also possible for custom data types.

- Flash Remoting uses AMF, which is a binary messaging protocol, ensuring the
  smallest packet size of almost any option for data communication.

- AMF is a native messaging format understood by Flash Player, meaning that the data serialization and deserialization on the client are not only automatic, but also fast.

- Because a gateway receives requests on the server and delegates them to the correct services, the actual services can be standard classes on the server. This means little to no adaptation is required to use existing services with Flash Remoting.

Flash Remoting is supported natively by Flash Player, so no additional special libraries are necessary for the client-side implementation of Flash Remoting service calls. However, on the server, you'll need a gateway product capable of receiving and sending AMF packets over HTTP, serializing and deserializing AMF, and delegating requests to the appropriate services.

Because the focus of this book is on Flex, our discussion focuses on how to implement Flash Remoting service method calls from Flex applications rather than how to configure the server-side elements. However, the basic configuration is generally quite simple, and you can read more about the specifics based on the gateway product you select. Here's a list of popular Flash Remoting gateway products:

- AMFPHP (PHP, *http://www.amfphp.org*)
- OpenAMF (Java, *http://www.openamf.com*)
- WebORB (.NET, Java, Ruby on Rails, *http://www.themidnightcoders.com*)
- Fluorine (.NET, *http://fluorine.thesilentgroup.com*)
- Adobe Flash Remoting MX (Java, .NET, *http://www.adobe.com/products/flashremoting*)
- ColdFusion (the Flash Remoting gateway is part of a standard ColdFusion installation, *http://www.adobe.com/products/coldfusion.*)

 The Flex framework has a component called RemoteObject that enables you to make Flash Remoting calls. However, this component is designed to work best in conjunction with Flex Data Services, which is not discussed in this book. Although you can use RemoteObject without Flex Data Services, it does require a lot of extra work at the time of this writing. RemoteObject requires a Flash Remoting gateway that supports AMF3 (rather than AMF0), and it requires special XML files used by the compiler to determine the service locations. RemoteObject is a good solution in some cases, but it is outside the practical scope of this book to discuss it in detail.

Creating Flash Remoting connections

All Flash Remoting service calls are made using a native Flash Player class called flash.net.NetConnection. The first step is always to construct a new NetConnection instance:

```
var netConnection:NetConnection = new NetConnection( );
```

Next, you must specify the location of the Flash Remoting gateway. You can accomplish this by calling the connect( ) method, passing it the URL to the gateway:

```
netConnection.connect("http://www.server.com/flashremoting/gateway");
```

Calling Flash Remoting methods

You can call Flash Remoting methods using the call( ) method of a NetConnection object. The call( ) method requires, at a minimum, that you pass it two parameters: the name of the service method to call and a flash.net.Responder object that specifies what listeners should handle the response.

The name of the service method should include the full name of the service and the method name, delimited by dots. The name of the service is always the name by which the service is known to the gateway. Generally this is the fully qualified class name or an alias. For example, if the service is a Java class called com.oreilly. Example, the service name would be com.oreilly.Example. If the service method is named testMethod, the full name of the service method (as specified in the first parameter of the call( ) method) should be com.oreilly.Example.testMethod.

The Responder class allows you to specify the listeners that handle responses from the service method call. The Responder constructor requires at least one parameter referencing the listener method to handle the result response. Optionally, you can specify a second parameter referencing the listener method to handle a fault response. Here's an example that calls a service method and specifies a result handler:

```
netConnection.call("com.oreilly.Example.testMethod", new Responder(resultHandler));
```

Passing parameters to Flash Remoting methods

When a service method expects parameters, you can pass those parameters via the call( ) method. Any parameters passed to the call( ) method beyond the two required parameters are passed to the service method as parameters. Here's an example that passes a string and a number to the service method:

```
netConnection.call("com.oreilly.Example.testMethod",
                new Responder(resultHandler), "a", 1);
```

Using Flash Remoting remote proxies

You can (and generally should) use Flash Remoting in the context of a remote proxy class. Example 16-16 is based on the example from the section "Using HTTPService with ActionScript." This example uses the same MXML document and data model class, but the remote proxy class needs to be changed to use Flash Remoting. Here's the new remote proxy class.

Example 16-16. The new proxy class

```
package com.oreilly.programmingflex.remotedata {

    import flash.net.NetConnection;
    import flash.net.Responder;
    import mx.collections.ArrayCollection;
    import com.oreilly.programmingflex.remotedata.ApplicationDataModel;

    public class StatesService {

        private var _service:NetConnection;

        public function StatesService() {
            _service = new NetConnection();
            _service.connect("http://www.rightactionscript.com/states/flashremoting/
gateway.php");
        }

        public function getCountries():void {
            _service.call("StatesService.getCountries",
                        new Responder(countriesResultHandler));
        }

        public function getStates(country:String):void {
            _service.call("StatesService.getStates", new Responder(statesResultHandler),
country);
        }

        private function countriesResultHandler(countries:Array):void {
            ApplicationDataModel.getInstance().countryNames = new
ArrayCollection(countries);
        }

        private function statesResultHandler(states:Array):void {
            ApplicationDataModel.getInstance().statesNames = new ArrayCollection(states);
        }


    }
}
```

Real-Time/Socket Connection

Flash Player supports lower level, persistent socket connections, allowing you to create low-latency, real-time applications. Furthermore, with the use of binary sockets you can create Flex applications that communicate directly with services not otherwise directly accessible to Flash Player. For example, binary socket connections allow for the creation of mail clients, VNC clients, and more.

Essentially three types of socket connections are available from Flex applications:

XML sockets
Socket connections that require a specific communication protocol.

Binary sockets
Raw binary sockets.

RTMP
Real Time Messaging Protocol is used not only for media (video, audio, etc.), but also for real-time data communication. RTMP is supported by Flex Data Services, Flash Media Server, and other third-party applications.

Each of these persistent socket connection options is quite specialized and nonspecific to Flex applications. Entire books can be (and have been) written about these topics. Therefore, our goal in this chapter is simply to make you aware of their existence rather than to detail their use. You can learn more about using ActionScript to communicate using socket connections in the *ActionScript 3.0 Cookbook* (O'Reilly).

File Upload/Download

Flex applications support file upload and download using the Flash Player flash. net.FileReference class. You can enable the user to download one file at a time, as well as select and upload one or more files at the same time.

Downloading Files

Use the download( ) method of a FileReference object to download a file. The download( ) method requires at least one parameter: a URLRequest object. The URLRequest object should point to the URL from which you want to download the file. Here's an example that downloads a file called *test.txt*:

```
var fileReference:FileReference = new FileReference( );
fileReference.download(new URLRequest("test.txt"));
```

As soon as the download( ) method is called, Flash Player opens a dialog prompting the user to accept the file. The user has complete control over whether to save the file, where to save the file, and what to name the file. However, by default, the filename field in the dialog will be filled out with the name of the file as it exists on the server. If you want to customize the default filename in the dialog, you can do so with a second parameter in the download( ) method. This is particularly useful when the URL from which the file is requested is a script that generates the file or proxies the request to the file. For example, if the URL from which you request the file is *test.cgi*, a script that outputs a text file, you likely will want to use a custom filename rather than allow it to default to *test.cgi*. Here's an example:

```
fileReference,download(new URLRequest("test.cgi"), "test.txt");
```

The download() method can potentially throw errors. The two most common error types are IllegalOperationError and SecurityError. An IllegalOperationError occurs when a save dialog is already open (because only one can be open at a time). The SecurityError type occurs when the *.swf* is untrusted in the domain to which it is trying to make the request.

Uploading Files

The FileReference.browse() method allows you to enable the user to browse his files and select one for upload. Optionally, you can use FileReferenceList.browse() to allow the user to select one or more files at a time.

In either case (FileReference or FileReferenceList), the browse dialog has two buttons allowing the user to close the dialog: Open and Cancel. The FileReference or FileReferenceList object dispatches different events depending on which button the user clicks. If the user clicks the Cancel button, it dispatches a cancel event (Event.CANCEL). If the user clicks the Open button, it dispatches a select event (Event.SELECT).

When the user has selected a file or files (the select event has been dispatched), you can start to upload the file or files using the upload() method. The method requires that you pass it a URLRequest object specifying the URL to which to upload the file:

```
fileReference.upload(new URLRequest("upload.php"));
```

If you're using a FileReferenceList object, you must call the upload() method of each instance stored within the fileList property:

```
var request:URLRequest = new URLRequest("upload.php");
for(var i:int = 0; i < fileReferenceList.fileList.length; i++) {
    fileReferenceList.fileList[i].upload(request);
}
```

In order to upload files from Flash Player, you must have a script on the server that can receive the requests. When a file upload request is made to the server-side script, it is made in exactly the same way as a standard request from an HTML form submit request with a file field: using POST with a content type of multipart/form-data. The Content-Disposition header value is Filedata by default. If you need to customize this setting, you can specify a Content-Disposition header value using the second parameter in the upload() method:

```
fileReference.upload(request, "UploadFile");
```

Summary

In this chapter, you learned how to work with remote data communication. Remote data communication consists of HTTP request/response, sockets, and file upload/download. The HTTP request/response category can be further broken down into the different messaging formats, such as plain text, XML, SOAP, and AMF, each of which you learned about in this chapter.

Application Debugging

One of the strengths of Flex is its modern debugging. Debugging client-side code in web applications has traditionally been cumbersome. The Flash Debug Player, provided with Flex, allows developers to debug applications in the same way they have been accustomed to with other modern development platforms.

In this chapter, we will cover runtime errors, debugging applications using FDB, debugging applications using the Flex Builder debugger, remote debugging, and tracing and logging.

The Flash Debug Player

The Flash Debug Player is at the core of the debugging capabilities provided to Flex. The Debug Player provides several benefits specific to developers, and is required for most types of debugging you will need to do. The browser plug-in and standalone editions of the Debug Player are included in the free SDK in the */player/debug* folder, and in the *Path to Flex Builder 2/Player/debug* folder if you are using Flex Builder 2. Also, if you installed Flex Builder 2, the Debug Player browser plug-in is typically installed during the install process. You can always check to ensure that you have the latest edition of the Debug Player by visiting *http://www.adobe.com/support/flashplayer/downloads.html*.

If you are unsure whether you have the Debug Player installed within a browser, you can build a simple application to check the version of the player installed. Here's an example:

```
<?xml version="1.0" encoding="utf-8"?>
<mx:Application xmlns:mx="http://www.adobe.com/2006/mxml">
 <mx:Label text="Flash Player Version: {flash.system.Capabilities.version},
Debug Player: {flash.system.Capabilities.isDebugger}"/>
</mx:Application>
```

When you open the application in your browser, you should be presented with the version of Flash Player and whether it is the debug edition. flash.system.Capabilities is a class Flash Player provides that allows you to retrieve information about the runtime environment in which an application is executing. In this example, we are checking the isDebugger property, which should return true if you have the Debug Player installed. You can also use this property to enable additional debugging type features of an application only when they are running within a Debug Player.

The Debug Player provides several additional capabilities on top of the traditional player, as we'll see in the next section. This functionality allows a developer access to runtime behavior of a running application and is required for some debugging tools, including the command-line debugger and the Flex Builder 2 debugger.

 Running an application in the Debug Player, especially when it is being debugged, will impact runtime performance. You should install the Debug Player only for debugging purposes and never in a production environment.

Runtime Errors

Flash Player 9 supports runtime type checking and exceptions, capabilities developers have become accustomed to in any modern runtime. Runtime errors when identified during the development process can greatly help in debugging applications. Runtime errors are not presented to users with the non-Debug Player installed, but for development and testing purposes, you should have the Flash Debug Player installed (along with any team members that are involved in application testing). The Debug Player will display runtime errors by presenting you with a dialog as errors occur in your application. You may wonder why such errors are not presented to the user with the regular Flash Player. This is because Adobe silently hides such errors from regular users to minimize their impact on the application experience. The runtime errors still occur, but rather than interrupt the user with a dialog and halt the applications, Flash Player attempts to silently continue code execution. This does not guarantee that an application will always continue running; some exceptions are fatal and will cause an application to halt. Because of this, it is generally not advisable to deploy any application that contains runtime exceptions that are not handled. This also does not guarantee that an application will respond as expected when a nonfatal exception occurs. In general, it is good practice to properly handle exceptions to prevent unexpected results.

If you execute this code in the Debug Player, you will receive a runtime error:

```
<?xml version="1.0" encoding="utf-8"?>
<mx:Application xmlns:mx="http://www.adobe.com/2006/mxml"
initialize="initializeHandler()">
    <mx:Script>
        <![CDATA[
            private function initializeHandler():void
            {
```

```
            var loader:Loader = new Loader( );
            loader.load(new URLRequest("foo"));
        }
    ]]>
  </mx:Script>
</mx:Application>
```

The runtime error you will receive is IOErrorEvent, because the example does not handle such an exception. Figure 17-1 is the dialog that results when running the Debug Player.

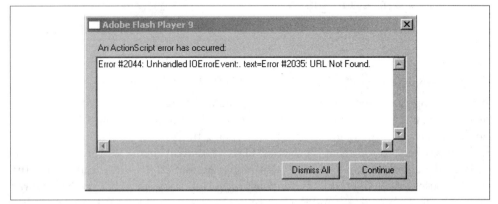

Figure 17-1. Flash Debug Player error dialog

You can find a list of runtime error codes, along with descriptions, in the Flex 2 Language Reference documentation, under Appendixes → Run-Time Errors.

The Debugging API

Although runtime errors are useful, often you will require more than just runtime errors to identify bugs. For such cases, the Flash Debug Player exposes an API for debuggers to interact with an application at runtime. This includes the ability to set breakpoints, step through code, set and retrieve variables at runtime, as well as other debugging-related tasks. As of this writing, two debuggers are available on the market, both provided by Adobe. The first is the free FDB command-line debugger provided by the Flex SDK, and the other is the integrated GUI debugger that is part of Flex Builder 2. The debuggers communicate with the Flash Debug Player through a TCP socket connection. Typically, this happens on the same machine, but it is possible to also do remote debugging whereby one machine is the client and the other is running the debugger.

To allow the Debug Player to initiate a debug session, the application must be compiled with the debug data included within the SWF. To do this, you need to set the -debug mxmlc compiler flag to true:

```
mxmlc -debug=true main.mxml
```

This flag generates a debug-enabled SWF. Although you may not experience any side effects from using a debug-enabled SWF for production, this is strongly discouraged because the -debug compiler flag produces larger SWF files, and exposes the internals of an application. If a user has the Debug Player installed, he could inspect the internals of your application and even change client-side variable values. Later in this chapter, we will discuss how to use debug-enabled SWF files using various debuggers available today.

Using Show Redraw Regions

Even with modern hardware, you can run into rendering performance bottlenecks with graphics-intensive applications. Isolating such bottlenecks can be challenging, especially considering all the variables involved in how Flash Player renders content. For this reason, the Debug Player exposes an option called Show Redraw Regions.

When this option is enabled, the player will highlight areas of a running application that are being redrawn, which can help you identify graphical regions of an application that may be drawing inefficiently. You enable this option by selecting the Show Redraw Regions option from the Debug Player's context menu, or through Action-Script. To enable this option through ActionScript you can call the `showRedrawRegions()` method of the `flash.profiler` package. This method works only with the Debug Player and doesn't require a debug-enabled SWF. Here's a simple example that will allow you to experiment with how this feature works:

```
<?xml version="1.0" encoding="utf-8"?>
<mx:Application xmlns:mx="http://www.adobe.com/2006/mxml" initialize="flash.profiler.
showRedrawRegions(true)">
    <mx:HSlider width="100%"/>
</mx:Application>
```

Compile and run this example in the Debug Player. Drag the slider to see how the Debug Player highlights what areas are being redrawn. This is especially helpful with Flex applications because the Flex framework provides a lot of functionality that you don't need to implement and often may not even know how it is implemented. Using the Show Redraw Regions feature can help you identify rendering bottlenecks in Flash Player.

 By default, the `showRedrawRegions()` method highlights regions by drawing a blue rectangle outline around the regions being redrawn and the player context menu will use a red outline. However, sometimes you might find the default color difficult to identify. If so, you can specify your own color values by passing in a color value for the second parameter of the `showRedrawRegions()` method.

Using FDB

As part of the Flex 2 SDK, Adobe includes FDB, a free command-line debugger. This debugger is fully featured, although usually you will opt to use the Flex Builder 2 debugger if available. With that said, it is great to have access to a free debugging tool included as part of the SDK. This allows developers who do not want to purchase Flex Builder 2 access to a fully featured debugger. We won't be covering FDB in depth, but we will discuss the basics and some of the possible benefits it has to offer.

You launch FDB from the command line as you would any other command-line application. Once it is started, you are prompted with the FDB prompt (fdb). You can type **help** at the prompt for a list of available commands.

The starting point for a debug session with FDB is to launch a SWF compiled with debugging enabled in the Debug Player and establish a connection with FDB. You do this by first executing the run command at the FDB prompt. Once the command is executed, FDB will confirm that it is waiting for the player to connect. To connect Flash Player to FDB, open a debug-enabled SWF with the Debug Player. When a debug-enabled SWF is opened, the player will attempt to auto-connect to the local debugger, if available.

If you open an application without the debugger listening for a connection from the player, the Flash Debug Player will prompt you to select the debugger you want to use. Although typically a user will be running the application and the debugger on the same machine, which means you may never receive the prompt requesting you to select the debugger, it is possible to initiate a *remote debugging* session. Remote debugging allows you to execute an application on a machine that is separate from the debugger, allowing you to debug problems that are reproducible on only certain machines, or even debug across platforms wherein a Mac OS X machine executes an application with the debugger running on a Windows machine. For this purpose, all debugging communication occurs through TCP on port 7935. Remote debugging is covered later in this chapter.

Once a connection is established, you can set breakpoints or instruct the debugger to continue execution of the application. To continue execution you can issue the continue command. Application trace messages are shown in the debugger as they are encountered.

Breakpoints can be set using several methods. The most typical method of setting a breakpoint is to specify the class and line number for the breakpoint, which you can achieve by issuing the break command. For example, if you wanted to insert a breakpoint in line 56 of the class MainApp, you would use input the command break MainApp.mxml:56. If you want a breakpoint when a button is pressed but you are not sure of the method that will be called when the event occurs, you could enter **break button**. This will return a list of methods that begin with the word *button*. From the list, you should see buttonPressed and the location of the method. With that information, you could set the breakpoint by calling break buttonPressed. Once done, you will need to call the command continue, which will tell the debugger to allow the player to continue executing the application. There are other methods of setting breakpoints with FDB, which you can find by issuing the command help breakpoint.

When an application is executing, the debugger will inform you when it encounters a breakpoint. Once a breakpoint is encountered, you have several options. You can issue the continue command, which will continue execution of the application, step through the application using the step command, and set the value of a variable using the set command. When done debugging, you can exit FDB to end the debugging session, which will automatically end the active connection with the Debug Player, or you can execute the kill command.

As discussed, FDB makes it easy to search for methods on which you want to set breakpoints. Some of the other nice features of FDB which Flex Builder's debugger doesn't support are the ability to set conditional breakpoints using the condition command, and the ability to review a list of all the loaded types and functions with the info functions command.

FDB can be a powerful tool and is worth exploring, but as you will see in the next section, Flex Builder provides a more practical method of application debugging, which you will likely opt for over FDB.

Debugging with Flex Builder 2

One of the best selling points of Flex Builder 2 is the integrated GUI debugger. FDB is free, but for day-to-day debugging, Flex Builder's debugger makes it much easier to debug applications.

A default Flex Builder 2 installation (see Figure 17-2) will configure the tasks needed to get you up and running for debugging applications. To debug an application you are working on, you just need to select Run → Debug from the main menu (or press F11). This will compile the application, launch it within the browser, and connect the application to the debugger. The first time you debug an application you will be prompted to switch perspectives to the debugging perspective in Flex Builder, which usually is recommended.

When in the debugging perspective, you have access to the currently running application. Often you will set a breakpoint to stop the application at a point during the execution process in which you are interested. You can set breakpoints by right-clicking on the left margin of a source line in Flex Builder. You can do this during a debug session or even before a session is started in the development perspective. You can navigate through a list of breakpoints by using the Breakpoints panel (see Figure 17-3). The Breakpoints panel contains a list of all breakpoints currently set, and will allow you to navigate directly to a breakpoint or disable a breakpoint. This panel can also be very useful if you aren't sure what breakpoints you have set in your application.

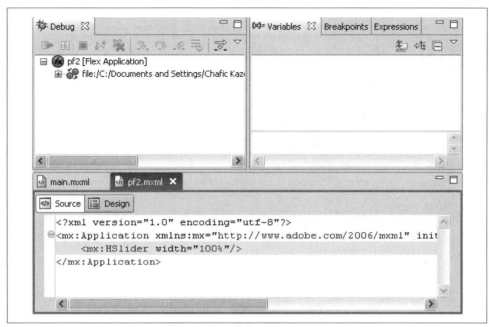

Figure 17-2. Default debugging perspective

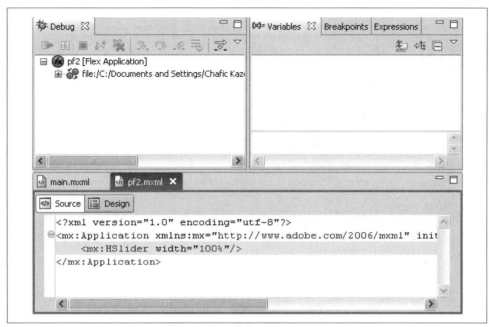

Figure 17-3. The Breakpoints panel

When Flash Player encounters a breakpoint, as in Figure 17-4, execution will halt, the debugger will gain focus, and the call stack will be displayed. As you would expect, when a breakpoint is reached, execution halts. You then will have the option of having the application continue execution, step through code, set variables, and evaluate expressions.

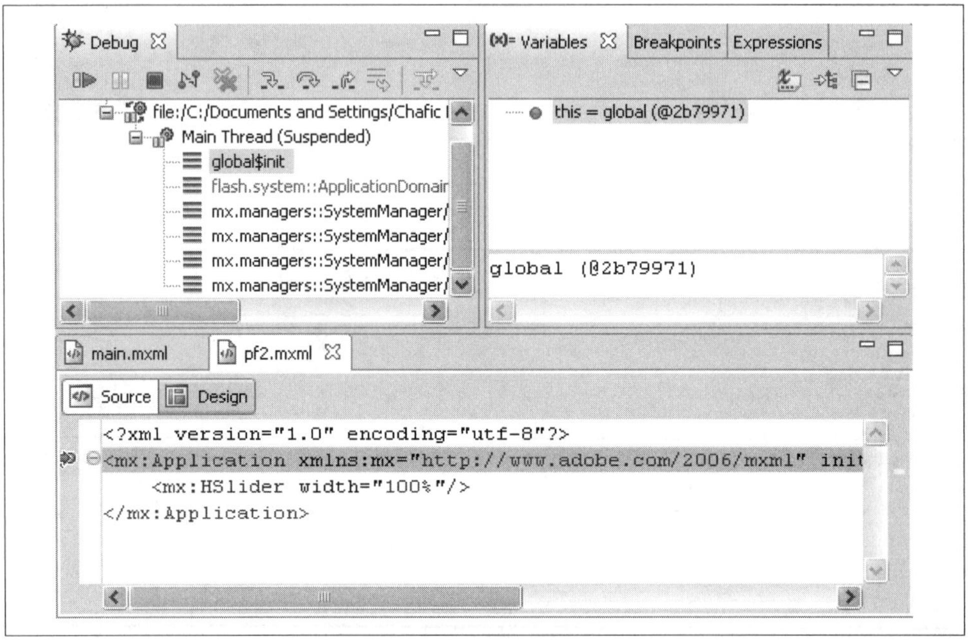

Figure 17-4. Debugging view when a breakpoint is reached

Breakpoints are typically set on ActionScript portions of the code. Setting breakpoints on MXML portions of the code typically will result in an invalid breakpoint. Because of this, Flex Builder attempts to find the nearest valid breakpoint, if one exists. It does so by scanning the application's next 10 lines of execution for points where a breakpoint would be valid, and automatically moves the breakpoint to that location.

To help speed up the debugging process, Flex Builder 2 offers the following default keyboard shortcuts for stepping through code:

- Stepping into (F5)
- Stepping over (F6)
- Step return (F7)
- Resume execution (F8)

While stepping through code, the debugger will have control over the player. At times, this may cause the player and browser to seem as though they are frozen. This is normal as you step through code. To suspend the debugger from having control until the next breakpoint, you have to tell the debugger to resume execution by clicking on the Play button or by using the F8 keyboard shortcut.

While debugging, you also have the ability to review values of variables at runtime. The Variables panel (see Figure 17-5) will list all object instances as well as their child properties and values. To change a value, right-click on the variable and select Change Value. This will prompt you for the new value.

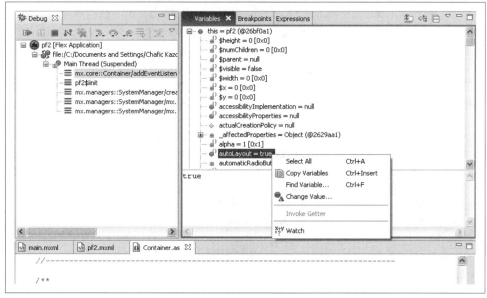

Figure 17-5. The Variables panel

 When debugging an application, you also have the ability to set breakpoints in and step through Flex framework code. Stepping through framework code will happen automatically when needed. To set breakpoints within the framework, you will need to open the class file. An easy way to do this is to use the shortcut Ctrl-Shift-T within Flex Builder 2 and select the appropriate type. Once the class file is opened, you can set breakpoints as you would normally.

You can have only a single active debug session running at once. To end a debug session you can either close Flash Player or your browser, or you can click on the red square within the Debug panel. Caution should be taken when closing an active debug session by closing the browser when it is executing within a browser, as sessions that are in a halted state can cause a web browser to close unexpectedly.

This book does not fully cover all the functionality possible with the debugger within Flex Builder 2. For full coverage, you can review the documentation provided with Flex Builder 2.

Remote Debugging

When attempting to isolate a bug in an application, it is possible that you will encounter a case where a bug is reproducible on only a specific machine. For such a case, you can use the Flash Debug Player's remote debugging feature. This feature can also be useful if you would want to use the Flex Builder debugger on a Windows or Mac-based machine while the application is executed under Linux, which does not have a native version of Flex Builder available.

As mentioned earlier, debugging occurs over a TCP connection on port 7935. Such a connection is typically established on the same machine transparently, but with remote debugging it is established from one machine to another. One machine will typically be running the debugger and can be referred to as the server, while the other will be running the application and can be referred to as the client machine. Once a connection is established between the client and the server, all of the features of using a debugger function in the same manner. It's important to remember that in a typical workstation, the the client machine may not be configured properly for remote debugging. Remember that the Flash Debug Player is required for a debug session, so you will need to ensure that it is installed on the client machine. It is also important to keep in mind that the client machine will need to be executing a debug-enabled SWF in the same manner as we discussed earlier in the chapter.

To initiate a debug session, follow these steps:

1. Initialize the debugger on the server machine.
   - With FDB: One benefit of using FDB when initializing a remote debugging session is that the steps for initializing FDB are exactly the same as initializing a local session. You initialize FDB by launching FDB and executing the run command.
   - With Flex Builder's Debugger: Initializing a remote debugging session with Flex Builder is more involved. Flex Builder's debugger doesn't formally support remote debugging, although it is possible. We will cover remote debugging with Flex Builder in the next section.

2. Initialize the debug-enabled SWF on the client machine and ensure that the debug player is installed.

3. Once initialized, the player will prompt you for a debugger, because the debugger is not running on the client machine. Input the IP address of the server running the debugger and select Connect.

4. If the server is running the debugger and listening for a connection, the client and server will connect. Note here that you will also need to ensure that the server is not blocking port 7935.

Once a connection has been established, debugging can be performed in the same manner discussed earlier in this chapter.

Establishing a Remote Debugging Session with the Flex Builder Debugger

As mentioned earlier, debugging sessions—both local and remote—are established over a TCP connection on port 7935. Flex Builder uses the same connection to establish debug sessions. Although by default Flex Builder does not expose remote debugging capabilities, it still is possible to do so.

To initiate a remote debug session with Flex Builder, follow these steps:

1. Compiled a debug-enabled *.swf*.
2. Copy the debug-enabled *.swf* to the remote client machine.
3. On the machine that will run the Flex Builder debugger (server), create an empty HTML file (typically within your project's *bin* folder).
4. Ensure that no firewall is actively blocking port 7935.
5. Edit the debug configuration within Flex Builder (select Run → Run).
6. Select the target debug configuration.
7. Uncheck the "Use defaults" checkbox.
8. Click on the Browse button for the debug file path.
9. Select the blank HTML page.
10. Click on Run (at this point, Flex Builder is waiting for a remote connection, in the same manner FDB does).
11. Open the debug-enabled *.swf* on the remote machine and, when prompted for a remote host address, input the host address of the machine with the Flex Builder debugger.

Logging Using trace( ) Within an Application

Although not an advanced debugging technique, at one time or another a developer will find a need to trace (also referred to as *log*) messages from within an application. For this purpose, Flash Player exposes a global trace( ) method. Messages can be logged from anywhere within an application simply by calling the trace( ) method and passing any parameter of type string:

```
trace("application initialized");
```

Trace messages are typically displayed by attaching the debugger to an application. With an active FDB debug session, trace messages will be displayed in the console. With Flex Builder, launching a debug session will automatically do this and trace messages will be shown in the Console panel in the debugging perspective (see Figure 17-6).

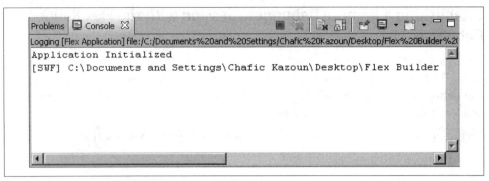

Figure 17-6. Flex Builder Debugger Console panel

One of the great benefits of using the trace statement in this manner is the ability to receive the messages in real time while an application is running. The trace( ) method also supports passing in arrays or multiple arguments (REST-style arguments). This can be very useful in dumping data for informational purposes—for example, if you wanted to be able to easily track what children are currently in the Display Child list.

Example 17-1 contains two children. When you click the button, the clickHandler( ) function is called and an array of children is displayed in the output window.

Example 17-1. Calling the clickHandler() function

```
<?xml version="1.0" encoding="utf-8"?>
<mx:Application xmlns:mx="http://www.adobe.com/2006/mxml">
    <mx:Script>
        <![CDATA[

            private function clickHandler( ):void
            {
                trace(this.getChildren( ));
            }

        ]]>
    </mx:Script>
    <mx:Button id="buttonOne" click="clickHandler( )" label="Dump Data"/>
    <mx:Label id="labelTwo"/>
</mx:Application>
```

As with other debugging methods we have seen thus far, using the trace( ) function requires the Flash Debug Player. Although often you will just use the Flex Builder Debugger to output trace messages, with the debug version of the player you have the option of outputting the trace messages to a file. You may want to use this feature if you are having a hard time isolating user-reported bugs by having the user configure his machine to log all trace calls to a file and allow you to review the logfiles at a later time for clues on what sequence of events may have caused the bug.

This also is useful for when a tester isolates a bug in an application and provides corresponding log information.

By default, installing the Debug Player does not enable trace logging. You will need to configure the player to enable logging. The configuration filename is *mm.cfg*. Under Windows XP, it is located at *C:\Documents and Settings\user_name*, and under Mac OS X, it is located in */Application Support/Macromedia/Flash Player/*. For other operating systems, consult the Flash Player documentation.

First review your operating system-specific path for an existing *mm.cfg*. If none already exists, you will need to create one. The configuration file is a plain text file that supports several options. Most important, you will be interested in the ErrorReportingEnable, MaxWarnings, TraceOutputFileEnable, and TraceOutputFileName configuration properties.

A basic *mm.cfg* file that enables the trace output includes the following:

```
TraceOutputFileEnable=1
```

Once the configuration file is updated and saved to the proper location with the filename *mm.cfg*, the Flash Debug Player will log trace messages to the same location as the *mm.cfg* file with a log filename of *flashlog.txt*. You may also be interested in logging all errors; if so, you just need to enable ErrorReportingEnable:

```
TraceOutputFileEnable=1
ErrorReportingEnable=1
```

If you prefer to create a logfile not in the default location, or if you want to use a different filename, you may do so using the TraceOutputFileName property. Here we are creating a logfile in the root drive with the filename *weirdBug.txt*:

```
TraceOutputFileEnable=1
ErrorReportingEnable=1
TraceOutputFileName=c:/weirdBug.txt
```

The Logging Framework

The trace( ) statement can be a powerful method of logging, but if you have any formal logging experience, you likely used some sort of logging framework or built your own. Flex includes a logging framework that offers several benefits over using the trace( ) statement alone.

The logging framework consists of two main components: the logger and the target. The logger is used by an application to configure the logging framework and to send messages which are output via a target.

A target is used to specify where log messages are output. They can be output to any mechanism that Flash Player supports. The logging framework includes a TraceTarget, which inherits from LineFormattedTarget and AbstractTarget and implements the ILoggingTarget interface.

TraceTarget internally sends messages via the global trace( ) function. This will often be the target you use. Here's an example using the logging framework with TraceTarget:

```
<?xml version="1.0" encoding="utf-8"?>
<mx:Application xmlns:mx="http://www.adobe.com/2006/mxml"
initialize="initializeHandler( )">
    <mx:Script>
    <![CDATA[
        import mx.logging.Log;
        import mx.logging.targets.TraceTarget;

        private var _target:TraceTarget;

        private function initializeHandler( ):void
        {
            _target = new TraceTarget( );
            _target.includeTime = true;
            _target.includeLevel = true;
            _target.includeCategory = true;
            Log.addTarget(_target);
        }

        private function sendToLog( ):void
        {
         Log.getLogger("com.oreilly.programmingflex.MainClass").info("Log Message");
        }
    ]]>
    </mx:Script>
    <mx:Button click="sendToLog( )" label="Log Message"/>
</mx:Application>
```

In this example, clicking on a button will send a message in the same manner as calling trace( ) would. The main distinction to just using trace( ) is the ability to configure the target to include extra information, supply a category for a message, and have different levels of errors.

> The Flex framework internally uses the logging framework within the mx.rpc.* package with the WebService, RemoteObject, and HTTPService components. This allows you to retrieve details of the communication between the Flex client and the server. We will cover debugging remote data communication later in this chapter.

A target can support extra functionality. In the preceding example, the date, category, and level were enabled. This will instruct the target to include the time, category of message, and level with the messages. The built-in targets support other properties which you may want to explore.

Specifying the Logging Options

A log message must define two values: the level of the message, which we discussed, and the category. The category is required to define the origins of a message and, in return, allow you to filter what is displayed by the logging framework. In the preceding example, the category was `com.oreilly.programmingflex.MainClass`. It is a good idea to specify a category based on the package and class, as this will allow you to easily filter and identify the origins of logged messages.

The built-in targets support the ability to filter the messages so that only messages you are interested in are displayed. This is useful in cases where you are interested only in log messages within a certain package, and is achieved via the `filters` property of the target. The `filters` property accepts an array of categories. A category filter can be any text value, but it is recommended that you follow package-naming conventions. You may also specify an * (wildcard) filter—for example, the following category filter of `com.oreilly.*` will instruct the target to output all messages in the `com.oreilly` package and within its subpackages:

```
_target.filters = ["com.oreilly.*"];
```

You also can define multiple filters as well as redefine the filters at any time. Setting the level is achieved in a similar manner.

The default logging level is `ALL`, but you can define another level by setting the `level` property:

```
_target.level = LogEventLevel.FATAL;
```

The logger supports sending several levels of messages with the `debug( )`, `error( )`, `fatal( )`, `info( )`, and `warn( )` methods. Alternatively, you can call the `log( )` method of the logger and pass in a log level. You can find the different levels with the constant values `LogEventLevel.FATAL`, `LogEventLevel.ERROR`, `LogEventLevel.WARN`, `LogEventLevel.INFO`, and `LogEventLevel.DEBUG`. This can be useful if you want to output all messages during development and debugging, but limit what is output in a production environment. When setting a log level, all messages in that level and above are logged. For example, setting the level to `WARN` will log all messages with that level as well as messages with a `FATAL` or `ERROR` level.

Defining a Custom Target

If the built-in targets are not sufficient, you can define your own. To define your own target you need to implement the `ILoggingTarget` interface. For convenience, the logging framework includes the `AbstractTarget` class, which already implements a default set of behaviors that you can easily subclass to define your own target. Example 17-2 is a custom target that will send a message to a remote server via the Socket class rather than via `trace( )`.

Example 17-2. Custom target sending a message to a remote server via the Socket class

```
package com.oreilly.programmingflex.logging.targets
{
    import flash.net.Socket;
    import mx.logging.LogEvent;
    import mx.logging.AbstractTarget;

    public class SocketTarget extends AbstractTarget
    {
        private var _host:String;
        private var _port:int;
        private var _socket:Socket;

        public function SocketTarget(host:String = "localhost",port:int = 18080)
        {
            _host = host;
            _port = port;
            //This example ommits the error handling, for production you will
            //need to handle errors when creating the socket and when sending
            //messages
            _socket = new Socket(host,port);
            super();
        }

        override public function logEvent(event:LogEvent):void
        {
            _socket.writeUTF(event.message);
            _socket.flush();
        }
    }
}
```

Example 17-3 is updated to use the new SocketTarget.

Example 17-3. Example 17-2 updated to use the new SocketTarget

```
<?xml version="1.0" encoding="utf-8"?>
<mx:Application xmlns:mx="http://www.adobe.com/2006/mxml"
initialize="initializeHandler()">
    <mx:Script>
        <![CDATA[
            import com.oreilly.programmingflex.logging.targets.SocketTarget;
            import mx.logging.Log;

            private var _target:SocketTarget;

            private function initializeHandler():void
            {
                _target = new SocketTarget();
                Log.addTarget(_target);
            }

            private function sendToLog():void
```

Example 17-3. Example 17-2 updated to use the new SocketTarget (continued)

```
            {
                Log.getLogger("com.oreilly.programmingflex.MainClass").info("Log Message");
            }
        ]]>
    </mx:Script>
    <mx:Button click="sendToLog()" label="Log Message"/>
</mx:Application>
```

With Flex's built-in logging framework, you will be able to log messages, easily change options so that you can more easily debug an application, and integrate the framework within your application.

Debugging Remote Data

Although you can use the debugger to inspect data after Flex has received it and before Flex sends it, you may want to find out more details regarding what data is being sent and received. You can achieve this by using the logging framework, or a data inspector.

Debugging with the Flex Logging Framework

The `WebService`, `HTTPService`, and `RemoteObject` components use the Flex logging framework, which can greatly assist debugging applications. Messages are automatically logged to the Flex logging framework, so you won't need to enable the components to explicitly begin logging. Messages that are logged are within the `mx.messaging.*` filter. Example 17-4 is an `HTTPService` call with a `TraceTarget` that will only show log messages related to the server calls.

Example 17-4. HTTPService call with a TraceTarget that shows log messages related to server calls

```
<?xml version="1.0" encoding="utf-8"?>
<mx:Application xmlns:mx="http://www.adobe.com/2006/mxml"
initialize="initializeHandler()">
    <mx:Script>
    <![CDATA[
        import mx.logging.Log;
        import mx.logging.targets.TraceTarget;

        private var _target:TraceTarget;

        private function initializeHandler():void
        {
            _target = new TraceTarget();
            _target.includeTime = true;
            _target.includeLevel = true;
            _target.includeCategory = true;
            _target.filters = ["mx.messaging.*"];
            Log.addTarget(_target);
        }
```

Example 17-4. HTTPService call with a TraceTarget that shows log messages related to server calls

```
            private function sendToLog():void
            {
                Log.getLogger("com.oreilly.programmingflex.Logging").info("Log Message");
            }
        ]]>
    </mx:Script>
    <mx:Button click="sendToLog()" label="Log Message"/>
    <mx:Button click="service.send();" label="Send HTTPService"/>
    <mx:HTTPService id="service" url="http://www.w3c.org"/>
</mx:Application>
```

This example will log messages from the HTTPService but not from the button click handler, which can be very useful when you are working with a larger application and you are only interested in viewing the log information from the mx.rpc components. The server component logs useful information on both the data that is being sent and received, as well as the information that can be used for profiling messaging performance. For the WebService component, this can be especially useful in gauging Flex's performance in terms of serializing and deserializing SOAP messages.

Debugging Using a Data Inspector

When debugging network programming code, using a data inspector (packet sniffing tools or a proxy) is invaluable. With Flex, these tools can also be very useful. Adobe does not provide such a built-in tool, but many tools exist that work with Flex. If you are already comfortable with a tool, you can continue to use that tool. Some common network debugging tools include the following:

ServiceCapture
This cross-platform proxy tool for debugging RPC communication supports AMF3 (*http://kevinlangdon.com/serviceCapture*).

Charles
This cross-platform proxy tool for debugging RPC communication also supports AMF3 (*http://www.xk72.com/charles/download.php*).

Wireshark (similar to Ethereal)
This is a feature-complete packet sniffer that is capable of inspecting all traffic for both real-time applications as well as RPC (*http://www.wireshark.org*).

Fiddler
This is a quick HTTP proxy debugger that is free. It supports RPC debugging, but does not support AMF3 (*http://www.fiddlertool.com*).

Summary

In many ways, a development platform is only as good as the debugging capabilities available to the developer. In this chapter, we covered many of the methods you can use to debug Flex applications.

Application Components

As the scope of your applications grows, sooner or later you will need a better way to organize all their different components. One principle that is known to be effective in this task is the component-based development principle.

This chapter focuses on application components. Application components are logically modular elements (not to be confused with Flex modules) within an application that you typically define using MXML and that behave in a manner similar to the components described throughout this book.

Component-based development allows a developer to divide an application into components. Doing so provides several benefits:

- It helps to promote many object-oriented design principles, including code reuse, loose coupling, encapsulation, and reduced bugs.
- It allows you to simplify a large problem into smaller ones.
- It allows different team members to focus on their own components, which allows teams to be more efficient.

Traditionally when developers think of components, they think of prepackaged components that have been developed by a third party. In component-based development, third-party components are important, but so are user-developed components. Instead of allowing application development using just third-party components, an effective component-based development platform should allow you to mix third-party and user-developed components. In earlier chapters, we discussed how Flex and MXML allow rapid application development using several components. In this chapter, we'll discuss the reasons application components are important and useful. We'll also discuss how to write application components.

The Importance of Application Components

To understand the importance of application components, let's examine where they would be helpful. In this example, we will study a typical application: a contact manager. Figure 18-1 shows the completed contact manager application.

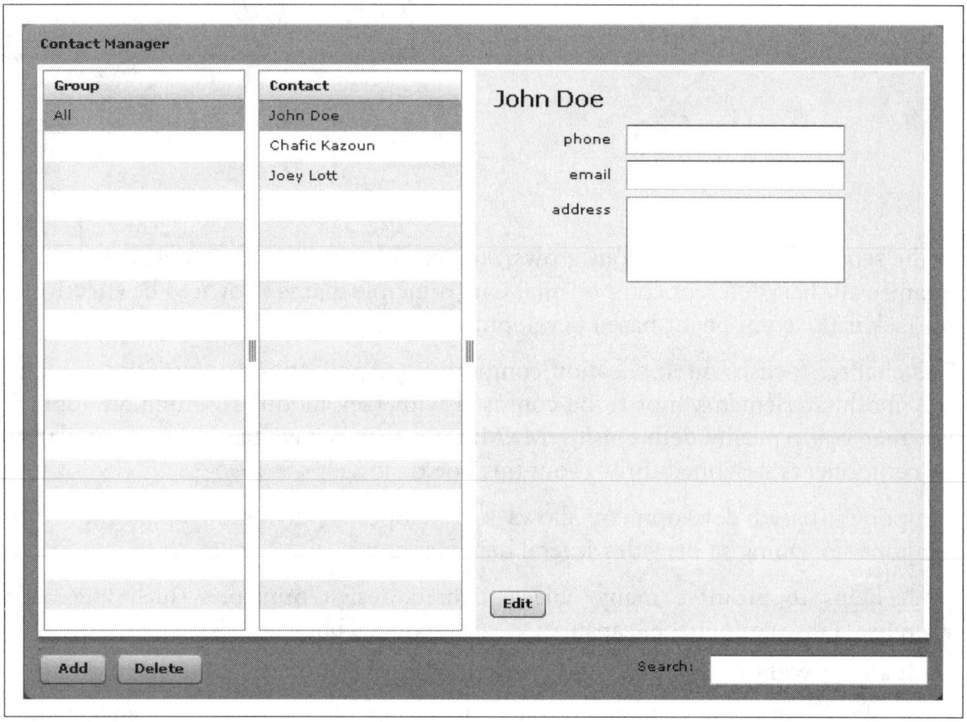

Figure 18-1. Contact manager application

This application is considered to be simple, but even a simple application can benefit from application components. If you were to build this application while making sure to separate your presentation code from your data communication and business logic, you would typically structure the application using many Flex components. The result would be one large MXML file, with many event handlers, associated UI code, and many ActionScript class files.

Although this book does not cover the popular Model View Controller (MVC) design pattern, it is assumed that you understand the benefits of separating the data access and business logic outside of your presentation code. Flex allows you to rapidly develop applications using MXML. However, if application architecture is important, ideally you should use MXML mainly for the view, and use ActionScript for the model and controller. This does not mean that all applications should have such a structure, but if you are working on a large application, we recommend that you consider separating different parts of your application appropriately. If you are interested in learning more about design patterns and ActionScript 3, you can find good coverage in *Advanced ActionScript 3 with Design Patterns*, by Joey Lott and Danny Patterson (Adobe Press).

Although such a structure isn't bad, imagine if you were working on a team and one team member was responsible for the contact details area. Working on such an application would not be ideal because it would be built with one large MXML file that is difficult to manage. Taking this one step further, imagine if the contact details were used by other applications. You would ideally want to be able to write such code as a component once, and not have to rewrite it. The component would encompass the highlighted area in Figure 18-2.

There are even more benefits to creating an application out of many components. Imagine how large and unmanageable this single MXML file would become. You would have to have different event handlers for when a user selects a group, selects a contact, attempts to edit the user details, adds and deletes a user, and so on. This doesn't even include the complexity involved with nesting containers. It could easily become confusing to keep track of everything. Instead, this application would be simpler to manage if you could focus on the contact details alone as one component that almost lives in its own world. This is where application components come in.

You can develop application components in MXML or ActionScript. This chapter covers application component development with MXML because it's easier to build such components from existing components using MXML than it is using ActionScript. That does not mean you cannot develop application components in ActionScript. However, ActionScript-based components tend to be more advanced and more ideal for custom components, which we cover in Chapter 19, whereas MXML-based components are typically ideal for application components.

MXML Component Basics

To understand MXML components it helps to understand that MXML files are just classes behind the scenes. When an MXML file is compiled, the compiler translates the file to ActionScript and then compiles it into native Flash Player bytecode. This means that everything you can build in MXML you can also build in ActionScript.

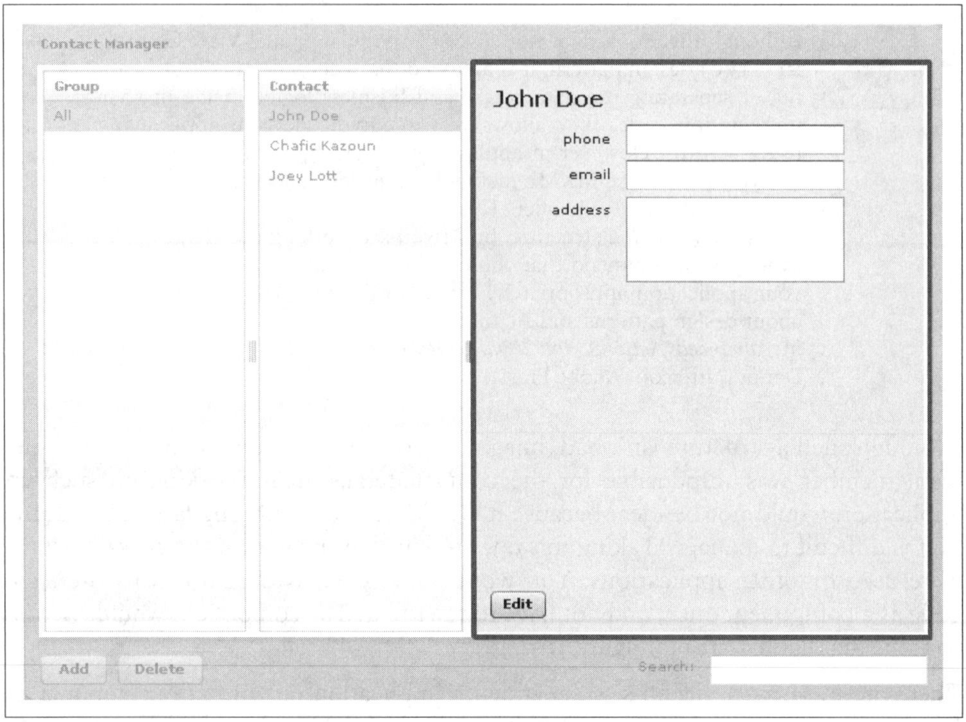

Figure 18-2. Contact details highlighted

MXML code usually is shorter and easier to read than the equivalent ActionScript code. This makes MXML more convenient to work with than ActionScript in many cases. At the same time, because MXML is ultimately compiled to the same byte-code as ActionScript is, there is no loss in performance or features. This makes MXML ideal for application layout.

Now that you understand the benefits of working with MXML over ActionScript, let's discuss how to create a class, optimally implement its common features, and decouple application components written in MXML within an application.

Creating and Using a Component

To create a component in MXML, you create a new file with the root tag corresponding to the class you want to extend, and with a filename corresponding to the class name of the component. Typically when segmenting an application, the base class (root tag) will be a container component. In Figure 18-2, our contact details component example, the base class is the Canvas container. Example 18-1 provides the code for the Canvas container.

Example 18-1. ContactDetails.mxml

```
<?xml version="1.0" encoding="utf-8"?>
<mx:Canvas xmlns:mx="http://www.adobe.com/2006/mxml">
    <!-- Contact Details Implementation Details -->
</mx:Canvas>
```

The code in Example 18-1 should look very similar to a basic MXML application file, except that it uses the Canvas component as the root tag rather than the Application component. Also note that as each MXML file is a separate component, you need to reference the MXML namespace as you would in the application's root MXML file.

Although we do not cover it in this book, MXML components are also ideal for when you want to extend an existing component. By declaring your own MXML file that is based on an existing component and just adding your own additional logic where needed, you can customize the existing Flex framework components. Extending components requires an understanding of the underlying component framework and the component you want to extend. To learn more about the component framework, see Chapter 19, as well as the Flex SDK documentation.

Once the component is created, you can reference it using the filename used for the MXML file, as shown in Example 18-2.

Example 18-2. Main MXML application file

```
<?xml version="1.0" encoding="utf-8"?>
<mx:Application xmlns:mx="http://www.adobe.com/2006/mxml" xmlns:pf2="*">
    <pf2:ContactDetails/>
</mx:Application>
```

In Example 18-2, we declared an instance of the ContactDetails component as we would any other component. Notice the addition of the pf2 namespace prefix. To inform the compiler of available components, you will need to reference the package, which in this case is just the root package, *.

In ActionScript, you would typically use the package keyword to declare the package of a class. In MXML, you declare a package simply via the directory structure. Because we placed the main MXML file and the MXML component in the same directory in Example 18-2, the compiler defaults to the top-level package. Although this is usable, you should specify a package for all your components. For example, to create the package com.oreilly.programmingflex.contactmanager.views you would just create the corresponding directory structure, com/oreilly/programmingflex/contactmanager/views/, and place the component's MXML file within the *views* directory. You can find more details on the source paths in Chapter 2.

Now, to update the main application file, we need to update the namespace reference to reflect the new package (see Example 18-3).

Example 18-3. Updating the namespace to reflect the new package

```
<?xml version="1.0" encoding="utf-8"?>
<mx:Application xmlns:mx="http://www.adobe.com/2006/mxml" xmlns:pf2="com.oreilly.
programmingflex.contactmanager.views.*">
    <pf2:ContactDetails/>
</mx:Application>
```

When dividing an application into several components, you will want to place many of the components together within the same folder (package). This allows you to create a single package for all your components. There is nothing wrong with having multiple packages; however, you will want to have a logical reason for doing so. One such reason could be to separate components created for use within the application you are developing versus shared components you develop to be shared across many applications.

Going back to the understanding that an MXML file is a class, you can also reference the newly created component in ActionScript classes as you would any class, as shown in the following code:

```
package com.oreilly.programmingflex.foo {
    //Import the ContactDetails component
    import com.oreilly.programmingflex.contactmanager.ContactDetails;

    public class SampleClass {
        //Instance variable of the ContactDetails type
        private var _contactDetails:ContactDetails;
        //Class code omitted for brevity
    }
}
```

As you can see, the basics of creating a new component are straightforward. The ability to quickly create components is one of the biggest benefits of Flex and MXML, and it helps support the component-based development nature of Flex.

Adding and Laying Out Controls

When creating an application component, typically you will base your component on an existing Flex container, and the new component will be composed of existing components. Adding and laying out components in an MXML component requires almost the same techniques we covered in Chapter 6 regarding the main MXML file.

In the ContactDetails component from Figure 18-2, we created a component based on the Canvas layout component. As we discussed in Chapter 6, the Canvas layout component allows you to place components using absolute positioning or constraint-based layout rules. Because this is the Canvas tag of the component rather than the Application, as you saw in the main application MXML file, we will use the layout rules for Canvas to lay out children that are added to the component.

Although not required, Flex Builder 2 allows you to view the layout of a component in design mode, as well as visually lay out the component's contents in design mode. This can be helpful when working with application components, as there is no other mechanism to easily view a component's layout without needing to compile an application with your component.

Reviewing ContactDetails in Figure 18-2, you can see that the component is built from Labels, TextInputs, a TextArea, and a Button. You can add components using the same techniques we used previously. Here is the earlier component, with the needed components added and positioned:

```
<?xml version="1.0" encoding="utf-8"?>
<mx:Canvas xmlns:mx="http://www.adobe.com/2006/mxml" width="100%" height="100%">
    <mx:Label id="heading" styleName="heading" x="10" y="10"/>
    <mx:Button id="edit" bottom="10" left="10" label="Edit" toggle="true"/>
    <mx:Label x="62" y="42" text="phone"/>
    <mx:Label x="53" y="94" text="address"/>
    <mx:Label x="66" y="68" text="email"/>
    <mx:TextArea x="110" y="93" editable="false" enabled="true" width="160"
height="60" id="address"/>
    <mx:TextInput x="110" y="40" editable="false" id="phone"/>
    <mx:TextInput x="110" y="66" editable="false" id="email"/>
</mx:Canvas>
```

In the preceding code, we added the components and set their properties. We positioned the components using the properties for positioning (x,y, left, and bottom, in this example), as we would any child within a container. We set the root Canvas tag's width and height properties to 100%. In the ContactDetails component, we positioned the children using absolute positioning relative to the edges of the parent. By setting the Canvas width and height properties to 100%, we helped to ensure that the container would grow to the maximum space allowed for it. It is important to note that setting the values on the root tag of an MXML component doesn't disallow a parent from overriding the values. Because of this, the value set on the root MXML component is said to be the default value.

Understanding Interaction

When you create an MXML file, it lives isolated in its own world. When you build an application using one large MXML file, it is easy to reference component instances using the id attribute, data-bind directly to controls, and pretty much access anything within the same MXML file. When an application is split into multiple components, each component will be able to access its members, but it should not access another component's members, even though component instances in MXML are declared public by default. Although this may seem like a limitation, it helps to promote a key object-oriented programming principal: encapsulation.

Encapsulation is the process of hiding implementation details. With components, you can set properties and call methods, but a component should not access another component's internal workings.

With that said, when you are working with application components, you will need to communicate to and from each component instance. To communicate with a component, you interact with the interface it has defined—in other words, the methods and properties that are accessible. For example, in the following code, we are setting the `toolTip` property. We are able to do so because the `toolTip` property is defined by part of the `ContactDetails` API (in this case, it is inherited from the existing Flex framework).

```
<?xml version="1.0" encoding="utf-8"?>
<mx:Application xmlns:mx="http://www.adobe.com/2006/mxml" xmlns:pf2="com.oreilly.
programmingflex.contactmanager.views.*">
    <pf2:ContactDetails toolTip="Contact Details"/>
</mx:Application>
```

This code should look familiar to you in that you can work with the component in the same way you are used to working with the Flex component. In addition, because the `ContactDetails` component extends `Canvas`, its public API is inherited, including all methods, properties, events, and styles. This allows you to set the width and height properties even though you did not define them yourself. You also can use all the MXML features available with other components, including data binding.

When deciding on the component's interface, it is important to step back for a moment and think about the purpose of the component. The interface may initially be used for one specific purpose, but with time you will find that a good interface will improve reusability of your newly created component. A good interface also allows a developer to accomplish his goals without having to access the internals of the component.

Defining component properties

Component properties can aid in communicating to and from a component. You create properties by defining fields or getter/setter functions. You define properties in the same manner you would in ActionScript.

Although it is possible to define properties using `<mx:DataType>` syntax, it is generally recommended that you declare properties within the ActionScript `<mx:Script>` block. This will allow you to organize all public methods, properties, and getter and setter functions together. This chapter focuses on real-world usage rather than all possible methods of developing a component. You can review the Flex 2 documentation for details on all possible methods of implementing component properties, methods, and metadata.

It is good practice to not declare fields as public, but instead to declare getter/setter functions, as shown in the following code. This helps you to guarantee that if the implementation of the property changes in the future, the public interface will not change.

```xml
<?xml version="1.0" encoding="utf-8"?>
<mx:Canvas xmlns:mx="http://www.adobe.com/2006/mxml">
    <mx:Script>
        <![CDATA[

        private var _mode:String;

        [Bindable]
        public function set mode(value:String):void
        {
            _mode = value;
        }

        public function get mode( ):String
        {
            return _mode;
        }
        ]]>
    </mx:Script>
    <!-- contents omitted for brevity-->
</mx:Canvas>
```

An alternative for not creating many getter/setter functions needlessly is to create public fields and, when needed, to refactor by adding getter/setter functions with the same name while renaming or removing the previously declared property.

In the preceding code, we declared a public property mode. You can use this property to set the mode property of the component from the parent. In the code, we declared the property as bindable using the [Bindable] metadata tag. It is a good idea to use [Bindable] whenever you declare a public property because it is likely that a developer will want to use the data-binding features of Flex with your new component. Finally, we declared a private _mode variable. It is a good practice to declare private properties with a preceding single underscore. This allows you to distinguish a public property from a private one, especially if you are exposing a private property via a public getter/setter function.

As you learned when adding ActionScript within MXML files in earlier chapters, you can add properties and methods using ActionScript within MXML as well, as within <mx:Script/>. This chapter covers inline ActionScript within a Script tag, but it is important to note that you can also use the other methods to add ActionScript to an MXML component just as you would reference an external ActionScript file via the Script tag's source property.

Once you've declared a property, you can access the property from the parent container as you would any other property. In the following code, we have set the property value from the parent container:

```
<?xml version="1.0" encoding="utf-8"?>
<mx:Application xmlns:mx="http://www.adobe.com/2006/mxml" initialize="init( )" xmlns:
pf2=" com.oreilly.programmingflex.contactmanager.views.*">
    <pf2:ContactDetails mode="view" />
    <!-- contents omitted for brevity -->
</mx:Application>
```

Most of the time, you will want a property to accept any value of a data type, and in such cases, this method works well. Sometimes, though, you will want to restrict the possible values. In the code we've been building on throughout this chapter, the mode value can accept only an enumeration of values. However, ActionScript does not support enumerations. It is good practice, therefore, to provide the user with static variables. This reduces the possibility of user error and improves ease of use because static variables are a form of self-documentation for possible values. Adding such values helps the developer and allows Flex Builder to provide code hinting for the possible values, but does not provide any sort of compile time or runtime type checking at this time. Example 18-4 is updated to make use of enumerations for the component, and Example 18-5 is the updated *Main.mxml*.

Example 18-4. Adding enumerations to a component

```
<?xml version="1.0" encoding="utf-8"?>
<mx:Canvas xmlns:mx="http://www.adobe.com/2006/mxml" width="100%"
backgroundColor="#f8f8f8" height="100%">
    <mx:Script>
        <![CDATA[

            public static const VIEW_MODE:String = "view";
            public static const EDIT_MODE:String = "edit";

            private var _mode:String;

            [Bindable]           [Inspectable(enumeration="{ContactDetails.VIEW_
MODE},{ContactDetails.EDIT_MODE}")]

            public function get mode( ):String
            {
                return _mode;
            }

            public function set mode(value:String):void
            {
                _mode = value;
            }
        ]]>
    </mx:Script>
    <!-- contents omitted for brevity -->
</mx:Canvas>
```

Example 18-5. Updated Main.mxml file referencing the enumeration value

```
<?xml version="1.0" encoding="utf-8"?>
<mx:Application xmlns:mx="http://www.adobe.com/2006/mxml" initialize="init( )" xmlns:
pf2="com.oreilly.programmingflex.contactmanager.views.*">
    <pf2:ContactDetails mode="{ContactDetails.VIEW_MODE}"/>
</mx:Application>
```

So far in this section, we covered using properties to pass and retrieve values with a component. You also can use a property to pass an instance of an object with which you would like the component to communicate. For example, you could pass an instance of the root application to a component and have the component call methods directly on the root application. At first, this may seem like an appropriate method of communicating from child to parent, but it actually results in a tight coupling between the child and the passed object. This is not an absolute rule, but later in this chapter we will discuss how to use events to communicate with other objects. Although this requires more work, it will typically be the more appropriate method of communicating from a component as it helps promote loose coupling and reusability.

 Tight coupling is where components are reliant on each other and cannot be separated without a fair amount of recoding.

Defining component methods

In the same way you declare a property, you can declare a component method within part of a component. Although you do not have to add any methods with the ContactDetails component, Example 18-6 shows how you would add a clear( ) method.

Example 18-6. Adding a clear( ) method to ContactDetails

```
<?xml version="1.0" encoding="utf-8"?>
<mx:Canvas xmlns:mx="http://www.adobe.com/2006/mxml">
    <mx:Script>
        <![CDATA[
            public function clear( ):void
            {
                address.text = null;
                phone.text = null;                email.text = null;
            }
        ]]>
    </mx:Script>
</mx:Canvas>
```

This method clears the text within the input components. Once you've defined a method with a proper accessor keyword, you can call the new method from the parent, as shown in Example 18-7.

Example 18-7. Calling the new method from the parent

```
<?xml version="1.0" encoding="utf-8"?>
<mx:Application xmlns:mx="http://www.adobe.com/2006/mxml" initialize="initializeHandler(
)" xmlns:pf2="com.oreilly.programmingflex.contactmanager.views.*">
    <mx:Script>
        <![CDATA[
            private function initializeHandler():void
            {
                //In this example, calling clear is redundant
                contactDetails.clear();
            }
        ]]>
    </mx:Script>
    <pf2:ContactDetails id="contactDetails"/>
</mx:Application>
```

In Example 18-7, the composing object creates an instance of the component and calls the clear( ) method. The parent has no knowledge of the internal workings of the component; it only knows of the publicly accessible interface and it trusts that the component knows how to do what it needs to do. This further helps to decouple the parent and child relationship between components built in an application.

Defining component events

When creating an MXML component, you will typically be composing other objects within the component, as you did in the ContactDetails component. These child components dispatch their own events, and the application will be interested in some of the events or a custom event that is specific to ContactDetails. Because the children reside within the component, their events won't be seen by the world outside of the component. Actually, you wouldn't even want them to be seen. Doing so would allow any internal component to dispatch any event, and you would have no control over what events your component dispatches.

For this reason, and to be able to define custom events that do not depend on existing events, you will need to define your own events for your component. In the ContactDetails component, one event that would be useful to define is when a user clicks on the edit button. Although a lot can happen within the component, you are only interested in knowing when a user has changed the data or maybe when the user is about to change the data (in edit mode). For this reason, it would be ideal for this component to have an EditChange event, with a description of "begin" and "end," depending on whether the user has begun or finished editing the component.

All components in the Flex framework inherit from EventDispatcher, a class that implements the capability of an object to subscribe to and receive event notification. To add an event to a custom component, you need to define and dispatch the event.

To define an event, you first need to declare the event. You declare events using a metadata tag, and in MXML you do that using the <mx:Metadata/> tag, as shown in Example 18-8.

Example 18-8. ContactDetails with event metadata tag added

```
<?xml version="1.0" encoding="utf-8"?>
<mx:Canvas xmlns:mx="http://www.adobe.com/2006/mxml" width="100%"
backgroundColor="#f8f8f8" height="100%">
    <mx:Metadata>
        [Event(name="editChange", type="com.oreilly.programmingflex.contactmanager.events.
EditChangeEvent")]
    </mx:Metadata>
    <!-- contents omitted for brevity -->
</mx:Canvas>
```

In Example 18-8, we added an event with the name editChange, and the type EditChangeEvent. EditChangeEvent is the object type passed to the handler function when an event occurs. You could have used a generic event class here, but it is a good idea to create your own events for components. Doing so will allow you to provide added functionality that is specific to your component.

Now let's create the EditChangeEvent class in the com.oreilly.programmingflex. contactmanager.events package. It is good practice as usual to specify a package for a class and for events, and to place all events in an events package. This is consistent with the Flex framework and allows users to import a single package that will contain all events. Here is the definition of the EditChangeEvent class:

```
package com.oreilly.programmingflex.contactmanager.events
{
    import flash.events.Event;

    public class EditChangeEvent extends Event
    {
        public static const EDIT_CHANGE:String = "editChange";
        public var edit:Boolean;

        public function EditChangeEvent(edit:Boolean=false)
        {
            super(EDIT_CHANGE);
            this.edit = edit;
        }

        override public function clone():Event
        {
            return new EditChangeEvent(this.edit);
        }
    }
}
```

With the custom event type created, now you can dispatch the new event (see Example 18-9). We will incorporate the new event into the ContactDetails component later in the chapter.

Example 18-9. Dispatching EditChangeEvent

```
var eventEditing:EditChangeEvent = new EditChangeEvent(true);
dispatchEvent(eventEditing);
```

Component Styles

When working with an application component and styles, the application component can define its own style values for components within. The easiest way to specify such styles is to define cascading style sheets (CSS) within the application component as you would within an application (however, you will still have the limitation of not being able to specify CSS type selectors other than in ActionScript). When working with styles within a component, keep in mind why application components exist. They don't exist to be as fully featured and flexible as distributed components. They exist to allow you to build an application more efficiently. As such, you may find that defining styles within an application component is acceptable.

 With application components, you can also define your own custom styles, as discussed in Chapter 19.

Also, as we saw in Chapter 14, styles in Flex support inheritance, which is also supported by application components. When defining a global style or CSS custom class, these styles are applied to all display items in Flex. This allows you the benefit of providing one master CSS file for an application. In the CSS file, you can define your custom style, and for any component in your application you can apply the style by setting the styleName property.

In this example, we first set the styleName property of the Label component:

```
<mx:Label id="contactName" styleName="heading" x="10" y="10" text="John Doe"/>
```

Once the styleName value is set, we can define style values anywhere within our application, including within the application component itself. Here a style definition is created in an <mx:Style> tag:

```
<mx:Style>
    .heading
    {
        font-size:16;
        font-weight:bold;
    }
</mx:Style>
```

Internal States

Application components can also define states internally. In the `ContactDetails` component, we want the ability to support two modes: an edit mode and a view mode. By default, the component will be in view mode, but with the public mode property defined earlier in this chapter, a user can change the state of the `ContactDetails` component easily.

You define the states, as discussed in Chapter 10:

```
<mx:states>
    <mx:State name="{VIEW_MODE}"/>
        <mx:State name="{EDIT_MODE}" basedOn="{VIEW_MODE}">
        <mx:SetProperty target="{address}" name="editable" value="true"/>
        <mx:SetProperty target="{email}" name="editable" value="true"/>
        <mx:SetProperty target="{phone}" name="editable" value="true"/>
    </mx:State>
</mx:states>
```

To set the default state of the component, you set the `currentState` property of the root node of the `ContactDetails` component:

```
<mx:Canvas xmlns:mx="http://www.adobe.com/2006/mxml" width="100%"
backgroundColor="#f8f8f8" height="100%" currentState="view">
```

With the states defined, providing a mechanism to set the state is easy. We just need to update the mode setter to set the component's `currentState` property and the getter to return the value `currentState` property:

```
[Inspectable(enumeration="{ContactDetails.VIEW_MODE},{ContactDetails.EDIT_MODE}")]
public function set mode(value:String):void
{
    this.currentState = value;
}

[Bindable]
public function get mode():String
{
    return this.currentState;
}
```

Declaring your own public API to set the component's state isn't required, but it is a good practice. The `currentState` property is declared publicly, and defining your own setter with valid values reduces the likelihood of errors and is a form of documentation that can help others use a component.

Because we've been working on the code in snippets throughout the chapter, we thought it might help you to understand the utility of application components by providing you with the component code in its entirety:

```
<?xml version="1.0" encoding="utf-8"?>
<mx:Canvas xmlns:mx="http://www.adobe.com/2006/mxml" width="100%"
backgroundColor="#f8f8f8" height="100%" currentState="view">
    <mx:Metadata>
    [Event(name="editChange", type="com.oreilly.programmingflex.contactmanager.
events.EditChangeEvent")]
    </mx:Metadata>
    <mx:Script>
        <![CDATA[
            import com.oreilly.programmingflex.contactmanager.events.EditChangeEvent;
            import mx.controls.Alert;
            import mx.states.State;

            public static const VIEW_MODE:String = "view";
            public static const EDIT_MODE:String = "edit";

            [Bindable]
            public function get mode():String
            {
                return this.currentState;
            }

            public function clear():void
            {
                address.text = null;
                phone.text = null;
                email.text = null;
            }

[Inspectable(enumeration="{ContactDetails.VIEW_MODE},{ContactDetails.EDIT_MODE}")]
            public function set mode(value:String):void
            {
                this.currentState = value;
            }

            private function clickHandler(e:Event):void
            {
                if(this.currentState == VIEW_MODE)
                {
                    this.mode = EDIT_MODE;
                    phone.setFocus();
                    var eventEditing:EditChangeEvent = new EditChangeEvent(true);
                    dispatchEvent(eventEditing);
                }
                else if(this.currentState == EDIT_MODE)
                {
                    this.mode = VIEW_MODE;
                    var eventDoneEditing:EditChangeEvent = new
EditChangeEvent(false);
```

```
                dispatchEvent(eventDoneEditing);
            }
        }
    ]]>
</mx:Script>
<mx:Style>
    .heading
    {
        font-size:16;
        font-weight:bold;
    }
</mx:Style>
<mx:states>
    <mx:State name="{VIEW_MODE}"/>
    <mx:State name="{EDIT_MODE}" basedOn="{VIEW_MODE}">
        <mx:SetProperty target="{address}" name="editable" value="true"/>
        <mx:SetProperty target="{email}" name="editable" value="true"/>
        <mx:SetProperty target="{phone}" name="editable" value="true"/>
    </mx:State>
</mx:states>
<mx:Label id="contactName" styleName="heading" x="10" y="10" text="John Doe"/>
<mx:Button id="edit" bottom="10" left="10" label="Edit" width="41" height="20"
toggle="true" click="clickHandler(event)"/>
<mx:Label x="62" y="42" text="phone"/>
<mx:Label x="53" y="94" text="address"/>
<mx:Label x="66" y="68" text="email"/>
<mx:TextArea x="110" y="93" editable="false" enabled="true" width="160"
height="63" id="address"/>
<mx:TextInput x="110" y="40" editable="false" id="phone"/>
<mx:TextInput x="110" y="66" editable="false" id="email"/>
</mx:Canvas>
```

Summary

This chapter discussed how to build application component with a public API, events, and internal implementation details. Application components can greatly help improve how you build and architect applications.

CHAPTER 19

Building Custom Components

At some point, you may want to build advanced components. For instance, you may want to create a truly custom component or a commercial-grade distributed component, or you may just want a much deeper understanding of and level of control over the underlying framework. Although Flex allows you to build components rapidly, as we saw in Chapter 18, developing advanced components requires a deeper understanding of the component framework and methodology.

In this chapter, you will learn about the component framework life cycle and develop an understanding for what it has to offer. You will do so through theory as well as by developing a custom component. You will also learn about ways to implement functionality within the component framework.

Component Framework Overview

Understanding what the component framework implements, as well as how and where it does so, is key to building good components. Flex contains a sophisticated framework that aims to abstract many of the underlying details of Flash Player and add many features not supported natively by Flash Player. A majority of the framework is built to support a rich set of features for the UI components that the Flex components use. This framework allows components to share a common set of APIs, and it allows components to function in a predictable manner based on the needs of the Flex framework. Using this framework will allow you to develop your own custom components that also behave and operate in a consistent manner with other Flex components.

As with developing components for any platform, it is important to do some initial planning. This book doesn't cover the theories and methodologies of designing components, but it is important to note that when developing custom components, it is highly recommended that you define requirements and the public interface, and that you plan things more carefully before writing any code. This is not as important with application components (discussed in Chapter 18), but it is critical when developing custom components that others will consume. Also keep in mind that when developing custom components, there is always a chance that a user may extend your component.

The Flex component framework contains many classes, most of which we won't be covering in detail here. Instead, we will focus on the most important classes for developing custom components: the UIComponent and Container classes. Figure 19-1 shows those classes and their inheritance chain.

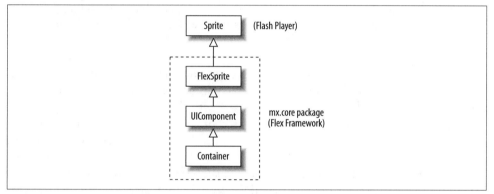

Figure 19-1. Component framework classes

All interface components in Flex inherit from UIComponent, which itself inherits from many classes, including Sprite. When developing a custom component you will have to decide which of the following two classes to use: the UIComponent class or the Container class. Generally speaking, you will use the UIComponent class unless you are developing your own container (for instance, if you need scrolling and clipping support built in). The UIComponent class is essentially an abstract class. It implements most of the common sets of behaviors, leaving you to implement the parts that are pertinent to your component.

 You could use an existing component as the base class. In such a case, you would be extending the existing component rather than developing a completely custom component. We will not cover the specifics of how to extend components in this chapter, but many of the lessons you will learn in this chapter apply to extending components as well.

UIComponent has several requirements that you will need to understand; we will cover those requirements later in the chapter. For now, it's important to note that UIComponent implements what your component needs in order to participate in the Flex framework and behave appropriately. It also provides you with a predefined component life cycle, as well as event handling, sizing, skinning, styling, invalidation, and rendering techniques.

Component Life Cycle

The life cycle that the component framework provides is an important aspect of the Flex framework. By understanding the component life cycle, you will be able to build better components more quickly.

 Most of the Flex framework, and particularly the built-in component, is based on the same component life cycle discussed in this chapter. As such, not only is it helpful to learn the component life cycle for building custom components, but it is also helpful for understanding the Flex framework as a whole for building applications.

The component life cycle comprises three phases: initialization, update, and destruction. The initialization phase consists of three main steps: construction, attachment, and initialization (the latter not to be confused with the initialization phase of which it is a part). The initialization step is composed of its own steps. For instance, during the initialization step, the component dispatches the preinitialize event, calls the createChildren( ) internal method, dispatches the initialize event, goes through a full invalidation and validation, and finally dispatches the creationComplete event. At this point, the component has completed the initialization step. Figure 19-2 outlines the initialization phase and its steps.

The update phase comprises everything that occurs between the initialization and destruction phases, and it is the phase during which the component responds to changes. The update phase begins right after the initialization phase and goes through a repeated set of steps to keep the component updated. Typically in the update phase, the component is initially in the waiting step, during which it awaits a request to change. If a component is initialized and never changes, it will stay in the waiting step. If the component receives a request to change—for example, if it receives a request to set a new value for Button.label—it goes through an invalidation step, then through validation, and finally back to the waiting step.

 Flash Player renders on a frame-by-frame basis. Because of this, it is important to merge the rendering updates together rather than process them immediately.

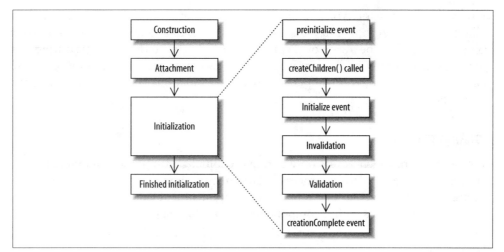

Figure 19-2. Component life cycle during the initialization phase

The invalidation and validation steps in the update phase are the same steps as those in the initialize phase. Also important to note is that a component can go through an update phase many times throughout its lifetime. If many updates to a component are requested at different times, the component will go through the same cycle each time and return to the waiting step. That is why, for performance considerations, you will need to ensure that the validation step is optimized to handle many calls, and you will need to reduce the processing required to satisfy this step. Figure 19-3 outlines the update phase and the repeated cycle of validation. You will learn more about the details of the each step in the life cycle of a component in the next section.

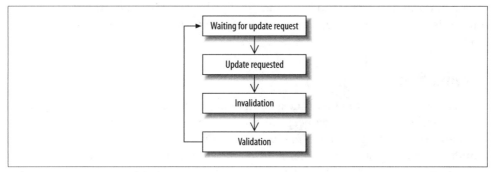

Figure 19-3. The steps during the update phase

Construction

In this step of the life cycle, the component is instantiated, the constructor is called, and the component begins beginsits life cycle. The component is instantiated either by being declared in MXML or through the new operator in ActionScript. The component constructor typically does not contain any implementation other than calling super( ), and sometimes it adds event listeners to application events that your component needs to be aware of. Typically you will want to do very little during this step because it is early in the component's life, and most parts of the component are not ready yet. Instead, you will perform the other functions in other methods, as we will see later.

Configuration

During this step, which occurs only during the initialization phase, component properties are set internally to be processed later in the component's life cycle. The values are set using the setter functions of the component defined. We will cover how to handle setter functions within components later in this chapter.

Attachment

When a component is instantiated, it does not automatically complete the entire initialization phase until it is added to the display list and it has a parent. Once a component is attached using addChild or addChildAt, or is declared via MXML (which internally calls addChild automatically), this step of the cycle begins and the internal initialize( ) function of the component is called.

Initialization

This step occurs after attachment. In this step, the preinitialize event is dispatched, the createChildren( ) method is called, the initialize event is dispatched, invalidation and validation occur, and finally the creationComplete event is fired. After this step, the component has finished the initialization phase and will enter the update phase.

Invalidation

This step occurs both the first time a component is initialized and during the update phase. Invalidation is a key concept in the component framework. Invalidation is a mechanism by which changes made to a component are queued and processed simultaneously. Flash Player internally renders on a frame-by-frame basis. Therefore, there is no benefit to immediately updating values that will affect the rendered view of a component. With invalidation, all changes are noted within the component and the component is marked for validation. In the validation step, the values that were noted are actually rendered. This occurs when the next frame is reached in Flash Player.

When a component is first initialized, it is automatically marked for full validation. But after a component is initialized, it is marked for validation during the update phase by calling the invalidateProperties( ), invalidateSize( ), or invalidateDisplayList( ) method. Later in this chapter, we will examine the role these methods play and how to implement proper invalidation.

Validation

When a component is being initialized, the last step before the creationComplete event is dispatched is the validation step. This step also occurs when a component is invalidated using one of the invalidate methods. The validation phase is where the commitProperties( ), measure( ), or updateDisplayList( ) method of the component is called. During initialization all three methods are called. We will cover how to implement the validation methods properly later in this chapter.

Destruction

The destruction phase (also sometimes referred to as the detachment phase) occurs when a component is removed from the display list. At this point, the component no longer participates in the layout events, and if it is no longer referenced anywhere, it will be garbage-collected and removed from memory.

Component Implementation

Now that you have a good understanding of the component life cycle, we will discuss how to implement a component.

Throughout this chapter, you will develop a custom instant messenger status icon component (StatusIcon) that uses many of the features of the component framework. Figure 19-4 shows the finished component.

Figure 19-4. Finished StatusIcon component

StatusIcon allows the user to set his name, his status (available, busy, idle), and a font color. It also should automatically resize to display the entire name, and allow the user to data-bind to the value of the username, dispatch an event when the status is changed, and set icons for the different statuses.

Implementing the Constructor

The first step in building a component is to decide on the base class and constructor. For this component, we will use UIComponent. The UIComponent class gives us a basic implementation for writing a custom component and allows us to build on top of it as we please. Here are the beginnings of the component:

```
package com.oreilly.programmingflex.controls
{
    import mx.core.UIComponent;

    public class StatusIcon extends UIComponent
    {
        public function StatusIcon()
        {
            super();
        }
    }
}
```

> In this chapter, you will be developing custom components using ActionScript. Although it is possible to build the same components in MXML, you will find that for custom components, you will often opt to use ActionScript.

In this example, we have created the component's main class, StatusIcon, which contains the basic implementation for the constructor. The constructor calls super() and nothing else. Although at this point the component doesn't perform any useful function, it already has inherited many capabilities from the component framework, including the component life cycle. For every custom component, this will be a basic starting point on which to build. The constructor is one of the first things to be called when a component is instantiated. Because of this, many things may not be ready for you to work with. For this reason, it is advisable that you do very little within the constructor and instead save most of the implementation for other steps in the component's life cycle.

In addition to the constructor, every component should also implement four other methods: createChildren(), commitProperties(), measure(), and updateDisplayList(), which we will cover shortly. These methods are called in that order during initialization, as seen in Figure 19-5.

The initialization step includes the call to the constructor as well as the createChildren(), commitProperties(), measure(), and updateDisplayList() methods. Within the initialization step, a validation step occurs. This validation step includes where the calls to the commitProperties(), measure(), and updateDisplayList() methods occur. This same validation step is used in the update phase as well, which occurs several times during the life of a component. The only difference between the validation step in the initialization and the update is that in

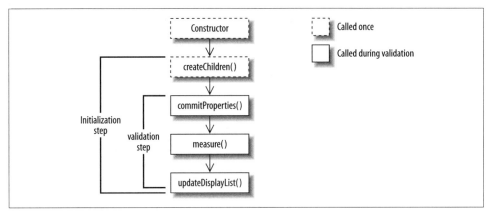

Figure 19-5. UIComponent required methods, and their order

the initialization step, all the methods are calls. In the update phase, the methods that get called depend on many factors, which we will cover throughout different parts of this chapter.

Implementing createChildren( )

The createChildren( ) method is called during the initialization phase. Its purpose is to attach subobjects to your component at the beginning of the life of the component. Unlike containers and components in Flex, in which a child needs to be a UIComponent (or needs to implement the IUIComponent interface), children of a custom component can be any type of Flash Player display object.

As you can see in Figure 19-5, createChildren( ) is called only once throughout a component's life cycle. Because this method is typically called only once, though, it is ideal for adding children that are required through the life of a component, as instantiating new objects is one of the most intensive operations in Flash Player. The createChildren( ) method doesn't have many rules. All you have to do is decide what children you would like to create early in the life of the component; typically these would include the children that will be needed throughout the life of the component, or at least at the beginning of the component's life. Then you simply set their initial states, check to ensure that the children have not been instantiated already (in cases where your component has been subclassed), and call super.createChildren( ).

Our StatusIcon component has two child objects: the status icon and the user's label. In the createChildren( ) method, we will need to add both children to the display list because they are required at all times. To implement the createChildren( ) method you override the UIComponent base class implementation. Here is the code to implement the createChildren( ) method:

```
[Embed(source="/images/available.gif")]
private var IconAvailable:Class;
[Embed(source="/images/busy.gif")]
```

```
private var IconBusy:Class;
[Embed(source="/images/idle.gif")]
private var IconIdle:Class;

private var currentIcon:DisplayObject;
private var displayNameLabel:Label;

override protected function createChildren():void
{
    super.createChildren();

    if(currentIcon == null)
    {
        currentIcon = new IconAvailable();
    }
    addChild(currentIcon);

    if(displayNameLabel == null)
    {
        displayNameLabel = new Label();
    }
    addChild(displayNameLabel);
}
```

In the createChildren( ) body, you call super.createChildren( ), then instantiate both children and add them to the display list using addChild( ) while ensuring that the children have not already been instantiated. Notice that for the icon, we referenced the IconAvailable bitmap class, and for the display name, we used an existing Flex component, the Label component.

Understanding Invalidation

In addition to the initialization phase, during which a component automatically goes through a full validation, a component also goes through validation via update requests. An update request can occur when a user interacts with a component and triggers an event, when methods and properties are set, and when the application or parent it is a part of can interact with a component. To handle such interaction efficiently, the Flex component framework implements an invalidation routine.

Invalidation routines can handle several constraints and assumptions for you. For example, invalidation routines assume that when a component needs to be redrawn, only parts of it may need to be redrawn, not the entire component. Because of this, the component framework divides the view update routines into three types: those that update subobject properties, those that update component sizing, and those that update drawing.

To understand this better, let's take the example of a component that is a child of another component. At some point within the component's lifetime, its parent may ask to resize it. When that occurs, the component may not have to change any values or do any redrawing; instead, it may require only that a component measure its size. For this purpose, there exist a specific invalidation method, `invalidateSize()`, and a corresponding validation method, `measure()`. Figure 19-6 shows the invalidation methods and their corresponding validation methods.

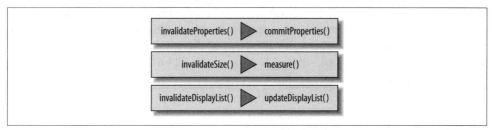

Figure 19-6. Invalidation methods and their corresponding validation methods

You may be wondering why you need an invalidation method if you can call the validation method directly. The reason concerns another key aspect of invalidation and it relates to Flash Player behavior.

Flash Player renders on a frame-by-frame basis. Thus, if a value is changed in the middle of a frame several times, although the value is set several times, only the last value set is rendered to the user in the next frame. For this reason, it is a waste to call a validation more than once per frame. Thus, the invalidation routines (also sometimes referred to as marking the component as dirty) have the job of merging changes needed together into a single frame which the component renders in the next frame during validation (the validation step). With this process, an invalidation method may be called several times during a single frame, and the corresponding validation method will be called only once in the next frame.

For this process to work properly, you will need to cache data changes and allow the validation methods to make the actual change. For component properties, you should follow the pattern of defining a private variable for every public property that will hold the new value until the validation methods are called. For the `StatusIcon` component, a property label is used to set the username by updating the values of the `_displayNameLabel.text` property. Rather than setting the `_displayNameLabel.text` property directly, however, we will store the new value in a private property, `_label`.

 Another reason to have setter functions store values in a temporary property is that setter functions could be called before children are instantiated. If you attempt to set the value of the child immediately before the child is instantiated, this could cause an error.

Here are the label setter and getter functions for `StatusComponent`:

```
private var _label:String;

public function set label(value:String):void
{
```

```
        _label = value;
        invalidateProperties();
        invalidateSize();
    }
```

In the label setter function, we set the `private _label` property with the new value, then call the invalidation methods `invalidateProperties()` and `invalidateSize()`. Although we haven't looked at how to implement the validation methods, it's easy to understand that when the label value is changed, the value of the internal label component will need to be changed as well. Thus, when you call the `invalidateProperties()` method, the size of the component may change because of the new values of the label, so you call the `invalidateSize()` method. Although it may not be clear when to call which invalidation method, after reviewing how to implement the three invalidation methods, keeping in mind Figure 19-6 and what invalidation methods cause a call to what validation method, and gaining some experience, you will have a clear understanding when building your own component.

Implementing commitProperties( )

The validation method that corresponds to calling the `invalidateProperties()` invalidation method, and the first validation method to be called during initialization, is `commitProperties()`. This method's purpose is to commit any values typically set by using a setter function. Often the `commitProperties()` method is as simple as calling `super.commitProperties()` and setting the cached values:

```
    override protected function commitProperties():void
    {
        super.commitProperties();
        displayNameLabel.text = _label;
    }
```

If your component contains many public properties, you may find that your `commitProperties()` method becomes inefficient as it attempts to set values for every value even though only a single value was changed. To work around this, it is recommended that you not only store the new value of the set data in a temporary property, but also track what has changed. You do so by declaring a Boolean property (also referred to as a *dirty flag*) for each public property that serves as a flag for the `commitProperties()` method to help it know how to conditionally set values. Here is the updated setter and the `commitProperties()` method which adds this optimization:

```
    private var _label:String;
    private var labelChanged:Boolean = false;

    public function set label(value:String):void
    {
        _label = value;
        labelChanged = true;
        invalidateProperties();
```

```
    invalidateSize( );
}
```

And here is the updated implementation of `commitProperties( )`:

```
override protected function commitProperties():void
{
    super.commitProperties( );
    if(labelChanged)
    {
        //reset to false as the value is being commited
        labelChanged = false;
        displayNameLabel.text = _label;
    }
}
```

Sometimes when a component value is changed, it may require that new children be created or existing children be removed. In addition to updating the values of existing children, the `commitProperties( )` method also serves to add and remove children. Keep in mind that if a child is going to be required through the entire life of a component, it should be instantiated and added to the display list in the `createChildren( )` method. In the `StatusIcon` component, this isn't required, but if, for example, you wanted to display a label only if it contained a value, and that use case was the norm, you would add logic to handle such a case in the `commitProperties( )` method.

Implementing measure( )

When the `invalidateSize( )` invalidation method is called, the corresponding validation method, `measure( )`, will be called, and as with other validation methods, `measure( )` is always called during the initialization phase of a component as well. The purpose of this method is to perform measurement calculation and define sizing information for the framework. Flex provides a sophisticated set of layout containers whose underlying implementation requires that each component perform appropriate size measurements. Specifically, the framework requires that a component specify the optimal size of the component and, optionally, the minimum size. In Chapter 6, we covered how to use containers to lay out components. With containers and components, you can specify the width and height of components explicitly, by percentage, or not at all, and the framework will automatically do its best to decide on the sizing for you. This is why the `measure( )` method exists. If your component is used, and its size is not defined or is defined using constraint-based layout logic, your component will need to tell the layout containers what it would like its size to be (the default size). Also, when the layout logic is attempting to size a component, it will need to tell its container how small the component can be sized. Because of this, the `measure( )` method also has a mechanism for defining the minimum size of the component.

Both the default and minimum sizes of the component are set to a width and height of zero. You may find that having a minimum width and height of zero is acceptable, but typically you will at least want to define the default width and height yourself. Defining the default and minimum values in the measure( ) method requires that you set the values of the measuredWidth, measuredHeight, and optionally, measuredMinWidth and measuredMinHeight properties:

measuredWidth, measuredHeight

These are the component's default width and height. You should set these values to the width and height that your component requires.

measuredMinWidth, measuredMinHeight

These are the component's minimum width and height. You will often set their values to the same as the measured value.

Here is the measure( ) method implemented for the StatusIcon component:

```
override protected function measure():void
{
    super.measure();
    measuredHeight = measuredMinHeight = currentIcon.height;
    measuredWidth = measuredMinWidth = currentIcon.width + displayNameLabel.
getExplicitOrMeasuredWidth();
}
```

In this measure( ) implementation, we override the existing implementation and call super.measure( ). This is typically how most measure( ) implementations will begin. We also set measuredHeight, measuredMinHeight, measuredWidth, and measuredMinWidth. measuredHeight and measuredMinHeight are set to the height of the icon image and measuredWidth and measuredMinWidth are set to the total width of the children within the component (icon and label).

When performing measurement in order to decide on sizing, you will often need to retrieve the size of the children along with any chrome/padding that needs to be taken into account. As a general rule, you will typically use the children's width and height properties to retrieve the size values of children that do not inherit from UIComponent. For children that do inherit from UIComponent, you will want to use the getExplicitOrMeasuredWidth( ) and getExplicitOrMeasuredHeight( ) methods.

Implementing updateDisplayList( )

The last validation method is updateDisplayList( ). This validation method is called as a result of calling the invalidateDisplayList( ) invalidation method, and by the Flex framework internally (typically the LayoutManager class). The purpose of this validation method is to lay out the contents of the component and perform any needed drawing and redrawing. Typically this method contains a lot of the implementation of a component.

In `StatusComponent`, we will implement the basic `updateDisplayList()` method. The method will position the `displayNameLabel` and then set its size:

```
override protected function updateDisplayList(unscaledWidth:Number, unscaledHeight:
Number):void
{
    super.updateDisplayList(unscaledWidth,unscaledHeight);
    displayNameLabel.move(currentIcon.x + currentIcon.width,0);
    displayNameLabel.setActualSize(unscaledWidth-currentIcon.width,
unscaledHeight);
}
```

The `updateDisplayList()` method is implemented by overriding the existing implementation. Notice that this method receives two arguments: `unscaledWidth` and `unscaledHeight`. You begin by calling `super.updateDisplayList()`, passing in the two arguments. Then typically you will perform any drawing API rendering before measuring and positioning children.

 The `updateDisplayList()` method can get very long, especially when you need to handle many children and styles. For this reason, you may want to break up parts of the method into smaller functions.

In the `measure()` validation method we retrieved the size, and in the `updateDisplayList()` method we will set the size and position the children. When positioning and sizing children, if a child does not inherit from `UIComponent` you will want to use the `x` and `y` properties for positioning and the `width` and `height` properties for sizing. If a child does inherit from `UIComponent`, you should use the `setActualSize(width,height)` method for sizing and the `move(x,y)` method for positioning.

Adding Custom Properties and Events

When creating components, you will often want to declare some sort of public API. It is typically advisable that you create properties rather than methods with components. Doing so will allow component properties to be set more naturally within MXML as attributes, because methods are not declaratively called within MXML.

You create a public property in a custom component by creating a getter/setter. For the `StatusIcon` component, one feature you might want to have is the ability to set the status of the component. The status could be a public property that you can set and whose value you could retrieve. Also, the property should be bindable. To create the property you first declare the getter/setter function and make it bindable via `[Bindable]` metadata:

```
public static const STATUS_AVAILABLE:String = "available";
public static const STATUS_BUSY:String = "busy";
public static const STATUS_IDLE:String = "idle";
```

```
private var _status:String;
private var statusChanged:Boolean = false;

[Bindable]
public function set status(value:String):void
{
    _status = value;
    statusChanged = true;
    invalidateProperties();
}

public function get status():String
{
    return _status;
}
```

Next, you will need to update the commitProperties() method to support the new property. You first declare public constant values for the different values that the setter supports. Although ActionScript 3 does not support enumerations, declaring public properties for valid values is a good practice when a setter can accept only a limited set of values. Then you should check for a change in the statusChanged value. If the value evaluates to true, you handle the new status as follows:

```
override protected function commitProperties():void
{
    //code omitted for brevity

    if(statusChanged)
    {
        statusChanged = false;
        removeChild(currentIcon);

        switch (_status)
        {
            case STATUS_AVAILABLE:
                currentIcon = new IconAvailable();
                break;
            case STATUS_BUSY:
                currentIcon = new IconBusy();
                break;
            case STATUS_IDLE:
                currentIcon = new IconIdle();
                break;
        }
        addChild(currentIcon);
    }
}
```

With the property added and set to bindable, users can manipulate the value and data-bind to the new property easily.

One other common need may be to dispatch an event whenever the status is changed. You can dispatch events within components using the same techniques we discussed throughout this book. Remember that UIComponent inherits from EventDispatcher, which implements the event system.

 A custom event class is not always required. If you are dispatching an event that already exists within the Flex framework or another component, you may opt to reuse the existing event object rather than create your own.

To create an event, you first should create a custom event class:

```
package com.oreilly.programmingflex.events
{
    import flash.events.Event;

    public class StatusChangeEvent extends Event
    {
        public static const STATUS_CHANGE:String = "statusChange";
        public var status:String;

        public function StatusChangeEvent(status:String,bubbles:Boolean = false,
cancelable:Boolean = false)
        {
            super(STATUS_CHANGE,bubbles,cancelable);
            this.status = status;
        }

        public override function clone( ):Event
        {
            return new StatusChangeEvent(status, bubbles, cancelable );
        }
    }
}
```

Next, you can dispatch the new event for when the status value is set. Here is the updated status setter function:

```
[Bindable(event="statusChanged")]
public function set status(value:String):void
{
    _status = value;
    statusChanged = true;
    invalidateProperties( );
    dispatchEvent(new StatusChangeEvent(value))
}
```

When developing custom components, it is good practice to create events that you think your users may find useful. This helps to promote good application design principles and helps to decouple a component from an application.

Adding Styling Support

One of the key features of Flex that Flash Player does not inherently support is styles. As we discussed earlier in the book, styles in Flex are a robust mechanism for defining component styles on an instance, class, or global basis, within MXML, Action-Script, and CSS. Styling support is built into the Flex framework and is exposed to custom components that inherit from UIComponent. Because of this, the complexity for integrating styling support for our components is greatly reduced.

To add support for styles you need to add a style metadata tag and override the styleChanged() method. After you do that, you can use the getStyle() utility method from within your component to retrieve the value of the style. In this section, we will build the code to add a horizontalGap style that will control the space between the icon and the label in our instant messenger status icon component.

First, you need to define the style metadata tag by preceding the class declaration, specifying the style's name and type, and usually disable inheritance:

```
[Style(name="horizontalGap",type="int", inheriting="false")]
public class StatusIcon extends UIComponent
{
```

Next, you need to implement the styleChanged() method:

```
override public  function styleChanged(styleProp:String):void
{
    super.styleChanged(styleProp);
    if(styleProp == "horizontalGap")
    {
        invalidateSize();
        invalidateDisplayList();
    }
}
```

In styleChanged(), we first call super.styleChanged(), passing it the styleProp value. Then we check for the changed value. Because styleChanged() is called whenever a style is changed, you need to check what style has changed and handle each type of style change separately. If you do not conditionally check for this you will likely run into performance issues, as the framework calls styleChanged() at different times throughout the application life cycle.

In the implementation of styleChanged(), after you check for the properly styled property, you call the invalidate methods. Although you could handle the required style changes with styleChanged(), typically it is best to call the proper invalidation methods and have the component redraw what it needs to. In this case, the component needs to recalculate its size and perform the drawing and layout functions.

With basic implementation of styling added to the StatusIcon, now we can update the rest of the component to support the new style. The simplest way to retrieve the style value from within our validation methods is to call the getStyle() function. The getStyle() function retrieves the value of a particular style. For example, it will automatically handle instance- versus class-based style values for you. However, if getStyle( ) cannot find a value for a style you request, it will return undefined. You should make sure that you handle such cases by providing a default value of your own if none exists. A common way to do this is to define a private getter function for the style. In our example, the getter should be called horizontalGapDefault. Here is the getter function that attempts to retrieve a valid value from getStyle( ). If it does not find a valid value, it will return a default value of 5.

```
private function get horizontalGapDefault( ):int
{
    var horizontalGap:Number = getStyle("horizontalGap");
    return  (horizontalGap == undefined ? 5 : horizontalGap);
}
```

Now that we have a convenient method of retrieving the style, let's update the validation methods to support the new style:

```
override protected function measure( ):void
{
    super.measure( );
    measuredHeight = measuredMinHeight = currentIcon.height;
    measuredWidth = measuredMinWidth = currentIcon.
width+horizontalGapDefault+displayNameLabel.getExplicitOrMeasuredWidth
( );
}

override protected function updateDisplayList(unscaledWidth:Number, unscaledHeight:
Number):void
{
    super.updateDisplayList(unscaledWidth,unscaledHeight);
    displayNameLabel.move(currentIcon.x + currentIcon.width +
horizontalGapDefault,0);
    displayNameLabel.setActualSize(unscaledWidth-currentIcon.width-
horizontalGapDefault,unscaledHeight);
}
```

When child components exist that contain their own styles, you will often want to allow the child styles to be set as well. For example, it would be convenient if our status icon component supported styling of the label component's font type and font size. There are two methods you can use to achieve this. You can have the label component inherit the same style values from its parent, or you can define a custom style that only that child will use.

To allow children to inherit directly from their parents, you only need to add a metadata tag, like so:

```
[Style(name="fontSize", type="Number", format="Length", inherit="yes")]
```

This method is very useful when a component does not contain many types of children. In the status icon component, this method works well because only one component uses the fontSize value. If there were many children, you might run into a situation where you want some children to have different styles than others. For such a case, you can define a custom style for a child. For our status icon component, the name of the style would be `labelFontSize`. The naming convention is to prefix the style with the component type. To add support for this style, you will first need to define the style metadata tags in the same way you did the other methods:

```
[Style(name="labelFontSize", type="Number", format="Length", inherit="no")]
```

Next, you need to manually handle this new style and set the style of the child. Here is the updated code:

```
Private var labelFontSizeChanged:Boolean = false;

override protected function commitProperties():void
{
        //code omitted for brevity

        if(labelFontSizeChanged)
        {
            displayNameLabel.setStyle("fontSize",labelFontSizeDefault);
            labelFontSizeChanged = false;
        }
    }
}

private function get labelFontSizeDefault():Number
{
    return (getStyle("labelFontSize") == undefined ? 12 : getStyle("labelFontSize"));
}

override public  function styleChanged(styleProp:String):void
{
    super.styleChanged(styleProp);
    if(styleProp == "horizontalGap")
    {
        invalidateSize();
        invalidateDisplayList();
    }

    if(styleProp=="labelFontSize")
    {
        labelFontSizeChanged = true;
        invalidateProperties();
    }
}
```

Summary

The Flex framework greatly simplifies the task of developing custom components. In this chapter, you learned the basics of custom components—the component life cycle, validation mechanisms, adding styles, and adding events. Although these are some of the key topics when it comes to developing components, developing custom components is a vast subject that takes time to master, and a whole book can be written on the subject.

Index

We'd like to hear your suggestions for improving our indexes. Send email to *index@oreilly.com*.

About the Authors

Chafic Kazoun has worked with Flash-related technologies since 1998. He has been involved with Flex Server 1.0 since its pre-alpha stage, has a deep understanding of the internals of the Flex Framework, and has additional experience with Action-Script 3.0 and Zorn.

Joey Lott is the author of *Flash 8 Cookbook*, *Programming Flash Communication Server*, and *ActionScript 3 Cookbook* (all O'Reilly titles). He is also the author of *Complete Flash Remoting MX* as well as the coauthor of the *Flash 8 ActionScript Bible* (both from Wiley). Joey has worked in the Internet industry since 1996, including cofounding RightSpring, Inc. and consulting for YourMobile/Premium Wireless Services and Ads.com. He has been teaching Flash and ActionScript since 1999.

Colophon

The animal on the cover of *Programming Flex 2* is a krait snake. The krait (*Bungarus caeruleus*) is one of the deadliest venomous snakes in the world. Their native habitat is limited to Asia, and they are nocturnal. The snake's bands are white or yellow on a blue/black body, the head is narrow, and a krait can grow to nearly three feet in length.

Fairly common in the fields and jungles of India, Pakistan, and Sri Lanka, the krait is also known to seek shelter in human encampments. They are fond of hiding out in sleeping bags, footwear, and piles of clothing or rags. Their venom contains a neuro-toxin that causes respiratory failure; victims often feel little pain from the bite itself, but the death rate of victims is 85 percent without administration of anti-venom, and nearly 50 percent even when medication is available.

The 2006 film *Snakes on a Plane* features a snake smuggler named "Kraitler," and the krait makes an appearance in several Sherlock Holmes stories.

The cover image is from the *Dover Pictorial Archive*. The cover font is Adobe ITC Garamond. The text font is Linotype Birka; the heading font is Adobe Myriad Condensed; and the code font is LucasFont's TheSans Mono Condensed.

Related Titles from O'Reilly

Web Authoring and Design

ActionScript 3.0 Cookbook

Ajax Hacks

Ambient Findability

Creating Web Sites: The Missing Manual

CSS Cookbook, *2nd Edition*

CSS Pocket Reference, *2nd Edition*

CSS: The Definitive Guide, *3rd Edition*

CSS: The Missing Manual

Dreamweaver 8: Design and Construction

Dreamweaver 8: The Missing Manual

Dynamic HTML: The Definitive Reference, *3rd Edition*

Essential ActionScript 2.0

Flash 8: Projects for Learning Animation and Interactivity

Flash 8: The Missing Manual

Flash Hacks

Head First HTML with CSS & XHTML

Head Rush Ajax

HTML & XHTML: The Definitive Guide, *6th Edition*

HTML & XHTML Pocket Reference, *3rd Edition*

Information Architecture for the World Wide Web, *3rd Edition*

Information Dashboard Design

JavaScript: The Definitive Guide, *5th Edition*

Learning JavaScript

Learning Web Design, *2nd Edition*

PHP Hacks

Programming Flash Communication Server

Web Design in a Nutshell, *3rd Edition*

Web Site Measurement Hacks

O'REILLY®

Our books are available at most retail and online bookstores.

To order direct: 1-800-998-9938 • *order@oreilly.com* • *www.oreilly.com*

Online editions of most O'Reilly titles are available by subscription at *safari.oreilly.com*